Street by Stre

EAST SUSSEX

PLUS BURGESS HILL, EAST GRINSTEAD, ROYAL TUNBRIDGE WELLS

Enlarged Areas Brighton, Eastbourne, Hastings, Lewes, Newhaven

lst edition May 2001

© Automobile Association Developments Limited 2001

This product includes map data licensed from Ordnance Survey® with the permission of the Controller of Her Majesty's Stationery Office. © Crown copyright 2000. All rights reserved. Licence No: 399221.

Published by AA Publishing (a trading name of Automobile Association Developments Limited, whose registered office is Norfolk House, Priestley Road, Basingstoke, Hampshire, RG24 9NY. Registered number 1878835).

Mapping produced by the Cartographic Department of The Automobile Association.

A CIP Catalogue record for this book is available from the British Library.

Printed by in Italy by Printer Trento srl

Ref: MD022

Key to map pages	ii-iii
Key to map symbols	iv-1
Enlarged scale pages	2-11
Street by Street	12-237
Index – towns & villages	238-240
Index – streets	241-273
Index – featured places	273-280

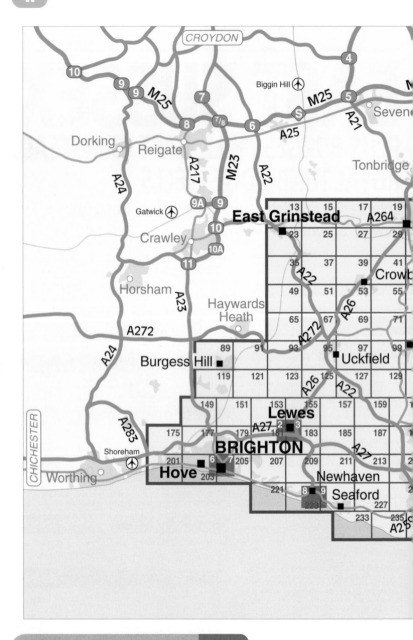

ii

CROYDON

10

9

9

M25

7

Biggin Hill ✈

M25

5

A21

Seven

8

7/8

6

A25

Dorking

Reigate

A217

M23

A22

Tonbridge

A24

Gatwick ✈

9A

9

East Grinstead

A264

13 15 17 19

Crawley

10

23 25 27 29

10A

35 37 39 41

A22

Crowb

11

49 51 53 55

Horsham

A23

Haywards
Heath

A26

65 67 69 71

A272

A24

A272

A272

89 91 93 95 97 99

Burgess Hill

Uckfield

119 121 123 A26 125 127 129

A22

149 151 153 155 157 159

A283

Lewes

175 177 179 A27 181 2 3 183 185 187

BRIGHTON

A27

Shoreham ✈

201 6 7 205 207 209 211 213

Worthing

Hove 203

Newhaven

221 8 9 Seaford

223 227

233 235

A25

CHICHESTER

Enlarged scale pages 1:17,500 3.6 inches to 1 mile

0   1/2   miles   1

0   1/2   1   kilometres   1 1/2

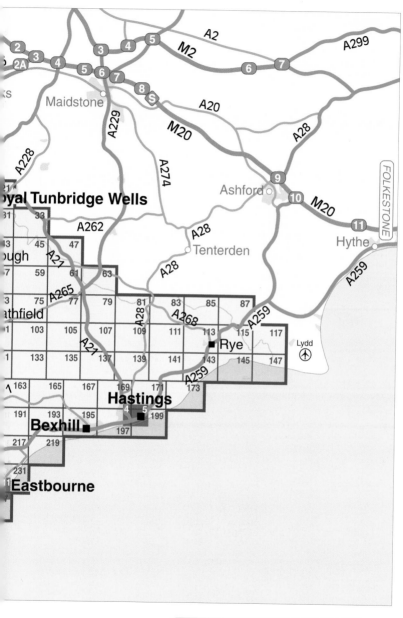

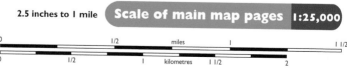

iv

Junction 9	Motorway & junction	P+🚌	Park & Ride
Services	Motorway service area	🚌	Bus/coach station
	Primary road single/dual carriageway		Railway & main railway station
Services	Primary road service area		Railway & minor railway station
	A road single/dual carriageway	⊖	Underground station
	B road single/dual carriageway	⊖	Light railway & station
	Other road single/dual carriageway	++++++++++	Preserved private railway
	Restricted road	*LC*	Level crossing
	Private road	●━●━●	Tramway
← ←	One way street	----------	Ferry route
	Pedestrian street	....	Airport runway
----------	Track/ footpath	— · — · —	Boundaries- borough/ district
	Road under construction	|||||||	Mounds
⊱ - - - ⊰	Road tunnel	**93**	Page continuation 1:25,000
P	Parking	**7**	Page continuation to enlarged scale 1:17,500

	River/canal lake, pier	♿	Toilet with disabled facilities
	Aqueduct lock, weir	⬛	Petrol station
▲ 465 Winter Hill	Peak (with height in metres)	PH	Public house
	Beach	PO	Post Office
	Coniferous woodland	📖	Public library
	Broadleaved woodland	ℹ	Tourist Information Centre
	Mixed woodland	♜	Castle
	Park	🏛	Historic house/ building
	Cemetery	Wakehurst Place NT	National Trust property
	Built-up area	Ⓜ	Museum/ art gallery
	Featured building	✝	Church/chapel
⊓⊔⊓⊔⊓	City wall	♈	Country park
A&E	Accident & Emergency hospital	🎭	Theatre/ performing arts
🚻	Toilet	👥	Cinema

2

A   154   B   C

I

A3
1 Sheepfair

B3
1 Arundell Gn
2 Segrave Cl

B4
1 Irelands La
2 Nunnery Stable
3 St Anne's Crs
4 Shelley Cl

2

B5
1 Cleve Ter
2 Juggs Cl
3 Juggs Rd
4 Winterbourne Cl

C2
1 Hoopers Cl
2 Mealla Cl
3 Peckham Cl

3

C3
1 Landport Rd
2 Weald Cl

181

4

C4
1 Banks Castle
2 Castle Ditch La
3 Paddock Rd
4 Precincts Castle
5 Queen Anne's Cl
6 Sackville Cl
7 St Peters Pl
8 Well House Pl

*Houndean
Bottom*

5

C5
1 Antioch St
2 Potter's La
3 St Peters Pl
4 St Swithun's Ter
5 S'thover High St
6 Stewards Inn La
7 Well House Pl
8 Westgate St

6

A   182   B   C

I grid square represents 500 metres

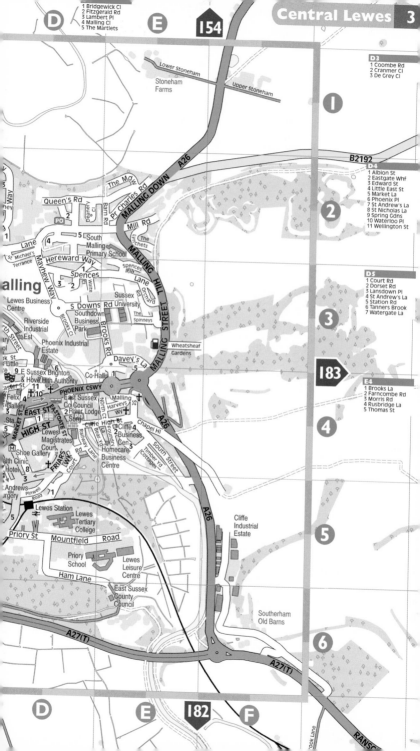

154

Lower Stoneham

Stoneham
Farms

Upper Stoneham

I

B2192

D3
1 Coombe Rd
2 Cranmer Cl
3 De Grey Cl

The Mq

Pr Charles Rd

Queen's Rd

Barn Rd

MALLING DOWN

2

D4
1 Albion St
2 Eastgate Whf
3 Edward St
4 Little East St
5 Market La
6 Phoenix Pl
7 St Andrew's La
8 St Nicholas La
9 Spring Gdns
10 Waterloo Pl
11 Wellington St

PO

Mill Rd

The
Pechets

Lane

St Michael's
Terrace

South
Malling
Primary School

5

Hereward Way

Spences
Field

MALLING HILL STREET

Mayhew Way

Spences
Lane

alling

3 2

Waite

Sussex
University

Orchard

The
spinneys

D5
1 Court Rd
2 Dorset Rd
3 Lansdown Pl
4 St Andrew's La
5 Station Rd
6 Tanners Brook
7 Watergate La

Lewes Business
Centre

S Downs
Rd

Southdown
Business
Park

3

Riverside
Industrial
Est

Brooks Rd

Phoenix Industrial
Estate

Davey's La

Wheatsheaf
Gardens

183

E Sussex Brighton
& Hove Hlth Authority

Co Hall

5

E4
1 Brooks La
2 Farncombe Rd
3 Morris Rd
4 Rusbridge La
5 Thomas St

11 10

PHOENIX CSWY

Felix
Gallery

Malling
Harvey's
Wy

A26

EAST ST

East Sussex
Co Council

River Lodge

MARKET ST

HIGH ST

Cliffe
High St

Chapel Hi

4

Lewes
Magistrates
Court

Cliffe

Business
Gen

Homecare
Business
Centre

South
Street

Shoe Gallery

Railway Lane

Beer Yd

Timber Yd
Cottages

lth Clinic
Hotel

FRIARS

Court

Andrews
urgery

Pinwell
Road

Lewes Station

Lewes
Tertiary
College

Priory St

Mountfield   Road

Priory
School

A26

Lewes
Leisure
Centre

Cliffe
Industrial
Estate

5

Ham Lane

East Sussex
County
Council

Southerham
Old Barns

6

A27(T)

A27(T)

D

E

182

F

RANSC

Brook Lane

Broomsgrove

West Hill

Old Town

Belle

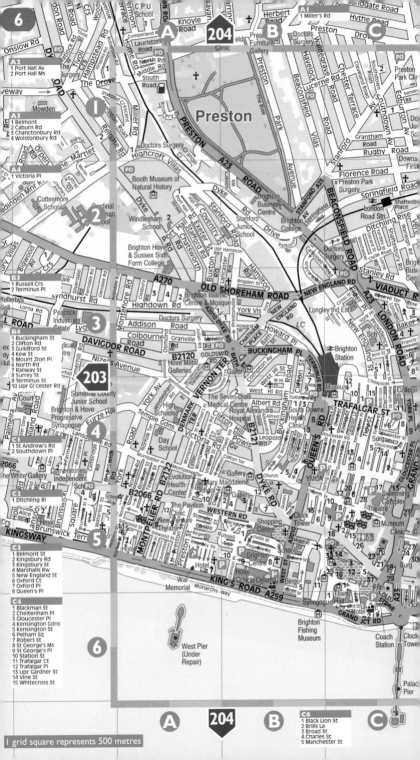

A2
1 Port Hall Av
2 Port Hall Ms

A3
1 Belmont
2 Caburn Rd
3 Chanctonbury Rd
4 Wolstonbury Rd

A4
1 Victoria Pl

B3
1 Russell Crs
2 Terminus Pl

B4
1 Buckingham St
2 Clifton Rd
3 Guildford St
4 Kew St
5 Mount Zion Pl
6 North Rd
7 Railway St
8 Surrey St
9 Terminus St
10 Upr Gl'cester Rd

B5
1 St Andrew's Rd
2 Southdown Pl

C2
1 Ditchling Ri

C3
1 Belmont St
2 Kingsbury Rd
3 Kingsbury St
4 Marshalls Rw
5 New England St
6 Oxford Ct
7 Oxford Pl
8 Queen's Pl

C4
1 Blackman St
2 Cheltenham Pl
3 Gloucester Pl
4 Kensington Gdns
5 Kensington St
6 Pelham Sq
7 Robert St
8 St George's Ms
9 St George's Pl
10 Station St
11 Trafalgar Ct
12 Trafalgar Pl
13 Upr Gardner St
14 Vine St
15 Whitecross St

C6
1 Black Lion St
2 Brills La
3 Broad St
4 Charles St
5 Manchester St

Preston

West Pier
(Under
Repair)

Brighton
Fishing
Museum

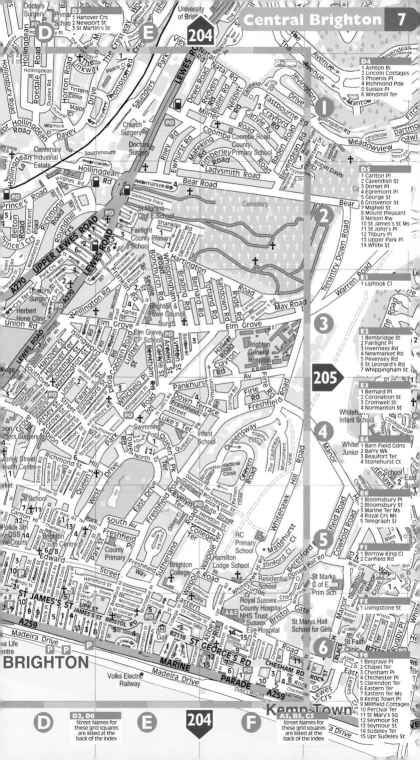

8

B2
1 Piddinghoe Mead

223

Nore Down

Cemetery

Cemetery

BN9

Bush Road

Lewes Road

Robinson Rd

Firdick Road

Valley Close

Willow Wk

Lee Way

Evelyn Av

Lawes Av

Metcalfe Av

Anderson Close

Kennedy Way

Valley Road

Fullwood Av

Elm Ct

Va Dene

Maple Leaf Cl

Meeching Valley CP School

Chestnut Way

Braxen Close

Rothwell Ct

Rose Wk Cl

The Rose Wk

BRIGHTON ROAD

Nore Rd

Upr Valley Rd

East Sussex County Council

Church Hill

First Avenue

Second Av

Third Avenue

Rectory Close

222

Links Avenue

The Fairway

Cresta Road

Blakeney Avenue

Outlook Avenue

Ringmer Road

Highway

Northdown Road

Western Hill

Gibbon Road

Hanson Road

Crest Road

Chelwood Road

The Leas

Park Road

Highway

The

Charlston Avenue

Pevensey Road

Wilmington Way

Jugler Road

Southdown Road

Tideway School

Harbour View Road

Cuckmere Rd Av

Westdean Avenue

Cornelius Avenue

Friars' Bay

Court

The Dr

Farm

Quay

Harbour Heights

A259

Cliff Pk Close

Chichester Close

223

223

I grid square represents 500 metres

D1
1 Cottage Cl
2 St Martins Crs

+ 223

Heighton

Rookery Way

Hill Rise

Drive Close

Denton

D3
1 Bay Vue Rd
2 Bridge St
3 Chapel St
4 Dacre Rd
5 Hill Side
6 Lorraine Rd
7 Senlac Rd
8 South La
9 South Wy

M
PI

D

E

Iveagh Crescent

Heighton

New Rd

Powell Gdns

B2109

NEW ROAD

A26(T)

Paradise Park

Estate Road

North Quay

LC

Denton County Primary School

Denton Drive

Avis Close

Beresford

King's Avenue

Arundel Road

Avis Rd

Station Road

Claremont Road

Denton Rd

Fairholme Road

Seaview Road

Crest Road

Palmerston Rd

Howard

Holmdale

E1
1 Powell Gdns

Rich Industrial Est

Avis Way

Euro Business Park

Ranalah Estate

Bross Estate

East Sussex Co Council

THE DROVE

A259

Mount Road

Mount Close

Seaview Road

Oaklands Road

2

E2
1 Estate Rd

East Sussex Health Authority

A259

B2109

DROVE RD

A259

1

Estate Rd

SEAFORD

3 Stud Farm

A259
WY

Railway Approach

LC

B2109

Railway Road

RAILWAY ROAD

Newhaven Town Station

Newhaven Health Centre

CLIFTON RD

B2109

Norton Terrace

Eastbridge Rd

224

A259 ROAD

Elizabeth Close

Hurdis

Meagles Close

St Andrew

Chapel St

Riverside

Newhaven Harbour Station

Norton Road

PO

Ferryfield Industrial Estate

NEWHAVEN

Holmes Close

3

Rosemount Close

St Margaret's Rd

St Andrew

Viking

Drive

4

Fort

Geneva Rd

ourt

haven

Council

Flea

ays County

ants School

Beach Road

Newhaven Marine Station

Transit Rd

Beach Road

Fort Road

Marina

Beach Road

Mill Creek

Mill

Drove

LC

NEWHAVEN R

Marine

5

Mills

Fort Rd

Fort R

Fort

6

DIEPPE SUMMER ONLY

D

E

223

F

Roselands

230

D

E

D1
1 Churchdale Pl

Northbourne Road
Churchdale Road
Bowood Avenue
Kinfauns Av
Marlow Av
Astaire Avenue
Harding Avenue
Southbourne Road
Brydges Cl
Roselands Avenue
Windermere Crescent
Fitzmaurice Avenue
Baillie Avenue
Huntloke Av
Brook mead
Saint Philip's Avenue
Woodgate Road
Kerrara Ter
Annington Road
Infants School Road

Finmere Road
Fort Lane
Myrtle Rd
Lottbridge Droy

Willoughby Crescent
Infant School
Vine Square
Martello Rd
Monsey
Alexandra Rd
Brede
Winchelsea Rd
Rye St
Sandwich St
Wartling Road

Winifred Lee Health Centre
Channel View Road
Seaside
Seabeach Lane
Fairlight Road
Seaford Road
Latimer Road
Bexhill Road
Sidley Rd
Wannock Rd
Penhale
Desmond Rd

Eastbourne United Football Club
Guestling Rd

Royal Parade

WHITLEY RD A2021
Dudley Rd
Mona Rd
Vista
Clarence Rd
Gilbert Road
School
Carlton Road
Glennys Est
Beamsley Rd
Barden Rd
Addingham Rd
Redoubt Road
Hanover Rd
Cambridge Road
Latimer Road

Eastbourne Sovereign Sailing Club

The Redoubt

Western Road
Avondale Road
Leslie Street
Belmore Road
Firle Road
Seaside Medical Centre
Cavendish Avenue
TA Centre
Belmore Road
Meads Rd
New Road
Melbourne Road
Pevensey Road
Seaside Road
Ceylon Place
Marine Parade
Royal Parade

Primary School
Salvation Army
PO
Royal Hippodrome Theatre
Bus Depot
Webster's
Gallery
Mon
Elms Av

TERMINUS
B2106
Hotel of Shops
Bandstand
Eastbourne Pier

A259
SEASIDE
BEACH RD
SIDLEY RD
ROYAL PARADE
SEASIDE
MARINE PARADE
SEASIDE ROAD

D
1
2 Avondale Rd
2 Clarence Rd

Cunningham Cl
Hood Cl
Raleigh
Jervis
Collingwood Cl
Prince
Wartling Road
Royal Parade

231

I

D3
1 Albion Rd
2 Beltring Ter
3 Chawbrook Rd
4 Havelock Rd
5 Hoad Rd
6 Neville Rd
7 Oxford Rd
8 St George's Rd
9 Sheen Rd
10 Springfield Rd
11 Stanley Rd
12 Willowfield Rd

2

D4
1 Burfield Rd
2 Cavendish Pl
3 Colonade Rd
4 Leaf Hall Rd
5 Lion La
6 Marine Rd
7 Qu's Col'ade Gdns
8 St Aubyn's Rd
9 Willowfield Sq

3

D5
1 Burlington Rd
2 Cavendish Pl
3 Elms Rd

4

E1
1 Burleigh Pl
2 Roseveare Rd

5

E2
1 Belle Vue Rd
2 Romney St
3 Roselands Cl

6

D

E3
1 Bayham Rd
2 Halton Rd
3 St James Rd
4 Taddington Rd

E

237

F

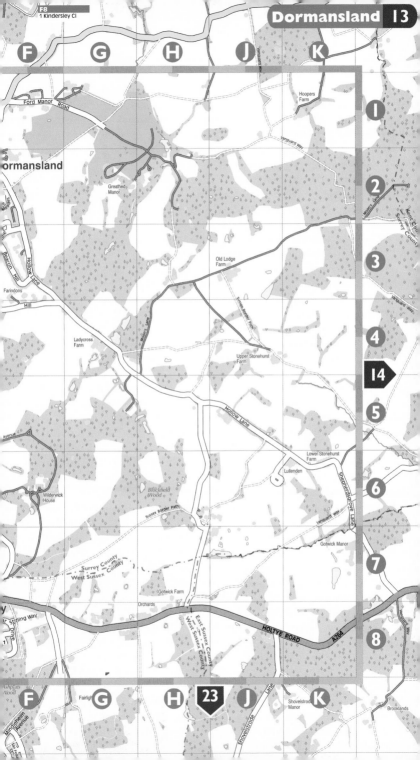

Stick
Hill

F G H J K

Wilderness
Farm

Markbeech

Cow

Lane

Eden Hall
(Convent)   Falconhurst

Cowden
Pound

Gilridge

Horshoe
Green

Edells

Blower's Hill

Polefields

Claydene   Pyle Gate
Farm

B2026

Cowden
Station

Wicke

The
Paddocks

B2026

Moat Lane

Saxbys

Leighton
Manor
Farm

Glover's
Hawes

North Street

Spode Lane

Kent County

East Sussex County

Holywych
House

Cowden

Chantlers
Mead

Church
Street

HARTFIELD ROAD

Holywych
Farm

Cowden
Mews

High Street

Holtye
Common

Holtye House

Sussex House
Farm

Hethe

Cullinghurst
Farm

B2026

F G H 25 J K

Edenbridge
Road

EDENBRIDGE ROAD

Goodtrees

Chantlers
Farm

Tye Farm

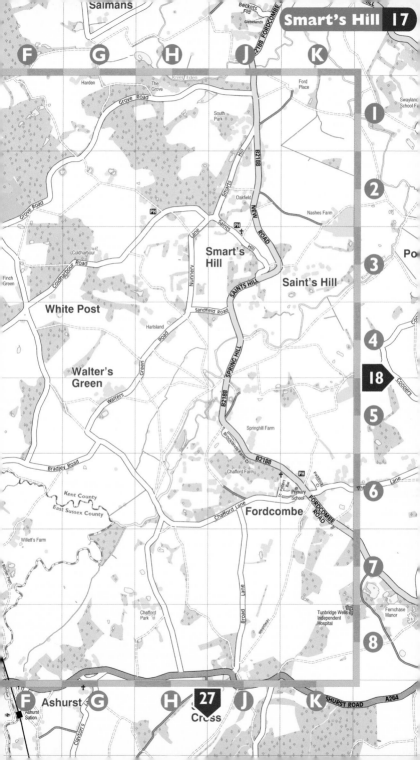

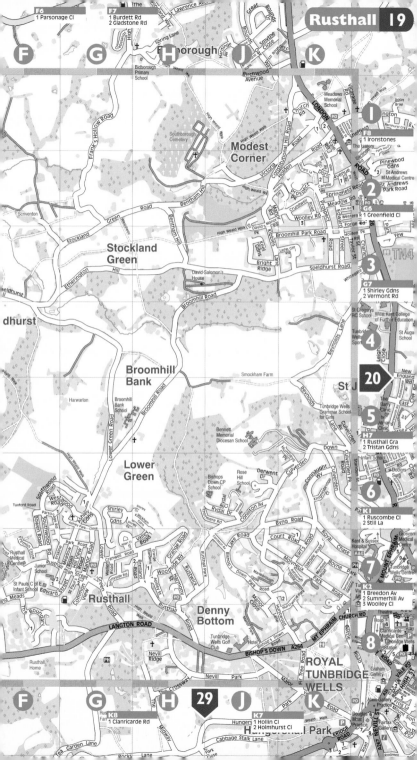

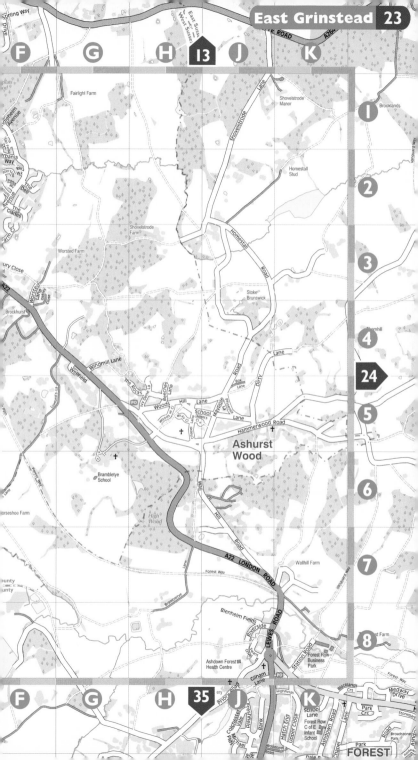

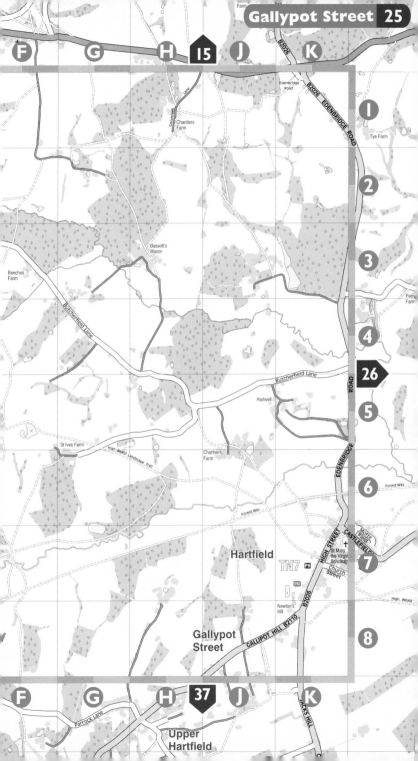

I grid square represents 500 metres

1 grid square represents 500 metres

ROYAL
TUNBRIDGE
WELLS

A2
1 Broad Gv
2 Clarendon Gdns

A1
Street Names for
these grid squares
are listed at the
back of the index

B1
1 Cambridge Gdns
2 Clifton Pl
3 Farmcombe Cl
4 Grecian Rd
5 Madeira Pk
6 Norfolk Rd

B2
1 Beau Nash Wy

B3
1 Elphick's Pl

C1
1 Camden Hl
2 Hollyshaw Cl

C3
1 Cypress Gv

D1
1 Camden Pk
2 Hawkenbury Cl
3 Polesden Rd
4 Rookley Cl

D2
1 Hawkenbury Md

Camden Park

Hawkenbury

adwater Down

Frant

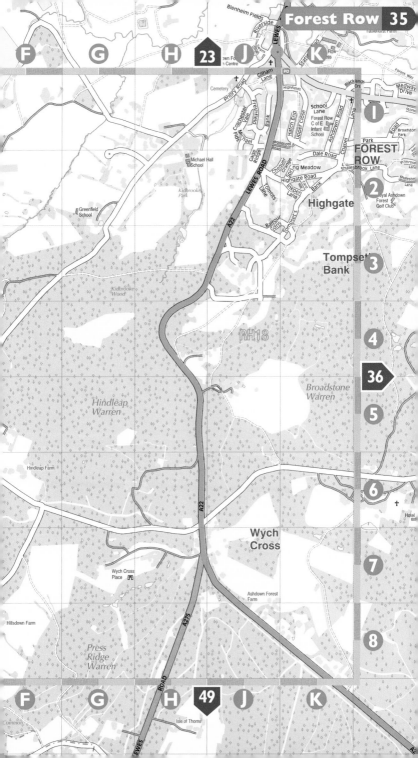

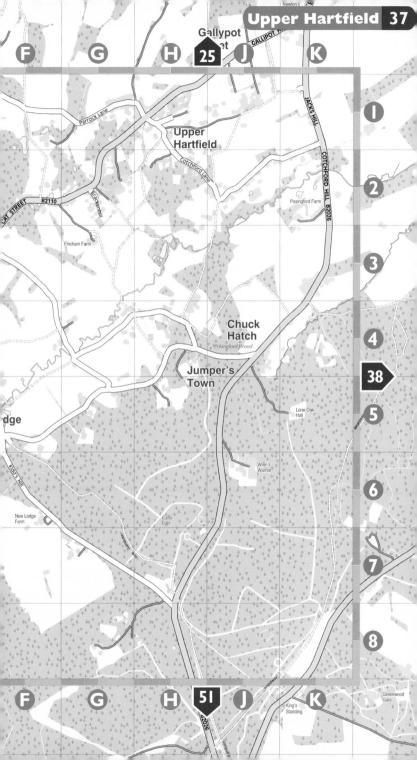

F G H 25 J K

Newton's

I

Gallypot
et

GALLIPOT HILL

JACKS HILL

COTCHFORD HILL B2026

2

Parrock Lane

**Upper
Hartfield**

Cotchford Lane

Posingford Farm

CAT STREET B2110

Blackenhill

Fincham Farm

3

**Chuck
Hatch**

Posingford Wood

4

38

**Jumper's
Town**

Lone Oak
Hall

5

dge

KING'S HILL

Wren's
Warren

6

New Lodge
Farm

Gills
Lap

Newnham Park

7

8

F G H 51 J K

B2026

Wealdway

King's
Standing

Greenwood
Gate

Withynam

38

A   B   **26**   C   D   E
Buckhurst
Park

Forstal Farm

1

JACK'S HILL

COTCHFORD

2

osingford Farm

Buckhurst Farm   Fisher's
Gate

3

Wealdway

4

37

Friar's
Gate

Lone Oak
Hall

5

Five
Hundred
Acre Wood

Marden's
Hill

B2188

6

Marden's Hill

7

Saint John's Road

Wood
Eaves

8

A   B   **52**   C   D   E
Home Farm

1 grid square represents 500 metres

Crowborou
W

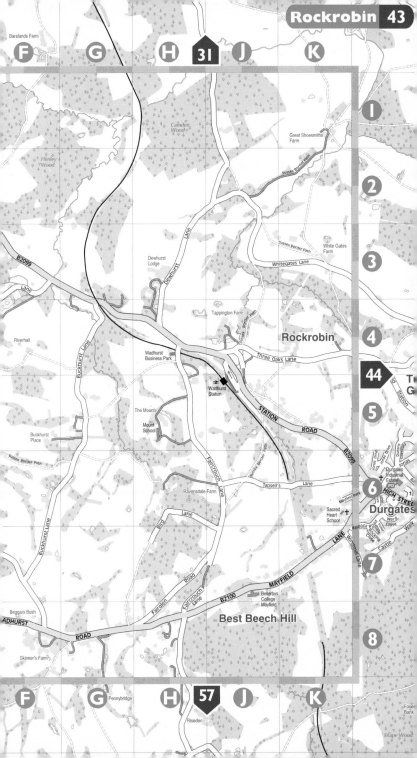

F G H **33** J K

A21(T)

I

Nellis Road

Road

Owls Castle Farm

Hognole Lane

Sweetings Lane

2

Bewlbridge Lane

Wiskett's Wood

Kent County
East Sussex County

B2100

Markwicks

3

COUSLEY WOOD ROAD

Ladymeads Farm

Hook Farm

4

46 ▶

Sussex Border Path

**Lower
Cousley Wood**

Sussex Border Path

Bewl Water

Little Butts Farm

5

Bryant's Farm

Hook Hill

Beaumans

Sussex Border Path

Ward's Lane

Clapmatch Lane

6

Chesson's Farm

Lower Hazelhurst

7

Lower Hazelhurst

Rowley

Whilgh

Birchetts Green Lane

Penton Hill

**Birchett's
Green**

Ward's Lane

8

Lane

Tolhurst

F G H **59** ▽ J K

Holbeam Wood

Birchetts Green Lane

Lodge Lane

Broomden

Vineyard Lane

46

Spray Hill

Scotney Castle Garden (NT)

River Bewl

Kilndown Wood

West Road

Church Road

Chicks Lane

Rough

Kilndow

A21(T)

A **B** **C** **D** **E**

Wilsley's Wood

Bewl Bridge Farm

Bewlbridge Lane

A21(T)

Shearnf Wood

I

2

3

Chingley Wood

Gats Wood

A21(T)

4

45

Chingley Manor

Stonecrouch

5

Sussex Border Path

Kent County

East Sussex County

County

Sussex Border Path

Rosemary Farmhouse

Rosemary Lane

6

Hazelhurst Farm

Overy's Farm

7

Lower Hazelhurst

Rowley

Kelley Farm

8

Boarders Lane

Huntley

Mill Road

Mill Road

Tinkers Lane

Downash House

Three Leg Cross

Sutton Hill

Three Leg Cross Road

PH

Vine

Broomden

Copse

A **B** **60** **C** **D** **E**

B2087

Tin

Perne

Dale Hill

Ticehurst

1 grid square represents 500 metres

A B **38** C D E

King's Standing

Greenwood Gate

Home Farm

Crowboro Warren

Warren Road

1

2

Old Mill House

3

Crabtree Farm

Heaven Road

4

Poundgate

A26

◀ **51**

UCKFIELD ROAD A26

The Doves Nest

5

Sw

6

rnsgate

Vanguard Way

Newnham Park Wood

7

A26

Chillies

Strood

Grovehurst

8 Heron's yll

Chillies Lane

Vanguard Way

Temple Grove with St Nicholas School

Sweetlands

Burnt Ga

A B **68** C D E

Road

Cross Fields

F1
1 The Drive
2 Rannoch Rd West
3 Warren Rdg

F2
1 Winscote Cl

Old Lane

Beacon Garden

HIGH ST

THE BROADWAY

Wealden Way

Setton Place

Charity Farm Way

Owl

Court

Beacon Community College

K

GREEN LA

B2157

F More East

Shell Road

G Highlands Close

Doctors Surgery

Hotel Grove

H Hill Drive

39

J

Hoadswood Road

Saxonborough Surgery

Pine Lane

Mill Lane

Saxonbury Close

The Park

The Crabelands

Fermor School

Beacon Community College

Beeches East

Beeches West

Poundfield Road

1
Poundfield

G1
1 Holly Ct
2 Warren Gdn

2

The Broo

G2
1 Pratt's Folly La
2 Southview Cl
3 Twyfords

Church Road

Tennis Club

Grove Park School

Myrtle Road

St Maria Primary Catholic School

CROWBOROUGH

Cornford Close

Oliver Cl

Beaver Close

Beeches Farm

CROWBOROUGH HILL

B2100

Rochester Road

Medway

Hillrise

Osborne Lane

Windsor Road

3

Wealden Industrial Estate

H1
1 Chapel Gn
2 Graycoats Dr
3 Lower Saxonbur
4 Pollington Pl

The Twitten

Pastens Close

South View Road

Whitehill Road

Queens Road

The Martlets

Montargis

Nye

Bridger Way

Blackness

Buller Close

Whitehill County Infant School

Belvedere Gardens

St Michaels Cl

Southridge Rise

Springhead Way

Stonecott Cl

Wealden College

Edge Lane

Blackness Road

Fermor Road

Harlequin Lane

Manor Way

Whitehill Road

Queens Road

Cemetery

Heathland Way

Luxford Lane

4

Western

Tubwell Farm

Whin Croft Park

Crowborough Beacon Golf Club

Whitehill

Hurtis Hill

Springhead Way

Herne School

Herne Down

Broadsmith

Fermor Road

St Richards Rd

Weald Close

54

5

Haywa

H2
1 Little Sunnyside
2 Sandridge

High Broom Lane

Broom Road

Bright Road

Alderbrook

Alder Cottages

Alderbrook Close

Adam Close

Alderbrook Way

Walshes Road

Finnart House

6

I1
1 Chequers Cl

Stone Cross

Stone Lane

Sandhill Farm

S

Alfriston Lane

Redbridge Farm

ridge Lane

Pick Pale

Lotmans Farm

Owlsbury Farm

7

J2
1 Coldharbour La
2 Simons Cl
3 Tanners Wy
4 Troy Cl
5 Wallis Cl

8

Burnt Oak

Brook House

Fordbrook Lane

Mill Lane

Inchreed Farm

Fordb

F

G

H

69

J

K

K2
1 Kemps Farm Rd
2 Shawfield

K1
1 Springfield Cl

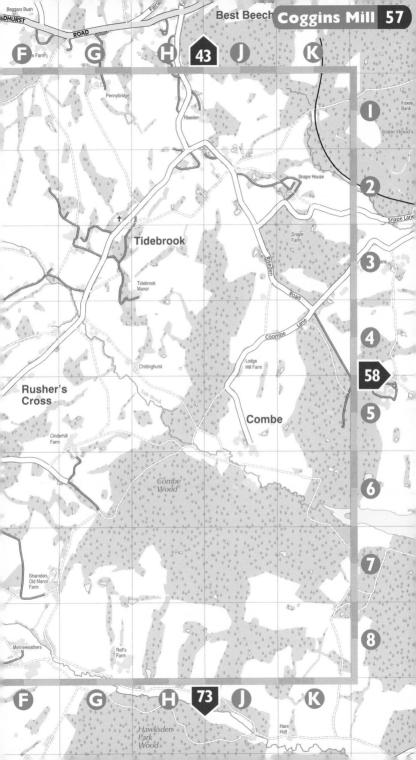

F

Birchetts Green Lane

Ward's Lane

Birchett's Green

G

H

45

Tolhurst

J

K

I

Holbeam Wood

Birchetts Green Lane

Lodge Lane

Broomden

Burnt

Vineyard Lane

Tolhurst Lane

Ridgeway Farm

Ticehurst House

Wallcrouch

TN5

HIGH STREET

B2099

HIGH STREET

B2099

Brick Kiln Farm

2

3

Lymden Lane

Storrers Farm

4

Bricklehurst Manor

Lymden

Wedd's Farm

Bardown

60

Bardown Road

Stonegate

5

The Acorns

Linden Close

Myskyns

Cottenden

Stonegate C of E Primary School

6

Station Road

Hill

Shrub Lane

Bearhurst Farm

7

Pearrtree

Stonegate Station

Hammerden

Battenhurst Farm

8

F

G

H

75

J

K

LC

C2
1 Lavender Gdns
2 Reeves Ter

Downash
House

Three
Leg Cross

Tinkers Lane

Berner
Hill

Dale Hill

Ticehurst

Dale Hill Hotel
& Golf Club

Broomden

Vineyard Lane

Ridgeway Farm

Ticehurst House

Cross Lane Gardens

B2099

Brick Kiln
Farm

Hillbury
Gardens

The
Surgery

Farthing
Hill

The Warren

Springfields

Acres End

HIGH STREET

Steellands Rise

Hazelgrove Avenue

LOWER PLATTS

B2099

St Mary's Lane

PO

Doctors Surgery

Ticehurst
C of E Primary School

Oakover

Birchenwood
Farm

Gibbs
Reed Farm

Wardsbrook
Farm

Wadhurst Road

Wedd's

Chestnutfield
Wood

Cottenden

Myskyns

Bearhurst
Farm

Burgham

Sheepstreet Lane

Fox Farm

Shoyswell
Manor

Shortridge Farm

She

Old Shoyswell
Manor

Battenhurst
Farm

Furzes
Farm

1 grid square represents 500 metres

F **G** **H** `49` **J** **K**

I

2

3

4

`66`

5

6

7

8

Tanyard Farm

Broomhouse Bottom

Wilmshurst

Woolpack Farm

Sheffield Forest

Furner's Green

Sheffield Mill

Holmesdale Farm

Searles

Sheffield Green

Moyse's Farm

Spring Farm

Sheffield Park Farm

Knabbs Farmhouse

Spl Gre

Sheffield Park Garden (NT)

Atherall's Farm

PH

Fletching

Sheffield ridge

Fletching C of E School

Parsonage Farm

F **G** **H** `93` **J** **K**

Mill Farm

River Ouse

Netherall Farm

F G **Burnt Oak** H 53 J K

Grouse

I

2

3

4

70

5

6

7

8

Inchreed Farm

Fordbrook

Hastingford Farm

River Uck

Howbourne Farm

Smallberry Hill

Foxhole Farm

Stockland Lane

Stockland Farm

Five Chimneys

A272

Five Chimneys

Pound Green

Saxon Court

Waste Wood

Popeswood Farm

Hole Wood

Had Dow

Hall Lane

Wilderness Farm

Wilderness Lane

Sleeches

Fordbrook Hill

Harlow Down Road

Mill Lane

Tubbs

Howbourne Lane

Buxted Wood Lane

Howbourne Lane

Redbrook Lane

Vanguard Way

Lane

otter's een

F G H 97 J K

Hole Farm

Warren Farm

Sleeves Wood

Huggett's Furnace

School Lane

Wagmoans Lane

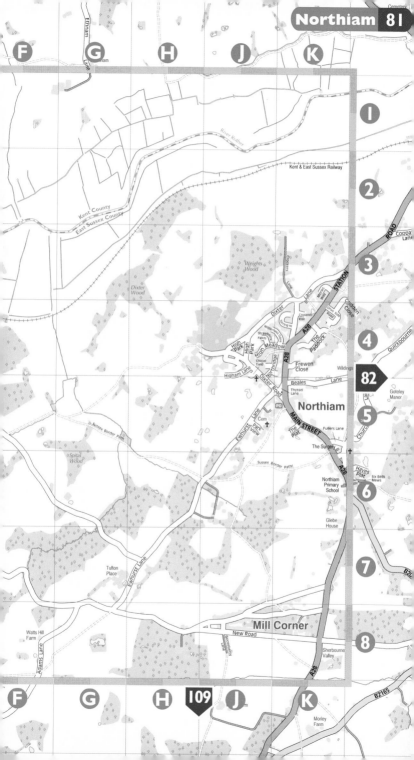

F
G
H
J
K

I

LC

Fairfield Court

Becket Barn
Farm

Brattle
House

Fairfield

2

Old Farm

Salters Wall
Lane

3
Salter's L

Poplar
Hall

Puddock

4 (A??)

Dean Court

Hook Lane

New Buildings
Farm

5

6
Whitehouse
Farm

A259 (T)

7

GUILDFORD LANE

8

F
G
H
J
K

Guildeford
Lane Corner

Farm

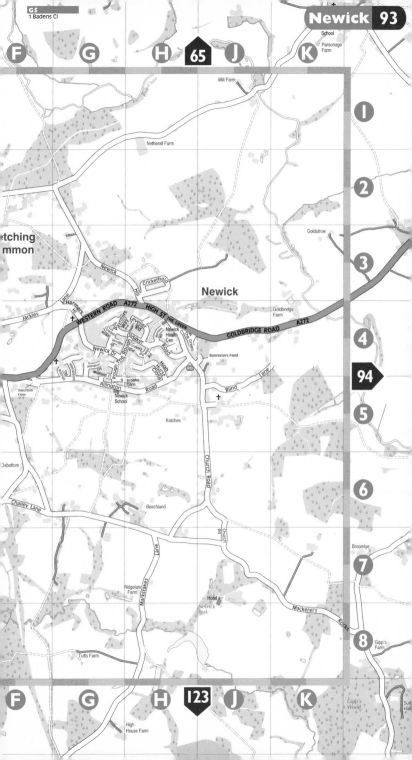

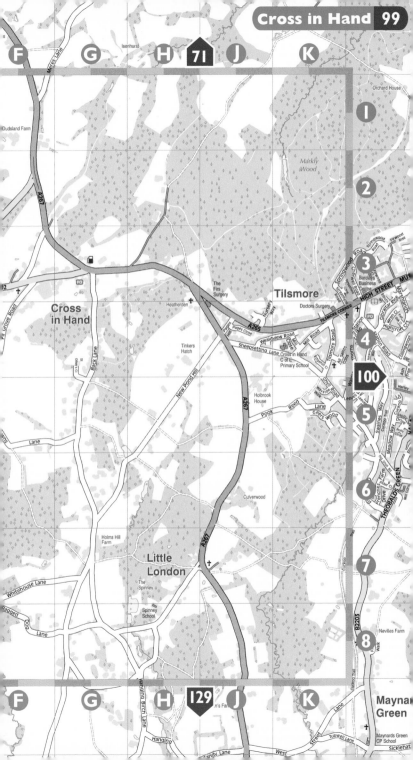

F G H **73** J K

I

2

3

4

102

5

6

7

8

F G H **131** J K

Barklye

Holbar
Farm

Kingsdo
Farm

Broad
Oak

Oak Hall (Sch)

Old
Tottingworth Farm

Binglett
Wood

Glendale Ma
Farm

Hugletts
Farm

B2096

Punnett's
Town

Blackdown

North Street

Forest Lane

B2096

Greenwoods

Lane

Chapel
Cross

Punnetts
Town School

Upper

Pont
Close

Flitterbrook Lane

Barley Mow Lane

Three Cups
Corner

St Dunstan's Farm

Kemp's
Wo

Caller's
Corner

Beaconland

Marlove

Lane

Flitterbrook Lane

TN21

Stone House

Chapman's

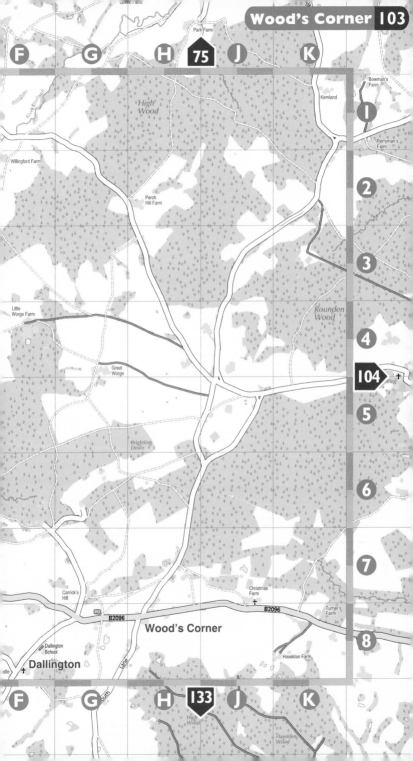

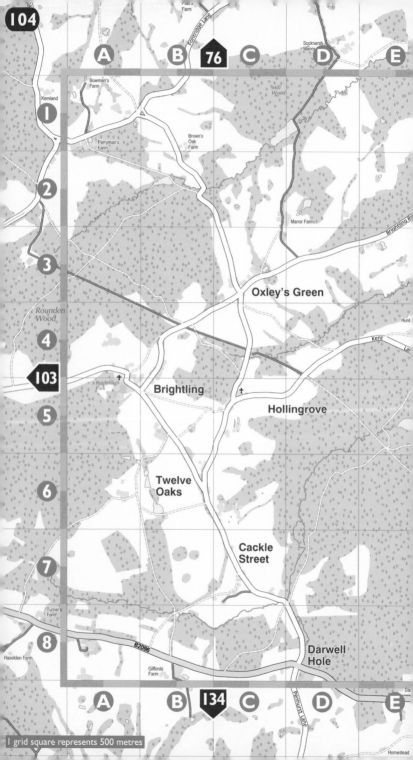

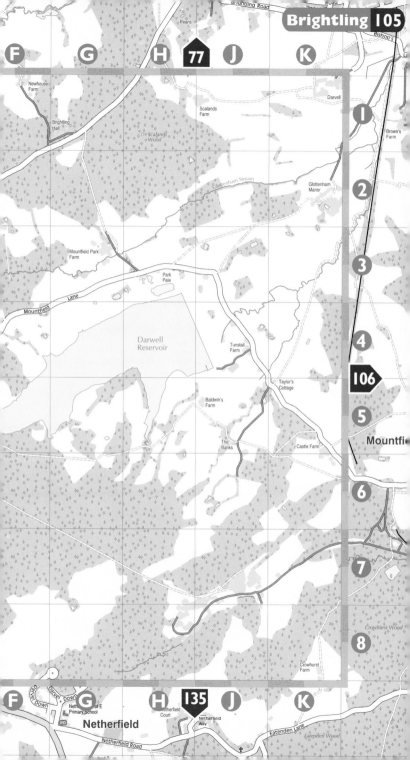

F G H **77** J K

Peans

Newhouse Farm

Brightling Hall

Scalands Farm

Scalands Wood

Darvell

Brown's Farm

1

Glottenham Stream

Glottenham Manor

2

Mountfield Park Farm

3

Park Pale

Mountfield Lane

Darwell Reservoir

Tunstall Farm

4

106

Baldwin's Farm

Taylor's Cottage

5

Mountfi

The Banks

Castle Farm

6

7

Crowhurst Wood

8

Crowhurst Farm

Darvell Down

Darvell Down

Neth of E Primary School

Netherfield Court

Netherfield Way

Netherfield

Netherfield Road

Eatenden Lane

Eatenden Wood

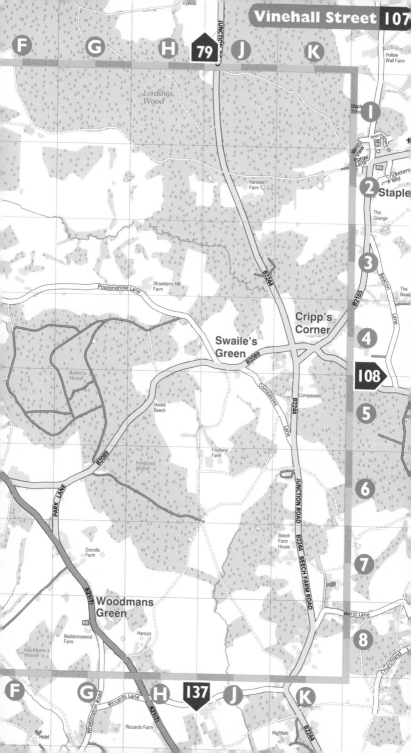

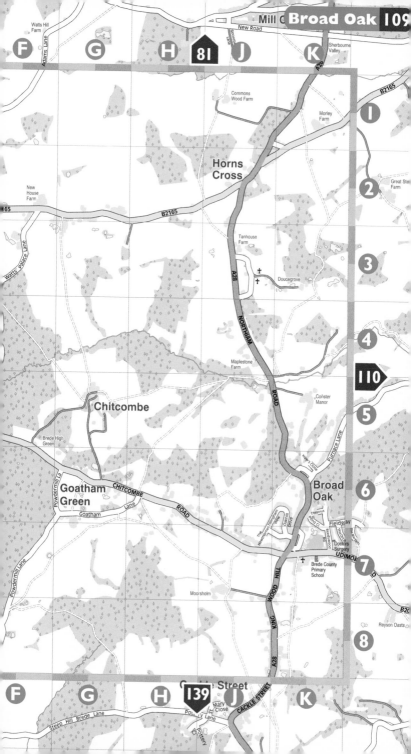

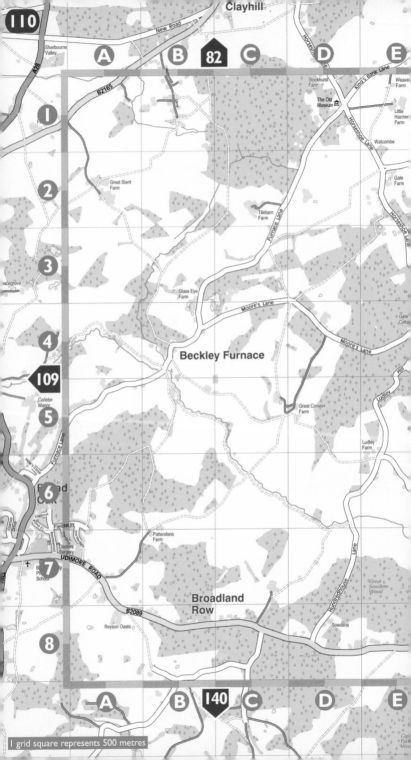

Flackley
Ash

Pea

Peasma
Place

Woodlands
Farm

The
Hermitage

starvecrow Lane

New

Pelsham

Groves

Lower Gate
Farm

Beckley
Woods

crow Lane

Partridge Farm

Hayes Lane

Dinglesden

Hayes
Farm

Hayes Lane

River Tillingham

Billingham
Farm

Newman's
Farm

Little Park
Wood

Court
Lodge

Udim

Knellstone

Cock Marling

Winchelsea Lane

Bixley Lane

Mill Lane

Tanhouse

A268

Dew Lane

Tillingham Lane

Billingham Lane

F **G** **H** 83 **J** **K**

I

2

3

4

112

5

6

7

8

F **G** **H** 141 **J** **K**

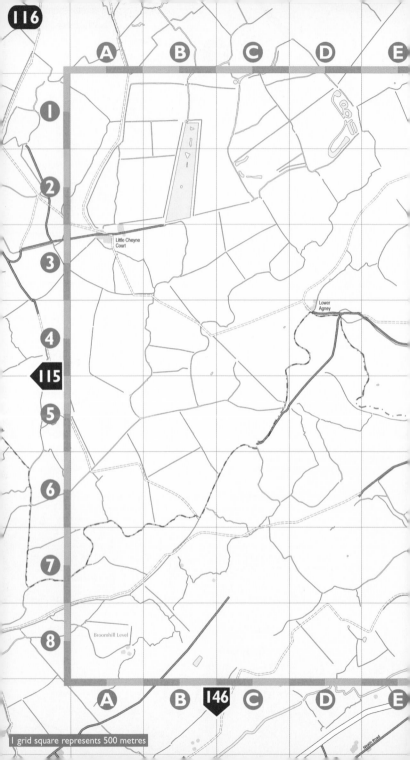

A　　　B　　　C　　　D　　　E

1

2

3

Little Cheyne
Court

Lower
Agney

4

115

5

6

7

8

Broomhill Level

A　　　B　　　C　　　D　　　E

146

Heath Road

1 grid square represents 500 metres

F G H J K

Corner

I

Newland
Farm

2
Bones
Farm

Newland

3

4

Little Scotney

5

Pigwell

Kent County
East Sussex County

6 JURY'S GAP

7 LC LC
West
Ripe

Scotney
Court

JURY'S GAP Road

The Forelands

8

F G H **147** J K

North Road stone

Ferguson Road Ferguson Road LC

Invicta Road

G5
1 The Paddocks

G6
1 Station Cl

F G H 91 J K

I

H6
1 South Downs

2

Southam

3

4

Honeypot
Lane

Shepherds Way

122

Yokehurst

5

F G H 152 J K

Heath
Farm

Helena
m

Shaw
Park

Great
Home
Wood

Inholms Farm

Chapel
Rd

Woodgate
Row

Homewoodgate
Farm

Wells
Cl

West
Gate

Station
Road

Plumpton Green

North Barnes
Farm

North
Hall

North   Barnes   Lane

Riddens
Lane

Riddens
La
Gardens

PO

Plumpton New
Primary
School

Barnfield

East Dw
Fields

LC

LC

Plumpton
Station

6

Mount
Pleasant
Lane

Highbridge Lane

7

Plumpton
Race Course

Plumpton
Lane

Rylands

Brookhouse

East
Chiltington

Novington Lane

8

Chiltingto.

Ashurst

The Old
Mill Ho

Chapel
Lane

PH

Woolton Farm

LC

Chi

A   B   92   C   Chailey   D   E

C4
1 Appledene Cnr
2 Grantham Cl
3 Green La
4 Hornbuckles Cl

B4
1 Whitegates Cl

1

The Hooke

2

Southam

South Street

Markstakes Lane

Markstakes Farm

3

Caveridge Lane

Markstakes Common

South Common

St John Bank Lane

4

Honey Lane

Chailey Comprehensive School

South Chailey

Balneath Manor

Shepherds Way

121

Yokehurst

Old Barns Farm

Swan Close

A275

5

North Hall

6

Hurst Barns

Woodbrooks Farm

Mount Pleasant

Highbridge Lane

7

Noverton

Chiltington Lane

Hewenstreet Farm

LC

8

Wootton Farm

Chiltington   153   Wickham Lane   Resting Oak Hl

A   B   C   D   E

A275

Wilding Wood

RESTING OAK

124

A   B   **94**   C   D   E

Mackerel's Rocks

Vuggles Farm

Gipp's Farm

Constantia Manor

New House Farm

1

Gipp's Wood

Sutton Hall

2

Longford Stream

Beaks Farm

Longford Farm

River Ouse

3

Spithurst

Station Road

Tile Barn Cl

Isfield

PO

4

Burtenshaw Farm

123

Birch

Mount Pleasa

Lewes Road

5

Dallas Lane

Anchor Lane

Scufflings

Boathouse Farm

Lane

Delves Farm

6

Banks Farm

Oaklands Park

7

Isfield Road

PH

8

Cinder Hill

Upper Clay Hill Farm

Barcombe Mills Road

Barcombe House

A   B   **155**   C   D   E

Iron River

1 grid square represents 500 metres

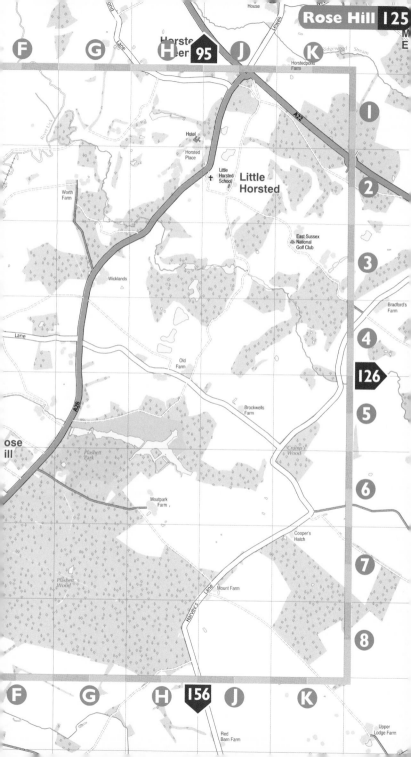

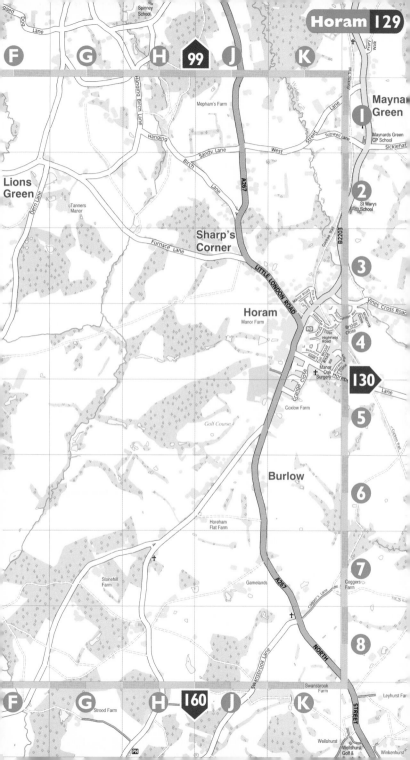

F
G
H
99
J
K

Dog Lane
Spinney School
Mepham's Farm
Mayna Green
Friary Walk
Cuckoo Trail

I
Maynards Green CP School

Hanging Birch Lane
Hanging
Sandy Lane
West
Street
Tubwell Lane
Sicklehat

Lions Green

Dern Lane
Tanners Manor
Birch Lane
A267

2
St Marys School

Furnace Lane
Sharp's Corner

Little London Road
Cuckoo Trail
B2203

3

Horam
Manor Farm
Manor Road
Vines Cross Road

PO
Highfield Road
Bridge Close
Maldron

4

Grange Close
Manor Oak Surgery
Horebs

130
Lane

Coxlow Farm

5

Golf Course

Burlow

6

Horeham Flat Farm

Stonehill Farm
Gamelands
A267
Coggers Lane

7
Coggers Farm

8

Swanbrook Lane
North

F
G
H
160
J
K

Strood Farm
Swansbrook Farm
Leyhurst Far

Street

PH
Wellshurst
Wellshurst Golf &
Winkenhurst

TN21

F G H 101 J K

Beaconland

Markly Lane

Fitterbrook Lane

I

Stone House

Chapman's Town

Rushlake Green PH
PD

2

Great Iwood

Warbleton

PH

Chapmans Town Road

Back Lane

3

Kingsley Hill Farm

Hammer Lane

Bathurst Farm

4

Tilement Farm

132

Iwood Place Farm

5

Durrants Farm

Beech Hill Farm

6

Egypt Farm

Cralle Place

7

Foul Mile

Furnace Brook

8

Court Horeham

Hammer Lane

F G H 162 J K

Bemzells Lane

Trolliloes

Lane

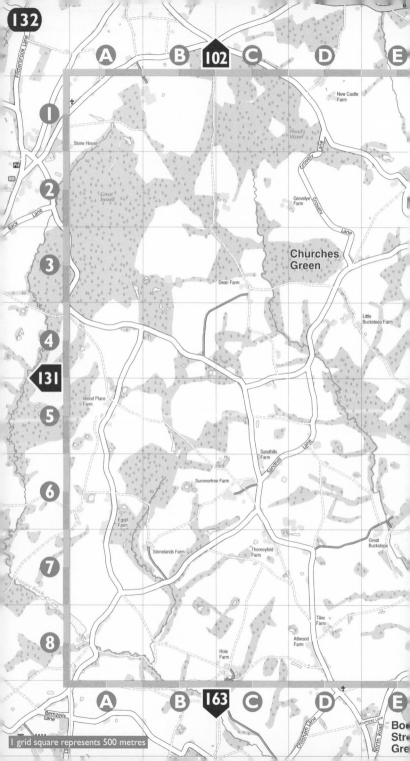

A B **102** C D E

1

Fittarbrook Lane

+

Stone House

PH
PD

Back Lane

2

Great Iwood

3

4

5

Iwood Place Farm

6

Egypt Farm

Furnace Brook

7

Stonelands Farm

8

Hole Farm

New Castle Farm

Road's Wood

Crovely Lane

Grovelye Farm

Crovely Lane

Churches Green

Dean Farm

Little Bucksteep Farm

Sandhills Farm

Sandhill Lane

Summertree Farm

Thorneyfold Farm

Great Bucksteep

Christ...

Tiles Farm

Althwood Farm

A B **163** C D + E

Bemzelis Lane

Chisham Lane

Trumpet Lane

North Road

**Bod...
Str...
Gre...**

| 1 grid square represents 500 metres |

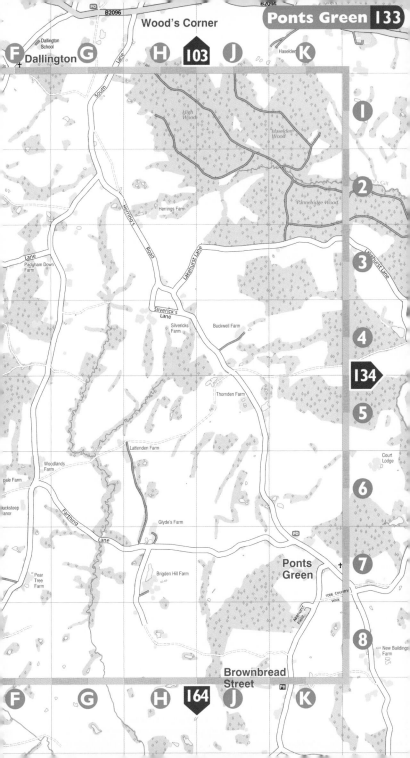

Wood's Corner

F **Dallington** **G** **H** **103** **J** **K**

Dallington School

B2096

Haselden

I

High Wood

Haselden Wood

2

Pinnelbridge Wood

Herrings Farm

3

Lavenhurst Lane

Padgham Down Farm

Lane

Silverick's Lane

Silvericks Farm

Buckwell Farm

4

134

Thornden Farm

5

Lattenden Farm

Court Lodge

Woodlands Farm

6

pale Farm

ucksteep anor

Glyde's Farm

Ponts Green

7

Farthing Lane

Pear Tree Farm

Brigden Hill Farm

1066 Country Walk

8

New Buildings Farm

Brownbread Street

F **G** **H** **164** **J** PH **K**

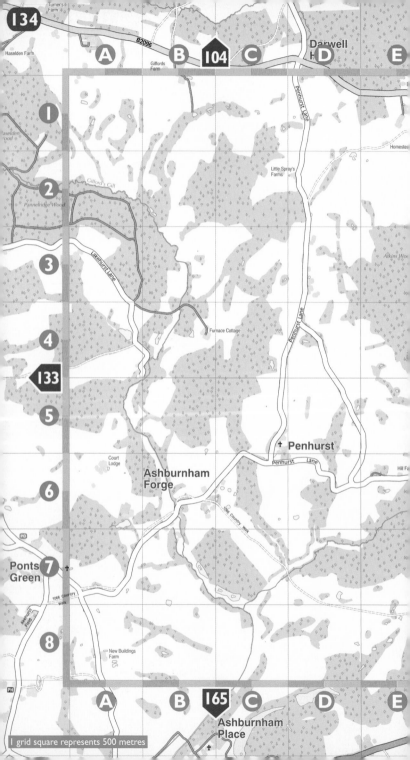

A

B

104

C

Darwell

D

E

Turners Farm

Haselden Farm

B2096

Giffords Farm

1

Haselden Wood

Penhurst Lane

Homestea

2

Gifford's Gill

Pannehidge Wood

Little Spray's Farms

3

Lakehurst Lane

Atkins Woo

4

Furnace Cottage

133

5

Penhurst Lane

Penhurst

Court Lodge

Ashburnham Forge

Penhurst Lane

Hill Fa

6

1066 Country Walk

7

Ponts Green

PO

8

1066 Country Walk

Resevr Field

New Buildings Farm

PH

A

B

165

C

D

E

Ashburnham Place

F G H **105** J K

Darvel Down

Darvel Down

Netherfield C of E
Primary School

PO

Netherfield

Netherfield
Court

Netherfield
Way

Netherfield Road

Eatenden Lane

Eatenden Wood

hurst
Farm

Ivyland Farm

B2096

HighWood

Netherfield Road

Netherfield
Place

Burnthouse Wood

Ashes Wood

Creep Wood

Spray's Wood

Foxhole
Farm

136

Beech
Farm

Lane

Westfurze

Tower
House

Beechdown Wood

B2096

A271 NORTH

Battle Hospital

TRA

Claverham
Community Co

A271

Crowders

Lane

B2204

Tellis Coppice

Steven's
Crouch

Freckley

CATSFIELD

TN3

F G **166** J ROAD K

Great
Farm

H

Parkgate
Manor

Country Walk

I
2
3
4
5
6
7
8

A **B** **106** **C** **D** **E**

Crowhurst
Eatenden Wood

Lenden Lane

1

Crowhurst
Farm

2

Burnthouse Wood

3

Ashes Wood

Netherfield

Canadia

Le Rette
Farm

Wood's Place

Woodsdale

Lower Gate
Farm

Canadia Road

A2100

LONDON ROAD

Whatlington Road

4

135

Kingswell
Farm

Hills

Beech Cl

Netherfield Road

Wattle's
Wish

Virgin's Lane

Oak West Rd

Whatlington Road

Uckham Lane

5

Beech
Farm

A2100

Bowman Drive

Dixies Hill

Caldbec Hill

BATTLE

6

Rother
District Council

Chain Lane

Mount Joy

Mount Street

Caldbec Hill

Little F
Farm

7

A271

NORTH TRADE ROAD

Battle Hospital

Claverham
Community College

Battle Gate's

Colgates

Hampden
Close

Claverham Crisp

Claverham Wy

Asten Flds

Battle & Langton
School

Martins
Oak
Surgery

Doctors Surgery

PO

Woodlands

Market Sq

A2100 HIGH STREET

Battle Museum

M

Park Lane

Battle Abbey
School

UPPER LAKE

Langton
Close

LOWER

8

Tower
Hill

North Country Walk

POWDERMILL LANE

Great Park
Farm

A **B** **167** **C** B2095 **D** **E**

Hotel

F G H 109 J K

Cackle Street

Steep Hill Brede Lane

Mary's Close

Pottery Lane

Pottery

CACKLE STREET

Steephill Wood

Park Wood

I

Stubb Lane

Brede

BREDE HILL

2

Hare Fa

River Brede

3

4

Rocks Farm

Crowham Manor

Little Knight's Oast

140

Miller's Hill Cottage Lane

Marlpits Farm

A28

5

Doleham Farm

Benskins

Doleham Lane

6

1066 C... alk

Westbrook Lane

Mill Lane

Mill

New Cut

Ferrens Cl.

Pattleton's Farm

7

New Cut

Downoak Farm

1066

ark Farm Estate

Westfield

MAIN ROAD

Moor Road

Oak Wood

Maxfield

Wheel Lane

Church Lane

Moor Lane

Heathlands

Greenacres

Vicarage Lane

New Moorsite

The Moor

8

A28

Stonestile Lane

F G H 170 J K

Lankh.. Farm

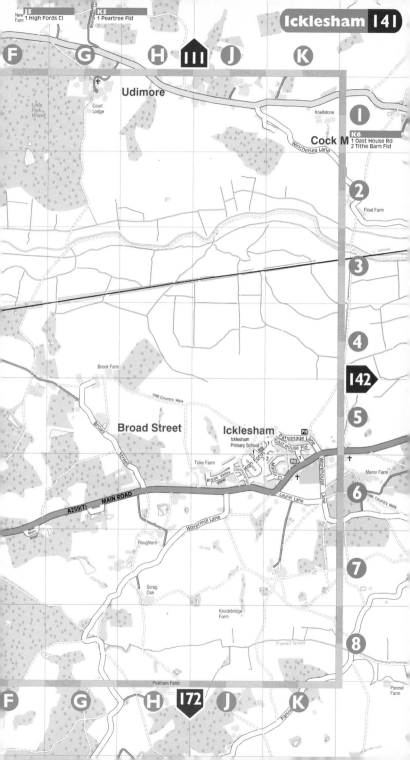

J5
New 1 High Fords Cl
Farm

K5
1 Peartree Fld

F G H J K

Udimore

Court
Lodge

Little
Park
Wood

Knellstone

Winchelsea Lane

Cock M

I6
1 Oast House Rd
2 Tithe Barn Fld

Float Farm

Brook Farm

1066 Country Walk

Broad Street

Icklesham

Icklesham
Primary School

Parsonage Lane

PH

1 Oast House Fld

Broad

Street

Toke Farm

Brede Valley
View

High
Fords

Manor Cl

Manor Farm

1066 Country Walk

Laurel Lane

Workhouse Lane

A259(T)   MAIN ROAD

Main
Road

Watermill Lane

Roughters

Scrag
Oak

Knockbridge
Farm

Pannel Sewer

Pannel
Farm

Pickham Farm

F G H J K

I42

Pannel

H4 1 Windmill Wy
H5 1 Greyfriars Pl

F G H **113** J K

I
2
3
4
144
5
6
7
8

Camber Castle
✗

Rye Marsh Farm

Nook Beach

Watch House

Castle Farm

Sutton Ind Park

Winchelsea Beach

Willow Lane

Rye Bay Club House

The Ridge

Saxon Shore Way

NEW WINCHELSEA ROAD

A259(T)

ROYAL MILITARY ROAD

A259(T)

Sea Road

Sea Road

Old River Way

Mortars Place

Morlais Ridge

Pett Level Road

Pools Hill Road

Dimsdale Sewer

Donald Way

Windsor Way

Victoria Way

Streatfield Lane

school

F G H J K

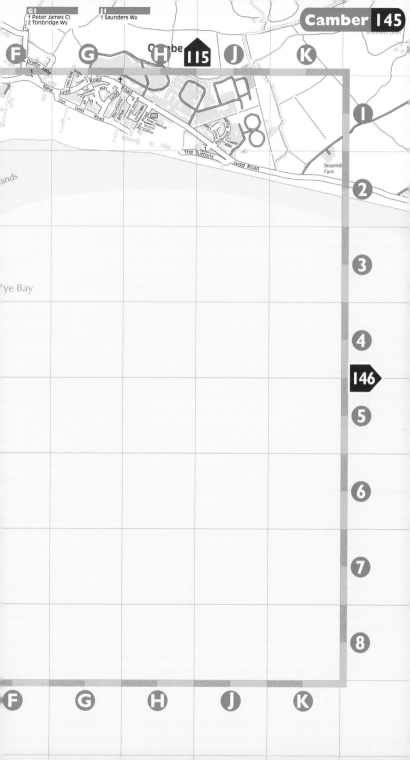

G1
1 Peter James Cl
2 Tonbridge Wy

J1
1 Saunders Wy

Cambe

Prann Lane

New Lydd Road
Old Lydd Road
Denham Way
Lydd Road
Links View
Dene
Dunes Avenue

First Avenue
Second Avenue

The Suttons

Lydd Road

Broomhill Farm

Broomhill Level

ands

'ye Bay

I

2

3

4

146 ▶

5

6

7

8

116

145

Broomhill Level

A   B   C   D   E

1

Broomhill Farm

2

Jury's Gap

Neath Road

Neath Road

Midrip

Lydd Road

Broomhill Sands

3

4

5

6

7

8

A   B   C   D   E

1 grid square represents 500 metres

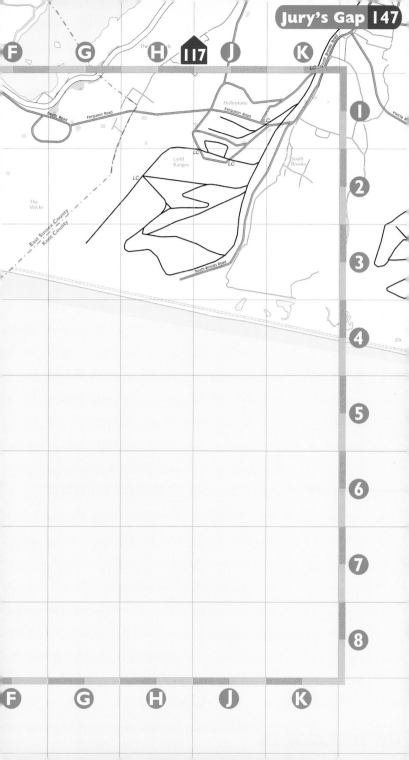

F G H **118** J K

I

Butcher's Wood

KEYMER ROAD

South B

Ockenden Wy

Lagwood Close

Bonny Wd Rd

Court Vie

Downlands School

BRIGHTON ROAD

Halfway

Hautboyes

Coldharbour Farm

NEW ROAD

B2112

2

New Way Lane

Theo Warenne

A273

Clayton

3

Underhill

Wolstonbury

Hill Fort

CLAYTON HILL

Clayton Windmills

Mill Lane

4

150

Clayton Tunnel

South Downs Way

South Downs Way

5

PYECOMBE HILL

Pyecombe

Church Hl

School La

Church La

Haresdean

6

145

ow Down

South Downs Way

West Sussex County
Brighton and Hove

Pangdean Farm

7

West Sussex County
Brighton and Hove

8

F G H **177** J K

uth Farm

Sussex

Chiltington

Ashurst

Chapel Lane

PH

Ⓐ   Ⓑ   Old   121   Ⓒ   ✝   Ⓓ   Ⓔ
          Mill Ho

Stantons
Farm

❶

Street Lane

❷

Plumpton Lane

Novington
Manor

Novington Lane

❸

Wales Farm

✝

Warningore
Farm

War
Hou

Plumpton

❹   B2116

Novington
Farm

❺   Plumpton Bostall

South Downs Way

Blackcap

Plumpton Plain

hill

❻

Ascombe
Bottom

❼   South Downs Way

❽   Buckland
    Bank

Ⓐ   Ⓑ   180   Ⓒ   Ⓓ   Ⓔ
            South Downs Way

I grid square represents 500 metres

Balmer
Down

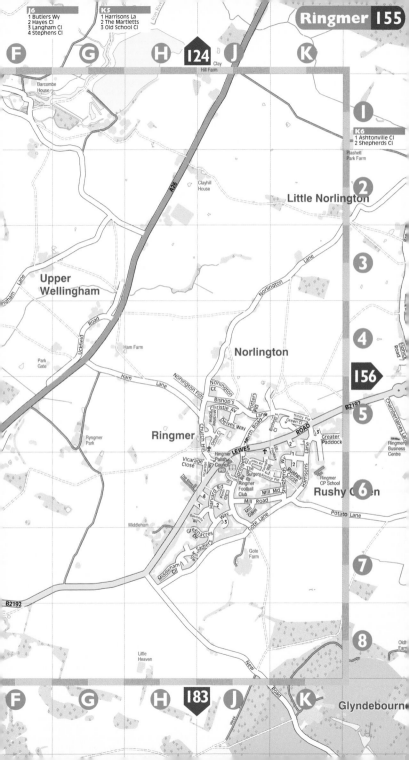

F G H **128** J K

I

2

3

4

160

5

6

7

8

Hilder's Court

Vanguard Way

Highlands Farm

Frith's Farm

Wealdway

Parsonage Farm

Chiddingly Place

Chiddingly

PH

PO

Chiddingly Cricket Club

Wealdway

Little Park Farm

Wealdway

Hale Green

Hamly Bridge

Scraper's Hill

Chiddingly CP School

Muddles Green

Thunder's Hill

House

Burgh Hill

Holmes's Hill

Vanguard Way

PO

PO

Golden Cross

Nash Street

A22

Hackhu Stud

New Cuckmere

The Old Farmhouse

Northfield Business Park

A22

Camberlot Hall

Camberlot Road

Hackhurst Lane

L E

Vanguard Way

Limekiln Farm

F G H **187** J K

Field House

Clover Farm

Road

160

A　**B**　**129**　**C**　**D**　**E**

1

Stream Mill

Hale Green

Strood Farm

PH

Gun Hill

Broadway

Swanbrook Lane

2

West Street Farm

Wholeway

3

Hamly Bridge

World's End Farm

Lea

4

159

Hill

Pekes House

5

Perryland Farm

Broad Farm

Granary Business Centre

6

Hackhurst Stud

Hackhurst Lane

Hell CP

7

thfield Business

A22

Lower Dicker

North Street B2104

Marsh Lane

Lower Horsebridge

A271

8

Camberlot Hall

Cott Road

Knight's Farm

A267

Hotel

Upper Horsebr

Hatches Farm

A　**B**　**188**　**C**　**D**　**E**

1 grid square represents 500 metres

Swanbrook Lane

N

Swans

A22

POUT ROAD

Stamash

F   **G**   **H**   **132**   **J**   **K**

I

Tiles Farm

Attwood Farm

Hole Farm

Chilsham Lane

Trumpet Lane

North Road

Bodle Street Green

2

Beard's Farm

Ale House Farm

Prinkle Lane

Prinkle Farm

3

Chilsham

Nunningham Farm

Bagham Lane

4   Cowden Farm

164

5

James Avenue

West Terrace

Fairfield

West Monceux Road

Bramah Lane

Herstmonceux

West End

PO

The Surgery

Windmill Hill

Darre

Airlawns

Dr

Road

CHILSHAM ROAD

GARDNER STREET

Herstmonceux C of E School

A271

Victoria Rd

Davis Orch

The Surgery

Hurst

Highview

Cl

Jiggs Lane

Nursery Lane

6

Chapel Row

Lime Park

PO

A271

Tiley Lane

Flowers Green

Comphurst Lane

Comphurst

Windmill Hill

7

Butler's Lane

Wartling Road

8

Herstmonceux Place

Golden Cross

F   Lower   **G**   **H**   **191**   **J**   **K**

Cherry Croft Farm

Church

Road

Wartling Wood

A B 133 C D E

Brownbread
Street

PH

Boot
Street
Green

Prinkle

2

Prinkle Farm

Huggetts Station

Bray's
Hill

3

Prinkle Lane

Brownings
Farm

4

Cowden
Farm

Tilley Lane

Ash Bourne

163

Tilley Farm

5

dmill

Gardners Farm

6

Tilley Lane

Nunningham Stream

A271

PO

7

Windmill
Hill Place

Boreham
Street

Sussex Country Way

BOREHAM HILL

8

Wartling Road

A271

Hotel

Wood Lane

Sussex Country Way

Lane

A B 192 C D E

Puddledock

Champneys Farm

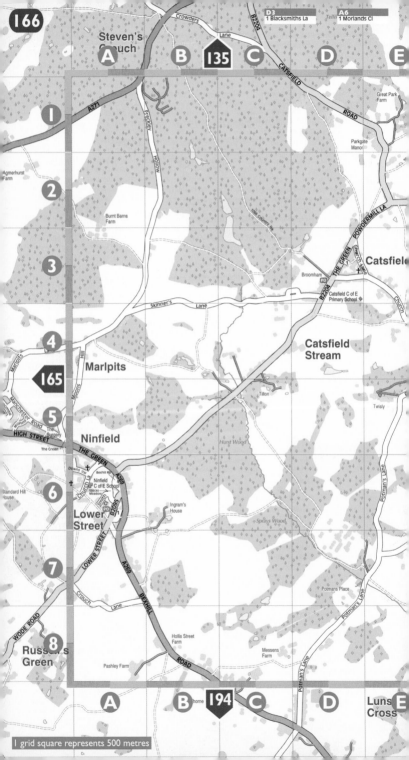

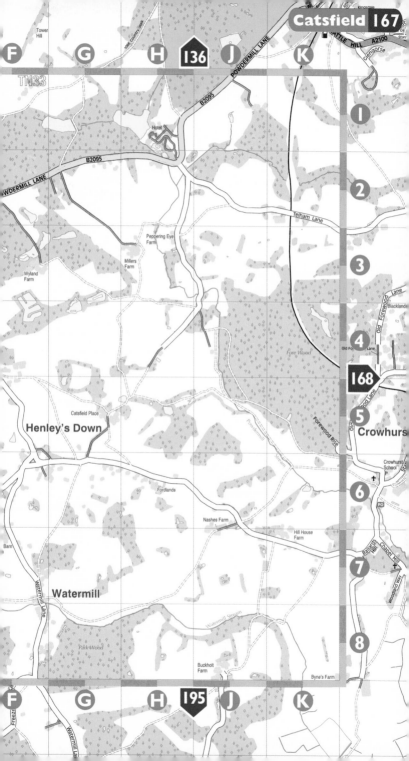

E8
1 Hartfield Mdw
2 Sandr'ham H'hts ay

A **B** **137** **C** **D** **E**

BATTLE HILL
Kingsdale
Close
The Spinney
Starrs
The Coppice
The Oak
A2100
Starr's On La

Branshill
Farm

Little
Hemingfold
Farm

Starr's
Green

Telham

1

Loose Farm

HASTINGS ROAD

A2100

†

2

Telham Lane

Telham   Lane

Crowhurst Park

Forewood Lane

3

Telham Place

Pye's
Farm

Lane

Blacklands

Brakes Coppice
Farm

Old Forewood

Fore Wood

4

Old Forewood Lane

167

Crowhurst
Station

Craig Close

5

Wood Rise

Crowhurst

Station Road

Park
Farm

Lane

Breadsell

6

Swaim

Crowhurst
School

†

Stonebridge Farm

Hill House
Farm

Swainham Lane

7

Ballard

Chapel Hill

†

Sampock Hill

**Green
Street**

Highfield
Business Park

Byne's Farm

8

Chowns Lane

Lower Wilting Farm

Crowhurst Road

Crowhurst Road

A **B** **196** **C** **D** **E**

Adam's Farm

Upper W
Farm

CROWHURST

K6
Street Names for
these grid squares
are listed at the
back of the index

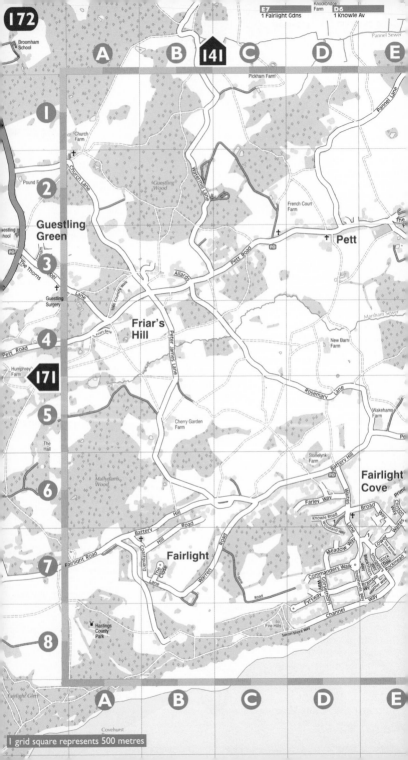

Pannel
Farm

Carter's
Farm

Lunsford

**Pett
Level**

Pett Road

Chick Hill

Pett Road

Cliff End

Cliff End Lane

Saxon Shore Way

Saxon Shore Way

Pett Level Road

Saxon Lovers Way

142

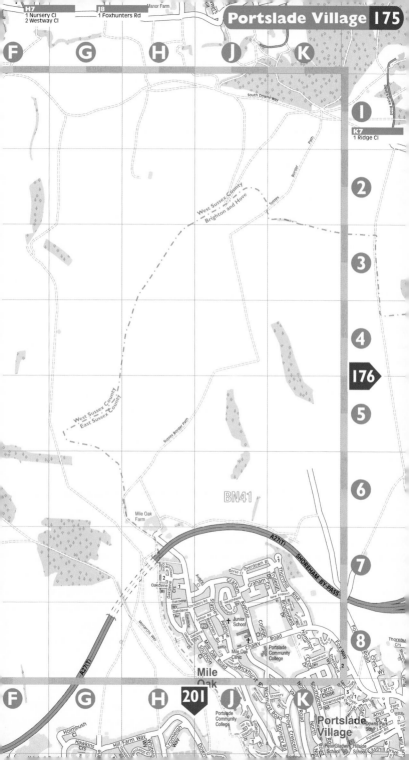

H7
1 Nursery Cl
2 Westway Cl

J8
1 Foxhunters Rd

Manor Farm

F G H J K

south downs way

I

K7
1 Ridge Cl

2

West Sussex County
Brighton and Hove

3

Sussex Border Path

4

176

5

West Sussex County
East Sussex County

Sussex Border Path

6

BN41

Mile Oak
Farm

A27(T)

SHOREHAM BY-PASS

7

Overdown Rd

Gorse Rd

Graham Avenue

Graham Cl

Oakdene

Oakdene Way

Christison's Rd

Heathfield Avenue

New England Rise

Thornhill Rise

Broomfield

Junior School

College Road

Hampton Rise

Chalky Road

8

Thornbu
Crs

Mile Oak
Clinic

Wickhurst Rd

Portslade
Community
College

Fox Way

Foxdown Road

Crest Way

Usha

Mile
Oak

F G H 201 J K

Portslade
Community
College

Hornbush
Cl

Hawkins
Crs

Hill Farm Way

Cornbush Way

Winter

Down

Tove Crescent

Stoney Rd

Stonery Road

West Way

Southdown Road

Farm
Close

Downsview

PeterGladwin Hillside
School School

Portslade
Village

Downs Park

Foxdov

Anvil

Flint

Easthill Drive

176

148

Saddlescombe

A   B   C   D   E

C8
1 The Dene

B8
1 Meads Cl
2 Meyners Cl
3 Sycamore Cl

A8
1 Juniper Cl
2 The Parks

1

D8
1 Harmsworth Crs
2 Northease Dr
3 Northease Gdns

2

E8
1 Findon Cl
2 Midhurst Wk
3 Nutley Cl

3

4

175

5

6

7

8

Portslade
Village

A   B   **202**   C   D   E

South Downs Way

Devil's Dyke Road

Devil's Dyke Farm

Devil's Dyke Road

Brighton and Hove / West Sussex County

Skeleton Hovel

Brighton & Hove Golf Course

Monarch's Way

Devil's Dyke Road

A27(T)

SHOREHAM BY-PASS

FOX WAY

Foredown Road

Benfield Valley Golf Course

Thornbush Crs

Hardwick Way

East Sussex County Council

Hangleton

Hangleton Lane

1 grid square represents 500 metres

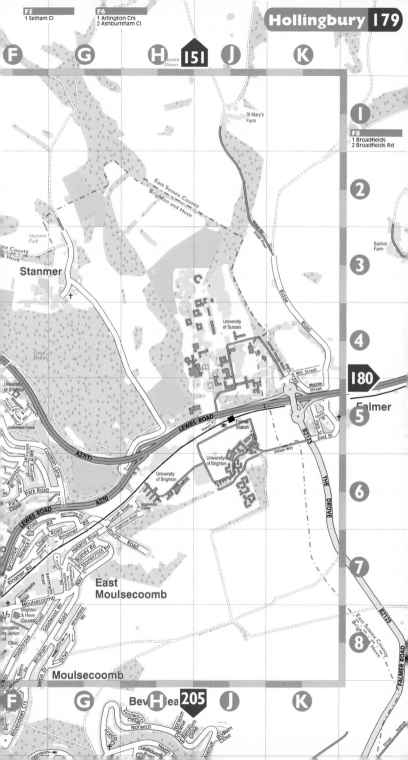

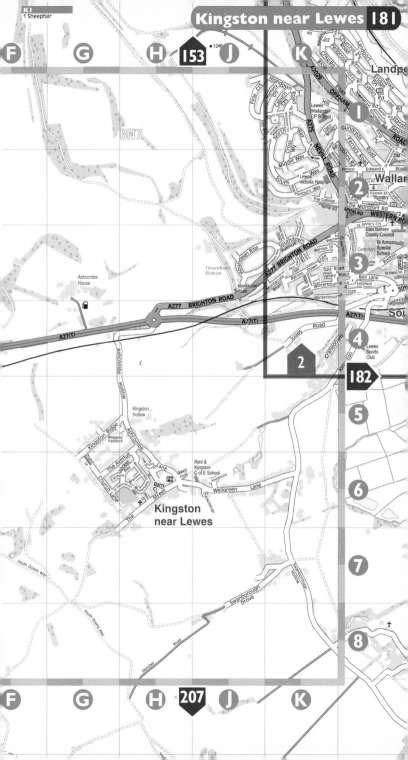

F G H **157** J K

1

Mark
Cross

2

3

Lulhams Farm

Hall
Court Farm

4

186

Middle
Barn

Sheeplands
Farm

5

Bushy
Lodge Farm

LC

6

Middle
Farm

Pookhill
Barn

7

Sherrington
Manor

8

F G **211** J K

Charleston
Farmhouse

A27(T)

Tilton Farm

F1
1 Ashburnham Pl

F2
1 Chesnut Cl
2 Lepeland

HAILSHAM

I

F3
1 Busheyfields
2 Hamelsham Ct

F5
1 Bl'ksmiths Copse
2 Oaklands Wy

2

F6
1 Quintin Cl

3

G1
1 Hawks Farm Cl
2 Lansdowne Gdns

G3
1 Beuzeville Av
2 Summercourt

4

190

5

G4
1 Downsview Wy

6

G5
1 Freshfield Cl
2 Holly Cl
3 Sandbanks Gv
4 Sherwood Gn

7

G6
1 Sandbanks Gdns

8

H1
1 Harebeating Cl
2 H'beating Gdns
3 North Heath Cl

215

H6
1 Beechwood Cl

H5
1 Compton Ter
2 Mount View Ter

H4
1 Ashford Cl
2 Chapel Barn Cl
3 Timbers Ct

H3
1 Greenacres Wy
2 Nursery Cl

Golden Cross

Lower Road

Church Road

Herstmonceux Place

Cherry Croft Farm

Church Farm

Airy Road

Flamstead Road

Middleyne Road

Church Road

Herstmonceux Castle

Halley Road

1066 Country Walk

Bradley Road

Wartling Road

Wartling Wood

Cha...

The Well House

Cooper's Farm

Wartling

Wartling Road

1066 Country Walk

Thorn Haven

1066 Country Walk

Walk

Marsh Foot Farm

Newhouse Farm

Pylons Farm

Butler's

163

217

192

F   G   H   J   K

I

2

3

4

5

6

7

8

A B C D E

Wartling Rd

Wood Lane

A271

Hotel

BOR-

1066 Country Walk

Boreham Lane

1

Wartling Wood

Champneys Farm

Puddledock

2

Wartling Road

The Well House

1066 Country Walk

Boreham Lane

Rocklands Farm

3

Cooper's Farm

Wartling Road

Nut Brown Farm

4 **Wartling**

Horsewalk

Horse Bridge

Horsewalk

Waller's Haven

5

New Barn Farm

B2095

Marsh Foot Farm

6

PH

7

A259(T)

8

A B C D E

A259(T)

iddle ge

Waller's Haven

A259(T)

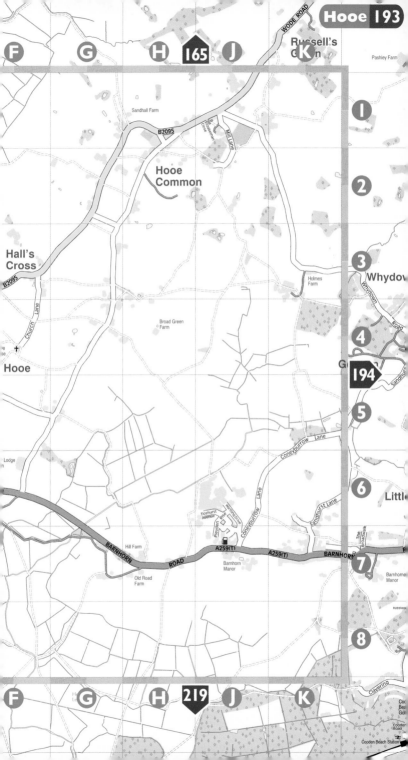

F3
1 Pankhurst Cl

F6
1 Leasingham Gdns

F7
1 Downlands Cl

G3
1 Faygate Cl
2 Morgan Cl
3 Redwell Av

G4
1 Oakwood Av

G5
1 Dane Court Cl

H4
1 Bank Rd

H5
1 Maberley Rd

H6
1 Bowrey Pl
2 Edinburgh Rd
3 Hanover Cl
4 Jacobs Acre
5 Pipers Cl

H7
1 Cookham Dene

K5
1 Gainsborough Rd

K6
1 Compton Cl
2 Gleneagles Cl
3 Martlets

K7
1 Brookfield Rd

170

197

A4
1 The Cloisters
2 Prince's Rd
3 St Paul's Pl
4 Victoria Rd

A3
1 De Cham Av
2 St Catherine's Cl
3 Summerfields

A2
1 Selmeston Cl

B1
1 Hole Farm Cl

B2
1 Piltdown Cl

B3
1 Braybrooke Ter
2 Cornwallis Ter
3 Hillyglen Cl
4 Hopgarden Cl
5 Linton Crs
6 Station Ap

B4
1 Claremont
2 Dorset Pl
3 Prospect Pl
4 Robertson St
5 Schwerte Wy
6 White Rock Gdns

C1
1 Hughenden Pl

D2
1 Becket Cl
2 Gladstone Rd
3 Saunders Cl

D3
1 Alpine Rd
2 Castledown Av
3 Exmouth Pl
4 Gordon Rd
5 Swan Ter

D4
1 Cutter La
2 East St
3 Pelham Crs
4 Shell La
5 Sun La

C3, C4, E3
Street Names for
these grid squares
are listed at the
back of the index

E1
1 Broomgrove Rd
2 Robertsons Hl

E2
1 The Glebe

I grid square represents 500 metres

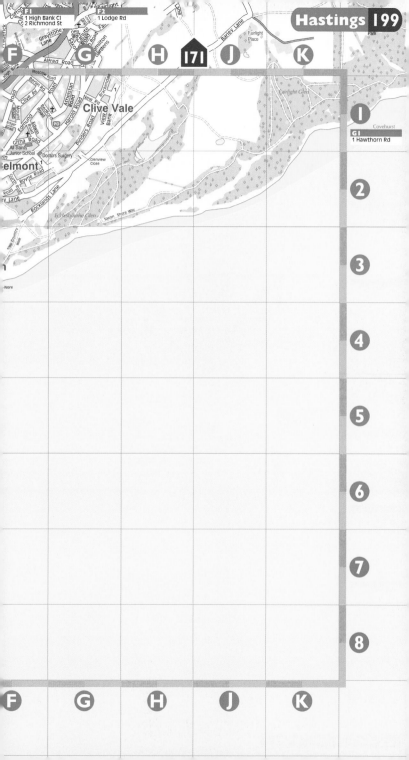

A4
1 Church St
2 St Aubyn's Crs

A3
1 Bampfield St
2 Barnes Rd
3 Buckler St

A1
1 Blackthorn Cl
2 Brackenbury Cl
3 Cornford Cl
4 Foredown Cl
5 Highways
6 Meadow Cl

A **B** **176** **C** **D** **E**

Hangleton

I Portslade Village

B1
1 Cottage Bush Cl

B3
1 Southdown Av

2

B4
1 George St
2 Symbister Rd

3

Souther Cross

1 Camden St
2 Clarendon Pl

B2194 VICTORIA ROAD

Portslade Stn.

4

A259

201

WELLINGTON ROAD

5

PORTSLADE-BY-SEA

C1
1 Dale View Gdns
2 Northease Cl

NEW CHURCH ROAD Aldrington

B2066

6

C4
1 Mornington Crs

7

D1
1 Ashlings Wy
2 Storrington Cl
3 Sunninghill Cl
4 Thornhill Cl

8

D4
1 Ingram Crs

A **B** **C** **D** **E**

E1
1 Fallowfield Cl

E2
1 Acacia Av
2 Torrance Cl
3 Wayfield Cl

E4
1 Mainstone Rd
2 Scott Rd

1 grid square represents 500 metres

HOVE

F4
1 Haybourne Cl

F5
1 Exceat Cl
2 School Rl

F
G
H
179
J
K

Moulsecoomb

Bevendean

Kenilworth
Norwich Close
Norwich
Bamford Close
Bodiam Close
Knepp
Heath Hi Av
Cleybourne
Bevendean County
Primary School
The Willow
Surgery
Taunton
Hornby
Auckland
Walmer Crs
Drive
Bodiam Avenue

Upper Bevendean

Drove
Ivor Rd
McWilliam Rd
Down parish church

I

F6
1 Flimwell Cl
2 Lwr Chalv'ton Pl

Norton Rd

2

F7
1 Eastern Rd

Warren Av
Barnwood
Downland
Avenue
Warren Farm
Vernon Avenue
Farm Hill
Warren Rd
Ridgway
Close
Warren Way
Falmer Gdns
The

Drove
Downland
2
Channel View Rd
Sexrey Rd
Midway
Heath
Avenue
1
Warren Road
3
Hazel
Cottage
Clinic
Downs
View
School

3

F8
1 De Courcel Rd

Bear Road
Warren Road
Sussex Nuffield
Hospital
Woodingdean
School

Cemetery
Warren Road
Brighton
Racecourse
Woodingdean

Pitt
Gdns
Briarcro
Road

Lodsworth Cl
Alburne
Cl
Swanborough
Wilson Avenue
Milvard Crs

Haybourne
Way
Wilson
Drive
Views Cross

4

206

Whitehawk
Infant School
Uphall
Wilson Avenue
Wick
Bottom
BN2

5

G4
1 Pulborough Cl
2 Sevelands Cl
3 Sompting Cl
4 Swanborough
Close

Whitehawk
Junior School
Secondary
School
Sheepcote
Valley
Golf Course

Whitehawk

6

G5
1 Horsham Cl
2 Pett Cl
3 Selmeston Pl

Whitehawk
Clinic
Stanley Deason
Leisure Centre

Orange
ndean
School

7

G6
1 Selmestone Rd

Manor
Way
Eldon Road
Broadway Surgery
Henley Rd
B2118
Bristol Gdns
Eastern Rd
Tower
End Est

8

Roedean
Road
The Cliff
Roedean
Crescent
Roedean
Road
Roedean
School

Black Rock
Marine Drive
Marina Way
A259
B2118
Roedean

Virgin Cinemas
Marina Way
Trafalgar
Gate
Victory
Mews
The
Strand
Brighton
Marina
MARINE
DRIVE
A259

F
G
H
J
K

D5, D7, E7
Street Names for
these grid squares
are listed at the
back of the index

J3
1 Downland Cl
2 Hylden Cl
3 Warren Cl

H2
1 Leybourne Cl
2 Taunton Wy

F G H 181 J K

I
2
3
4
208
5
6
7
8

Telscomb

South Downs Way

Whiteway
Bottom

Breaky
Bottom

Pickers Hill Farm

Coombe Farm

Brighton & Hove
East Sussex County

Coombe Vale

Westfield Av.
Westfield Vale
Sanner Av.
North
Coombe Rise
Westfield Rise
Hempstead Road
Upper Bannings Road
Hornbush Av.

F G H 221 J K

Saltdean County
School

Saltdean

Pedlersburgh

The Ridings
Rustic Rd

Iford

A B **182** C D E

I

Northease
Manor
School

White Way

Northease Farm

2

South Downs Way

Rodmell

3

The Dicklands

Badgers
Dene

The
Paddocks

Mill Lane

4

Breaky
Bottom

Rodmell
Primary School

Southease

207

5

6

7

Dean's Farm

Money Burgh

Telscombe

8

Bullock Down

The
Lookout

Halcombe Farm

A B **222** C D E

Valley

Waterford
Close

Johns
Cl

Telscombe
Tye Road West

Tor Road

Bretts
Field

Avenue

Heath
Cl

Wendale
Drive

Highfield
Park

Greenacre

Telscombe Road

Rustic Rd

The Walk

Broadway
Avenue North

F G H 183 J K

1
2
3
4
210
5
6
7
8

The Lay

White Lion Pond

South Downs Way

Red Lion Pond

ase

Well Bottom

ford Farm

rm

✝

Tarring Neville

hoe

Brookside

South Heighton

A26(T)

A26(T)

A26(T)

The Furlongs

A

B

184

C

D

Firle Place

West Firle

E

Street

PH

PO

The Dock

Firle Bostal

1

2

White Lion Pond

Maies Burgh

Firle Plantation

3

Blackcap Farm

4

Lord's Burghs

209

Well Bottom

5

6

7

8

South Heighton

A

Wellington

Rookery Way

Heighton

PO

The Drove

Cantercrow Hill

B

224

Pove Bottom

C

D

E

1 grid square represents 500 metres

F G H **185** J K

Charleston Farmhouse

Tilton Farm

I

south Downs Way

219 ▲ Firle Beacon

2

Bopeep Lane

3 Alcis

Bopeep Farm

Bopeep Lane

Bopeep Road

4

▶ **212**

5

Jerry's Pond

south Downs Way

6

7

Five Lord's Burgh

8

F G H **225** J K

190
215
230

C7
1 Eskdale Cl
2 Hickling Cl
3 Horning Cl
4 Ranworth Cl
5 Reedham Rd
6 Whitbread Cl

B7
1 Boship Cl
2 Broad Oak Cl
3 Caburn Cl
4 Chyngton Cl
5 Laughton Cl
6 Michelham Cl
7 Ringmer Wy

A8
1 Shepherds Cl

C8
1 Lavender Cl

D6
1 Blatch'ton Mill Dr

D7
1 Borrowdale Cl
2 Buttermere Wy
3 Coniston Rd
4 Elmwood Cl
5 Elmwood Gdns
6 Middleham Wy
7 Wildwood

D8
1 Cleveland Cl
2 Harebell Cl
3 Magdalen Cl
4 Milfoil Dr
5 Sorrel Cl

E8
1 Marlborough Cl
2 Pentland Cl

Glynleigh Level

Glynleigh Road

Glyndley Manor

Rickney

The Horns

Lusteds

Priesthawes

Montague

HAILSHAM ROAD

Hankham

Hankham CP School

Foords Lane

Hall Road

Milton Street

Hankham Street

Peelings

A27(T)

Peelings Lane

Mill

DITTONS ROAD

B2247

Barn Close

Rattle Road

Stone Cross

Windmill Gn

Mill View

Rattle Road

Regnum Cl

Catsfield Cl
Ditchling Cl

Rothyrfield Avenue

Stonegate

Burwash Cl

Doctors Surg

Sorrel

Olive

Pextill Way

Pennine

FRIDAY STREET

Causeway Secondary School

Health Centre

Old Sorrel Drive

Fern Close

Langney Shopping Cen

Hampden Park Infants School

Maywood Avenue

Brodrick

Lakelands Close

WILLINGDON DROVE

1 grid square represents 500 metres

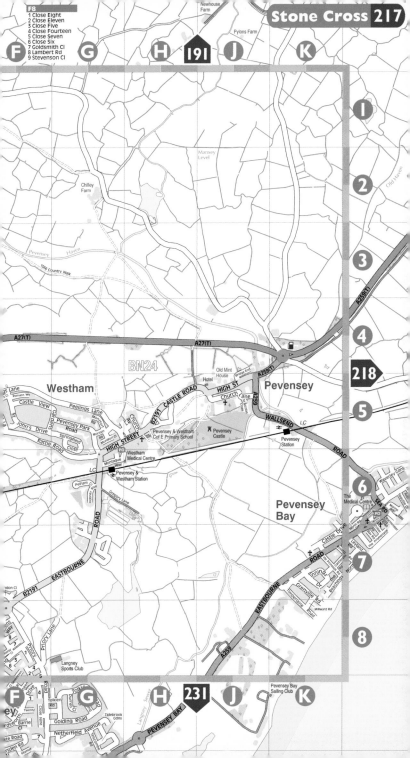

F G H 193 J K

Hoe
Level

Clavering

C
Be
G

Cood
Road

Cooden Beach Station

I

2

Herbrand Walk

3

Norman's Bay Station

Norman's
Bay

Road

4

5

6

7

8

F G H J K

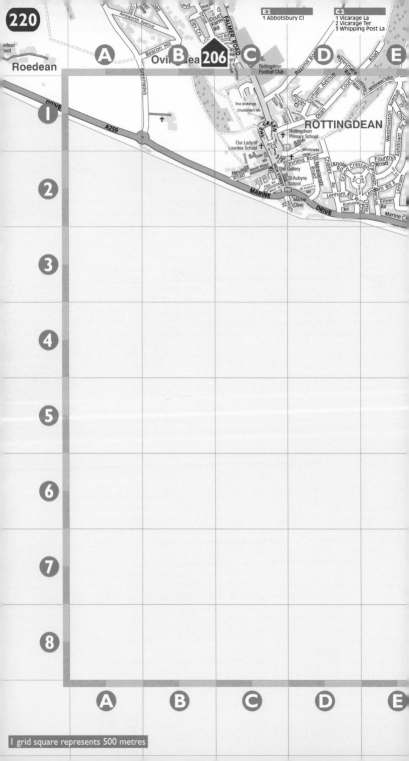

Roedean

E2
1 Abbotsbury Cl

C2
1 Vicarage La
2 Vicarage Ter
3 Whipping Post La

A

Ovi B ea 206 C

D

E

Ainsworth avenue

Beacon Hill

Greenways

PALMER ROAD

Rottingdean
Football Club

Bazehill Rd

Cottham Avenue

Corham Avenue

Court

Welesmere

Road

Whiteway Lane

1

DRIVE

A259

The Rotyngs

Challoners Ms

THE GREEN

Dean

Poyles

ROTTINGDEAN

Rottingdean
Primary School

Westmeston Avenue

Lashdown Av

Chaloch

2

Our Lady of
Lourdes School

Neville
Road

MARINE

Havisham Road

Steyning Road

The Gallery

St Aubyns
School

Whiteway
Lane

Newlands

Chailey

Knole Rd

Av

Grand Crescent

Carleton

Lenham Rd

Founthill
Road

Lenham Rd

Marine
Clinic

DRIVE

Romney
Rd

Little

Eileen
Av

Marine Ct

3

4

5

6

7

8

A

B

C

D

E

211

226

232

BN25

A   B   **212**   C   D   E

1

2

225

5

6

7

8

A   B   **233**   C   D   E

Alfriston

Lullington
Court

The
Rails

Frog Firle

Pingles Place

Church Farm

Litlington

PH

Clapham
House

Tile
Barn

Cow Lane

Cuckmere River

Cradle Hill

White
Horse

Alfriston Road

BN25

Westdea

Dymock
Farm

Exceat

Vanguard Way

Hythe Cl

EASTBOURNE   ROAD   A259

A259

PH

Exceat
Bridge

South Downs Way

Chyngton

Chyngton
Farm

South Downs Way

Seven
Sisters
Country Park

Long Burgh

North   Road

County Primary
School

The Broadway

The
Surgery

High St

Kings Ridge

South Downs Way

White Way

Vanguard Way

Alfriston Clergy
House (NT)

1 grid square represents 500 metres

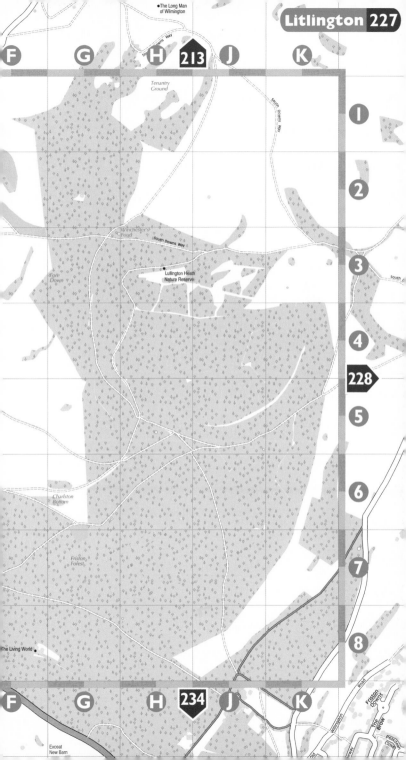

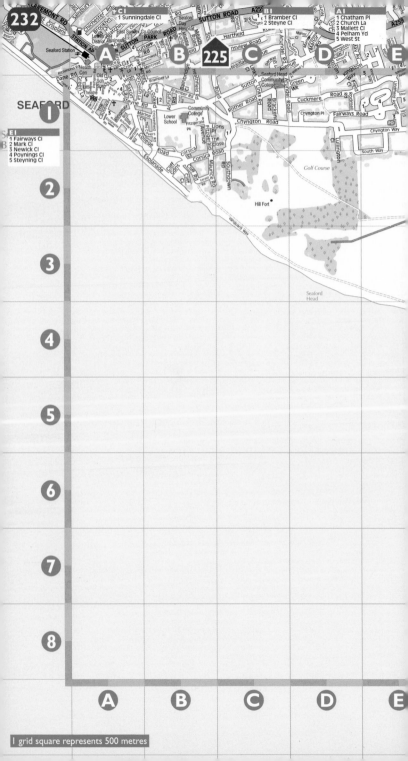

The Living World

ROAD

A259

PH

Exceat
Bridge

Cuckmere River

Vanguard Way

South Downs Way

Seven
Sisters
Country Park

Foxhole

South Downs Way

Nature Reserve

Cliff
End

Cuckmere Haven

Vanguard Way

South Downs Way

Seven
Sisters

234 South Do

F G H 226 J K

I 2 3 4 234 5 6 7 8

F G H J K

A
B
227
C
D
E

The Living World

Exceat
New Barn

Friston

Wire

Gayles

Crowlink

South Downs W

233

Seven
Sisters

South Downs Way

1
2
3
4
5
6
7
8

A
B
C
D
E

1 grid square represents 500 metres

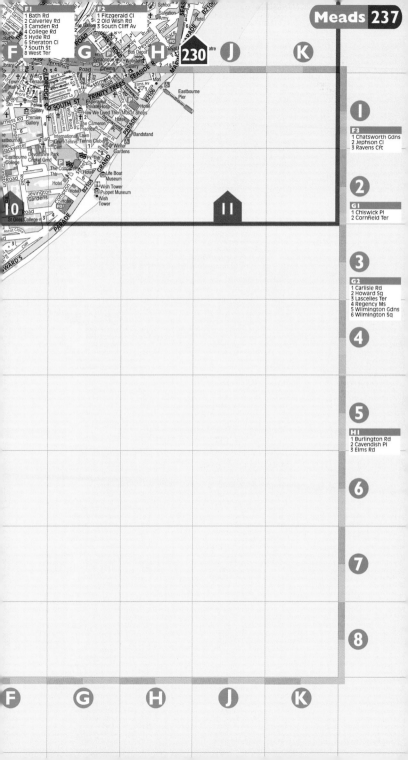

F1
1 Bath Rd
2 Calverley Rd
3 Camden Rd
4 College Rd
5 Hyde Rd
6 Sheraton Cl
7 South St
8 West Ter

F2
1 Fitzgerald Cl
2 Old Wish Rd
3 South Cliff Av

F3
1 Chatsworth Gdns
2 Jephson Cl
3 Ravens Cft

G1
1 Chiswick Pl
2 Cornfield Ter

G2
1 Carlisle Rd
2 Howard Sq
3 Lascelles Ter
4 Regency Ms
5 Wilmington Gdns
6 Wilmington Sq

H1
1 Burlington Rd
2 Cavendish Pl
3 Elms Rd

Abbotsford 88 E5
Alciston 212 A3
Alderbrook 53 H4
Aldrington 202 D4
Alfriston 226 C1
Argos Hill 55 J6
Arlington 187 J7
Ashburnham Forge 134 B6
Ashburnham Place 165 H1
Ashton Green 156 A7
Ashurst 27 F1
Ashurst Wood 23 J5
Bachelor's Bump 171 H5
Baldslow 169 J4
Baldwins Hill 12 A8
Balls Green 26 C6
Barcombe 154 D2
Barcombe Cross 123 J7
Bardown 59 F4
Battle 136 C5
Beachlands 218 C5
Beacon Down 98 E4
Beckley 82 E7
Beckley Furnace 110 B4
Beddingham 183 J7
Bells Yew Green 31 H6
Belmont 199 F2
Berner's Hill 60 E1
Berwick 212 C4
Best Beech Hill 43 J8
Bevendean 205 H1
Bexhill 195 F7
Birchden 28 B5
Birchett's Green 45 G8
Birchgrove 48 E2
Birling Gap 234 E6
Bishopstone 224 D4
Blackboys 97 K5
Blackham 16 C7
Blacklands 4 B2
Blackness 53 J2
Black Rock 205 H8
Blackwell 22 C1
Boarshead 39 K5
Bodiam 80 A3
Bodle Street Green 163 K1
Bohemia 4 A4
Boreham Street 164 B7
Bowler's Town 113 H1
Bray's Hill 164 D2
Brede 139 K2
Brightling 104 B5
Brighton 7 D6
Broadland Row 110 B7
Broad Oak 101 F2
Broad Oak 109 K6
Broad Street 141 G5
Broadwater Down 29 K3
Broomham 158 C5
Broomhill Bank 19 G4
Broomsgrove 5 E2
Brownbread Street 133 J8
Broyle Side 156 B3
Buckham Hill 94 E5
Budlet's Common 67 J8
Bulverhythe 196 E6
Burgess Hill 89 G8
Burgh Hill 61 J8
Burgh Hill 159 H5
Burlow 129 K6
Burnt Oak 53 H8
Burrswood 27 J3
Burwash 75 J5
Burwash Common 74 C8
Burwash Weald 74 E8
Butcher's Cross 71 G3
Buxted 68 C8
Cackle Street 66 E1
Cackle Street 104 C7
Cackle Street 139 H1
Cade Street 100 E5
Camber 115 H8
Camden Park 30 C1
Canadia 136 C3
Castle Hill 54 E7
Catsfield 166 E3
Catsfield Stream 166 D4
Chailey 92 C8
Chalvington 186 D4
Chapel Cross 101 G6
Chapel Row 163 G6
Chapman's Town 131 H1
Charlwood 34 C2
Chelwood Common 49 H5

Chelwood Gate 49 G2
Chiddingly 159 H2
Chiddingstone Hoath ... 16 C1
Chilsham 163 G3
Chiltington 153 F1
Chitcombe 109 G5
Chuck Hatch 37 J4
Churches Green 132 D3
Clayhill 82 C8
Clayton 149 K3
Cliff End 173 G4
Clive Vale 199 G1
Cock Marling 141 K1
Coggins Mill 56 C7
Coldean 178 E6
Coleman's Hatch 36 E2
Collier's Green 108 C2
Combe 57 J5
Cooden 194 C8
Cooksbridge 153 K3
Cooper's Green 67 K8
Cousley Wood 44 E4
Cowbeech 162 D2
Cowbeech Hill 162 C4
Cowden 15 G5
Cripp's Corner 107 K4
Cross in Hand 99 F4
Crowborough 53 H2
Crowborough Warren ... 52 E1
Crowhurst 168 A5
Dale Hill 60 D1
Dallington 103 F8
Danegate 41 G3
Danehill 48 E7
Darwell Hole 104 D8
Davis's Town 127 K4
Denny Bottom 19 H8
Denton 9 F1
Ditchling 119 K8
Dittons 215 K5
Dormansland 13 F2
Dormans Park 12 C4
Downside 229 H6
Down Street 66 D6
The Down 33 H8
Duddleswell 51 G7
Durgates 44 A6
Earl's Down 102 D7
Eason's Green 127 F2
East Blatchington 225 F7
Eastbourne 229 H6
East Chiltington 121 J7
East Dean 235 F3
East Grinstead 22 C2
East Guldeford 114 B4
East Hoathly 127 K6
East Moulsecoomb 179 G7
Eckington Corner 186 B3
Eridge Green 29 G7
Etchingham 77 F2
Etchingwood 97 F2
Ewhurst Green 80 D6
Exceat 226 C2
Fairfield 87 G2
Fairlight 172 B7
Fairlight Cove 172 E6
Fairwarp 67 H2
Falmer 180 A5
Felcourt 12 A3
Ferndale 20 C6
Fishersgate 201 J4
Five Ash Down 68 A6
Five Ashes 71 G4
Flackley Ash 83 K8
Fletching 66 A7
Fletching Common 93 F3
Flimwell 47 G8
Flowers Green 163 G7
Folkington 214 B7
Fordcombe 17 J6
Ford's Green 50 C8
Forest Row 35 K2
Foul Mile 131 J7
Foulride Green 215 G7
Four Oaks 83 G6
Four Throws 63 J5
Foxhunt Green 128 D2
Framfield 96 C5
Frant 30 C8
Friar's Gate 38 D4
Friar's Hill 172 A4
Friston 234 D2
Furner's Green 65 G2
Gallypot Street 25 H8

Ginger's Green 162
Glenleigh Park 195
Glynde 183
Glyndebourne 183
Glyne Gap 196
Goatham Green 109
Goddards' Green 88
Godleys Green 9
Golden Cross 159
Golden Cross 19
Gotham 193
Green Street 168
Groombridge 27
Grove Hill 16
Guestling Green 17
Guestling Thorn 140
Gun Green 63
Gun Hill 160
Hadlow Down 70
Hailsham 189
Hale Green 159
Halland 120
Hall's Close 193
Ham Green 84
Hammerwood 14
Hampden Park 22
Hamsey 154
Hangleton 20
Hankham 21
Harbour Heights ....
Harley Shute 19
Hartfield 2
Hassocks 11
Hastings ....
Hawkenbury 3
Hawkhurst 6
Hawkhurst Common 12
Hazard's Green 16
Heathfield 5
Heathfield 10
Hellingly 16
Henley's Down 16
Heron's Ghyll 5
Herstmonceux 16
High Brooms 2
High Cross 5
Highgate 3
Highgate 6
High Hurstwood 6
The Highlands 19
High Street 6
Hollingbury 17
Hollingdean 17
Hollingrove 10
Hollington 16
Holmes's Hill 15
Holtye 1
Hooe 19
Hooe Common 19
Hook Green 3
Horam 12
Horney Common 6
Horns Cross 5
Horshoe Green 1
Horsted Green 9
Horsted Keynes 4
Houghton Green 11
Hove 20
Hungershall Park 2
Hurst Green 6
Hurst Wickham 11
Icklesham 14
Iden 8
Iford 18
Isfield 12
Jarvis Brook 5
Jevington 22
John's Cross 10
Jumper's Town 3
Jury's Gap 14
Kemp Town 20
Keymer 11
Kilndown 4
Kingston by Sea 20
Kingston near Lewes ... 18
Lamberhurst 3
Lamberhurst Quarter ... 3
Landport ....
Langney 23
Langton Green 1
Laughton 15
Lewes ....
Lidham Hill 14
Lions Green 12

...ngton 226 D3
...e Bayham 32 B7
...e Common 194 A6
...e Horsted 125 J2
...e London 99 H7
...e Norlington 155 K2
...er Cousley Wood 45 G3
...er Dicker 160 A7
...er Green 19 C6
...er Green 21 K3
...er Horsebridge 160 D7
...er Street 166 A6
...er Willingdon 215 G8
...sford's Cross 194 E1
...Green 39 G2
...wood Common 26 D4
...ham Down 162 A7
...or Park 96 A2
...den's Hill 38 D6
...esfield Park 67 G6
...kbeech 15 K1
...k Cross 42 A7
...k Cross 185 K1
...le Green 130 B6
...lpits 50 D5
...lpits 166 A4
...field 72 A1
...nard's Green 130 A1
...ds 236 E3
...Oak 175 J8
...Corner 81 J8
...Hill 216 E5
...on Street 213 C6
...est Corner 19 J1
...Moor 63 F3
...t's Mill 27 J8
...alsecoomb 179 G8
...ant Ephraim 96 A8
...antfield 106 A5
...nt Pleasant 123 K5
...nt Pleasant 224 B2
...dles Green 159 H4
...ton Hall 100 B2
...n Street 159 J5
...herfield 135 G1
...vbridge 36 E5
...vhaven 9 E3
...vick 93 J3
...v Town 96 A5
...ield 166 A5
...lington 155 J4
...man's Bay 219 G3
...thbridge Street 78 C6
...th Chailey 92 B5
...th Common 92 C4
...thiam 81 K5
...th Moulsecoomb 178 E7
...ton 224 D3
...ley 50 C8
...iam 153 K6
...Heathfield 100 D5
...Shoreham 200 B2
...Town 5 F4
...Town 195 H5
...Town 229 J7
.... 171 F8
...gdean 206 B8
...ey's Green 104 C3
...house Common 126 D1
...k Corner 28 C6
...k Corner 158 C1
...cham 178 A5
...cehaven 222 B4
...cehaven Heights 222 D6
...smarsh 112 A1
...sham 196 A5
...Green 44 D4
...sbury 21 J5
...hurst 134 D5
... . 172 D3
...·Level 173 G3
...ensey 217 J5
...ensey Bay 217 K6
...linghoe 223 F1
...down 94 C2
...den 63 K2
...den 113 J3
...mpton 152 C4
...mpton Green 121 G5
...gate 215 F6
...ts Green 133 K7

Portslade-by-Sea 202 A5
Portslade Village 201 K1
Potter's Green 69 F8
Poundfield 53 K1
Poundford 70 E6
Poundgate 52 C4
Pound Green 69 F7
Poundsbridge 18 A3
Pounsley 97 J3
Poynings 148 A6
Preston 6 A1
Punnett's Town 101 J5
Pyecombe 149 G5
Quabrook 36 C2
Ramslye 29 H2
Rickney 216 E1
Ridgewood 95 J7
Ringles Cross 95 J1
Ringmer 155 H5
Ripe 186 B2
Robertsbridge 77 K7
Rockrobin 43 K4
Rocks Park 95 G4
Rodmell 208 C3
Roedean 205 K8
Rose Hill 125 F5
Roselands 230 D4
Roser's Cross 98 D5
Rotherfield 54 E3
Rottingdean 220 D1
Royal Tunbridge Wells 19 K8
Rusher's Cross 57 F5
Rushlake Green 131 J2
Rushy Green 155 K6
Russell's Green 165 K8
Rusthall 19 G7
Rye 113 J5
Rye Foreign 112 E2
Rye Harbour 144 B1
Saddlescombe 148 D8
St Helen's 170 D6
St Helen's Wood 170 B7
St John's 19 K5
St John's 38 E7
St Leonards 197 H4
Saint's Hill 17 K3
Salehurst 78 C6
Saltdean 221 G1
Sandown Park 21 F5
Sandy Cross 100 B6
Seacox Heath 61 J1
Sedlescombe 137 K2
Selmeston 186 B8
Sharpsbridge 94 C5
Sharp's Corner 129 J3
Sheffield Green 65 F4
Sherwood Park 20 E5
Shoreham Beach 200 E6
Shoreham-by-Sea 200 C6
Shortbridge 94 E3
Shortgate 126 D8
Shover's Green 58 E1
Sidley 195 G5
Silver Hill 78 B3
Silverhill 4 A1
Silverhill Park 169 K5
Skippers Hill 70 E4
Sleeches Cross 42 B1
Smart's Hill 17 H3
Snagshall 80 B6
Southborough 20 A2
South Chailey 122 C4
Southease 208 D4
Southern Cross 201 K3
South Heighton 223 K1
South Malling 2 C3
Southover 2 B6
Southover 74 E3
South Street 122 C2
Southwick 201 H3
Sparrow's Green 44 B6
Speldhurst 18 E4
Spithurst 123 K4
Splayne's Green 66 A6
Stanmer 179 F3
Staplecross 108 A2
Starr's Green 168 B1
Steel Cross 39 K8
Steven's Crouch 135 F8
Stockland Green 19 G3
Stone Cross 27 H1

Stone Cross 44 C8
Stone Cross 53 H5
Stone Cross 216 D6
Stonecrouch 46 C4
Stonegate 59 J5
Stonequarry 12 E8
Strawberry Hill 29 H3
Streat 120 D8
Stunts Green 162 E4
Summer Hill 189 F7
Sunnyside 22 C5
Sutton 225 H7
Swaile's Green 107 J4
Sweethaws 52 E5
Tarring Neville 209 J7
Teasley Mead 16 E8
Telham 168 C1
Telscombe 208 A8
Telscombe Cliffs 221 K3
Three Cups Corner 101 J6
Three Leg Cross 46 B8
Three Oaks 171 G1
Thunder's Hill 159 J4
Ticehurst 60 C1
Tidebrook 57 H3
Tilsmore 99 K3
Tolhurst 59 H1
Tompset's Bank 35 K3
Town Littleworth 123 G2
Town Row 55 G2
Trollilees 162 E1
Turner's Green 44 A5
Turner's Green 102 B7
Twelve Oaks 104 B6
Uckfield 95 K4
Udimore 141 H1
Union Street 47 F8
Upper Dicker 187 K3
Upper Hartfield 37 H1
Upper Horsebridge 160 D8
Upperton 10 A2
Upper Wellingham 155 F3
Vinehall Street 106 E5
Vines Cross 130 C3
Wadhurst 44 C7
Waldron 98 D8
Waldron Down 98 B3
Wallands Park 2 B4
Wallcrouch 59 H2
Walter's Green 17 G4
Wannock 214 E7
Warbleton 131 G2
Wartling 191 K4
Watermill 167 G7
Wellbrook 71 K2
West Blatchington 202 E2
Westdean 226 F7
Westdene 177 G6
Westfield 139 H7
West Firle 184 D8
Westham 217 F5
West Hill 5 E3
West Marina 197 G5
Westmeston 151 F3
Whatlington 137 G2
Whitehawk 205 G5
Whitehill 53 G3
White Post 17 F4
Whitesmith 158 E3
Whydown 194 A3
Wickstreet 187 H5
Willard's Hill 77 G6
Willingdon 229 F2
Wilmington 213 H5
Wilmington Green 213 H4
Winchelsea 142 D4
Winchelsea Beach 143 H5
Windmill Hill 163 J6
Winton 212 D7
Withdean 177 K7
Witherenden Hill 74 C2
Withyham 26 C8
Wivelsfield 90 C6
Woodingdean 205 K4
Woodmans Green 107 G8
Wood's Corner 103 H8
Wood's Green 44 B3
World's End 89 K7
Wych Cross 35 J7

USING THE STREET INDEX

Street names are listed alphabetically. Each street name is followed by its postal town or area locality, the Postcode District, the page number, and the reference to the square in which the name is found.

Example: **Abbey Wy** *BAT* TN3.................................. **136** D6 🔟

Some entries are followed by a number in a blue box. This number indicates the location of the street within the referenced grid square. The full street name is listed at the side of the map page.

GENERAL ABBREVIATIONS

ACC ....ACCESS	GA ....GATE	PL ....PL
ALY ....ALLEY	GAL ....GALLERY	PLN ....P
AP ....APPROACH	GDN ....GARDEN	PLNS ....PL
AR ....ARCADE	GDNS ....GARDENS	PLZ ....PL
ASS ....ASSOCIATION	GLD ....GLADE	POL ....POLICE STAT
AV ....AVENUE	GLN ....GLEN	PR ....PRI
BCH ....BEACH	GN ....GREEN	PREC ....PRECL
BLDS ....BUILDINGS	GND ....GROUND	PREP ....PREPARAT
BND ....BEND	GRA ....GRANGE	PRIM ....PRIM
BNK ....BANK	GRG ....GARAGE	PROM ....PROMEN
BR ....BRIDGE	GT ....GREAT	PRS ....PRINC
BRK ....BROOK	GTWY ....GATEWAY	PRT ....P
BTM ....BOTTOM	GV ....GROVE	PT ....P(
BUS ....BUSINESS	HGR ....HIGHER	PTH ....P
BVD ....BOULEVARD	HL ....HILL	PZ ....PIA
BY ....BYPASS	HLS ....HILLS	QD ....QUADR
CATH ....CATHEDRAL	HO ....HOUSE	QU ....QU
CEM ....CEMETERY	HOL ....HOLLOW	QY ....Q
CEN ....CENTRE	HOSP ....HOSPITAL	R ....RI
CFT ....CROFT	HRB ....HARBOUR	RBT ....ROUNDAB
CH ....CHURCH	HTH ....HEATH	RD ....R(
CHA ....CHASE	HTS ....HEIGHTS	RDG ....RI
CHYD ....CHURCHYARD	HVN ....HAVEN	REP ....REPU
CIR ....CIRCLE	HWY ....HIGHWAY	RES ....RESER\
CIRC ....CIRCUS	IMP ....IMPERIAL	RFC ....RUGBY FOOTBALL C
CL ....CLOSE	IN ....INLET	RI ....
CLFS ....CLIFFS	IND EST ....INDUSTRIAL ESTATE	RP ....R/
CMP ....CAMP	INF ....INFIRMARY	RW ....F
CNR ....CORNER	INFO ....INFORMATION	S ....SO
CO ....COUNTY	INT ....INTERCHANGE	SCH ....SCH
COLL ....COLLEGE	IS ....ISLAND	SE ....SOUTH E
COM ....COMMON	JCT ....JUNCTION	SER ....SERVICE A
COMM ....COMMISSION	JTY ....JETTY	SH ....SH
CON ....CONVENT	KG ....KING	SHOP ....SHOPP
COT ....COTTAGE	KNL ....KNOLL	SKWY ....SKY
COTS ....COTTAGES	L ....LAKE	SMT ....SUM
CP ....CAPE	LA ....LANE	SOC ....SOC
CPS ....COPSE	LDG ....LODGE	SP ....S
CR ....CREEK	LGT ....LIGHT	SPR ....SPR
CREM ....CREMATORIUM	LK ....LOCK	SQ ....SQU
CRS ....CRESCENT	LKS ....LAKES	ST ....STF
CSWY ....CAUSEWAY	LNDG ....LANDING	STN STA1
CT ....COURT	LTL ....LITTLE	STR ....STR
CTRL ....CENTRAL	LWR ....LOWER	STRD ....STR.
CTS ....COURTS	MAG ....MAGISTRATE	SW ....SOUTH V
CTYD ....COURTYARD	MAN ....MANSIONS	TDG ....TRAC
CUTT ....CUTTINGS	MD ....MEAD	TER ....TERR
CV ....COVE	MDW ....MEADOWS	THWY ....THROUGH
CYN ....CANYON	MEM ....MEMORIAL	TNL ....TUN
DEPT ....DEPARTMENT	MKT ....MARKET	TOLL ....TOLL
DL ....DALE	MKTS ....MARKETS	TPK ....TURNI
DM ....DAM	ML ....MALL	TR ....TR
DR ....DRIVE	ML ....MILL	TRL ....T
DRO ....DROVE	MNR ....MANOR	TWR ....TOV
DRY ....DRIVEWAY	MS ....MEWS	U/P ....UNDERF
DWGS ....DWELLINGS	MSN ....MISSION	UNI ....UNIVER
E ....EAST	MT ....MOUNT	UPR ....UF
EMB ....EMBANKMENT	MTN ....MOUNTAIN	V ....\
EMBY ....EMBASSY	MTS ....MOUNTAINS	VA ....VA
ESP ....ESPLANADE	MUS ....MUSEUM	VIAD ....VIAD
EST ....ESTATE	MWY ....MOTORWAY	VIL ....\
EX ....EXCHANGE	N ....NORTH	VIS V
EXPY ....EXPRESSWAY	NE ....NORTH EAST	VLG VILL
EXT ....EXTENSION	NW ....NORTH WEST	VLS VII
F/O ....FLYOVER	O/P ....OVERPASS	VW ....\
FC ....FOOTBALL CLUB	OFF ....OFFICE	W ....W
FK ....FORK	ORCH ....ORCHARD	WD ....W
FLD ....FIELD	OV ....OVAL	WHF ....WH
FLDS ....FIELDS	PAL ....PALACE	WK ....\
FLS ....FALLS	PAS ....PASSAGE	WKS ....W
FLS ....FLATS	PAV ....PAVILION	WLS ....W
FM ....FARM	PDE ....PARADE	WY ....\
FT ....FORT	PH ....PUBLIC HOUSE	YD ....Y
FWY ....FREEWAY	PK ....PARK	YHA ....YOUTH HOS
FY ....FERRY	PKWY ....PARKWAY	

OSTCODE TOWNS AND AREA ABBREVIATIONS

............Battle	HTHF.............Heathfield	RRTW...........Rural Royal Tunbridge Wells	
............Bexhill	HWH.........Haywards Heath	RTON............Rural Tonbridge	
KW............Bexhill west	LEW.................Lewes	RTW................Royal Tunbridge Wells	
............Brighton	LGNY..............Langney	RTWE/PEM.........Royal Tunbridge	
R/ETCH......Burwash/Etchingham	LING..............Lingfield		Wells east/Pembury
RH............Burgess Hill	LW/ROSE.....Lower Willingdon/Roselands	RYE.................Rye	
3K............Cranbrook	LYDD................Lydd	SBGH/RUST.....Southborough/Rusthall	
DW............Crowborough	MAYF.............Mayfield	SEAF.............Seaford	
T.............Eastbourne	NEWHV..........Newhaven	SHOR.............Shoreham	
EN............Edenbridge	NROM...........New Romney	SLVH.............Silverhill	
N/EASTW ......East Dean/Eastbourne west	PEAHV..........Peacehaven	STEY/UB........Steyning/Upper Beeding	
PIN............East Grinstead	PEV...............Pevensey	STHW.............Southwick	
W.............Forest Row	POLE..............Polegate	STLEO.............St Leonards	
L.............Hailsham	POY/PYE.......Poynings/Pyecombe	STPH/PW.......Staplehurst/Paddock Wood	
.............Hastings	PTSD.............Portslade	TENT.............Tenterden	
WK............Hawkhurst	RBTBR.........Robertsbridge	UCK...............Uckfield	
.............Henfield	RHAS.........Rural Hastings	WADH.............Wadhurst	
VE............Hove	RHWH.......Rural Haywards Heath	WSEA.............Winchelsea	
PT/KEY.......Hurstpierpoint/Keymer	RING/NEW.......Ringmer/Newick		
F.............Hartfield	ROTT...............Rottingdean		

106 - Arr

Index - streets

6 Country Wk *BAT* TN33............ 137 J7	
AIL BN27 .... 191 F5	
HAS TN35 .... 140 A8	
HAS TN35 .... 199 F3	
SEA TN36 .... 141 H5	

A

erton Fld *HPPT/KEY* BN6 .... 118 B6
ey Cl *PEAHV* BN10 .... 222 B2
ey Dr *STLEO* TN38................ 196 C6
ey Rd *EDN/EASTW* BN20 .... 229 C6
OTT BN2 .... 7 F6
ey Rd *EAST* TN40................. 195 J5
ey Wy *BAT* TN33 .... 136 D6 ⊞
ootsbury Cl *ROTT* BN2 .... 220 E2 ⊞
oots Cl *BAT* TN33 .... 137 F8
PPT/KEY BN6 .... 118 E7
otsfield La *HAS* TN34 .... 5 D1
erdale Rd *POLE* BN26 .... 215 H5
erdeen Rd *ROTT* BN2 .... 7 D2 ⊞
ergavenny Rd *LEW* BN7 .... 2 B4
nger Pl *LEW* BN7 .... 2 C4
nger Rd *PTSD* BN41 .... 202 A3
OTT BN2 .... 206 B5
cia Av *HOVE* BN3 .... 202 E2 ⊞
cia Rd *LW/ROSE* BN22 .... 229 J1
EWHV BN9 .... 223 K1
r Av *RTWE/PEM* TN2 .... 30 C3
rn Cl *EGRIN* RH19 .... 22 C3
LVH TN37 .... 169 K7
Acorns *HPPT/KEY* BN6 .... 88 D7
ADH TN35 .... 59 H5
rn Wy *BUR/ETCH* TN19 .... 62 A8
e Cl *HWH* RH16..................... 89 K1
es Ri *WADH* TN35 .... 60 C3
rn Cl *CROW* TN6.................... 53 J5
LEO TN38............................. 169 C7
ms Cl *BRI* BN1 .... 204 C1
ms La *RYE* TN31 .... 81 F8
stra Av *HPPT/KEY* BN6 .... 119 C7
lingham Rd *LW/ROSE* BN22 ...... 11 E3
lington Cl *STLEO* TN38............ 197 F6
lison Rd *HOVE* BN3 .... 6 A3
laide Cl *SEAF* BN25 .... 225 F6 ⊞
laide Crs *HOVE* BN3 .... 203 H6
laide Rd *STLEO* TN38 .... 169 J8
laide Sq *SHOR* BN43.............. 200 E4
ncourt Cl *STLEO* TN38.......... 169 G4
es St *ROTT* BN2 .... 7 E3
sworth Av *ROTT* BN2 .... 206 A8
sworth Cl *ROTT* BN2 .... 206 A7
r Rd *HAIL* BN27 .... 191 G2
hurst Fld *BAT* TN33 .... 133 K8
n Wy *ROTT* BN2 .... 205 G5
any Hl *RTWE/PEM* TN2 .... 20 C6
any Ms *HOVE* BN3 .... 203 G5
any Rd *BEX* TN40.................. 195 H8
EAF BN25 .... 224 C5
LEO TN38 .... 197 J3
any Vls *HOVE* BN3 .... 203 G6
ert Dr *BURH* RH15 .... 118 E1
ert Ms *HOVE* BN3 .... 203 G5

Albert Rd *BEX* TN40 .... 195 H8	
BRI BN1 .... 6 B4	
POLE BN26 .... 214 E4	
STHW BN42 .... 201 G4	
UCK TN22 .... 95 K5 ⊞	
Albert Ter *EAST* BN21 .... 229 H6	
Albion Cl *BURH* RH15 .... 119 F1 ⊞	
Albion Hl *ROTT* BN2 .... 7 D4	
Albion Rd *LW/ROSE* BN22 .... 11 D5 ⊞	
RTW TN1 .... 20 B6	
Albion St *LEW* BN7 .... 3 D4 ⊞	
PTSD BN41 .... 201 D5	
ROTT BN2 .... 7 D4	
STHW BN42 .... 201 D4	
Albourne Cl *ROTT* BN2 .... 205 F4	
STLEO TN38 .... 197 G3	
Aldborough Rd *SLVH* TN37 .... 4 A3	
Alderbrook Cl *CROW* TN6.......... 53 J5	
Alderbrook Wy *CROW* TN6......... 53 J5	
Alder Cl *HTHF* TN21 .... 100 A6	
RTWE/PEM TN2 .... 20 C2	
SLVH TN37 .... 169 K6	
Alders Av *EGRIN* RH19 .... 12 B8	
Alders View Dr *EGRIN* RH19 ..... 12 C7 ⊞	
Aldervale Cottages *CROW* TN6... 53 J4	
Aldrich Cl *ROTT* BN2 .... 205 G5	
Aldrington Av *HOVE* BN3 .... 203 F3	
Aldrington Cl *HOVE* BN3 .... 202 D4	
Alexander Dr *BEXW* TN39 .... 194 D7	
Alexandra Cl *SEAF* BN25 .... 225 F6 ⊞	
Alexandra Rd *BURH* RH15 .... 119 J1	
HTHF TN21 .... 100 B5	
LW/ROSE BN22 .... 11 F1	
MAYF TN20 .... 56 C8	
SLVH TN37 .... 4 A4	
UCK TN22 .... 95 K5	
Alexandra Vls *BRI* BN1 .... 6 B3	
Alford Wy *BEX* TN40 .... 195 K5	
Alfray Cl *BEX* TN40 .... 196 B6	
Alfred Rd *BRI* BN1 .... 6 B4	
LGNY BN23 .... 231 G3	
RHAS TN35 .... 171 F8	
Alfred St *STLEO* TN38 .... 4 A5	
Alfriston Cl *BEXW* TN39 .... 194 B5	
EDN/EASTW BN20 .... 236 C1	
ROTT BN2 .... 205 C5	
Alfriston Pk *SEAF* BN25 .... 225 K6	
Alfriston Rd *SEAF* BN25 .... 225 J6	
Alice Bright La *CROW* TN6........ 53 H4	
Alice St *HOVE* BN3 .... 203 J6	
Allan Cl *SBGH/RUST* TN4 .... 19 G7	
Allandale Rd *RTWE/PEM* TN2 .... 20 D5	
Allards *RHAS* TN35 .... 172 B3	
Allen's Cl *EGRIN* RH19 .... 23 H5	
Allen Wy *BEX* TN40 .... 196 A5	
Allfrey Rd *LW/ROSE* BN22 .... 11 F1	
Allfreys La *CROW* TN6............... 53 F5	
Allington Crs *RING/NEW* BN8 .... 93 G4	
Allington La *LEW* BN7 .... 153 F4	
Allington Rd *RING/NEW* BN8...... 93 G4	
All Saints Gdns *HTHF* TN21 .... 99 K4	
All Saints La *BEXW* TN39 .... 195 H4	
All Saints Rd *HAWK* TN18 .... 63 C2	
SBGH/RUST TN4 .... 20 A5	
All Saints' St *HAS* TN34 .... 5 F4	
Allwood Crs *RHWH* RH17 .... 90 E2	
Alma Ter *SLVH* TN37 .... 4 A2	
Alma Vls *SLVH* TN37 .... 4 A2	
Alpine Rd *HAS* TN34 .... 5 E4 ⊞	
HOVE BN3 .... 203 J6	
Alverstone Cl *LGNY* BN23......... 216 C7	
Amanda Cl *BEX* TN40 .... 196 A4	
Amberleaze Dr *RTWE/PEM* TN2 ... 21 K5	

Amberley Cl *BURH* RH15 .... 89 G7
SHOR BN43 .... 200 C2 ⊞
Amberley Dr *HOVE* BN3 .... 176 D8
Amberley Rd *LW/ROSE* BN22 .... 229 H2
Amberstone *HAIL* BN27 .... 161 K8
Amberstone Cl *HAS* TN34 .... 170 D7 ⊞
Amberstone Vw *HAIL* BN27....... 189 H1
Ambleside Av *PEAHV* BN10 ...... 221 K4
Amesbury Crs *HOVE* BN3 .... 202 D4
Amherst Cl *SLVH* TN37 .... 4 B3
Amherst Crs *HOVE* BN3 .... 202 E3
Amherst Gdns *HAS* TN34 .... 4 B3
Amherst Rd *BEX* TN40 .... 195 H7
SBGH/RUST TN4 .... 20 A6
SLVH TN37 .... 4 B3
Amhurst Rd *PEAHV* BN10 .... 221 J4
Anchor Cl *SHOR* BN43 .... 200 D5
Anchor Fld *RING/NEW* BN8 .... 155 J6
Anchor La *RING/NEW* BN8 .... 124 A5
Anderida Rd *LW/ROSE* BN22 ..... 215 C8
Anderson Cl *NEWHV* BN9 .... 8 B3
Andrew Rd *SBGH/RUST* TN4 .... 20 C3
Andrews Cl *RBTBR* TN32 .... 78 C6
RTWE/PEM TN2 .... 20 D6 ⊞
Angela Cl *BEX* TN40 .... 196 A4 ⊞
Anglesea Ter *STLEO* TN38 .... 4 A4 ⊞
Anglesey Av *HAIL* BN27 .... 189 F1
Angus Cl *EDN/EASTW* BN20 ...... 229 G3
Ann Cl *HPPT/KEY* BN6 .... 119 C6
Annington Gdns *SHOR* BN43 .... 200 C2 ⊞
Annington Rd *LW/ROSE* BN22 .... 11 D2
Ann St *BRI* BN1 .... 6 C3
HAS TN34 .... 5 F2
Anson Cl *LGNY* BN23 .... 231 F4
Ansty Cl *ROTT* BN2 .... 205 F6
Antioch St *LEW* BN7 .... 2 C5 ⊞
Antony Cl *SEAF* BN25 .... 224 C5
Antrona Cl *BEXW* TN39............. 194 B8
Anvil Cl *PTSD* BN41 .... 202 A1
UCK TN22 .... 95 H5
Anvil Ct *SLVH* TN37 .... 169 K6 ⊞
Anzac Cl *PEAHV* BN10 .... 222 B2
Appledene Cnr *RING/NEW* BN8 .. 122 C4 ⊞
Appledore Cl *LGNY* BN23 .... 230 E1 ⊞
Appledore Rd *ROTT* BN2 .... 179 C7
Applesham Av *HOVE* BN3 .... 202 D1
Applesham Wy *PTSD* BN41 .... 201 K2
Apple Tree La *RTWE/PEM* TN2 ..... 20 D3
Applewood Cl *SLVH* TN37 .... 169 J7
The Approach *BRI* BN1 .... 177 K8
EGRIN RH19 .... 12 D5
Apsley St *SBGH/RUST* TN4 .... 19 H7
Aquarius Cl *PEAHV* BN10 .... 222 B5 ⊞
Aquila Pk *SEAF* BN25 .... 225 H8 ⊞
Arbourvale *STLEO* TN38 .... 197 H2
Archery Rd *STLEO* TN38 .... 197 J4
Archery Wk *HAIL* BN27 .... 189 H5
Ardingly Rd *ROTT* BN2 .... 221 C3
Ardingly St *ROTT* BN2 .... 7 D5
Argent Cl *SEAF* BN25 .... 225 H4
Argos Hill Rd *MAYF* TN20 .... 55 H7
Argyle Rd *BRI* BN1 .... 6 B2
SBGH/RUST TN4 .... 20 A1
Arlington Crs *BRI* BN1 .... 179 F6 ⊞
Arlington Gdns *ROTT* BN2 .... 221 C1
Arlington Rd *EAST* BN21 .... 10 A1
Arlington Rd East *HAIL* BN27 ..... 188 E5
Arlington Rd West *HAIL* BN27 .... 188 E5
Armstrong Cl *STLEO* TN38 .... 169 F7
Armbury Ms *STLEO* TN38 .... 197 E5
Arnold St *ROTT* BN2 .... 7 E3
Arnside Rd *STLEO* TN38 .... 197 F5
Arran Cl *HAIL* BN27 .... 189 F1

Arthur Rd *BEXW* TN39 ..... 195 G7
Arthur St *HOVE* BN3 ..... 203 F3
Arundel Cl *HAIL* BN27 ..... 189 H1
  PEV BN24 ..... 218 C5
  SHOR BN43 ..... 201 F3
Arundel Dr East *ROTT* BN2 ..... 221 F2
Arundel Dr West *ROTT* BN2 ..... 220 E2
Arundell Gn *LEW* BN7 ..... 2 B3 🔲
Arundel Pl *ROTT* BN2 ..... 205 F7
Arundel Rd *EAST* BN21 ..... 10 B3
  NEWHV BN9 ..... 9 E1
  PEAHV BN10 ..... 222 B4
  ROTT BN2 ..... 205 F8
  RTW TN1 ..... 30 B1
  SEAF BN25 ..... 225 H8
Arundel Road Central *PEAHV* BN10.. 222 A4
Arundel Rd West *PEAHV* BN10 ..... 221 K3
Arundel St *ROTT* BN2 ..... 205 F8
Arundel Ter *ROTT* BN2 ..... 205 F8
Arun Wy *PEV* BN24 ..... 216 A6
Ascham Pl *EDN/EASTW* BN20 ..... 10 A6 🔲
Ascot Cl *EDN/EASTW* BN20 ..... 237 F3
Ascot Ms *STLEO* TN38 ..... 197 H3 🔲
Ashbrook Rd *SLVH* TN37 ..... 169 J7
Ashburnham Cl *BRI* BN1 ..... 179 F6 🔲
Ashburnham Dr *BRI* BN1 ..... 178 E3
Ashburnham Gdns *EAST* BN21 ..... 10 A2
Ashburnham Pl *HAIL* BN27 ..... 189 F1 🔲
Ashburnham Rd *EAST* BN21 ..... 10 A3
  RHAS TN35 ..... 199 F2
Ashby Cl *BEXW* TN39 ..... 195 F4
Ash Cl *HOVE* BN3 ..... 177 H8
  LW/ROSE BN22 ..... 215 K8
  RTWE/PEM TN2 ..... 30 D3
Ashcombe Dr *BEXW* TN39 ..... 194 C8
Ashcombe Hollow *LEW* BN7 ..... 181 G4
Ashcombe La *LEW* BN7 ..... 181 H5
Ash Ct *HAIL* BN27 ..... 189 H3
Ashcroft Cl *RING/NEW* BN8 ..... 155 J6
  SHOR BN43 ..... 201 G4
Ashdown Av *ROTT* BN2 ..... 220 E2
Ashdown Cha *LEW* BN7 ..... 50 C6
Ashdown Cl *FROW* RH18 ..... 36 A1
  SBGH/RUST TN4 ..... 19 K7
  STLEO TN38 ..... 197 K7
Ashdown Pl *HTHF* TN21 ..... 100 B5 🔲
Ashdown Rd *BEX* TN40 ..... 195 K3
  FROW RH18 ..... 35 K1
  ROTT BN2 ..... 7 D2
Ashdown Vw *EGRIN* RH19 ..... 22 C4
  UCK TN22 ..... 50 D5
Ash Dr *SEAF* BN25 ..... 225 K8
Ashenden Av *RTW* TN31 ..... 113 G6
Ashenden Wk *RTWE/PEM* TN2 ..... 20 E3
Asher Reeds *RRTW* TN3 ..... 18 E7
Ashford Cl *HAIL* BN27 ..... 189 H4 🔲
Ashford Rd *BRI* BN1 ..... 204 B3
  EAST BN21 ..... 10 C4
  HAS TN34 ..... 4 C1
Ashford Sq *EAST* BN21 ..... 10 C4
Ashford Wy *HAS* TN34 ..... 4 C1
Ashgate Rd *LGNY* BN23 ..... 231 F1
Ash Gv *HWH* RH16 ..... 89 K1
  PEV BN24 ..... 216 E5
Ashington Gdns *PEAHV* BN10 ..... 222 D5
Ashington Rd *LW/ROSE* BN22 ..... 230 B2
Ashleigh Gdns *CROW* TN6 ..... 39 G4
Ashley Cl *BRI* BN1 ..... 177 K4
Ashley Gdns *HAIL* BN27 ..... 161 H8
  MAYF TN20 ..... 72 A1
  SBGH/RUST TN4 ..... 19 G6
Ashley Park Cl *SBGH/RUST* TN4 ..... 19 C6
Ashley Rd *CROW* TN6 ..... 55 H2
Ashlings Wy *HOVE* BN3 ..... 202 D1 🔲
  SHOR BN43 ..... 200 E2
Ashmore Cl *PEAHV* BN10 ..... 222 C1
Ashton Ri *ROTT* BN2 ..... 7 D4 🔲
Ashtonville Cl *RING/NEW* BN8 ..... 155 K6 🔲
Ash Tree Cl *HTHF* TN21 ..... 100 A4
Ashurst Av *ROTT* BN2 ..... 221 H3
Ashurst Rd *ROTT* BN2 ..... 179 G6
  RRTW TN3 ..... 27 K1
  SEAF BN25 ..... 232 K1
Ashway *RHAS* TN15 ..... 119 G1 🔲
Aspen Rd *LW/ROSE* BN22 ..... 229 K1
Aspen Wk *HTHF* TN21 ..... 100 B6
Aspen Wy *BEXW* TN39 ..... 194 B5
  RTWE/PEM TN2 ..... 20 C2
Astaire Av *LW/ROSE* BN22 ..... 11 D1
Asten Cl *STLEO* TN38 ..... 197 F4
Asten Flds *BRI* TN21 ..... 136 B7 🔲
Athelstan Cl *LGNY* BN23 ..... 231 G3 🔲
Athelstan Rd *RHAS* TN35 ..... 199 G3
Atlantic Dr *LGNY* BN23 ..... 231 G4
Atlingworth St *ROTT* BN2 ..... 7 D6 🔲
Attree Dr *ROTT* BN2 ..... 7 E4
Auckland Dr *ROTT* BN2 ..... 205 G2
Auckland Rd *RTW* TN1 ..... 20 C5
Audrey Cl *BRI* BN1 ..... 177 K6
  SEAF BN25 ..... 224 E6
Augustus Wy *STLEO* TN38 ..... 169 G5
Austen Wy *RHAS* TN35 ..... 171 G6
Avard Cl *EDN/EASTW* BN20 ..... 229 G5
Avards Cl *HAWK* TN18 ..... 62 E3
Avenue La *EAST* BN21 ..... 10 B4

The Avenue *EAST* BN21 ..... 10 B4
  EGRIN RH19 ..... 12 E5
  HAIL BN27 ..... 189 G5
  HTHF TN21 ..... 100 B5 🔲
  HTHF TN21 ..... 129 K3
  LEW BN7 ..... 2 B4
  LEW BN7 ..... 181 G6
  MAYF TN20 ..... 72 B1
  RHAS TN35 ..... 172 K7
  ROTT BN2 ..... 204 E1
  SHOR BN43 ..... 200 D2
Avery Cl *PTSD* BN41 ..... 175 J7
Aviemore Rd *CROW* TN6 ..... 53 F1
Avis Cl *NEWHV* BN9 ..... 9 E1
Avis Rd *NEWHV* BN9 ..... 9 D1
Avis Wy *NEWHV* BN9 ..... 9 E2
Avondale Rd *HOVE* BN3 ..... 203 J4
  LW/ROSE BN22 ..... 11 D2 🔲
  SEAF BN25 ..... 225 G8
  STLEO TN38 ..... 197 H2
Avonhurst *BURH* RH15 ..... 89 H8
Avon St *RTW* TN1 ..... 20 C6
Aylesbury Av *LGNY* BN23 ..... 231 F3
Aymer Rd *HOVE* BN3 ..... 203 F5
Ayscue Cl *LGNY* BN23 ..... 231 G4 🔲

B

Babylon Wy *EDN/EASTW* BN20 ..... 229 G3
Back La *HTHF* TN21 ..... 99 G4
  HTHF TN21 ..... 131 K3
  UCK TN22 ..... 67 H1
  WSEA TN36 ..... 142 E4
Baden Rd *ROTT* BN2 ..... 7 F2
Badens Cl *RING/NEW* BN8 ..... 93 G5 🔲
Badger Cl *PTSD* BN41 ..... 202 A1
Badgers Brow *EDN/EASTW* BN20 ..... 229 G3
Badgers Cl *CROW* TN6 ..... 39 G8
Badgers Copse *SEAF* BN25 ..... 225 K8
Badgers Dene *LEW* BN7 ..... 208 C3
Badgers Fld *PEAHV* BN10 ..... 222 B2
Badgers Holt *RTWE/PEM* TN2 ..... 20 C6
Badgers Mt *BEXW* TN39 ..... 194 D6
Badgers Wk *BURH* RH15 ..... 119 K3 🔲
Badger Wy *BRI* BN1 ..... 179 F5
Badlesmere Rd *LW/ROSE* BN22 ..... 10 C1
Bagham La *HAIL* BN27 ..... 163 G5
Bahram Rd *POLE* BN26 ..... 214 D5
Bailey Crs *LW/ROSE* BN22 ..... 215 G8
Baillie Av *LW/ROSE* BN22 ..... 11 E2
Bainbridge Cl *CROW* TN6 ..... 55 H2
Baird Dr *HAS* TN34 ..... 4 C1
Baker's Rd *EAST* BN21 ..... 229 J8 🔲
Baker St *BRI* BN1 ..... 6 C3
  UCK TN22 ..... 95 K5
Bakewell Rd *EAST* BN21 ..... 229 J7
Balaclava La *WADH* TN5 ..... 44 B4
Balcombe La *RHWH* RH17 ..... 48 C1
Balcombe Rd *PEAHV* BN10 ..... 222 A3 🔲
Baldock Rd *WADH* TN5 ..... 43 K7
Baldslow Down *SLVH* TN37 ..... 169 K2
Baldslow Rd *HAS* TN34 ..... 5 D2
Baldwin Av *EAST* BN21 ..... 229 H5
Bale Cl *BEXW* TN39 ..... 194 D6
Balfour Gdns *FROW* RH18 ..... 35 J3
Balfour Rd *BRI* BN1 ..... 204 A1
Ballard Dr *RING/NEW* BN8 ..... 156 A3
Ballards Hl *BAT* TN33 ..... 168 A7
Ballsocks La *HTHF* TN21 ..... 130 C3
Balmoral Cl *SEAF* BN25 ..... 225 H5
Balsdean Rd *ROTT* BN2 ..... 206 A2
Bamford Cl *ROTT* BN2 ..... 205 H1
Bampfield St *PTSD* BN41 ..... 202 A3 🔲
Bancroft Rd *BEXW* TN39 ..... 195 G6
Bank Rd *BEXW* TN39 ..... 195 H4 🔲
Banks Castle *LEW* BN7 ..... 2 C4 🔲
Bankside *BRI* BN1 ..... 177 H6
  HPPT/KEY BN6 ..... 119 F6
  WADH TN5 ..... 44 A6
Banks Rd *RING/NEW* BN8 ..... 92 C2
Banner Farm Rd *RTWE/PEM* TN2 ..... 30 B1
Bannings V *ROTT* BN2 ..... 221 C3
Bannisters Fld *RING/NEW* BN8 ..... 93 J4
Baranscraig Av *BRI* BN1 ..... 178 B4
Barcombe Av *SEAF* BN25 ..... 225 K8
Barcombe Cl *SEAF* BN25 ..... 225 K8 🔲
Barcombe Mills Rd
  RING/NEW BN8 ..... 154 E1
Barcombe Rd *BRI* BN1 ..... 179 F7
Barden Rd *LW/ROSE* BN22 ..... 11 E3
  RRTW TN3 ..... 18 D1
Bardown Rd *WADH* TN5 ..... 59 G5
Bargate Cl *BEXW* TN39 ..... 195 H4
Barham Cl *HAS* TN34 ..... 170 A7
Barkdale *BURH* RH15 ..... 89 K6
Barley Cl *PEAHV* BN10 ..... 222 B1
Barley Dr *BURH* RH15 ..... 88 C7
Barley La *RHAS* TN35 ..... 199 F2
Barley Mow La *HTHF* TN21 ..... 101 H6

Barming Cl *LGNY* BN23 ..... 230 E
Barn Cl *HAIL* BN27 189
  LEW BN7 181
  PEV BN24 216
  SEAF BN25 225
  SLVH TN37 169
Barnes Rd *PTSD* BN41 ..... 202 A
Barnett Rd *BRI* BN1 204
Barnetts Cl *RTWE/PEM* TN2 20
Barnetts Wy *SBGH/RUST* TN4 20
Barnett Wy *UCK* TN22 95
Barnet Wy *HOVE* BN3 176
Barnfield *CROW* TN6 53
  LEW BN7 121
  RTWE/PEM TN2 29
Barnfield Cl *SLVH* TN37 4
Barnfield Gdns *HPPT/KEY* BN6 ..... 120 A
Barn Field Gdns *ROTT* BN2 ..... 7 E
The Barnhams *LEW* BN7 194
Barnhorn Cl *BEXW* TN39 194
Barnhorn Rd *BAT* TN33 193
  BEXW TN39 193
Barn La *UCK* TN22 97
Barn Ri *BRI* BN1 177
  SEAF BN25 225
Barn Rd *LEW* BN7 3
Barnside Av *BURH* RH15 119
Barons Cl *SEAF* BN25 225
Barons Ct *BURH* RH15 119
Barons Down Rd *LEW* BN7 2
Barons Wy *POLE* BN26 214
Barrack Rd *BEX* TN40 195
Barrack Sq *WSEA* TN36 143
Barretts Rd *HAWK* TN18 63
Barrhill Av *BRI* BN1 178
Barrie Cl *LGNY* BN23 231
Barrow Cl *BRI* BN1 ..... 204 D
Barrowfield Cl *HOVE* BN3 ..... 177 F
Barrowfield Dr *HOVE* BN3 203
Barrow Hl *BRI* BN1 204
Barrow La *RRTW* TN3 28
Barrow Ri *SLVH* TN37 169
Barry Wk *ROTT* BN2 ..... 7 E
Bartholomews *BRI* BN1 ..... 6 C
Bartley Mill Cl *PEV* BN24 216
Bartley Mill Rd *RRTW* TN3 32
Barton Crs *EGRIN* RH19 22
Basin Rd South *PTSD* BN41 201
Baslow Rd *EDN/EASTW* BN20 236
Bassetts Hl *LING* RH7 ..... 12 L
Bassetts La *CROW* TN6 42
  EDEN TN8 16
  MAYF TN20 55
Batchelor Wy *UCK* TN22 95
Bateman's La *BUR/ETCH* TN19 75
Batemans Rd *ROTT* BN2 221
Bates Rd *BRI* BN1 204
Bathford Cl *LGNY* BN23 ..... 230 E
Bath Rd *EAST* BN21 10
Bath St *BRI* BN1 6
Battery Hl *RHAS* TN35 172
Battle Cl *SEAF* BN25 225
Battle Crs *HAIL* BN27 189
  SLVH TN37 169
Battle Gates *BAT* TN33 136
Battle Hl *BAT* TN33 136
Battle Rd *BAT* TN33 169
  HAIL BN27 189
  SLVH TN37 169
Batts Bridge Rd *UCK* TN22 67
Bavant Rd *BRI* BN1 203
Baxter Rd *LEW* BN7 2
Baxters La *RHWH* RH17 49
Baxter St *ROTT* BN2 7
Bay Av *PEV* BN24 218
Bayencourt North *BEXW* TN39 195
Bayhall Rd *RTWE/PEM* TN2 20
Bayham Rd *HAIL* BN27 189
  LW/ROSE BN22 11
  RTWE/PEM TN2 30
Bayley's La *POLE* BN26 187
Baylis Crs *BURH* RH15 88
Bay Pond Rd *EAST* BN21 229
Bay Rd *PEV* BN24 218
Bay Tree Cl *HTHF* TN21 100
  SHOR BN43 201
Bay Tree La *POLE* BN26 214
Bayview Rd *PEAHV* BN10 222
Bay Vue Rd *NEWHV* BN9 9
Baywood Gdns *ROTT* BN2 205
Bazehill Rd *ROTT* BN2 206
Beach Cl *SEAF* BN25 224
Beach Gn *SHOR* BN43 200
The Beachings *PEV* BN24 217
Beach Rd *LW/ROSE* BN22 11
  NEWHV BN9 9
  SHOR BN43 200
Beachy Head Rd
  EDN/EASTW BN20 237
  EDN/EASTW BN20 23
Beacon Cl *BRI* BN1 20
  CROW TN6 5
  SEAF BN25 22
Beacon Dr *SEAF* BN25 224

acon Gdns *CROW* TN6 .... 39 G8
acon Hl *BEXW* TN39 .... 194 E3
ING RH7 .... 13 F3
OTT BN2 .... 206 B8
acon Hurst *HPPT/KEY* BN6 .... 119 H8
acon La *RBTBR* TN32 .... 108 A3
acon Rd *CROW* TN6 .... 52 E3
PPT/KEY BN6 .... 150 E2
HAS TN35 .... 171 H7
EAF BN25 .... 224 E7
acon Rd West *CROW* TN6 .... 53 F1
aconsfield Rd *BEX* TN40 .... 195 H5
RI BN1 .... 6 C2
AS TN34 .... 5 D2
TSD BN41 .... 202 A5
HWH RH17 .... 49 H5
aconsfield Vis *BRI* BN1 .... 6 B1
al Crs *BRI* BN1 .... 204 C1
ales La *RYE* TN31 .... 81 K5
ale St *BURH* RH15 .... 118 E2
amsley Rd *LW/ROSE* BN22 .... 11 E3
aney's La *HAS* TN34 .... 170 B5
HAS TN35 .... 170 C5
ar Rd *ROTT* BN2 .... 7 E2
ar Yd *LEW* BN7 .... 3 D4
atrice La *EAST* BN21 .... 10 B4
atrice Wk *BEXW* TN39 .... 195 F5
atty Av *BRI* BN1 .... 178 E4
atty Rd *LGNY* BN23 .... 231 F5
auchamp Rd *STLEO* TN38 .... 169 H8
TLEO TN38 .... 169 H7
auford Rd *HTHF* TN21 .... 129 K4
aufort Crs *SLVH* TN37 .... 4 A2
aufort Ter *ROTT* BN2 .... 7 E4
auharrow Rd *SLVH* TN37 .... 169 H5
aulieu Dr *PEV* BN24 .... 216 B6
aulieu Gdns *SLVH* TN37 .... 169 K5
au Nash Wy *RTWE/PEM* TN2 .... 30 B2
auport Gdns *SLVH* TN37 .... 169 H4
auport Home Farm Cl
SLVH TN37 .... 169 H5
aver Cl *CROW* TN6 .... 53 J2
ckenham La *HAIL* BN27 .... 161 G8
cket Cl *HAS* TN34 .... 5 E3
ckets Wy *UCK* TN22 .... 96 D6
ckett Wy *EGRIN* RH19 .... 22 D3
EW BN7 .... 2 C2
ckley Cl *ROTT* BN2 .... 205 F6
TLEO TN38 .... 196 E1
delands Cl *BURH* RH15 .... 89 H6
dford Av *BEX* TN40 .... 195 J7
dford Ct *UCK* TN22 .... 95 J3
dford Gv *EAST* BN21 .... 10 B3
dford Pl *BRI* BN1 .... 6 A5
dford St *ROTT* BN2 .... 7 E6
dfordwell Rd *EAST* BN21 .... 10 C3
BGH/RUST TN4 .... 20 A2
dford St *BRI* BN1 .... 6 A5
dford St *ROTT* BN2 .... 7 E6
dgebury Cl *STLEO* TN38 .... 169 C7
dgebury Cross *CRBK* TN17 .... 47 G1
echam Pl *STLEO* TN38 .... 169 C7
ech Cl *BAT* TN33 .... 136 B4
EW BN7 .... 194 B5
TSD BN41 .... 175 J8
echers Rd *PTSD* BN41 .... 175 J8
eches Cl *HTHF* TN21 .... 100 B3
CK TN22 .... 95 K3
eches Farm Rd *CROW* TN6 .... 53 J2
eches La *EGRIN* RH19 .... 23 H5
eches Rd *CROW* TN6 .... 53 K1
e Beeches *BRI* BN1 .... 177 J8
ech Farm Rd *BAT* TN33 .... 107 K7
echfield Cl *PEV* BN24 .... 216 D5
ech Flds *EGRIN* RH19 .... 12 D8
ech Green La *HRFT* TN7 .... 26 B3
ech Gv *ROTT* BN2 .... 179 F8
ech House La *RBTBR* TN32 .... 78 C4
ech Hurst *RTWE/PEM* TN2 .... 21 K4
eching Rd *BEXW* TN39 .... 195 G7
eching Wy *EGRIN* RH19 .... 22 C2
ech St *RTW* TN1 .... 20 B6
echwood Av *BRI* BN1 .... 178 A7
echwood Cl *BRI* BN1 .... 178 A7
UR/ETCH TN19 .... 75 K4
AIL BN27 .... 189 H6
echwood Crs
DN/EASTW BN20 .... 229 J8
echwood Gdns *HAS* TN34 .... 170 A6
echwood La *HTHF* TN21 .... 100 B6
EW BN7 .... 153 H2
echwood Ms *RTWE/PEM* TN2 .... 20 E7
echwoods *BURH* RH15 .... 119 G2
echy Av *EDN/EASTW* BN20 .... 229 G7
echy Gdns *EDN/EASTW* BN20 .... 229 G7
echy Rd *UCK* TN22 .... 127 H2
eding Av *HOVE* BN3 .... 176 E8
Rd *PEAHV* BN10 .... 222 B3
ggar's La *POY/PYE* BN45 .... 148 C6
ggar's Wood Rd *RING/NEW* BN8 .... 92 A5
fast St *HOVE* BN3 .... 203 G5
field Rd *RTWE/PEM* TN2 .... 21 K5
fry Orch *UCK* TN22 .... 95 K6
Belfry *HAIL* BN27 .... 189 F3

Belgrave Crs *SEAF* BN25 .... 225 G6
Belgrave Pl *ROTT* BN2 .... 7 F6
Belgrave Rd *RTW* TN1 .... 20 A7
SEAF BN25 .... 224 E7
Belgrave St *ROTT* BN2 .... 7 D4
Bell Alley Rd *BUR/ETCH* TN19 .... 75 K5
Bell Banks Rd *HAIL* BN27 .... 189 H4
Belle Hl *BEX* TN40 .... 195 H6
Bellevue Gdns *ROTT* BN2 .... 7 E5
Belle Vue Rd *LW/ROSE* BN22 .... 11 E2
Bell Hammer *EGRIN* RH19 .... 22 C3
Bellhurst Rd *RBTBR* TN32 .... 78 A7
Bellingham Cl *SLVH* TN37 .... 169 J7
Bellingham Crs *HOVE* BN3 .... 202 C5
Bell La *LEW* BN7 .... 2 B5
ROTT BN2 .... 50 A7
UCK TN22 .... 95 J5
UCK TN22 .... 95 H5
Bell Wk *UCK* TN22 .... 95 J5
Belmont *BRI* BN1 .... 6 A3
Belmont Cl *HPPT/KEY* BN6 .... 118 E6
Belmont La *HPPT/KEY* BN6 .... 118 C7
Belmont Rd *RHAS* TN35 .... 199 F2
UCK TN22 .... 95 J4
Belmont St *BRI* BN1 .... 6 C5
Belmore Rd *LW/ROSE* BN22 .... 11 D3
Belton Rd *ROTT* BN2 .... 7 D5
Beltring Rd *LW/ROSE* BN22 .... 11 D3
SBGH/RUST TN4 .... 20 A5
Beltring Ter *LW/ROSE* BN22 .... 11 D3
Belvedere Gdns *CROW* TN6 .... 53 J2
SEAF BN25 .... 225 H6
Belvedere Pk *STLEO* TN38 .... 197 H3
Bembridge Gdns *LGNY* BN23 .... 216 C8
Bembridge St *ROTT* BN2 .... 7 E2
Bembrook Rd *HAS* TN34 .... 5 F3
Benzells La *HAIL* BN27 .... 162 E1
Benbow Av *LGNY* BN23 .... 231 F5
Benbow Cl *SHOR* BN43 .... 200 C5
Benchfield Cl *EGRIN* RH19 .... 22 E3
Benenden Cl *EAST* BN21 .... 225 H7
Benenden Ri *HAS* TN34 .... 4 C1
Benett Av *HOVE* BN3 .... 203 G1
Benett Dr *HOVE* BN3 .... 203 G1
Benfield Cl *PTSD* BN41 .... 202 B3
Benfield Crs *PTSD* BN41 .... 202 B3
Benfield Wy *PTSD* BN41 .... 202 B3
Bengairn Av *BRI* BN1 .... 178 B4
Benhall Mill Rd *RTWE/PEM* TN2 .... 30 C3
Benjamin Cl *LW/ROSE* BN22 .... 230 A1
Bennett Rd *ROTT* BN2 .... 205 F7
Bentham Hl *RRTW* TN3 .... 19 H2
Bentham Rd *ROTT* BN2 .... 7 E3
Berberis Av *BRI* BN1 .... 178 B4
Beresford Rd *NEWHV* BN9 .... 9 E1
ROTT BN2 .... 7 F5
Bergamot Crs *SHOR* BN43 .... 201 F2
Beristede Cl *EDN/EASTW* BN20 .... 10 A6
Berkeley Rd *RTW* TN1 .... 30 A1
Berkley Rd *MAYF* TN20 .... 71 K2
Berlin Rd *RHAS* TN35 .... 199 G5
Bermuda Pl *LGNY* BN23 .... 231 H4
Bernard La *EAST* BN21 .... 10 B4
Bernard Pl *ROTT* BN2 .... 7 E3
Bernard Rd *ROTT* BN2 .... 7 E3
Bernhard Gdns *POLE* BN26 .... 214 E6
Berriedale Av *HOVE* BN3 .... 202 C5
Berry Cl *BURH* RH15 .... 89 G6
PEAHV BN10 .... 221 K2
Berwick Cl *BEXW* TN39 .... 194 B5
LW/ROSE BN22 .... 215 H8
SEAF BN25 .... 224 E7
Berwick Rd *ROTT* BN2 .... 207 G8
Betchley Cl *EGRIN* RH19 .... 12 C8
Bethune Rd *BEX* TN40 .... 195 K8
Bethune Wy *HAS* TN34 .... 5 D3
Beulah Rd *RTW* TN1 .... 20 C7
Beuzeville Av *HAIL* BN27 .... 189 G3
Bevendean Av *ROTT* BN2 .... 221 G2
Bevendean Crs *ROTT* BN2 .... 205 F1
Bevendean Rd *ROTT* BN2 .... 7 F2
Beverington Cl *EAST* BN21 .... 229 J5
Beverington Rd *EAST* BN21 .... 229 J5
Bewl Bridge Cl *WADH* TN5 .... 47 F8
Bewlbridge La *RRTW* TN3 .... 46 A2
Bexhill Rd *BAT* TN33 .... 166 A6
LW/ROSE BN22 .... 11 E2
ROTT BN2 .... 206 A2
STLEO TN38 .... 196 C6
Bexleigh Av *STLEO* TN38 .... 196 C6
Bexley Cl *HAIL* BN27 .... 189 G1
Bicton Gdns *BEXW* TN39 .... 194 D7
Biddenden Cl *LGNY* BN23 .... 230 E1
Bidwell Av *BEXW* TN39 .... 195 F5
Bigwood Av *HOVE* BN3 .... 203 J4
Billingham La *RYE* TN31 .... 111 G8
Binsted Cl *LW/ROSE* BN22 .... 229 K1
Birch Cl *RTWE/PEM* TN2 .... 20 D4
UCK TN22 .... 96 A3
Birches Cl *CROW* TN6 .... 39 H7
Birchetts Av *RRTW* TN3 .... 18 C3
Birchetts Green La *WADH* TN5 .... 45 G8
Birch Grove Crs *BRI* BN1 .... 178 B6
Birchgrove La *RHWH* RH17 .... 48 D2
Birchgrove Rd *RHWH* RH17 .... 48 B6

Birchington Cl *BEXW* TN39 .... 194 C7
Birch Rd *LGNY* BN23 .... 230 D4
Birch Vw *BEXW* TN39 .... 195 H5
Birch Wy *HAIL* BN27 .... 189 G5
HAS TN34 .... 4 C1
HTHF TN21 .... 100 A6
HWH RH16 .... 90 C1
RTWE/PEM TN2 .... 20 D4
Birchwood Grove Rd *BURH* RH15 .... 119 H2
Birdham Rd *ROTT* BN2 .... 179 F8
Bird In Eye Hl *UCK* TN22 .... 96 A5
Bird in Hand St *RRTW* TN3 .... 28 A3
Bird La *WADH* TN5 .... 43 H7
Birk Dl *BEXW* TN39 .... 194 C7
Birken Rd *RTWE/PEM* TN2 .... 20 D5
Birling Cl *ROTT* BN2 .... 7 H2
SEAF BN25 .... 224 E7
Birling Dr *RTWE/PEM* TN2 .... 30 A3
Birling Gap Rd *EDN/EASTW* BN20 .... 235 F6
Birling Park Av *RTWE/PEM* TN2 .... 30 B3
Birling Rd *RTWE/PEM* TN2 .... 30 B3
Birling St *EDN/EASTW* BN20 .... 229 H7
Bishop's Cl *RING/NEW* BN8 .... 155 K5
SEAF BN25 .... 224 D7
Bishop's Down *SBGH/RUST* TN4 .... 19 J8
Bishop's Down Park Rd
SBGH/RUST TN4 .... 19 J7
Bishop's Down Rd *SBGH/RUST* TN4 .... 19 J8
Bishops Dr *LEW* BN7 .... 2 A5
Bishop's La *RBTBR* TN32 .... 78 A8
RING/NEW BN8 .... 155 J5
Bishops Rd *HOVE* BN3 .... 203 H2
Bishopstone Dr *ROTT* BN2 .... 220 E1
Bishopstone La *HPPT/KEY* BN6 .... 88 A3
RHWH RH17 .... 88 A4
Bishopstone Rd *SEAF* BN25 .... 224 D5
Bishop's Wk *BEX* TN40 .... 196 A5
Bixley La *RYE* TN31 .... 110 E2
Blackberry La *LING* RH7 .... 12 A3
Blackberry Rd *EGRIN* RH19 .... 12 B1
Blackdon Hl *CROW* TN6 .... 41 G5
Blackdown Rd *HTHF* TN21 .... 101 K5
Blackfields Av *BEXW* TN39 .... 194 E6
Blackhouse La *BURH* RH15 .... 89 H7
Blackhurst La *RTWE/PEM* TN2 .... 21 G4
Blacklands Crs *FROW* RH18 .... 35 K1
Blacklands Dr *HAS* TN34 .... 5 D2
Black Lion St *BRI* BN1 .... 6 C6
Blackman Av *STLEO* TN38 .... 169 H8
Blackman St *BRI* BN1 .... 6 C4
Blackmill Cl *BEXW* TN39 .... 195 F3
Blackness Rd *CROW* TN6 .... 53 H2
Black Pth *POLE* BN26 .... 215 F5
Blacksmiths Copse *HAIL* BN27 .... 189 F5
Blacksmiths La *BAT* TN33 .... 166 D3
WADH TN5 .... 44 C6
Blackstone Wy *BURH* RH15 .... 89 G6
Blackthorn Av *RTWE/PEM* TN2 .... 20 C2
Blackthorn Cl *BRI* BN1 .... 177 J8
LW/ROSE BN22 .... 229 K1
PTSD BN41 .... 202 A1
SLVH TN37 .... 169 K7
The Blackthorns *BURH* RH15 .... 89 H6
Blackthorn Wy *RHAS* TN35 .... 172 E7
Blackwater Rd *EDN/EASTW* BN20 .... 10 B6
Blackwell Farm Rd *EGRIN* RH19 .... 12 D8
Blackwell Hollow *EGRIN* RH19 .... 22 D1
Blackwell Rd *EGRIN* RH19 .... 22 D1
Blakeney Av *NEWHV* BN9 .... 8 A4
Blaker St *ROTT* BN2 .... 7 D5
Blakes Wy *LGNY* BN23 .... 231 G5
Blake Wy *RTWE/PEM* TN2 .... 20 D4
Blatchington Cl *SEAF* BN25 .... 225 G7
Blatchington Hl *SEAF* BN25 .... 225 F7
Blatchington Mill Dr *PEV* BN24 .... 216 D6
Blatchington Rd *HOVE* BN3 .... 203 G4
RTW TN1 .... 30 A2
SEAF BN25 .... 225 F8
Blenheim Cl *EGRIN* RH19 .... 12 E8
Blenheim Flds *FROW* RH18 .... 23 J8
Blenheim Wy *POLE* BN26 .... 215 J5
WADH TN5 .... 47 G8
Bletchingley La *CROW* TN6 .... 55 J2
Blind La *RING/NEW* BN8 .... 93 J5
Blois Rd *LEW* BN7 .... 2 A2
Blomfield Rd *SLVH* TN37 .... 4 A4
Bloomsbury Pl *ROTT* BN2 .... 7 E6
Bloomsbury St *ROTT* BN2 .... 7 E6
Blount Av *EGRIN* RH19 .... 22 A2
Blowers Hl *EDEN* TN8 .... 15 K3
Blue Haze Av *SEAF* BN25 .... 225 J7
Bluemans La *BAT* TN33 .... 138 C8
Bluestone Cl *STLEO* TN38 .... 197 G1
Boarders La *WADH* TN5 .... 46 A8
Boast La *RING/NEW* BN8 .... 123 J6
Bocking Cl *WADH* TN5 .... 44 A7
Boddingtons La *HPPT/KEY* BN6 .... 119 K8
Bodiam Av *BEX* TN40 .... 195 J5
ROTT BN2 .... 205 J2
Bodiam Cl *ROTT* BN2 .... 205 J1
SEAF BN25 .... 225 K7
Bodiam Cres *LW/ROSE* BN22 .... 230 B1
Bodiam Dr *STLEO* TN38 .... 196 E1
Bodiam Rd *HAWK* TN18 .... 80 B1
Bodle Crs *BEXW* TN39 .... 195 G4

Bohemia Rd *SLVH* TN37 .... 4 B4
STLEO TN38.................... 197 J2
Bolding Wy *HWH* RH16 .... 89 K1
Bolebrooke Rd *BEX* TN40 .... 195 J8
Bolney Av *PEAHV* BN10 .... 222 B5
Bolney Rd *ROTT* BN2 .... 179 G7
Bolsover Rd *EDN/EASTW* BN20 .... 236 D5
HOVE BN3 .... 202 D4
Bolton Cl *UCK* TN22 .... 95 G5
Bolton Rd *EAST* BN21 .... 10 C5
Bonchurch Rd *ROTT* BN2 .... 7 E2
Bondfield Cl *SBGH/RUST* TN4 .... 20 A2
Bond St *BRI* BN1 .... 6 C5
Bonfire La *RHWH* RH17 .... 48 A7
Boniface Cl *PEV* BN24 .... 216 D5
Bonny Wood Rd *HPPT/KEY* BN6 ...... 118 E8
Booker Cl *CROW* TN6 .... 53 J2
Bopeep Bostal *POLE* BN26 .... 211 J4
Bopeep La *POLE* BN26 .... 211 J3
Border Ct *EGRIN* RH19 .... 12 D7
Borders La *BUR/ETCH* TN19 .... 76 E3
Boreham HI *HAIL* BN27 .... 164 D8
Boreham La *HAIL* BN27 .... 192 B2
Borough La *EDN/EASTW* BN20 .... 229 J8
Borough St *BRI* BN1 .... 6 A5
Borrowdale Cl *LGNY* BN23 .... 216 D7
Borrow King Cl *ROTT* BN2 .... 7 F1
Boscawen Cl *LGNY* BN23 .... 231 G4
Boscobel Rd *STLEO* TN38 .... 197 H4
Boscobel Rd North *STLEO* TN38 ...... 197 H3
Boship Cl *LGNY* BN23 .... 216 E7
Bostal Rd *RING/NEW* BN8 .... 184 C7
Boston Cl *LGNY* BN23 .... 231 G4
Boston St *BRI* BN1 .... 6 C3
Bough Beeches *BURH* RH15 .... 119 J2
Boughey Pl *LEW* BN7 .... 2 C2
The Boulevard *PEV* BN24 .... 218 B5
Boundary & Station Roads
PTSD BN41 .... 202 B5
Boundary Rd *ROTT* BN2 .... 205 F8
RTWE/PEM TN2 .... 30 D2
The Boundary *RRTW* TN3 .... 19 F8
SEAF BN25 .... 232 A1
Bourg-de-péage Av *EGRIN* RH19 ...... 22 E2
Bourne La *RBTBR* TN32 .... 79 F3
Bourne St *LW/ROSE* BN22 .... 10 C4
The Bourne *HAS* TN34 .... 5 F4
HPPT/KEY BN6 .... 118 E8
Bowden Ri *SEAF* BN25 .... 225 F5
Bowen Ri *SBGH/RUST* TN4 .... 19 F6
Bower Cl *SLVH* TN37 .... 169 J7
Bowley Rd *HAIL* BN27 .... 189 H4
Bowmans Dr *BAT* TN33 .... 136 D5
Bowood Av *LW/ROSE* BN22 .... 11 D1
Bowrey Pl *BEX* TN40 .... 195 H6
Bowring Av *ROTT* BN2 .... 7 F6
Bowsprit Ms *STLEO* TN38 .... 169 F4
Boxes La *RHWH* RH17 .... 48 A7
Boxgrove Cl *BEX* TN40 .... 196 A7
Box La *EGRIN* RH19 .... 23 J5
Box's La *RHWH* RH17 .... 49 C5
Boyce's St *BRI* BN1 .... 6 B5
Boyne Rd *SBGH/RUST* TN4... .... 19 K7
Boyne Rd *RHAS* TN35 .... 199 F2
Brackenbury Ct *PTSD* BN41 .... 202 A1
Bracken Cl *CROW* TN6 .... 54 A2
RTWE/PEM TN2 .... 20 E6
Brackendale *RHAS* TN35 .... 199 G3
Brackenhill *HRTF* TN7 .... 37 G2
Bracken Rd *EDN/EASTW* BN20 ...... 230 A1
RTWE/PEM TN2 .... 20 E6
SEAF BN25 .... 232 C1
Bracken Wy *HTHF* TN21 .... 100 E2
Bradford Rd *LEW* BN7 .... 2 B4
Bradford St *EAST* BN21 .... 229 H8
Brading Cl *HAS* TN34.. .... 4 C2
LGNY BN23 .... 216 C2
Brading Rd *ROTT* BN2 .... 7 E3
Bradley Rd *HAIL* BN27 .... 191 K2
RRTW TN3 .... 17 F6
Braemore Rd *HOVE* BN3 .... 202 D5
Braeside Av *BRI* BN1 .... 178 A4
Braeside *HOVE* BN3 .... 176 E8
PEAHV BN10 .... 222 B5
Bramber Av *North *PEAHV* BN10... 222 B3
Bramber Cl *PEAHV* BN10 .... 222 B3
SEAF BN25 .... 232 B1
Bramber La *SEAF* BN25 .... 232 B1
Bramber Rd *SEAF* BN25 .... 232 B1
Bramber Wy *BURH* RH15 .... 89 G7
Bramble Cl *LGNY* BN23 .... 216 C8
Bramble Cft *CROW* TN6 .... 53 J1
Brambledean Rd *PTSD* BN41 ...... 202 A4
Bramble Dr *HAIL* BN27 .... 189 F4
Bramble Gdns *BURH* RH15 .... 88 D7
Bramble Ri *BRI* BN1 .... 177 H6
Brambles *HPPT/KEY* BN6 .... 119 F6
Brambleside *UCK* TN22 .... 95 G5
Brambletye La *FROW* RH18 .... 23 H8
Brambletyne Av *ROTT* BN2 .... 221 G2
Bramble Wy *RHAS* TN35 .... 172 E2
Bramley Rd *POLE* BN26 .... 215 H5
Bramleys *LEW* BN7 .... 181 H6
Brampton Av *BEXW* TN39 .... 194 E7
Brampton Rd *LW/ROSE* BN22 ...... 230 A2

Brand Rd *LW/ROSE* BN22 .... 229 K2
Brands Cl *NEWHV* BN9 .... 223 J1
Brangwyn Av *BRI* BN1 .... 177 K5
Brangwyn Crs *BRI* BN1 .... 177 K5
Brangwyn Dr *BRI* BN1 .... 177 J5
Brangwyn Wy *BRI* BN1 .... 177 K6
Branksome Rd *STLEO* TN38 ...... 197 H3
Branston Rd *LW/ROSE* BN22 ...... 229 K2
Brassey Av *LW/ROSE* BN22 ...... 229 K2
Brassey Rd *BEX* TN40 .... 195 J8
Brasslands Dr *PTSD* BN41 ...... 201 J2
Braybon Av *BRI* BN1 .... 178 A7
Braybrooke Rd *HAS* TN34 .... 4 C4
Braybrooke Ter *HAS* TN34 .... 4 C4
Braypool La *BRI* BN1 .... 177 J3
Brazen Cl *NEWHV* BN9 .... 8 A3
Breadsell La *BAT* TN33 .... 168 D6
Brede La *LW/ROSE* BN22 .... 11 F1
ROTT BN2 .... 205 F6
STLEO TN38 .... 169 G4
Brede HI *RYE* TN31 .... 139 K3
Brede La *BAT* TN33 .... 158 B2
Brede Valley Vw *WSEA* TN36... 141 J2
Breedon Av *SBGH/RUST* TN4 ...... 19 K2
RTWE/PEM TN2 .... 20 D6
Brendon Cl *LGNY* BN23 .... 217 F7
RTWE/PEM TN2 .... 20 D6
Brendon Ri *HAS* TN34. .... 5 F1
Brentwood Cl *BRI* BN1 .... 178 C8
Brentwood Crs *BRI* BN1 .... 178 C8
Brentwood Rd *BRI* BN1 .... 178 C8
Bretland Rd *SBGH/RUST* TN4 ...... 19 H7
Brett Dr *BEX* TN40 .... 196 A6
Bretton *BURH* RH15 .... 88 E6
Bretts Fld *PEAHV* BN10 .... 222 B1
Brewers Gv *MAYF* TN20 .... 72 B1
Brewer St *ROTT* BN2 .... 7 D3
RRTW TN3 .... 33 J6
Brian Crs *SBGH/RUST* TN4 ...... 20 B3
Briar Cl *RHAS* TN35 .... 173 F6
ROTT BN2 .... 206 A3
Briarcroft Rd *ROTT* BN2 .... 206 A4
Briar Pl *LGNY* BN23 .... 216 C8
Brickhurst La *RING/NEW* BN8 ...... 157 K3
Brick Kiln La *UCK* TN22 .... 70 B5
Brickyard La *CROW* TN6 .... 41 K7
The Bricky *PEAHV* BN10 .... 222 C3
Bridge La *BURH* RH15 .... 89 J7
HTHF TN21 .... 130 A4
Bridge End *PEV* BN24. .... 217 J5
Bridge Farm Rd *UCK* TN22 ...... 95 J5
Bridgelands *RING/NEW* BN8 ...... 123 H7
Bridgemere Rd *LW/ROSE* BN22 ... 11 D1
Bridger Wy *CROW* TN6 .... 53 J2
Bridge St *NEWHV* BN9 .... 9 D3
Bridge Wy *STLEO* TN38 .... 196 D5
Bridgewick Cl *LEW* BN7 .... 3 D2
Bridle Wy *PEAHV* BN10 .... 221 K2
Briers Av *SLVH* TN37 .... 4 A1
Briers Gdns *SLVH* TN37 .... 4 A1
Brigden St *BRI* BN1 .... 6 B3
Brightland Rd *EDN/EASTW* BN20 .. 229 J8
Brightling Av *RHAS* TN35 .... 171 G7
Brightling Rd *POLE* BN26 .... 215 F6
RBTBR TN32 .... 104 E3
Brighton Pl *BRI* BN1 .... 6 C5
Brighton Rd *HPPT/KEY* BN6 ...... 148 C1
HPPT/KEY BN6 .... 149 J1
LEW BN7 .... 181 H4
NEWHV BN9 .... 8 B4
SHOR BN43 .... 200 A5
Bright Rdg *SBGH/RUST* TN4 ...... 19 J3
Brills La *ROTT* BN2 .... 6 C6
Brincliffe *CROW* TN6 .... 39 G8
Brinkers La *WADH* TN5 .... 58 C1
Bristol Gdns *ROTT* BN2 .... 205 F7
Bristol Ga *ROTT* BN2 .... 7 F6
Bristol Ms *ROTT* BN2 .... 205 F7
Bristol Pl *ROTT* BN2 .... 205 F7
Bristol Rd *ROTT* BN2 .... 7 E6
STLEO TN38 .... 169 H8
Bristol St *ROTT* BN2 .... 205 F7
Brittany Ms *STLEO* TN38 .... 197 J4
Brittany Rd *HOVE* BN3 .... 202 C5
STLEO TN38 .... 197 J4
Britten Cl *LGNY* BN23 .... 216 E8
Brittenden La *HTHF* TN21 .... 98 C6
Britts Farm Rd *UCK* TN22 .... 68 E8
Broadcroft *RTWE/PEM* TN2 ...... 29 K3
Broadfields *ROTT* BN2 .... 179 F8
Broadfields Rd *ROTT* BN2 .... 179 F8
Broad Gn *ROTT* BN2 .... 206 B5
Broad Green Av *BURH* RH15 ...... 119 J1
Broad Gv *RTWE/PEM* TN2 ...... 30 A2
Broadhill Cl *HTHF* TN21 .... 100 E2
Broadlands *BURH* RH15 .... 119 H3
RHAS TN35 .... 171 G7
Broad La *RRTW* TN3 .... 17 J8
Broadmead *RTWE/PEM* TN2 ...... 29 J3
Broadmead La *RTWE/PEM* TN2 .. 29 K3
Broad Oak *RRTW* TN3 .... 27 K5
Broad Oak Cl *LW/ROSE* BN22 ...... 216 B7
RTWE/PEM TN2 .... 29 K2
Broadoak La *BEXW* TN39 .... 194 D6
Broad Rig Av *HOVE* BN3. .... 176 C7

Broad Rd *EDN/EASTW* BN20 214
Broadstone Pk *FROW* RH18 36
Broad St *ROTT* BN2 .... 6 C
SEAF BN25 225
WSEA TN36 141
Broad Vw *BEXW* TN39 194
HTHF TN21 100
Broadview Cl *EDN/EASTW* BN20 .. 214 E
The Broadwalk *BEXW* TN39 194
Broadwater Down
RTWE/PEM TN2 29
Broadwater La *RTWE/PEM* TN2 .. 29
Broadwater Ri *RTWE/PEM* TN2 .. 29
Broadwater Wy *LW/ROSE* BN22 .. 230
Broad Wy *RHAS* TN35 172
The Broadway *CROW* TN6 53
LW/ROSE BN22 229
POLE BN26 212
RHAS TN35 .... 171 C
RRTW TN3 33
Brockley Rd *BEXW* TN39 195
Brocks Gyhll *EDN/EASTW* BN20 .. 215 F
Brodie Pl *EAST* BN21 .... 229 J
Brodrick Cl *LW/ROSE* BN22 230
Brodrick Rd *LW/ROSE* BN22 229
Brokes Wy *SBGH/RUST* TN4 20
Bromley Cl *HPPT/KEY* BN6 119
LGNY BN23 230
Bromley Rd *ROTT* BN2 7
SEAF BN25 225
Brompton Cl *BRI* BN1. 177
The Brontes *EGRIN* RH19 .... 22 E
Brook Av *HPPT/KEY* BN6 119
Brook Cl *CROW* TN6 53
EGRIN RH19 23
Brooke Gdns *RING/NEW* BN8 93
Brooker Pl *HOVE* BN3 203
Brooker St *HOVE* BN3 203
Brookfield Rd *BEX* TN40 .... 195 K
Brookhouse Bottom *RHWH* RH17 ... 49
Brookhouse La *UCK* TN22 96
Brookland Cl *HAS* TN34 5
PEV BN24 218
Brooklands *RTWE/PEM* TN2 ...... 20 D
Brooklands Av *CROW* TN6 53
Brooklands Farm Cl *RRTW* TN3 .. 17
Brooklands Wy *EGRIN* RH19 22
Brook La *RING/NEW* BN8 183
Brooklyn Rd *SEAF* BN25 225
Brookmead Cl *LW/ROSE* BN22 .. 11
Brook Rd *RTWE/PEM* TN2 20
Brooks Cl *LEW* BN7 3
NEWHV BN9 8
Brookside *NEWHV* BN9 223
UCK TN22 95
Brookside Av *POLE* BN26 214
Brooks La *LEW* BN7 .... 3 E
Brooks Rd *LEW* BN7 3
The Brooks *BURH* RH15 88
Brook St *HAS* TN34 .... 5 D
LEW BN7 2
POLE BN26 214
Brookway *BURH* RH15. 89
Broom Cl *LW/ROSE* BN22 229
Broomfield Av *PEAHV* BN10 221
Broomfield Dr *PTSD* BN41 201
Broomfield St *EDN/EASTW* BN20 .. 229
Broomgrove Rd *HAS* TN34 .... 5 F
Broomham La *RING/NEW* BN8 158
Broomhill Park Rd *SBGH/RUST* TN4.. 19
Broomhill Rd *RRTW* TN3 19
Broom La *RRTW* TN3 28
Broom Pk *RRTW* TN3 18
Browning Rd *HTHF* TN21 100
The Brownings *EGRIN* RH19 .... 22 A
Brown Jack Av *POLE* BN26 ...... 214 E
Brownleaf Rd *ROTT* BN2 206
Browns Cl *UCK* TN22 95
Browns La *HTHF* TN21 99
UCK TN22 95
Browns Wd *EGRIN* RH19 12
The Brow *BURH* RH15 119
EDN/EASTW BN20 235
ROTT BN2 206
Broyle Cl *RING/NEW* BN8 156
Broyle La *RING/NEW* BN8 156
Broyle Paddock *RING/NEW* BN8 156
The Broyle *RING/NEW* BN8 156
Brunel Rd *STLEO* TN38 169
Brunswick Ms *HOVE* BN3 203
Brunswick Pl *HOVE* BN3 203
Brunswick Rd *HOVE* BN3 203
SHOR BN43 200
Brunswick Sq *HOVE* BN3 203
Brunswick St East *HOVE* BN3 203
Brunswick St West *HOVE* BN3 .. 203 J
Brunswick Ter *HOVE* BN3 203
Bryants Fld *CROW* TN6. 39
Brydges Cl *LW/ROSE* BN22 11
Buci Crs *SHOR* BN43 201
Buckholt Av *BEX* TN40 196
Buckholt La *BEXW* TN39 195
Buckhurst Cl *EDN/EASTW* BN20 .. 229
EGRIN RH19 12
LEW BN7 2

ckhurst La CROW TN6 .... 43 F7
ckhurst Rd BEX TN40 .... 195 H7
PEAHV BN10 .... 221 J4
ckhurst Wy EGRIN RH19 .... 12 A8
ckingham Av SHOR SN43 .... 200 B2
ckingham Cl SEAF BN25 .... 225 F7 ⬚
SHOR SN43 .... 200 D3 ⬚
ckingham Dr EGRIN RH19 .... 22 E4
ckingham Ms SHOR SN43 .... 200 C2 ⬚
ckingham Pl BRI BN1 .... 6 B3
ckingham Rd BRI BN1 .... 6 B4
RTW TN1 .... 30 E1
SHOR SN43 .... 200 C4
STLEO TN38 .... 169 H7
ckingham St BRI BN1 .... 6 B4 ⬚
SHOR SN43 .... 200 B4 ⬚
ckland Rd SEAF BN25 .... 225 C6 ⬚
ddens Gn RYE TN31 .... 83 F7
gsell La RBTBR TN32 .... 77 K6
ibeck Cl BURH RH15 .... 118 E2
iler Cl CROW TN6 .... 53 J2
iler Rd ROTT BN2 .... 7 F1
llfinch Cl UCK TN22 .... 95 K7
llingstone La RRTW TN3 .... 18 D4
lls Pl STLEO TN38 .... 197 F2
lrush Pl STLEO TN38 .... 197 F2
e Bungalows UCK TN22 .... 96 D6
rchetts Cl HWH RH16 .... 89 K1
rden Pl STLEO TN38 .... 169 H8
rdett Rd CROW TN6 .... 54 A2
SBGH/RUST TN4 .... 19 F7 ⬚
rfield Rd LW/ROSE BN22 .... 11 D4 ⬚
rgh Hl BUR/ETCH TN... .... 77 J1
rgh La RING/NEW BN8 .... 184 E6
rhill Wy STLEO TN38 .... 197 G4
rleigh Pl LW/ROSE BN22 .... 11 E1 ⬚
e Burrells SHOR SN43 .... 200 E5
rrow Down EDN/EASTW BN20 ... 229 J5
rry Rd SLVH TN37 .... 4 A1
rslem La RRTW TN3 .... 20 E5
rstead Cl BRI BN1 .... 178 C6
rston Gdns EGRIN RH19 .... 22 A2
ROTT BN2 .... 205 F4
rners Cl BURH RH15 .... 119 K2
rnham Cl ROTT BN2 .... 206 C4
rnside POLE BN26 .... 215 F5 ⬚
rnthouse Bostall
HPPT/KEY BN... .... 150 D4
rnt House La RRTW TN3 .... 18 D6
rnt Lodge La WADH TN5 .... 59 K2
rnt Oak Rd UCK TN22 .... 68 D2
rrells La UCK TN22 .... 67 G4
rry Rd NEWHV BN9 .... 8 B2
rsh Cl PEAHV BN10 .... 221 K2
ROTT BN2 .... 206 A2
sheyfields HAIL BN27 .... 189 F3 ⬚
sh Cl PEAHV BN10 .... 221 K2
sh Farm Dr PTSD BN41 .... 202 A1
sh Gill RRTW TN3 .... 18 E8
tcherfield La HRTF TN7 .... 25 G4
tcher's La RHAS TN35 .... 171 C1
te St ROTT BN2 .... 7 F5
tler's La HAIL BN27 .... 163 F8
tlers Wy RING/NEW BN8 .... 155 J6 ⬚
tterbox La RHWH RH17 .... 64 B7
ttercup Wk BRI BN1 .... 178 C5
ttermere Wy LGNY BN23 .... 216 D7 ⬚
tts Fll HAIL BN27 .... 189 H5
ttsfield La RING/NEW BN8 .... 127 J6
tts La EDN/EASTW BN20 .... 229 F2
VADH TN5 .... 44 E4
tts Rd STHW BN42 .... 201 H4
xted Cl BRI BN1 .... 178 C6
xted Wood La UCK TN22 .... 69 F6
xton Dr BEXW TN39 .... 195 C5
xton Rd BRI BN1 .... 6 A3
DN/EASTW BN20 .... 236 E3
town SEAF BN25 .... 225 H7
e Byeways SEAF BN25 .... 225 G7

The Byeway BEXW TN39 .... 194 C6
HAS TN34 .... 170 C7
Byfields Cft BEXW TN39 .... 194 E6
Byland Cl LW/ROSE BN22 .... 215 K8
Byng Rd SBGH/RUST TN4 .... 19 J6
Byron Gv EGRIN RH19 .... 22 A3
Byron St HOVE BN3 .... 203 F4
Byways HAS TN34 .... 170 A5
The Byway BRI BN1 .... 179 F5
Byworth Cl BEXW TN39 .... 194 B5
ROTT BN2 .... 205 G5

C

Cabbage Stalk La SBGH/RUST TN4... 29 J1
Cabot Cl LGNY BN23 .... 231 H5
Caburn Cl LW/ROSE BN22 .... 216 B7 ⬚
Caburn Crs LEW BN7 .... 2 A3
Caburn Rd HOVE BN3 .... 6 A3 ⬚
Caburn Wy HAIL BN27 .... 189 F5
Cacklebury Cl HAIL BN27 .... 189 F5
Cackle St RYE TN31 .... 139 J1
UCK TN22 .... 66 E2
Cadborough Cliff RYE TN31 .... 113 F7
Cade St LW/ROSE BN22 .... 230 A1
Cairngorm Cl LGNY BN23 .... 216 E8
Cairo Av PEAHV BN10 .... 221 K4
Cairo Av South PEAHV BN10 .... 221 K4
Caister Cl HOVE BN3 .... 203 H3
Caldbec Hl BAT TN33 .... 136 D6
Caldicotts La HAIL BN27 .... 160 B8
Caledonian Rd ROTT BN2 .... 7 D2 ⬚
Caley Rd RTWE/PEM TN2 .... 20 D3 ⬚
Calgary Rd BEXW TN39 .... 195 G4
Callums Wk BEX TN40 .... 195 K6
Calverley Ct RTWE/PEM TN2 .... 20 C8 ⬚
Calverley Pk RTWE/PEM TN2 .... 20 B8
Calverley Park Crs
RTWE/PEM TN2 .... 20 B8 ⬚
Calverley Park Gdns RTW TN1 ..... 20 B8
Calverley Rd EAST BN21 .... 10 B5 ⬚
RTW TN1 .... 20 B7 ⬚
RTWE/PEM TN2 .... 20 B8
Calverley St RTW TN1 .... 20 B7
Calvert Cl UCK TN22 .... 95 G4
HAS TN34 .... 5 E2
UCK TN22 .... 95 G4
Camber Cl BEX TN40 .... 195 K5
Camber Dr PEV BN24 .... 218 C5
Camberlot La HAIL BN27 .... 187 K2
Camber Rd RYE TN31 .... 114 B7
Camber Wy PEV BN24 .... 218 C5
Cambrian Rd SBGH/RUST TN4 ...... 20 A5
Cambridge Gdns HAS TN34 .... 4 C4
RTWE/PEM TN2 .... 30 B1 ⬚
Cambridge Gv HOVE BN3 .... 203 H4
Cambridge Rd BEXW TN39 .... 195 H5
HAS TN34 .... 4 C5
HOVE BN3 .... 203 J5
LW/ROSE BN22 .... 11 D3
Cambridge St RTWE/PEM TN2 ..... 20 C8 ⬚
Cambridge Wy UCK TN22 .... 95 J2
Camden Av RTWE/PEM TN2 .... 21 J5
Camden Hl RTWE/PEM TN2 .... 20 B8 ⬚
RTWE/PEM TN2 .... 30 C1 ⬚
Camden Pk RTWE/PEM TN2 .... 20 B8 ⬚
RTWE/PEM TN2 .... 30 D1 ⬚
Camden Rd EAST BN21 .... 10 B5 ⬚
RTW TN1 .... 20 B7
Camden St PTSD BN41 .... 202 B5 ⬚
Camelford St ROTT BN2 .... 7 D6 ⬚
Cameron Cl HAIL BN27 .... 189 F5
Campbell Cl UCK TN22 .... 95 J2
Campbell Rd BRI BN1 .... 6 B2
SBGH/RUST TN4 .... 20 A5 ⬚
Camperdown St BEXW TN39 .... 195 F4
Canada Cl PEAHV BN10 .... 222 A2 ⬚
Canada Wy BEXW TN39 .... 195 G4
Canadia Rd BAT TN33 .... 136 D3
Canfield Cl ROTT BN2 .... 7 F1
Canfield Rd ROTT BN2 .... 7 F1 ⬚
Canning St ROTT BN2 .... 7 E5
Cannon Pl BRI BN1 .... 6 B5 ⬚
Cansiron La EDEN TN8 .... 24 E1
FROW RH18 .... 24 B6
Cantelupe Rd BEX TN40 .... 195 J8
EGRIN RH19 .... 22 D2
Canterbury Cl LW/ROSE BN22 .... 229 H1 ⬚
Canterbury Dr ROTT BN2 .... 7 C1
Canterbury Ri HAS TN34 .... 4 D1
Cantercrow Hl NEWHV BN9 .... 224 A1
Cants Cl BURH RH15 .... 89 J8
Cants La BURH RH15 .... 89 J7
Canute Cl LGNY BN23 .... 231 G3 ⬚
Canute Rd RHAS TN35 .... 171 G8
Capel Av PEAHV BN10 .... 222 A5
Capenors BURH RH15 .... 119 F2
Caple Gdns STLEO TN38 .... 197 J4
Carden Av BRI BN1 .... 178 A6
Carden Cl BRI BN1 .... 178 B5
Carden Crs BRI BN1 .... 178 B5
Carden Hl BRI BN1 .... 178 C6

Card Hl FROW RH18 .... 35 K2
Cardiff Rd STLEO TN38 .... 4 A5 ⬚
Cardinals Cl BEX TN40 .... 196 A5
Carew Rd EAST BN21 .... 10 A3
Carey Down PEAHV BN10 .... 222 A2 ⬚
Carfax Cl BEXW TN39 .... 195 G3
Carinus Gdns STLEO TN38 .... 169 H6 ⬚
Carisbrooke Cl LGNY BN23 .... 216 C7
Carisbrooke Rd ROTT BN2 .... 7 F3
STLEO TN38 .... 197 J4
Carisbrooke Rd STLEO TN38 .... 197 J4
Carlisle Pde HAS TN34 .... 4 C5
Carlisle Rd EAST BN21 .... 10 C6 ⬚
EDN/EASTW BN20 .... 10 A6
HOVE BN3 .... 202 E5
Carlton Cl SEAF BN25 .... 224 E7
Carlton Crs RTWE/PEM TN2 .... 20 C7 ⬚
Carlton Hl ROTT BN2 .... 7 D5
Carlton Pl ROTT BN2 .... 7 D5 ⬚
Carlton Rd LW/ROSE BN22 .... 11 E2 ⬚
RTWE/PEM TN2 .... 20 C7
SEAF BN25 .... 224 E6
Carlton Ter HOVE BN3 .... 202 E5 ⬚
Carlyle Av ROTT BN2 .... 7 F1
Carlyle St ROTT BN2 .... 7 E3
Carmel Cl BEXW TN39 .... 194 C8
Carol Cl BRI BN1 .... 178 A5
Caroline Cl SEAF BN25 .... 224 E6 ⬚
Carpenter Dr STLEO TN38 .... 169 G7
Carpenters Cft RING/NEW BN8 ... 127 J6 ⬚
Carpenters Wy HAIL BN27 .... 189 F5
Carville Av SBGH/RUST TN4 .... 19 K3
Castle Ditch La LEW BN7 .... 2 E4 ⬚
Castledean Av HAS TN34 .... 5 C4 ⬚
Castle Dr PEV BN24 .... 217 K7
Castlefields HRTF TN7 .... 25 K7
Castle Gdns HAS TN34 .... 5 D5 ⬚
Castle Hl MAYF TN20 .... 54 E6
Castle Hill Pas HAS TN34 .... 5 D4 ⬚
Castle Hill Rd HAS TN34 .... 5 E4
Castle Hurst RBTBR TN32 .... 79 H3
Castle Ri UCK TN22 .... 95 K7
Castle Rd PEV BN24 .... 217 K7
SBGH/RUST TN4 .... 19 K8
Castleross Rd PEV BN24 .... 217 K7
Castle St BRI BN1 .... 6 A5
HAS TN34 .... 5 D5 ⬚
RTW TN1 .... 30 A1 ⬚
SBGH/RUST TN4 .... 19 K1
WSEA TN36 .... 143 F4
Castle View Gdns PEV BN24 .... 217 F5
Castle Wk WADH TN5 .... 44 A7
Castle Wy UCK TN22 .... 95 K7 ⬚
Catherine Pl RTW TN1 .... 20 B8 ⬚
Catherine V ROTT BN2 .... 206 B3
Catsfield Cl POLE BN26 .... 216 A7
STLEO TN38 .... 196 E1 ⬚
Catsfield Rd BAT TN33 .... 135 H8
Cat St HRTF TN7 .... 37 F2
Catt's Hl CROW TN6 .... 55 H2
The Causeway ROTT BN2 .... 7 F4
SEAF BN25 .... 232 A1
Cavalier Wy EGRIN RH19 .... 22 D4
Cavalry Crs EDN/EASTW BN20 ... 229 G6
Cavell Av PEAHV BN10 .... 222 A4
Cavell Av North PEAHV BN10 ...... 222 B3
Cavendish Av LW/ROSE BN22 ..... 11 D5 ⬚
STLEO TN38 .... 197 H4
Cavendish Cl PEAHV BN10 .... 222 A3
Cavendish Dr RTWE/PEM TN2 ..... 30 D1 ⬚
Cavendish Pl BRI BN1 .... 6 A5 ⬚
EAST BN21 .... 11 D4 ⬚
EAST BN21 .... 11 D5 ⬚
Cavendish St ROTT BN2 .... 7 D5 ⬚
Caveridge La RING/NEW BN8 ..... 122 C3
Caves Rd STLEO TN38 .... 197 H5
Cedar Cl BURH RH15 .... 89 H6
HAS TN34 .... 170 A6
LW/ROSE BN22 .... 229 H1
Cedar Rdg RTWE/PEM TN2 .... 20 D5
Cedars Cl UCK TN22 .... 95 J3 ⬚
Cedars Gdns BRI BN1 .... 177 J8
The Cedars HAIL BN27 .... 189 G2
PEAHV BN10 .... 222 B2 ⬚
UCK TN22 .... 95 K3
Cedarwell Cl NEWHV BN9 .... 223 G1 ⬚
Celandine Dr STLEO TN38 .... 197 H2
Central Av EDN/EASTW BN20 ...... 229 G6
POLE BN26 .... 221 K4
POLE BN26 .... 215 C4
Centurion Rd BRI BN1 .... 6 A4
Centurion Rd BRI BN1 .... 6 B4
Ceylon Pl EAST BN21 .... 11 D4
Ceylon Wk BEXW TN39 .... 194 D8
Chadborn Cl ROTT BN2 .... 7 F6
Chaffinch Cl BURH RH15 .... 88 D7 ⬚
Chaffinch Rd LGNY BN23 .... 230 D1
Chaffinch Wk UCK TN22 .... 95 K7
Chafford La RRTW TN3 .... 17 J6
Chailey Av ROTT BN2 .... 220 D2
Chailey Cl HAS TN34 .... 170 B6
LGNY BN23 .... 231 F2 ⬚
Chailey Crs ROTT BN2 .... 221 H2
Chailey La RING/NEW BN8 .... 93 F6
Chailey Rd ROTT BN2 .... 179 F1

Chain La BAT TN33 .... 136 C6
Chalfont Dr HOVE BN3 .... 177 H8
Chalkers La HPPT/KEY BN6 .... 118 B3
Chalket La RTWE/PEM TN2 .... 21 J6
Chalk Farm La RTWE/EASTW BN20 .... 229 G2
Chalkland Ri ROTT BN2 .... 206 B3
Chalky Rd PTSD BN41 .... 175 J8
Challoners RHWH RH17 .... 48 A7
Challoners Cl ROTT BN2 .... 220 C1
Challoners Ms ROTT BN2 .... 220 C1
Challow Cl RHWH BN6 .... 118 E7
Chalvington Cl BRI BN1 .... 179 F5
  SEAF BN25 .... 225 G5
Chalvington Dr SLVH TN37 .... 169 K5
Chalvington Rd EAST BN21 .... 229 H4
Chamberlaines La RING/NEW BN8 ... 156 A5
Chamberlain Rd EAST BN21 .... 229 H7
Chambers Crs STLEO TN38 .... 169 G8
Chambers Rd STLEO TN38 .... 197 G1
Chancellors Pk HPPT/KEY BN6 .... 119 F7
Chanctonbury Dr HAS TN34 .... 170 B3
  SHOR BN43 .... 200 B2
Chanctonbury Rd BURH RH15 .... 119 J3
  HOVE BN3 .... 6 A3
Chandler Rd BEXW TN39 .... 195 F6
Chandler's Md RING/NEW BN8 .... 153 K4
Chandos Rd RTW TN1 .... 20 C6
Channel Vw East BEX TN40 .... 195 H8
Channel View Rd LW/ROSE BN22 ...... 11 E2
  PEV BN24 .... 218 B6
  ROTT BN2 .... 205 J3
Channel Vw West BEX TN40 .... 195 H8
Channel Wy RHAS TN35 .... 172 D8
Channers La RING/NEW BN8 .... 186 A3
Chant La CROW TN6 .... 55 F2
Chantlers Cl EGRIN RH19 .... 22 A1
Chantlers Md EDEN TN8 .... 15 G6
Chantry Av BEX TN40 .... 195 H5
Chantry La BEX TN40 .... 195 H6
Chapel Barn La HAIL BN27 .... 189 H4
Chapel Cl BURH RH15 .... 89 F6
  SEAF BN25 .... 225 F7
Chapel Fld RYE TN31 .... 81 J4
Chapel Gn CROW TN6 .... 53 H1
Chapel Hl BAT TN33 .... 138 A3
  BAT TN33 .... 168 A7
  LEW BN7 .... 3 E4
Chapel La EGRIN RH19 .... 23 H5
  FROW RH18 .... 35 K2
  LEW BN7 .... 121 J8
  RHAS TN35 .... 171 K3
  RHWH RH17 .... 48 A6
  UCK TN22 .... 97 K4
Chapel Ms HOVE BN3 .... 203 J6
Chapel Park Rd SLVH TN37 .... 4 A4
Chapel Pl PTSD BN41 .... 202 A4
Chapel Rd LEW BN7 .... 121 G4
  PTSD BN41 .... 201 L4
Chapman's La EGRIN RH19 .... 22 B2
Chapmans Town Rd HTHF TN21 ...... 131 H2
Chapman Wy RTWE/PEM TN2 .... 20 C3
Charity Farm Wy CROW TN6 .... 39 J4
Charles Av BURH RH15 .... 118 E1
Charles Cl HOVE BN3 .... 177 F8
  SEAF BN25 .... 224 E6
Charles Rd STLEO TN38 .... 197 J3
Charles Rd West STLEO TN38 .... 197 J3
Charles St ROTT BN2 .... 6 C6
  SBGH/RUST TN4 .... 20 A3
Charleston Rd EAST BN21 .... 229 H7
Charlotte St ROTT BN2 .... 7 D6
Charlston Av NEWHV BN9 .... 8 A5
The Charlton's BRI BN1 .... 178 E5
Charlton's Wy SBGH/RUST TN4 ...... 29 J2
Charlwood Gdns BURH RH15 .... 89 J6
Charlwood Rd BURH RH15 .... 89 J6
Charlwoods Business Centre
  EGRIN RH19 .... 22 B1
Charlwoods Pl EGRIN RH19 .... 12 C8
Charlwoods Rd EGRIN RH19 .... 22 B1
Chartfield HOVE BN3 .... 203 F1
Chartres BEX TN40 .... 195 J5
Chartres Cl BEX TN40 .... 195 J5
Chartwell Cl SEAF BN25 .... 225 F5
Chatfield Crs LW/ROSE BN22 .... 229 H2
Chatham Pl BRI BN1 .... 6 B3
  SEAF BN25 .... 232 A1
Chatham Rd SLVH TN37 .... 197 J1
Chatsfield Cl STLEO TN38 .... 169 F7
Chatsworth Av PEAHV BN10 .... 221 K2
Chatsworth Rd BRI BN1 .... 6 A2
Chatsworth Gdns
  EDN/EASTW BN20 .... 237 F3
Chatsworth Pk PEAHV BN10 .... 222 A2
Chatsworth Rd BRI BN1 .... 6 A2
Chaucer Av EGRIN RH19 .... 22 A3
Chawbrook Rd LW/ROSE BN22 .... 11 D3
Cheal Cl SHOR BN43 .... 200 D5
Cheapside BRI BN1 .... 6 C2
Cheeleys RHWH RH17 .... 48 A6
Chelsea Cl BEX TN40 .... 195 J7
Chelston Av HOVE BN3 .... 202 C4

Cheltenham Pl BRI BN1 .... 6 C4
Chelwood Cl BRI BN1 .... 178 D5
Chelwood Gate Rd UCK TN22 .... 49 K5
Chelworth Rd LW/ROSE BN22 .... 229 H1
Chene Rd PEAHV BN10 .... 222 E5
Chenies Cl RTWE/PEM TN2 .... 30 A3
Chepbourne Rd BEX TN40 .... 195 G7
Chequer Gra FROW RH18 .... 35 J2
Chequer Rd EGRIN RH19 .... 22 D2
Chequers Cl CROW TN6 .... 53 J1
Chequers Wy CROW TN6 .... 53 J1
Cherington La HPPT/KEY BN6 .... 118 B6
Cherry Cl BURH RH15 .... 88 E8
Cherry Garden Rd
  EDN/EASTW BN20 .... 229 G8
Cherry Gdns HTHF TN21 .... 100 B6
Cherry Side HAIL BN27 .... 189 F4
Cherry Tree Cl SLVH TN37 .... 4 A4
Cherry Tree Gdns BEX TN40 .... 196 A5
Cherry Tree Rd RTWE/PEM TN2 ...... 29 J2
Cherwell Cl POLE BN26 .... 216 A6
Cherwell Rd HTHF TN21 .... 100 A3
Chesham Pl ROTT BN2 .... 7 F6
Chesham Rd ROTT BN2 .... 7 F6
Chesham St ROTT BN2 .... 7 F6
Chesnut Cl HAIL BN27 .... 189 F2
Chester Av RTWE/PEM TN2 .... 30 D1
Chesterfield Gdns
  EDN/EASTW BN20 .... 236 E3
Chesterfield Rd EDN/EASTW BN20 .. 236 E3
Chester Ter BRI BN1 .... 6 C1
Chesterton Av SEAF BN25 .... 225 J8
Chesterton Cl EGRIN RH19 .... 22 D4
Chesterton Dr SEAF BN25 .... 225 J8
Chestnut Av SBGH/RUST TN4 .... 20 B3
Chestnut Cl BURH RH15 .... 89 H6
  EGRIN RH19 .... 22 E2
  HAIL BN27 .... 163 F5
  RYE TN31 .... 109 K6
  SBGH/RUST TN4 .... 20 B3
Chestnut Dr POLE BN26 .... 215 F5
The Chestnuts HAWK TN18 .... 62 E3
Chestnut Wk BEXW TN39 .... 194 B6
  EGRIN RH19 .... 12 A4
Chestnut Wy NEWHV BN9 .... 8 B3
Cheviot Rd LGNY BN23 .... 216 D8
The Cheviots HAS TN34 .... 170 E7
Chichester Cl BEXW TN39 .... 195 G5
  HOVE BN3 .... 176 D7
  LW/ROSE BN22 .... 229 G1
  PEAHV BN10 .... 222 E4
Chichester Dr East ROTT BN2 .... 221 F3
Chichester Dr West ROTT BN2 .... 220 E2
Chichester Pl ROTT BN2 .... 7 F6
Chichester Rd SEAF BN25 .... 225 F8
Chichester Ter ROTT BN2 .... 7 F6
Chichester Wy BURH RH15 .... 89 J6
Chick Hl RHAS TN35 .... 173 G3
Chicks La CRBK TN17 .... 46 E1
Chiddingley Cl ROTT BN2 .... 205 G6
Chievelev Dr RTWE/PEM TN2 .... 30 C2
Chilcomb BURH RH15 .... 119 J2
Chilham Cl LGNY BN23 .... 230 E1
Chillies La UCK TN22 .... 68 C2
Chilsham La HAIL BN27 .... 162 E4
Chilston Cl SBGH/RUST TN4 .... 20 A6
Chilston Rd SBGH/RUST TN4 .... 20 A6
Chiltern Cl LGNY BN23 .... 216 E8
  SHOR BN43 .... 201 F3
Chiltern Dr HAS TN34 .... 5 F1
Chiltington Cl BURH RH15 .... 89 F6
  ROTT BN2 .... 221 F1
Chiltington La LEW BN7 .... 122 A8
Chiltington Wy ROTT BN2 .... 221 F1
Chiswick Pl EAST BN21 .... 10 C5
Chitcombe Rd RYE TN31 .... 109 G6
Chorley Av ROTT BN2 .... 220 E1
Chown's Hl HAS TN34 .... 170 D5
Chrisdory Rd PTSD BN41 .... 175 H8
Christie Av RING/NEW BN8 .... 155 J5
Christie Rd LEW BN7 .... 2 A4
Christies EGRIN RH19 .... 22 B3
Christopher Rd EGRIN RH19 .... 22 C2
Church Av PEV BN24 .... 217 H5
Church Cl BRI BN1 .... 178 A6
  BURH RH15 .... 89 G8
  EDN/EASTW BN20 .... 215 F7
Churchdale Pl LW/ROSE BN22 .... 11 D1
Churchdale Rd LW/ROSE BN22 ...... 11 D1
Church Farm Cl BUR/ETCH TN19 .... 77 G2
Churchfields UCK TN22 .... 50 C6
Church Gn SHOR BN43 .... 201 F4
Church Hl BRI BN1 .... 177 K5
  BUR/ETCH TN19 .... 77 G2
  NEWHV BN9 .... 8 C3
  POY/PYE BN45 .... 149 H5
  RING/NEW BN8 .... 155 J5
Church Hill Av BEXW TN39 .... 194 B7
Church House Cl STHW BN42 .... 201 H2
Churchill Av RHAS TN35 .... 171 G6
Churchill Cl EDN/EASTW BN20 .... 229 J8
Churchill Rd HTHF TN21 .... 100 B5
  LEW BN7 .... 2 B2
  SEAF BN25 .... 224 E6
Churchill Wy BURH RH15 .... 119 J1

Church In the Wood La
  STLEO TN38 .... 165 H1
Churchland La BAT TN33 .... 108 D7
Church La BAT TN33 .... 166 A7
  BAT TN33 .... 166 C3
  BAT TN33 .... 193 J2
  BUR/ETCH TN19 .... 77 F5
  EAST BN21 .... 229 G5
  EGRIN RH19 .... 22 E5
  HAIL BN27 .... 161 G5
  HPPT/KEY BN6 .... 119 F7
  HWH RH16 .... 90 D5
  LEW BN7 .... 2 C4
  LEW BN7 .... 181 H4
  PEV BN24 .... 217 J3
  POLE BN26 .... 228 B2
  POY/PYE BN45 .... 148 E1
  POY/PYE BN45 .... 149 F4
  RBTBR TN32 .... 78 D6
  RHAS TN35 .... 139 K3
  RHAS TN35 .... 172 A6
  RHWH RH17 .... 48 A6
  RHWH RH17 .... 48 B6
  RING/NEW BN8 .... 157 F2
  RING/NEW BN8 .... 186 E1
  RRTW TN3 .... 30 E1
  RYE TN31 .... 82 B8
  RYE TN31 .... 82 E7
  RYE TN31 .... 85 G8
  RYE TN31 .... 112 B6
  SEAF BN25 .... 232 A5
  STHW BN42 .... 201 J2
  UCK TN22 .... 68 A1
Church Marks La RING/NEW BN8 .... 127 K5
Church Md HPPT/KEY BN6 .... 119 F7
Church Pl ROTT BN2 .... 205 K1
Church Rd BAT TN33 .... 166 C3
  BURH RH15 .... 89 G8
  BURH RH15 .... 119 K1
  CRBK TN17 .... 46 D5
  CROW TN6 .... 53 H1
  HAIL BN27 .... 191 F1
  HOVE BN3 .... 203 J6
  POLE BN26 .... 215 F5
  PTSD BN41 .... 202 A4
  RBTBR TN32 .... 106 A4
  RING/NEW BN8 .... 96 E1
  RING/NEW BN8 .... 154 A1
  RRTW TN3 .... 33 F5
  SBGH/RUST TN4 .... 19 K4
  SBGH/RUST TN4 .... 19 K5
  SLVH TN37 .... 4 A4
  UCK TN22 .... 68 B1
Churchsettle La WADH TN5 .... 58 B5
Church Sq RYE TN31 .... 113 G6
Church St BEX TN40 .... 195 K3
  BRI BN1 .... 6 D4
  CROW TN6 .... 54 A2
  EDEN TN8 .... 15 G6
  EDN/EASTW BN20 .... 229 H7
  EDN/EASTW BN20 .... 229 J5
  HRTF TN7 .... 25 J5
  HTHF TN21 .... 100 A4
  LW/ROSE BN22 .... 229 H1
  PTSD BN41 .... 202 A4
  RHAS TN35 .... 171 F5
  SEAF BN25 .... 225 J8
  SHOR BN43 .... 200 E4
  UCK TN22 .... 68 A1
Church Vale Rd BEX TN40 .... 195 J8
Church Wood Dr STLEO TN38 .... 169 H1
Church Wood Wy STLEO TN38 .... 197 H1
Chyngton Av SEAF BN25 .... 225 K7
Chyngton Cl LGNY BN23 .... 216 E8
Chyngton Gdns SEAF BN25 .... 225 K8
Chyngton La SEAF BN25 .... 226 A8
Chyngton La North SEAF BN25 ...... 225 K8
Chyngton Pl SEAF BN25 .... 232 A1
Chyngton Rd SEAF BN25 .... 232 A1
Chyngton Wy SEAF BN25 .... 232 B1
Cinderford La HAIL BN27 .... 161 J4
Cinder Hl RING/NEW BN8 .... 92 A1
  RING/NEW BN8 .... 93 F1
Cinquefoil PEAHV BN10 .... 222 E5
Cinque Ports St RYE TN31 .... 113 G5
Cinque Ports Wy SEAF BN25 .... 225 J8
  STLEO TN38 .... 197 H3
Circus St ROTT BN2 .... 6 E4
The Circus LGNY BN23 .... 230 B1
Cissbury Av PEAHV BN10 .... 222 C5
Cissbury Crs ROTT BN2 .... 221 G3
Cissbury Rd BURH RH15 .... 88 E8
  HOVE BN3 .... 6 A1
Civic Ap UCK TN22 .... 95 H6
Civic Wy BURH RH15 .... 89 J8
Clackhams La CROW TN6 .... 54 E1
Clanricarde Gdns RTW TN1 .... 20 A4
Clanricarde Rd SBGH/RUST TN4 .... 19 K5
Clapham La POLE BN26 .... 226 D8
Claphatch La WADH TN5 .... 45 J4
The Clappers RBTBR TN32 .... 78 E2
Claremont HAS TN34 .... 4 C3
Claremont Gdns RTW TN1 .... 30 A4
Claremont Ri UCK TN22 .... 95 H2
Claremont Rd BEXW TN39 .... 195 F4

EWHV BN9 ... 9 F1
TW TN1 ... 30 B1
EAF BN29 ... 224 E8
ence Dr EGRIN RH19 ... 22 D4
ence Rd LW/ROSE BN22 ... 11 D2
TW TN1 ... 20 A8
ence Rw RTW TN1 ... 20 A7
ence Sq BRI BN1 ... 6 B5
endon Cl SLVH TN37 ... 169 J7
endon Gdns RTWE/PEM TN2 ... 30 A2
endon Pl PTSD BN41 ... 202 B5
endon Rd HOVE BN3 ... 203 G4
HOR BN43 ... 201 F3
endon Ter HOVE BN3 ... 7 F6
endon Vls HOVE BN3 ... 203 F4
e Rd LEW BN7 ... 2 A3
idge Gdns LING RH7 ... 12 E1
idges Md LING RH7 ... 12 E1
ke Av HOVE BN3 ... 176 E8
erham Cl BAT TN33 ... 136 B7
erham Wy BAT TN33 ... 136 B7
kton Cl EAST BN21 ... 229 J6
kton Rd BEX TN40 ... 196 B6
fields PEAHV BN10 ... 222 A4
ford LING RH7 ... 12 E1
y Hill Rd RRTW TN3 ... 33 F6
ys Cl EGRIN RH19 ... 22 C5
yton Av HPPT/KEY BN6 ... 118 E8
yton Dr BURH RH15 ... 119 F2
yton Hl POY/PYE BN45 ... 149 J4
yton Mill Rd PEV BN24 ... 216 C6
yton Rd HPPT/KEY BN6 ... 150 D1
OTT BN2 ... 7 F3
yton's La RRTW TN3 ... 27 C1
yton Wy HOVE BN3 ... 176 E8
arwaters La BURH RH15 ... 89 K3
eve Av RTWE/PEM TN2 ... 30 C1
evelands LW/ROSE BN22 ... 229 G1
gg St HAS TN34 ... 5 D4
ment Hill Rd HAS TN34 ... 5 F1
mentine Av SEAF BN25 ... 224 E8
ment La POLE BN26 ... 215 F6
ks Acre HPPT/KEY BN6 ... 119 G7
mont Rd BRI BN1 ... 203 J1
mont Ter BRI BN1 ... 203 K1
ve Cl UCK TN22 ... 96 D6
edon Rd BEXW TN39 ... 194 E5
veland RTWE/PEM TN2 ... 20 D6
veland Cl LGNY BN23 ... 216 D8
veland Gdns BURH RH15 ... 119 H1
veland Rd BRI BN1 ... 6 C1
e Ter LEW BN7 ... 2 B5
f Ap ROTT BN2 ... 205 G7
f Av PEAHV BN10 ... 222 D6
f Cl SEAF BN25 ... 232 B2
fe High St LEW BN7 ... 3 D4
f End La RHAS TN35 ... 173 G4
f Gdns PEAHV BN10 ... 221 J3
EAF BN25 ... 232 B2
ford Av EAST BN21 ... 229 H5
ford Rd BEX TN40 ... 195 H7
f Park Cl PEAHV BN10 ... 222 D6
f Rd EDN/EASTW BN20 ... 236 E4
OTT BN2 ... 205 G8
EAF BN25 ... 232 B2
Cliff ROTT BN2 ... 205 G7
f Wy RHAS TN35 ... 172 E6
ton Cl LW/ROSE BN22 ... 229 J3
ton Hl BRI BN1 ... 6 A4
ton Pl BRI BN1 ... 6 B4
TW TN1 ... 30 B1
ton Rd BEX TN40 ... 196 A6
ton Ter BRI BN1 ... 6 B4
onville Rd STLEO TN38 ... 196 E5
ton Wy PEAHV BN10 ... 221 K5
ch Green Av BEXW TN39 ... 194 E4
ton Crs STLEO TN38 ... 197 J2
e Av RHAS TN35 ... 199 F1
ton Hl LING RH7 ... 12 E1
ton La SEAF BN25 ... 225 F8
ton Pl SEAF BN25 ... 225 F8
ton Wy RHAS TN35 ... 172 E6
e Av RHAS TN35 ... 199 F1
ckhouse RTWE/PEM TN2 ... 30 C5
ck House La UCK TN22 ... 50 C7
sters NEWHV BN9 ... 8 C3
Cloisters BAT TN33 ... 135 D5
W/ROSE BN22 ... 229 H1
LVH TN37 ... 4 B5
se Eight LGNY BN23 ... 217 F8
se Eighteen LGNY BN23 ... 231 F1
se Eleven LGNY BN23 ... 217 F8
se Fifteen LGNY BN23 ... 231 F1
se Five LGNY BN23 ... 217 F8
se Four LGNY BN23 ... 231 F1
se Fourteen LGNY BN23 ... 217 F8
se Nine LGNY BN23 ... 231 F1
se One LGNY BN23 ... 230 E1
se Seven LGNY BN23 ... 217 F8

Close Seventeen LGNY BN23 ... 231 F1
Close Six LGNY BN23 ... 217 F8
Close Sixteen LGNY BN23 ... 231 F1
Close Ten LGNY BN23 ... 231 F1
The Close BRI BN1 ... 177 J6
BURH RH15 ... 89 J7
CROW TN6 ... 59 G8
EDN/EASTW BN20 ... 229 G3
EDN/EASTW BN20 ... 234 E2
EGRIN RH19 ... 22 B3
HPPT/KEY BN6 ... 119 F7
NEWHV BN9 ... 224 A1
RHAS TN35 ... 172 B7
RRTW TN3 ... 28 A5
RYE TN31 ... 113 G5
SEAF BN25 ... 232 B1
SHOR BN43 ... 200 C3
UCK TN22 ... 97 K5
Close Three LGNY BN23 ... 230 E1
Close Twelve LGNY BN23 ... 231 F1
Close Twenty LGNY BN23 ... 231 F1
Close Twentyfive LGNY BN23 ... 230 E1
Close Twentyfour LGNY BN23 ... 231 F1
Close Two LGNY BN23 ... 230 E1
Cloudesley Rd SLVH TN37 ... 4 A4
Cloverlea HAS TN34 ... 170 B6
Clovers End BRI BN1 ... 178 C4
Clover Wy PTSD BN41 ... 202 A1
Cluny St LEW BN7 ... 2 C5
Clyde Rd BRI BN1 ... 6 C2
STLEO TN38 ... 4 A5
Coach & Horses La RHWH RH17 ... 49 G5
Coach La RHWH RH17 ... 49 G5
Coastguard La RHAS TN35 ... 172 A7
Coastguard Sq RYE TN31 ... 114 C3
Coast Rd PEV BN24 ... 218 B6
Cobald Rd PEV BN24 ... 218 B6
Cobbett's Ride RTWE/PEM TN2 ... 29 K2
Cobbold Av EAST BN21 ... 229 H5
Cobden Rd ROTT BN2 ... 7 E3
Cobdown La UCK TN22 ... 67 J7
Cobhams RRTW TN3 ... 18 E5
Cobton Dr HOVE BN3 ... 177 F8
Cochrane Cl LGNY BN23 ... 231 F4
Cockcrow Wd HAS TN34 ... 170 A6
Cockmount La WADH TN5 ... 44 A5
Cockshut Rd LEW BN7 ... 2 C6
Cogger's La HTHF TN21 ... 129 K8
Coggins Mill Rd MAYF TN20 ... 56 C8
Coghurst Rd RHAS TN35 ... 171 F7
Colbourne Av ROTT BN2 ... 204 E1
Colbourne Rd HOVE BN3 ... 6 A3
Colchester Cl FROW RH18 ... 35 J1
Colchins BURH RH15 ... 119 F2
Coldean La BRI BN1 ... 178 D3
Coldharbour Cl CROW TN6 ... 53 J2
Coldharbour La RING/NEW BN8 ... 92 C3
RYE TN31 ... 85 F7
Coldharbour Rd HAIL BN27 ... 188 A1
RTON TN11 ... 17 F3
Coldthorn La HAIL BN27 ... 189 F6
Coldwaltham La BURH RH15 ... 119 K2
Colebrooke Rd BEXW TN39 ... 195 F8
Colebrook Rd BRI BN1 ... 177 J7
SBGH/RUST TN4 ... 20 C4
STHW BN42 ... 201 J4
Coleman Av HOVE BN3 ... 202 D4
Colemans Hatch Rd FROW RH18 ... 36 B6
Coleman St ROTT BN2 ... 7 D4
Coleridge St HOVE BN3 ... 203 F5
Colgate Cl BRI BN1 ... 205 G5
College Cl EGRIN RH19 ... 22 D2
PTSD BN41 ... 175 J8
College Dr RTWE/PEM TN2 ... 20 D7
College Gdns ROTT BN2 ... 7 E6
College Gn EAST BN21 ... 10 A3
College La EGRIN RH19 ... 22 D2
HPPT/KEY BN6 ... 118 C6
College Pl HPPT/KEY BN6 ... 118 C5
ROTT BN2 ... 7 E6
College Rd BEX TN40 ... 195 K7
EAST BN21 ... 10 B5
ROTT BN2 ... 7 E6
SEAF BN25 ... 232 A1
College St ROTT BN2 ... 7 E6
College Ter ROTT BN2 ... 7 E5
Collier Cl LW/ROSE BN22 ... 230 C4
Collier Rd HAS TN34 ... 5 E4
PEV BN24 ... 218 A7
Collingford La RHWH RH17 ... 49 F7
Collington Av BEXW TN39 ... 194 E8
Collington Cl BEXW TN39 ... 10 A6
Collington Gv BEXW TN59 ... 194 D7
Collington La East BEXW TN39 ... 194 D7
Collington La West BEXW TN39 ... 194 C8
Collington Park Crs BEXW TN39 ... 194 E7
Collington Ri BEXW TN39 ... 194 D7
Collingwood Av HTHF TN21 ... 100 A4
Collingwood Cl SHOR BN43 ... 200 C5
Collingwood Ri HTHF TN21 ... 100 A4
Collinstone Rd STLEO TN38 ... 197 H4
Collinswood Dr STLEO TN38 ... 197 H4

Colmer Ct BURH RH15 ... 88 E8
Colmer Pl BURH RH15 ... 88 E8
Colonade Rd LW/ROSE BN22 ... 11 D4
Colonel's Wy SBGH/RUST TN4 ... 20 A1
Coltstocks Rd
EDN/EASTW BN20 ... 236 D3
Columbus Dr LGNY BN23 ... 231 G5
Colvill Av SHOR BN43 ... 200 A5
Colwell La RHWH RH17 ... 90 B2
Colwell Rd HWH RH16 ... 90 B1
Colwood Crs EDN/EASTW BN20 ... 229 G5
Combe End CROW TN6 ... 53 H5
Combe La BAT TN33 ... 165 J5
EDN/EASTW BN20 ... 236 D4
Combe Ri EDN/EASTW BN20 ... 229 F1
Combermere Rd STLEO TN38 ... 197 J2
The Combe EDN/EASTW BN20 ... 229 F4
Commanders Wk RHAS TN35 ... 172 D7
Command Rd EDN/EASTW BN20 ... 229 G6
Commercial Rd BURH RH15 ... 89 F8
EAST BN21 ... 10 C4
RTW TN1 ... 20 B6
Common La HPPT/KEY BN6 ... 119 G6
POLE BN26 ... 212 D2
Common Vw SBGH/RUST TN4 ... 19 G8
Common Wood Ri CROW TN6 ... 39 H7
Compasses La RBTBR TN32 ... 107 J5
Comphurst La HAIL BN27 ... 163 J7
Compton Av BRI BN1 ... 6 B4
Compton Cl BEX TN40 ... 195 K6
Compton Dr EDN/EASTW BN20 ... 236 C1
Compton Place Rd
EDN/EASTW BN20 ... 229 J8
Compton Rd BRI BN1 ... 203 J2
Compton St EDN/EASTW BN20 ... 10 C6
Compton Ter HAIL BN27 ... 189 H5
The Compts PEAHV BN10 ... 222 A2
Concord Cl RTWE/PEM TN2 ... 20 C7
Concorde Cl BEXW TN39 ... 194 E5
Condor Wy BURH RH15 ... 88 E5
Conduit Hl RYE TN31 ... 113 J5
Coneyburrow Gdns STLEO TN38 ... 169 F7
Coneyburrow La BEXW TN39 ... 193 J7
Coneyburrow Rd RTWE/PEM TN2 ... 20 E6
Coney Furlong PEAHV BN10 ... 222 C2
Conghurst La HAWK TN18 ... 63 G6
Conifer Cl HAS TN34 ... 5 D1
The Conifers EAST BN21 ... 10 B3
Coniston Av SBGH/RUST TN4 ... 19 J7
Coniston Rd LGNY BN23 ... 216 D7
Connaught Av SHOR BN43 ... 200 B3
Connaught Rd EAST BN21 ... 10 C5
HOVE BN3 ... 203 F5
SEAF BN25 ... 224 D8
Connaught Ter HOVE BN3 ... 203 G4
Connaught Wy SBGH/RUST TN4 ... 19 K6
Connell Dr ROTT BN2 ... 206 B4
Conqueror Rd STLEO TN38 ... 197 G4
Consort Wy BURH RH15 ... 118 E1
Constable La LGNY BN23 ... 230 E2
Constable Wy BEX TN40 ... 195 J5
Constitutional Hill Rd
SBGH/RUST TN4 ... 19 J2
Conway Pl HOVE BN3 ... 203 G3
Conway St HOVE BN3 ... 203 G3
Cooden Cl BEXW TN39 ... 194 B8
Cook Av LGNY BN23 ... 231 F5
Cookham Dene BEX TN40 ... 195 H7
Cooksbridge Rd ROTT BN2 ... 205 F5
Cookstown Cl BAT TN33 ... 165 J5
Coolham Dr ROTT BN2 ... 205 F5
Coombe Cl HAIL BN27 ... 163 J6
Coombe Hill Rd EGRIN RH19 ... 22 A5
Coombe La WADH TN5 ... 57 J4
Coombe Ri ROTT BN2 ... 207 G8
Coombe Rd EDN/EASTW BN20 ... 229 H7
LEW BN7 ... 3 D5
ROTT BN2 ... 7 F1
Coombe Shaw BAT TN33 ... 165 K5
Coombe V ROTT BN2 ... 207 G8
Coombs Cl RYE TN31 ... 83 G6
Cooper Dr BEXW TN39 ... 195 F3
Cooper Ri STLEO TN38 ... 169 H6
Cooper Rd RYE TN31 ... 113 G6
Coopers Cl BURH RH15 ... 89 H6
Coopers La CROW TN6 ... 39 F7
RRTW TN3 ... 18 A5
Coopers Wy HAIL BN27 ... 189 F5
Coopers Wd CROW TN6 ... 39 F7
Copestake Dr BURH RH15 ... 89 K8
Coplands Ri RYE TN31 ... 81 K4
Coppards Cl RHWH RH17 ... 90 E7
Coppards La RYE TN31 ... 82 A3
Copper Beeches SLVH TN37 ... 169 K7
Coppice Av EDN/EASTW BN20 ... 215 F7
Coppice Cl EDN/EASTW BN20 ... 215 F7
The Coppice BAT TN33 ... 137 G8
HAS TN34 ... 4 C3
RTWE/PEM TN2 ... 21 K4
Coppice Vw HTHF TN21 ... 100 B5
Copse Cl EGRIN RH19 ... 12 D8
STLEO TN38 ... 168 E8
Copse Hl BRI BN1 ... 177 J6
Copse Rd BEXW TN39 ... 194 D7

Copthall Av *HAWK* TN18 .... 63 F2
Copwood Av *UCK* TN22 .... 95 H4
Copyhold Rd *EGRIN* RH19 .... 22 B3
Corbyn Crs *SHOR* BN43 .... 200 D4
Cordons *LEW* BN7 .... 181 G6
Cormorant Cl *LGNY* BN23 .... 230 D1
Cornelius Av *NEWHV* BN9 .... 8 A5
Cornfield Cl *SEAF* BN25 .... 225 G8 🄴
Cornfield La *EAST* BN21 .... 10 C5
Cornfield Rd *EAST* BN21 .... 225 G8
SEAF BN25 .... 225 G8
Cornfield Ter *EAST* BN21 .... 10 C5 🄴
SLVH TN37 .... 4 A3
Cornford Cl *BURH* RH15 .... 88 E6
CROW TN6 .... 53 J2
PTSD BN41 .... 202 A1 🄴
RTWE/PEM TN2 .... 21 H5 🄴
Cornford La *RTWE/PEM* TN2 .... 20 E7
Cornford Pk *RTWE/PEM* TN2 .... 21 J5
Cornish Cl *LGNY* BN23 .... 216 C7
Cornmill Gdns *POLE* BN26 .... 214 C7
Cornwall Av *PEAHV* BN10 .... 222 D5
Cornwall Gdns *BRI* BN1 .... 177 K8
EGRIN RH19 .... 22 D3
Cornwallis Cl *LGNY* BN23 .... 231 G4 🄴
Cornwallis Gdns *HAS* TN34 .... 4 C4
Cornwallis St *HAS* TN34 .... 5 D4 🄴
Cornwallis Ter *HAS* TN34 .... 4 C4 🄴
Cornwall Rd *BEXW* TN39 .... 195 G8
Coronation Cottages *RBTBR* TN32 .... 78 C6
BUR/ETCH TN19 .... 61 K8
Coronation Gdns *BAT* TN33 .... 137 F6
Coronation Rd *EGRIN* RH19 .... 22 C4
Coronation St *ROTT* BN2 .... 7 E3 🄴
Corseley Rd *RRTW* TN3 .... 27 J8
Corsica Cl *SEAF* BN25 .... 232 B5
Corsica Rd *SEAF* BN25 .... 232 B2
Cotchford Hl *HRTF* TN7 .... 37 K2
Cotchford La *HRTF* TN7 .... 37 H2
Cotswold Cl *HAS* TN34 .... 170 E7
LGNY BN23 .... 216 D7
The Cotswolds *STHW* BN42 .... 201 H4 🄴
Cottage Bush Cl *PTSD* BN41 .... 202 B1 🄴
Cottage Cl *NEWHV* BN9 .... 9 D1 🄴
Cottage La *BAT* TN33 .... 138 A4
PEV BN24 .... 215 K2
Coulstock Rd *HPPT/KEY* BN6 .... 88 C7
County Oak Av *BRI* BN1 .... 178 C5
The Course *LEW* BN7 .... 2 B5
Court Cl *BRI* BN1 .... 177 K4
EGRIN RH19 .... 22 E2
Court Crs *EGRIN* RH19 .... 22 E2
Court Farm Cl *NEWHV* BN9 .... 209 G8
Court Farm Rd *HOVE* BN3 .... 202 E1
NEWHV BN9 .... 8 C5
ROTT BN2 .... 206 B8
Courthope Av *WADH* TN5 .... 44 B7
Courthope Dr *BEXW* TN39 .... 194 D6
Courthouse St *HAS* TN34 .... 5 F4 🄴
Courtland Rd *POLE* BN26 .... 215 F6
Courtlands *UCK* TN22 .... 66 D1
Courtlands Pl *CROW* TN6 .... 53 G2
Courtlands Rd *LW/ROSE* BN22 .... 10 C2
Court Meadow *CROW* TN6 .... 55 F3
Court Ord Rd *ROTT* BN2 .... 206 B8
Court Rd *LEW* BN7 .... 3 D5 🄴
LW/ROSE BN22 .... 230 A1
SBGH/RUST TN4 .... 19 J7
The Courtyard *EGRIN* RH19 .... 23 F2
Cousley Wood Rd *WADH* TN5 .... 44 C5
Coventry Rd *STLEO* TN38 .... 169 H8
Coventry St *BRI* BN1 .... 6 A2
Coverdale Av *BEXW* TN39 .... 194 B8
The Covers *SEAF* BN25 .... 232 B1
Cowden Cl *HAWK* TN18 .... 62 E3
Cowden Hall *HTHF* TN21 .... 130 C1
Cowden La *HAWK* TN18 .... 62 E4
Cowden Ms *EDEN* TN8 .... 15 G6
Cowden Rd *ROTT* BN2 .... 221 G3
Cowdens Cl *HOVE* BN3 .... 176 C3
Cowdray Cl *BEXW* TN39 .... 194 C5
Cowdray Park Rd *BEXW* TN39 .... 194 B5
Cowfold Rd *ROTT* BN2 .... 205 F6
Cowhurst La *BEXW* TN39 .... 195 H4
Cow La *EDEN* TN8 .... 15 K1
POLE BN26 .... 226 D5
Cowley Dr *ROTT* BN2 .... 206 B5
Cowper St *HOVE* BN3 .... 203 F4
Cox Gv *BURH* RH15 .... 88 E6
Crabtree Av *BRI* BN1 .... 178 C5
Cradle Hill Rd *SEAF* BN25 .... 225 H5
Craig Cl *BAT* TN33 .... 168 B5
Craignair Av *BRI* BN1 .... 178 A4
Cranborne Av *EDN/EASTW* BN20 .... 236 C3
Cranbrook Rd *SLVH* TN37 .... 4 A3 🄴
Cranedown *LEW* BN7 .... 2 A6
Cranfield La *BEX* TN40 .... 195 H7
Cranleigh Av *ROTT* BN2 .... 220 E2
Cranleigh Cl *BEXW* TN39 .... 195 F2
Cranmer Av *HOVE* BN3 .... 202 E2
Cranmer Cl *LEW* BN7 .... 3 D3 🄴
Cranston Av *BEXW* TN39 .... 194 E7
Cranston Cl *BEXW* TN39 .... 194 E7
Cranston Ri *BEXW* TN39 .... 194 E7
Cranston Rd *EGRIN* RH19 .... 22 D1

Cranwell Rd *SBGH/RUST* TN4 .... 19 G7
Craven Rd *ROTT* BN2 .... 7 F4
Crawford Wy *EGRIN* RH19 .... 12 D8 🄴
Crawley Crs *LW/ROSE* BN22 .... 229 K1
Crawley Rd *BRI* BN1 .... 178 E5
Crayford Rd *ROTT* BN2 .... 7 F1
Crazy La *BAT* TN33 .... 138 A4
Crecy Cl *SLVH* TN37 .... 169 G4
Crendon Pk *SBGH/RUST* TN4 .... 20 A2
Crescent Dr *BURH* RH15 .... 89 H8 🄴
ROTT BN2 .... 206 B3
Crescent Dr North *ROTT* BN2 .... 206 B3
Crescent Dr South *ROTT* BN2 .... 206 B3
Crescent Pl *ROTT* BN2 .... 7 E6
Crescent Rd *BURH* RH15 .... 89 G8
EGRIN RH19 .... 22 B2
ROTT BN2 .... 7 D2
The Crescent *EDN/EASTW* BN20 .... 215 F8
EDN/EASTW BN20 .... 229 G6
EGRIN RH19 .... 12 A3
HPPT/KEY BN6 .... 119 H8
ROTT BN2 .... 205 F1
SLVH TN37 .... 4 A1
STHW BN42 .... 201 J3
Crespin Wy *BRI* BN1 .... 7 E1
Cresta Cl *POLE* BN26 .... 215 F4
Cresta Rd *NEWHV* BN9 .... 8 A4
Crest Rd *NEWHV* BN9 .... 9 F1
Crest Wy *PTSD* BN41 .... 176 A8
The Crestway *BRI* BN1 .... 7 E1
Cricket Ct *EGRIN* RH19 .... 12 C8
Cricketers Fld *RBTBR* TN32 .... 108 A2
Cricketfield Rd *RING/NEW* BN8 .... 93 H3
Cricketfield Rd *SEAF* BN25 .... 232 B1
Cricketing La *HAIL* BN27 .... 162 D7
Criers La *MAYF* TN20 .... 70 D4
Crink Hl *RING/NEW* BN8 .... 123 K8
Cripps Av *PEAHV* BN10 .... 222 C2
Crisp Rd *LEW* BN7 .... 2 A2
Crockers La *RYE* TN31 .... 81 K3
Crocks Dean *PEAHV* BN10 .... 222 C1 🄴
Croft Av *STHW* BN42 .... 201 H4
Croft Cl *POLE* BN26 .... 214 E7
Croft Ct *SEAF* BN25 .... 225 F8 🄴
Croft Dr *PTSD* BN41 .... 175 K4
Croft La *SEAF* BN25 .... 225 F8
Crofton Park Av *BEXW* TN39 .... 198 D8
Croft Rd *BRI* BN1 .... 177 J7
CROW TN6 .... 53 H2
HAS TN34 .... 5 F4
The Croft *EDN/EASTW* BN20 .... 229 G2
HAS TN34 .... 5 E4
HPPT/KEY BN6 .... 119 F6
Croft Works *HAIL* BN27 .... 189 G4
Croham Rd *CROW* TN6 .... 39 H8
Cromer Wy *HAIL* BN27 .... 189 F1
Cromleigh Wy *STHW* BN42 .... 201 H1
Cromwell Pl *EGRIN* RH19 .... 22 D4 🄴
Cromwell Rd *BURH* RH15 .... 89 F8
HOVE BN3 .... 203 H4
RTWE/PEM TN2 .... 20 C8
Cromwell St *ROTT* BN2 .... 7 E3 🄴
Crooked La *SEAF* BN25 .... 232 B1
Crossbush Rd *ROTT* BN2 .... 205 F5
Cross Lane Gdns *WADH* TN5 .... 60 B2
Cross Levels Wy *EAST* BN21 .... 10 A1
Cross Rd *STHW* BN42 .... 201 G3
Crossroad Cl *STHW* BN42 .... 201 G3 🄴
Cross St *BRI* BN1 .... 6 C3
POLE BN26 .... 215 F5
SLVH TN37 .... 4 A5 🄴
Cross Wy *LEW* BN7 .... 2 A4
Crossways Av *EGRIN* RH19 .... 22 A2
The Crossways *PEV* BN24 .... 216 B6
The Crossway *BRI* BN1 .... 204 C1
PTSD BN41 .... 201 K1 🄴
SBGH/RUST TN4 .... 29 H1
Crouch La *EDN/EASTW* BN20 .... 229 G5
Crouch La *BAT* TN33 .... 166 A7
SEAF BN25 .... 232 B1
Crowborough Hl *CROW* TN6 .... 54 A3
Crowborough Rd *RHAS* TN35 .... 171 F3
ROTT BN2 .... 221 G3
UCK TN22 .... 51 F5
Crowders La *BAT* TN33 .... 135 G8
Crowhurst Cl *LGNY* BN23 .... 216 B7
Crowhurst Rd *BAT* TN33 .... 168 B8
STLEO TN38 .... 196 E1
Crowmere Av *BEX* TN40 .... 195 H6
Crowmere Ter *BEX* TN40 .... 195 H6
Crown Cl *HAIL* BN27 .... 189 F4
UCK TN22 .... 95 J3
Crown Hl *SEAF* BN25 .... 225 F5
Crown La *HAS* TN34 .... 5 F4
Crown Rd *PTSD* BN41 .... 201 K3
SHOR BN43 .... 200 E3
Crown St *BRI* BN1 .... 6 B5
Croxden Wy *LW/ROSE* BN22 .... 215 J8 🄴
Crunden Rd *EDN/EASTW* BN20 .... 229 G7
Crundwell Rd *SBGH/RUST* TN4 .... 19 K2
Cubitt Wy *STLEO* TN38 .... 169 G7
Cuckfield Cl *BEX* TN40 .... 196 B5
Cuckfield Rd *BURH* RH15 .... 88 E4

HPPT/KEY BN6 118
RHWH RH17 88
Cuckmere Dr *PEV* BN24 216
Cuckmere Ri *HTHF* TN21 100
Cuckmere Rd *NEWHV* BN9 8
SEAF BN25 232
Cuckmere Wk *LW/ROSE* BN22 229
Cuckmere Wy *BRI* BN1 178
Cuckoo Dr *HTHF* TN21 100
Cuckoo La *STPH/PW* TN12 33
Cuckoo Trail *HAIL* BN27 189
HTHF TN21 99
HTHF TN21 100
POLE BN26 215
Culpepper *BURH* RH15 88
Culpepper Cl *ROTT* BN2 .... 204 E7
Culver Cl *LGNY* BN23 216
Culverden Av *SBGH/RUST* TN4 19
Culverden Down *SBGH/RUST* TN4 19
Culverden Pk *SBGH/RUST* TN4 19
Culverden Park Rd
SBGH/RUST TN4 19
Culverden Sq *SBGH/RUST* TN4 20
Culverden St *RTW* TN1 .... 20 A2
Cumberland Dr *BRI* BN1 .... 203 K1
Cumberland Gdns *STLEO* TN38 197
Cumberland Rd *BEXW* TN39 195
BRI BN1 203
Cumberland Yd *RTW* TN1 .... 30 A1
Cunningham Cl *SBGH/RUST* TN4 .... 20 B8
Cunningham Dr *LGNY* BN23 231
Cunningham Rd *SBGH/RUST* TN4 20
Curlew Ct *STLEO* TN38 .... 169 F1
The Curlews *SHOR* BN43 200
Currie Rd *SBGH/RUST* TN4 20
Curwen Pl *BRI* BN1 177
Cuthbert Cl *BEXW* TN39 195
Cuthbert Rd *ROTT* BN2 7
Cutter La *HAS* TN34 .... 5 E8
The Cygnets *SHOR* BN43 .... 200 C1
Cypress Cl *SHOR* BN43 200
STLEO TN38 .... 197 H1
Cypress Gv *RTWE/PEM* TN2 .... 30 C1
Cyprus Pl *RTW* TN1 .... 113 H1
Cyprus Rd *BURH* RH15 89

D

Dacre Rd *EDN/EASTW* BN20 229
HAIL BN27 163
NEWHV BN9 .... 9 D1
Dagg La *RBTBR* TN32 80
The Dakins *EGRIN* RH19 .... 22 C1
Dale Av *BRI* BN1 178
HPPT/KEY BN6 119
Dale Crs *BRI* BN1 178
Dale Dr *BRI* BN1 178
Dale Hl *POY/PYE* BN45 177
Dalehurst Rd *BEXW* TN39 195
Dale Rd *FROW* RH18 35
LEW BN7 2
Dales Cl *HAIL* BN27 163
Dale St *RTW* TN1 20
Dale Vw *HOVE* BN3 202
Dale View Gdns *HOVE* BN3 .... 202 C1
Dalewood Gdns *BURH* RH15 119
Dallas La *RING/NEW* BN8 123
Dallaway Dr *PEV* BN24 216
Dallaway Gdns *EGRIN* RH19 22
Dallington Cl *BEX* TN40 196
Dallington Rd *HOVE* BN3 202
LW/ROSE BN22 230
Dalmeny Rd *BEXW* TN39 195
Dalton Rd *EDN/EASTW* BN20 236
Damian Wy *HPPT/KEY* BN6 119
Damon Cl *PEAHV* BN10 222
Dane Court Cl *BEXW* TN39 .... 195 G1
Danehill La *RHWH* RH17 48
Danehill Rd *ROTT* BN2 205
Dane Rd *STLEO* TN38 4
STLEO TN38 197
Daniel Wy *RYE* TN31 145
Danum Cl *HAIL* BN27 161
Danworth La *HPPT/KEY* BN6 88
Darby's La *WADH* TN5 58
Darcey Dr *BRI* BN1 178
Darent Cl *POLE* BN26 216
Daresbury Cl *BEXW* TN39 195
Darley Rd *EDN/EASTW* BN20 236
Dartmouth Cl *ROTT* BN2 205
Dartmouth Crs *ROTT* BN2 205
Darvel Down *BAT* TN33 135
Darwall Dr *SEAF* BN25 225
Darwell Cl *STLEO* TN38 197
Darwell Dr *POLE* BN26 216
Davey Dr *BRI* BN1 7
Davey's La *LEW* BN7 3
Davigdor Rd *HOVE* BN3 203
Davis Cl *BEXW* TN39 195
Dawlish Cl *ROTT* BN2 205
Dawson Ter *ROTT* BN2 7
Daynes Wy *BURH* RH15 118

...cons Dr *PTSD* BN41 .... 202 A1
...dmans La *RYE* TN31 .... 113 J5
...dmantree HI *RING/NEW* BN8 ... 123 F8
...l Av *SEAF* BN25 .... 225 K6
...Deals *RYE* TN31 .... 113 H6 🞂
...n Cl *PTSD* BN41 .... 202 B1
...n Court Rd *ROTT* BN2 .... 220 D1
...nery Cl *LEW* BN7 .... 3 D2
...am Gdns *PTSD* BN41 .... 202 B1
...n Rd *SEAF* BN25 .... 232 B1
...ns Cl *BEXW* TN39 .... 195 G4
...OTT BN2 .... 206 B3
...ns Dr *BEXW* TN39 .... 195 F5
...ns Meadow *RING/NEW* BN8 ... 123 J6
...ns Rd *POLE* BN26 .... 212 C8
...n St *BRI* BN1 .... 6 A5
...nway *HOVE* BN3 .... 177 C8
...n Wood Cl *LGNY* BN23 .... 216 B7
...ham Av *SLVH* TN37 .... 4 B4 🞂
...ham Rd *SLVH* TN37 .... 4 A4 🞂
...hardin La *HAS* TN34 .... 170 D6
...courcel Rd *PTSD* BN2 .... 205 F8 🞂
...by Dr *LW/ROSE* BN22 .... 229 J3
...odene *WADH* TN5 .... 44 B5
...odene Gdns *HAS* TN34 .... 5 F1
...rswood La *BEXW* TN39 .... 194 D6
...Deeside *BRI* BN1 .... 178 B4
...rey Cl *LEW* BN7 .... 3 D3 🞂
...aware Dr *STLEO* TN38 .... 169 C5
...ware Rd *LEW* BN7 .... 2 A5
...a Warr Pde *BEX* TN40 .... 195 J8
...a Warr Rd *BEX* TN40 .... 195 J6
...GRIN RH19 .... 22 D2
...Cl *STLEO* TN38 .... 197 H1
...Dr *RTWE/PEM* TN2 .... 20 D7
...Dell *EGRIN* RH19 .... 23 F2
...nonden Rd *HAWK* TN18 .... 62 C3
...es Av *RTWE/PEM* TN2 .... 30 C2
...es Cl *RING/NEW* BN8 .... 155 J5
...es Wy *RING/NEW* BN8 .... 155 J5
...oleyns Cl *BEX* TN40 .... 195 J7 🞂
...OTT BN2 .... 7 E3
...eside *BRI* BN1 .... 177 J6 🞂
...Dene *EDN/EASTW* BN20 .... 235 F2
...S TN34 .... 170 D6
...VE BN3 .... 176 C8 🞂
...e V *BRI* BN1 .... 177 J4
...e Wy *RRTW* TN3 .... 18 E4
...Deneway *BRI* BN1 .... 177 J7
...ham Cl *STLEO* TN38 .... 169 C5
...ham Rd *BURH* RH15 .... 88 D7
...ham Wy *RYE* TN31 .... 145 G1
...HI *EDN/EASTW* BN20 .... 229 F7
...mark Rd *PTSD* BN41 .... 202 B4
...mark Ter *BRI* BN1 .... 6 A4
...mark Vis *HOVE* BN3 .... 203 G4
...nis Hobden Cl *ROTT* BN2 .... 205 F2
...ton Cl *RYE* TN31 .... 113 C5
...ton Dr *BRI* BN1 .... 178 B6
...WHV BN9 .... 9 E1
...ton Ri *NEWHV* BN9 .... 223 K1
...ton Rd *EDN/EASTW* BN20 .... 236 D3
...WHV BN9 .... 9 E1
...Dentons *EDN/EASTW* BN20 ... 236 D3
...ek Av *HOVE* BN3 .... 202 C5
...La *HTHF* TN21 .... 128 E7
...oos Rd *EAST* BN21 .... 229 J7
...vent Cl *HAIL* BN27 .... 189 F2
...vent Dr *SBGH/RUST* TN4 ... 19 J6
...vent Rd *EDN/EASTW* BN20 ... 236 E3
...mond Rd *LW/ROSE* BN22 ... 11 F2
...mond Wy *ROTT* BN2 .... 205 G5
...l's Dr *HOVE* BN3 .... 176 E5
...Y/PYE BN45 .... 176 A1
...SD TN34 .... 176 B2
...onshire Cl *RTWE/PEM* TN2 ... 29 K3 🞂
...onshire Pl *EAST* BN21 .... 10 C5
...TT BN2 .... 7 D5
...onshire Rd *BEX* TN40 .... 195 H8
...S TN34 .... 5 D4
...alden Ms
...N/EASTW* BN20 .... 236 E3 🞂
...Varrenne Rd *LEW* BN7 .... 2 B4
...e Rd *ROTT* BN2 .... 7 E1
...hurst La *WADH* TN5 .... 43 H3
...ands HI *MAYF* TN20 .... 70 C2
...La *RYE* TN31 .... 112 A3
...Dewpond *PEAHV* BN10 .... 222 A2 🞂
...er Dr *EGRIN* RH19 .... 22 C3
...a Cl *BEX* TN40 .... 196 B5
...ens Cl *EGRIN* RH19 .... 22 A2
...ens Wy *HAWK* TN18 .... 63 C2
...VY BN23 .... 217 F8
...gburgh Rd
...N/EASTW* BN20 .... 229 H7
...n Wy *RTWE/PEM* TN2 .... 20 D5
...ck Cl *POLE* BN26 .... 214 E5 🞂

Diplocks Wy *HAIL* BN27 .... 189 F4
Dirty La *EGRIN* RH19 .... 23 J5
Ditchling Bostall *HPPT/KEY* BN6 ... 150 E4
Ditchling Cl *POLE* BN26 .... 216 A7
Ditchling Crs *BRI* BN1 .... 178 D6
Ditchling Gdns *BRI* BN1 .... 6 C1
Ditchling Ri *BRI* BN1 .... 6 C2 🞂
Ditchling Rd *BRI* BN1 .... 178 D3
ROTT BN2 .... 6 C4
Ditchling Wy *HAIL* BN27 .... 189 F5
Dittons Ms *STLEO* TN38 .... 197 F1 🞂
Dittons Rd *EAST* BN21 .... 10 A4
POLE BN26 .... 215 H5
Dixter La *RYE* TN31 .... 81 J4
Dixter Rd *RYE* TN31 .... 81 J4
The Dock *RING/NEW* BN8 .... 184 D8
Dodshill *CROW* TN6 .... 53 J2
Dog Kennel La *UCK* TN22 .... 70 C5
Dogs Hill Rd *WSEA* TN36 .... 143 H6
Doleham La *RHAS* TN35 .... 139 F2
Dolphin Rd *SHOR* BN43 .... 200 E4
Dolphin Wy *SHOR* BN43 .... 200 E4
Donald Hall Rd *ROTT* BN2 .... 7 F5
Donald Wy *WSEA* TN36 .... 143 G6
Donkey Ms *HOVE* BN3 .... 203 J6 🞂
Donnington Rd *ROTT* BN2 .... 206 B5
Doon Brae *SBGH/RUST* TN4 ... 20 A1
Dordrecht Wy *HAS* TN34 .... 4 C3
Doric Av *SBGH/RUST* TN4 ... 19 K2
Doric Cl *SBGH/RUST* TN4 ... 19 K2
Dorking Rd *RTW* TN1 .... 20 C5
Dormans Av *LING* RH7 .... 12 E1
Dorman's Cl *LING* RH7 .... 12 E3
Dormans High St *LING* RH7 ... 12 E4
Dormans Park Rd *EGRIN* RH19 ... 12 C5
EGRIN RH19 .... 12 E1
Dormans Station Rd *LING* RH7 ... 12 D4
Dornden Dr *RRTW* TN3 .... 18 E7
Dorothy Av *PEAHV* BN10 .... 222 B3
Dorothy Av North *PEAHV* BN10 ... 222 B3
Dorothy Rd *HOVE* BN3 .... 202 C3
Dorset Av *EGRIN* RH19 .... 12 A8
Dorset Gdns *EGRIN* RH19 ... 12 A8
ROTT BN2 .... 7 D5
Dorset Pl *HAS* TN34 .... 4 C5 🞂
ROTT BN2 .... 7 D5
Dorset Rd *BEX* TN40 .... 195 J7
LEW BN7 .... 3 D5
RTWE/PEM TN2 .... 30 D1
Dorset Rd South *BEX* TN40 ... 195 J7
Dorset St *ROTT* BN2 .... 6 C5
Doublegates *BURH* RH15 .... 119 H1
Doucegrove *STLEO* TN38 .... 197 H1
Douglas Cl *HAIL* BN27 .... 189 G1
Douglas Rd *CROW* TN6 .... 55 H7
Dove Ct *UCK* TN22 .... 95 J3
Dovedale Gdns *LW/ROSE* BN22 .. 230 A1 🞂
Dover Cl *SEAF* BN25 .... 225 K6
Dover Rd *BRI* BN1 .... 204 D1
POLE BN26 .... 215 G4
Dowding Wy *RTWE/PEM* TN2 ... 20 E2
Dower Cl *ROTT* BN2 .... 206 A8
Downash Cl *ROTT* BN2 .... 205 F5
Down Av *RRTW* TN3 .... 33 J8
Downey Cl *SLVH* TN37 .... 169 J5
Downland Av *PEAHV* BN10 ... 222 D5
STHW BN42 .... 201 C2
Downland Cl *ROTT* BN2 .... 205 J3 🞂
STHW BN42 .... 201 C2
Downland Copse *UCK* TN22 ... 95 J3
Downland Crs *HOVE* BN3 .... 176 E8
Downland Dr *HOVE* BN3 .... 176 E8
Downland Rd *ROTT* BN2 .... 205 J3
Downlands Av *BEXW* TN39 ... 195 G7
Downlands Cl *BEXW* TN39 ... 195 F7 🞂
Downlands Wy
EDN/EASTW BN20 .... 235 F2 🞂
Down La *RRTW* TN3 .... 42 C3
Down Rd *BEXW* TN39 .... 195 F6
Down Av *EDN/EASTW* BN20 ... 229 G5
Downs Cl *LEW* BN7 .... 2 A3
Downscroft *BURH* RH15 .... 89 K6
Downside *BRI* BN1 .... 177 J6 🞂
HOVE BN3 .... 177 G8
LEW BN7 .... 2 A3
SHOR BN43 .... 200 D2
Downside Cl *SHOR* BN43 .... 200 C2
Downs Rd *BURH* RH15 .... 88 E7
HAS TN34 .... 5 D1
LW/ROSE BN22 .... 229 G1
SEAF BN25 .... 225 H8
Down St *UCK* TN22 .... 66 C3
Downsvalley Rd
EDN/EASTW BN20 .... 215 F7
Downs Valley Rd *ROTT* BN2 ... 206 B3
Downs Vw *BAT* TN33 .... 165 K6
Downsview *HOVE* BN3 .... 176 C8
HTHF TN21 .... 100 B3
Downs Vw *PEAHV* BN10 .... 222 C9
Downsview Av *ROTT* BN2 ... 205 K2
Downs View Cl *EDN/EASTW* BN20 ... 235 G3
RING/NEW BN8 .... 92 C5

Downsview Crs *UCK* TN22 .... 95 K3
Downsview Dr *RHWH* RH17 ... 90 E7
Downs View La *EDN/EASTW* BN20.. 235 G3
Downsview Rd
EDN/EASTW BN20 .... 215 F8 🞂
Downs View Rd *HPPT/KEY* BN6 ... 119 F8
Downsview Rd *PTSD* BN41 ... 201 K1
SEAF BN25 .... 225 H8
Downsview Wy *HAIL* BN27 ... 189 G4 🞂
Downs Wk *PEAHV* BN10 .... 222 A1
Downsway *ROTT* BN2 .... 206 A3
SHOR BN43 .... 200 C2
STHW BN42 .... 201 J1
Down Ter *ROTT* BN2 .... 7 E4
The Down *HOVE* BN3 .... 176 B7
Draffin La *RYE* TN31 .... 115 F8
Drake Av *LGNY* BN23 .... 231 F4
Draper St *SBGH/RUST* TN4.... 19 K1
Drapers Wy *STLEO* TN38 .... 197 H1
Draxmont Wy *BRI* BN1 .... 178 A8
Drayton Ri *BEXW* TN39 .... 194 C7
The Drive *BURH* RH15 .... 89 H7
CROW TN6 .... 53 F1 🞂
HAIL BN27 .... 189 C5
HOVE BN3 .... 203 H4
NEWHV BN9 .... 8 C5
RTWE/PEM TN2 .... 30 A2
SHOR BN43 .... 200 C3
STHW BN42 .... 201 H2
STLEO TN38 .... 197 G3
UCK TN22 .... 67 G6
UCK TN22 .... 95 J3
The Driveway *SHOR* BN43 .... 200 C3
Drockmill Cl *POLE* BN26 .... 215 H5 🞂
Drove Av *ROTT* BN2 .... 206 A1
Drove Crs *PTSD* BN41 .... 201 K1
Drove Rd *NEWHV* BN9 .... 9 E2
PTSD BN41 .... 201 K2
ROTT BN2 .... 205 K2
Drovers Cl *PTSD* BN41 .... 202 B1
Drovers Wy *BURH* RH15 .... 119 J1
The Drove *BRI* BN1 .... 179 K6
BRI BN1 .... 203 J2
NEWHV BN9 .... 9 E2
RING/NEW BN8 .... 153 K6
The Droveway *HOVE* BN3 .... 205 H2
Duchess Dr *SEAF* BN25 .... 225 F5
Dudley Rd *BRI* BN1 .... 7 D1
LW/ROSE BN22 .... 11 D3
RHAS TN35 .... 5 F3
RTW TN1 .... 20 A7 🞂
Dudwell Rd *ROTT* BN2 .... 206 B4
Duke Ms *SLVH* TN37 .... 197 J1 🞂
Duke Rd *SLVH* TN37 .... 197 J1
Dukes Cl *SEAF* BN25 .... 224 E6
Duke's Dr *EDN/EASTW* BN20 ... 236 D4
Dukes HI *BAT* TN33 .... 136 D5
Duke's Mound *ROTT* BN2 .... 7 F6
Dukes Rd *RTW* TN1 .... 20 C6
Duke St *BEXW* TN39 .... 194 E6
BRI BN1 .... 6 B5
SLVH TN37 .... 197 J1
Duke Ter *SLVH* TN37 .... 197 J1
Dulwich Cl *SEAF* BN25 .... 225 J7 🞂
Dumbrells Court Rd
HPPT/KEY BN6 .... 119 K7
Dumbrills Cl *BURH* RH15 .... 89 G6
Dumb Woman's La *RYE* TN31 ... 112 D8
Dunbar Dr *HAIL* BN27 .... 189 F2
Dunclutha Rd *HAS* TN34 .... 170 C7
Dundale Rd *RRTW* TN3 .... 32 A2
Dunes Av *RYE* TN31 .... 145 H1
Dunning's Rd *EGRIN* RH19 ... 22 C4
EGRIN RH19 .... 22 C5
Dunstall Av *BURH* RH15 .... 88 E7
Dunstall Farm Rd *BURH* RH15 ... 89 F7
Dunstan Gv *SBGH/RUST* TN4 ... 20 B6
Dunstan Rd *SBGH/RUST* TN4... 20 B5
Dunstans Cft *MAYF* TN20 .... 56 C8
Dunster Cl *BRI* BN1 .... 7 D1
Dunvan Cl *LEW* BN7 .... 2 C2
Durham Cl *ROTT* BN2 .... 205 H2
Durkins Rd *EGRIN* RH19 .... 12 B8
Durrell Cl *LGNY* BN23 .... 231 G1
Dursley Rd *LW/ROSE* BN22 ... 10 C3
Dutchells Wy *LW/ROSE* BN22 ... 215 J7
Dyall Cl *BURH* RH15 .... 88 E7
Dyke Cl *HOVE* BN3 .... 177 G7
Dyke Rd *BRI* BN1 .... 6 B4
HOVE BN3 .... 6 A3
Dyke Road Av *HOVE* BN3 .... 177 G7
Dyke Road Dr *BRI* BN1 .... 6 A2
Dyke Road Pl *HOVE* BN3 .... 177 H8
Dymchurch Cl *POLE* BN26 ... 215 H4
SEAF BN25 .... 225 J6
Dymock Cl *SEAF* BN25 .... 225 K7 🞂
The Dymock's *HPPT/KEY* BN6 ... 119 K8 🞂
Dymond Rd *STLEO* TN38 .... 169 H8
Dynevor Rd *SBGH/RUST* TN4 ... 20 C4

E

Eagle Cl *UCK* TN22 .... 96 A6
Eagle Rd *RYE* TN31 .... 113 J5
Earls Cl *SEAF* BN25 .... 224 D6 🖾
Earl's Rd *SBGH/RUST* TN4 .... 19 K7
Earl St *HAS* TN34 .... 5 D4
East Albany Rd *SEAF* BN25 .... 225 G7
East Ascent *STLEO* TN38 .... 197 J5
Eastbank *STHW* BN42 .... 201 J2
East Beach St *HAS* TN34 .... 5 F4 🖾
East Beeches Rd *CROW* TN6 .... 53 J1
Eastbourne Av *PEV* BN24 .... 218 A6
Eastbourne La *POLE* BN26 .... 228 B4
Eastbourne Rd *EDN/EASTW* BN20 . 229 G1
  LGNY BN23 .... 217 G7
  LW/ROSE BN22 .... 229 H2
  PEV BN24 .... 217 J8
  POLE BN26 .... 215 F6
  RING/NEW BN8 .... 126 E5
  ROTT BN2 .... 7 F1
  SEAF BN25 .... 225 K8
  UCK TN22 .... 126 B2
East Bourne St *HAS* TN34 .... 5 F4 🖾
Eastbridge Rd *NEWHV* BN9 .... 9 E3
Eastbrook Rd *PTSD* BN41 .... 202 A4
Eastbrook Wy *STHW* BN42 .... 201 K4
East Cliff *RYE* TN31 .... 113 J6
East Cliff *SBGH/RUST* TN4 .... 20 A5
East Cl *POLE* BN26 .... 215 G5
Eastdale Rd *BURH* RH15 .... 89 J7
East Dean Ri *SEAF* BN25 .... 225 H6
East Dean Rd *EDN/EASTW* BN20 .. 235 H5 🖾
East Dr *ROTT* BN2 .... 7 E5
East End La *HPPT/KEY* BN6 .... 119 K8
Eastergate *BEXW* TN39 .... 194 C6
Eastergate Rd *ROTT* BN2 .... 179 F7
Eastern Av *POLE* BN26 .... 215 G5
  SHOR BN43 .... 200 D4
Eastern Cl *SHOR* BN43 .... 200 D4
Eastern Rd *ROTT* BN2 .... 205 F7
Eastern Rd *ROTT* BN2 .... 7 E6
  ROTT BN2 .... 205 F7 🖾
Eastern Ter *ROTT* BN2 .... 7 F6 🖾
Eastern Terrace Ms *ROTT* BN2 .... 7 F6 🖾
East Gdns *HPPT/KEY* BN6 .... 119 K8
Eastgate St *LEW* BN7 .... 3 D4
Eastgate Whf *LEW* BN7 .... 3 D4 🖾
East Hl *EGRIN* RH19 .... 12 C5
Easthill Dr *PTSD* BN41 .... 202 A2
Easthill Wy *PTSD* BN41 .... 202 A2
Eastlands Cl *SBGH/RUST* TN4 .... 29 J3
Eastlands Rd *SBGH/RUST* TN4 .... 29 J3 🖾
East Meadway *SHOR* BN43 .... 200 D5
Eastport La *LEW* BN7 .... 2 C5
East St *BRI* BN1 .... 6 C5 🖾
  BRI BN1 .... 179 K5
  HAS TN34 .... 5 E5 🖾
  LEW BN7 .... 3 D4
  MAYF TN20 .... 56 C8
  PTSD BN41 .... 202 B5
  RYE TN31 .... 113 J6 🖾
  SEAF BN25 .... 225 F8
  SHOR BN43 .... 200 C4
East View Flds *LEW* BN7 .... 121 G6
East View Ter *BAT* TN33 .... 138 B2
Eastway *BEXW* TN39 .... 194 B7
East Wy *LEW* BN7 .... 181 J1
Eastwick Cl *BRI* BN1 .... 178 C4
Eastwood Rd *BEXW* TN39 .... 195 F7
Eatenden La *BAT* TN33 .... 135 K1
Eaton Gdns *HOVE* BN3 .... 203 H4
Eaton Gv *HOVE* BN3 .... 203 H4 🖾
Eaton Pl *ROTT* BN2 .... 7 F6
Eaton Rd *HOVE* BN3 .... 203 H5
Eaton Vls *HOVE* BN3 .... 203 G4
Eaton Wk *BAT* TN33 .... 137 K2
Ebden's Hl *BAT* TN33 .... 169 J2
Ebenezer Rd *HAS* TN34 .... 5 F4 🖾
Ecmod Rd *LW/ROSE* BN22 .... 11 E1
Edburton Av *BRI* BN1 .... 6 C1
Edburton Gdns *SHOR* BN43 ...... 200 C2
Edenbridge Rd *EDEN* TN8 .... 25 K1
  HRTF TN7 .... 25 K1
Eden Dr *BEXW* TN39 .... 194 D7
Eden Rd *RTW* TN1 .... 30 A1
Edensor Rd *EDN/EASTW* BN20 ... 236 D4
Eden V *EGRIN* RH19 .... 12 C7
Edgar Rd *RHAS* TN35 .... 199 F1
Edgehill Cl *HTHF* TN21 .... 99 K4
Edgehill Wy *EGRIN* RH19 .... 201 J1
Edinburgh Rd *BEX* TN40 .... 195 H6 🖾
  ROTT BN2 .... 7 D2 🖾
  SEAF BN25 .... 224 E8
  STLEO TN38 .... 197 F4
Edinburgh Wy *EGRIN* RH19 ...... 22 D4
Edith Av *PEAHV* BN10 .... 222 A4
Edith Av North *PEAHV* BN10 .... 222 B3
Edith Rd *RHAS* TN35 .... 171 G8
Edmond Cl *LGNY* BN23 .... 231 F3
Edmonton Rd *BEXW* TN39 .... 195 G4
Edmund Rd *RHAS* TN35 .... 199 F1
Edward Av *HOVE* BN3 .... 177 F8

  ROTT BN2 .... 207 G8
Edward Cl *HOVE* BN3 .... 177 F8
  SEAF BN25 .... 224 B5 🖾
Edward Rd *SLVH* TN37 .... 4 B5
Edward St *LEW* BN7 .... 3 D4 🖾
  ROTT BN2 .... 7 D5
  SBGH/RUST TN4 .... 19 F7
  SBGH/RUST TN4 .... 19 K2
Edward Ter *STLEO* TN38 .... 169 H7 🖾
Edwin Cl *RHAS* TN35 .... 199 F1
Effingham Cl *ROTT* BN2 .... 221 F1
Effingham Dr *BEXW* TN39 .... 194 C8
Egerton Rd *BEXW* TN39 .... 195 G8
Egginton Cl *BRI* BN1 .... 179 H6
Egginton Rd *ROTT* BN2 .... 179 G7
Egles Gv *UCK* TN22 .... 95 H3
Egmont Rd *HOVE* BN3 .... 202 C2
Egremont Pl *HAS* TN34 .... 5 F2
  ROTT BN2 .... 7 D5 🖾
Eight Acre La *RHAS* TN35 .... 171 G2
Eight Bells Cl *UCK* TN22 .... 68 E7
Eileen Av *ROTT* BN2 .... 220 E2
Eisenhower Dr *STLEO* TN38 ...... 169 G5
Elder Cl *PTSD* BN41 .... 202 A1
Elder Pl *BRI* BN1 .... 6 C3
Elderwood Cl *BEXW* TN39 .... 195 H4
  LW/ROSE BN22 .... 229 J1
Eldon Rd *EAST* BN21 .... 229 H6
Eldred Av *BRI* BN1 .... 177 J6
Eleanor Cl *SEAF* BN25 .... 224 E6 🖾
Eley Crs *ROTT* BN2 .... 206 B8
Eley Dr *ROTT* BN2 .... 206 B7
Elford St *HAS* TN34 .... 5 D4 🖾
Elgar Wy *LGNY* BN23 .... 217 F8
Elgin Gdns *SEAF* BN25 .... 225 K7
Elim Court Gdns *CROW* TN6 ...... 39 G7
Elizabethan Cl *BAT* TN33 .... 193 J1
Elizabeth Av *HOVE* BN3 .... 177 F8
Elizabeth Cl *HOVE* BN3 .... 177 F8 🖾
  SEAF BN25 .... 224 B5
Elizabeth Crs *EGRIN* RH19 ...... 12 D8 🖾
Elizabeth Rd *SHOR* BN43 .... 201 F3
Ellenslea Rd *SLVH* TN37 .... 4 A5 🖾
Ellen St *HOVE* BN3 .... 203 G4
  PTSD BN41 .... 202 B4
Ellenwhorne La *RBTBR* TN32 .... 108 C4
Ellerslie La *BEXW* TN39 .... 194 E4
Elliots Wy *HTHF* TN21 .... 100 A3
Ellison Cl *CROW* TN6 .... 39 G7
Ellis Wy *UCK* TN22 .... 95 G4
Elm Cl *HOVE* BN3 .... 203 H1
  RING/NEW BN8 .... 157 K4
  SEAF BN25 .... 225 K8 🖾
  SHOR BN43 .... 200 C2
Elm Ct *NEWHV* BN9 .... 8 B5
Elm Dr *EGRIN* RH19 .... 22 E2
  HOVE BN3 .... 202 D2
Elm Gv *LW/ROSE* BN22 .... 230 A2
  ROTT BN2 .... 7 E3
Elmhurst Av *RTWE/PEM* TN2 .... 21 K3
Elmore Rd *ROTT* BN2 .... 7 D4
Elm Rd *PTSD* BN41 .... 202 A3
  SBGH/RUST TN4 .... 19 K2
Elms Av *EAST* BN21 .... 11 D5
Elmsdown Pl *HAIL* BN27 .... 189 H4
Elms La *RHAS* TN35 .... 172 E2
Elms Lea Av *BRI* BN1 .... 177 K8
Elmsmead *RYE* TN31 .... 85 H7
Elms Rd *EAST* BN21 .... 11 D5 🖾
Elmstead Rd *BEX* TN40 .... 195 K6
The Elms *RING/NEW* BN8 .... 155 H6
Elm Wy *HTHF* TN21 .... 100 B5
Elmwood Cl *LGNY* BN23 .... 216 D7 🖾
Elmwood Gdns *LGNY* BN23 ...... 216 D7 🖾
Elphick Pl *CROW* TN6 .... 39 H8 🖾
Elphick Rd *NEWHV* BN9 .... 8 C2
  RING/NEW BN8 .... 156 A4
Elphick's Pl *RTWE/PEM* TN2 .... 30 B3 🖾
Elphinstone Av *HAS* TN34 .... 5 D2
Elphinstone Gdns *HAS* TN34 .... 5 D1
Elphinstone Rd *HAS* TN34 ...... 170 D7
Elrington Rd *HOVE* BN3 .... 203 H2
Elsted Crs *BRI* BN1 .... 178 D5
Elven La *EDN/EASTW* BN20 ...... 235 G2 🖾
Elvin Crs *ROTT* BN2 .... 206 B7
Elwood Cl *BURH* RH15 .... 119 F2
Emerald Quay *SHOR* BN43 ...... 200 D5
Emmanuel Rd *HAS* TN34 .... 5 E3
Endwell Rd *BEX* TN40 .... 195 H8
Engalee *EGRIN* RH19 .... 22 A1
English Cl *HOVE* BN3 .... 202 D3
Enys Rd *EAST* BN21 .... 10 B3
Epsom Cl *STLEO* TN38 .... 197 H5 🖾
Erica Cl *LGNY* BN23 .... 230 C1
Eridge Cl *BEXW* TN39 .... 194 E7
Eridge Dr *CROW* TN6 .... 39 H8
Eridge Gdns *CROW* TN6 .... 39 J8
Eridge Gn *LEW* BN7 .... 2 B3
Eridge La *CROW* TN6 .... 55 F1
Eridge Rd *CROW* TN6 .... 40 A7
  EAST BN21 .... 229 H4
  HOVE BN3 .... 203 F1
  RRTW TN3 .... 28 B5
  SBGH/RUST TN4 .... 29 K1
Erin Wy *BURH* RH15 .... 88 E8

Erringham Rd *SHOR* BN43 200
Erroll Rd *HOVE* BN3 202
Ersham Rd *HAIL* BN27 18
Ersham Wy *HAIL* BN27 18
Erskine Park Rd *SBGH/RUST* TN4 .. 1
Esher Cl *SEAF* BN25 225
Eskbank Av *BRI* BN1 177
Eskdale Cl *LGNY* BN23 216
Esplanade *SEAF* BN25 23
Esplanade Ms *SEAF* BN25 .... 23.
The Esplanade *PEAHV* BN10 22
Essenden Rd *STLEO* TN38 19
Essex Cl *RTWE/PEM* TN2 2
Essex Rd *STLEO* TN38 16
Essex St *ROTT* BN2 7
Estate Rd *NEWHV* BN9 9
Estcots Dr *EGRIN* RH19 2
Etchingham Rd *LGNY* BN23 23
Ethelred Cl *LGNY* BN23 231
Ethel St *HOVE* BN3 20
Etherington Hl *RRTW* TN3 1
Etherton Wy *SEAF* BN25 22
Eton Cl *SEAF* BN25 22
Evelyn Av *NEWHV* BN9 9
Evelyn Rd *LEW* BN7 ....
Evelyn Ter *ROTT* BN2 ....
Eversfield Pl *SLVH* TN37 ....
Eversfield Rd *EAST* BN21 1
Eversley Cl *SLVH* TN37 ....
Eversley Rd *BEX* TN40 19
  SLVH TN37 ....
Ewart St *ROTT* BN2 ....
Ewehurst La *RRTW* TN3 1
Ewhurst Cl *HAS* TN34 17
Ewhurst La *RYE* TN31 8
Ewhurst Rd *ROTT* BN2 ....
Exceat Cl *ROTT* BN2 205
Exeat Cl *LGNY* BN23 21
Exeter Cl *LW/ROSE* BN22 22
Exeter St *BRI* BN1 ....
Exmouth Pl *HAS* TN34 5

F

Factory La *HAIL* BN27 18
Fairbridge Wy *BURH* RH15 8
Faircrouch La *WADH* TN5 4
Fairdene *STHW* BN42 20
Fairfax Av *STLEO* TN38 16
Fairfield *HAIL* BN27 16
Fairfield Av *RTWE/PEM* TN2 20
Fairfield Cha *BEXW* TN39 19
Fairfield Cl *BURH* RH15 8
  SHOR BN43 20
Fairfield Crs *HPPT/KEY* BN6 11
Fairfield Gdns *PTSD* BN41 20
Fairfield Rd *BURH* RH15 8
  EDN/EASTW BN20 1
  EGRIN RH19 2
  SLVH TN37 16
Fairglen Rd *WADH* TN5 4
Fairholme Rd *NEWHV* BN9 ....
Fairisle Cl *HAIL* BN27 18
Fair Isle Cl *LGNY* BN23 231
Fair La *RBTBR* TN32 7
Fairlawns *SHOR* BN43 20
Fairlawns Dr *HAIL* BN27 16
Fairlea Cl *BURH* RH15 8
Fairlie Gdns *BRI* BN1 17
Fairlight Av *PEAHV* BN10 17
  RHAS TN35 17
Fairlight Cl *BEX* TN40 19
  POLE BN26 215
  SBGH/RUST TN4 ....
Fairlight Fld *RING/NEW* BN8 15
Fairlight Gdns *RHAS* TN35 172
Fairlight Pl *ROTT* BN2 7
Fairlight Rd *LW/ROSE* BN22 1
  RHAS TN35 17
Fair Meadow *RYE* TN31 1
Fairmile Rd *RTWE/PEM* TN2 2
Fairmount Rd *BEX* TN40 19
Fair Oak Cl *HTHF* TN21 10
Fairstone Cl *RHAS* TN35 17
Fairview *HAWK* TN18 ....
Fairview La *CROW* TN6 ....
Fairview Ri *BRI* BN1 ....
Fairway Cl *EDN/EASTW* BN20 .. 23
Fairway Crs *PTSD* BN41 20
Fairways Cl *SEAF* BN25 232
Fairways Rd *SEAF* BN25 ....
The Fairways *SBGH/RUST* TN4 .. 20
The Fairway *BEXW* TN39 19
  NEWHV BN9 ....
  STLEO TN38 19
Falaise Rd *HAS* TN34 ....
Falconbury Dr *BEXW* TN39 19
Falcon Cl *SHOR* BN43 20
Falconer Dr *BAT* TN33 13
Falcon Wy *HAIL* BN27 18
Fallowfield Cl *HOVE* BN3 202

owfield Crs *HOVE* BN3 .... 202 D1
ner Av *ROTT* BN2 .... 206 E8
OTT BN2 .... 220 E1
ner Cl *EDN/EASTW* BN20 .... 229 C4
ner Gdns *ROTT* BN2 .... 206 A3
ner House Rd *BRI* BN1 .... 179 K4
ner Rd *BRI* BN1 .... 206 A1
nouth Cl *LGNY* BN23 .... 231 G3 🄸
nday Av *EGRIN* RH19 .... 22 C5
aine Rd *EAST* BN21 .... 229 H5
ey Bank *HAS* TN34 .... 5 F2
eys Wy *RTW* TN1 .... 112 B1
ner Wy *RHAS* TN35 .... 172 D6
n Cl *EGRIN* RH19 .... 23 F3
PT/KEY BN6 .... 118 E7
SD BN41 .... 201 K1
AF BN25 .... 225 J7
ncombe Cl *RTW* TN1 .... 30 B1
ncombe La *RTW* TN1 .... 30 B1
ncombe Rd *RTW* TN1 .... 30 B1
n Gdns *RYE* TN31 .... 112 C1
n HI *ROTT* BN2 .... 205 K3
n Wy *BURH* RH15 .... 119 J2
HW BN42 .... 201 K4
nway Cl *HOVE* BN3 .... 202 C1
acombe Cl *RHWH* RH17 .... 91 F6
acombe Rd *LEW* BN7 .... 3 E4
e Cl *HAIL* BN27 .... 189 F1
n Ms *HOVE* BN3 .... 203 J5 🄸
n Rd *HOVE* BN3 .... 203 J5
n Wy *BURH* RH15 .... 119 J2
HW BN42 .... 201 K4
ridge Cl *EGRIN* RH19 .... 12 A8
urt Rd *EGRIN* RH19 .... 12 A4
ws Rd *HAS* TN34 .... 5 E1
Farthings *CROW* TN6 .... 39 J8 🄸
net Cl *LGNY* BN23 .... 231 F3
kners Wy *BURH* RH15 .... 89 G6
ersham Rd *LEW* BN7 .... 2 A3
ate Cl *BEXW* TN39 .... 195 G3 🄸
ate Rd *LW/ROSE* BN22 .... 229 K1
e Meadow *RBTBR* TN32 .... 78 B7
on Rd *HAS* TN34 .... 5 D2
ridge Cl *EGRIN* RH19 .... 12 A8
urt Rd *EGRIN* RH19 .... 12 A4
ws Rd *HAS* TN34 .... 5 E1
ell's Cl *EAST* BN21 .... 10 A2
ies *RRTW* TN3 .... 18 E4 🄸
uson Rd *LYDD* TN29 .... 147 C1
nor Rd *CROW* TN6 .... 53 H4
nor Wy *CROW* TN6 .... 53 H3
Cl *LGNY* BN23 .... 216 D8
dale *RTWE/PEM* TN2 .... 20 D6
dale Cl *RTWE/PEM* TN2 .... 20 C7 🄸
WE/PEM TN2 .... 20 C7 🄸
dale Rd *BURH* RH15 .... 119 H2
VE BN3 .... 203 J4
st Cl *BRI* BN1 .... 178 D5
hurst Crs *BRI* BN1 .... 178 C6
GH/RUST TN4 .... 20 A1
ea Cl *RHAS* TN35 .... 139 G7
Rd *STLEO* TN38 .... 197 G2
side Av *STLEO* TN38 .... 197 G3
erns *RTW* TN1 .... 20 B7 🄸
wood Ri *BRI* BN1 .... 177 J6
ers Rd *LEW* BN7 .... 2 B3
ng Cl *RYE* TN31 .... 113 C5
y HI *WSEA* TN36 .... 142 E3
y Rd *RYE* TN31 .... 113 H6 🄸
OR BN43 .... 200 C5
rsham Cl *SHOR* BN43 .... 200 C5
r Cl *BURH* RH15 .... 88 E7
AF BN25 .... 232 C1
End *UCK* TN22 .... 67 G7
en La *CROW* TN6 .... 52 E2
en Rd *CROW* TN6 .... 52 E3
way *HPPT/KEY* BN6 .... 119 K8
E TN31 .... 109 K6
Wy *STLEO* TN38 .... 197 F5
ways *HAWK* TN18 .... 63 C2
es Rd *HAIL* BN27 .... 165 F5
a *CROW* TN6 .... 53 H4
ng Cl *POLE* BN26 .... 214 D8
ng Rd *EDN/EASTW* BN20 .... 229 C6
r Cl *LW/ROSE* BN22 .... 10 C1 🄸
am Dr *BEX* TN40 .... 196 B5
am Rd *STLEO* TN38 .... 197 G4
am Va *STLEO* TN38 .... 197 G4
inches *BEX* TN40 .... 196 A7
OR BN43 .... 200 D4
EO TN38 .... 169 H6 🄸
n Av *ROTT* BN2 .... 221 H2

Findon Cl *BEXW* TN39 .... 194 D8
 HOVE BN3 .... 176 E8 🄸
 SEAF BN25 .... 225 K8 🄸
Findon Rd *ROTT* BN2 .... 205 G6
Finistere Av *LGNY* BN23 .... 231 G3 🄸
Finmere Cl *LW/ROSE* BN22 .... 11 E1
Finmere Rd *LW/ROSE* BN22 .... 11 E1
Finsbury Rd *ROTT* BN2 .... 7 D4
Fir Cl *ROTT* BN2 .... 206 C4
Fircroft Cl *BRI* BN1 .... 177 K8
Fir Grove Rd *HTHF* TN21 .... 99 F4
Firle Bostal *RING/NEW* BN8 .... 210 C1
Firle Cl *RHAS* TN35 .... 171 H7
 SEAF BN25 .... 225 F6
Firle Crs *LEW* BN7 .... 181 J1
Firle Dr *SEAF* BN25 .... 225 F6
Firle Gra *SEAF* BN25 .... 225 F6
Firle Rd *BEXW* TN39 .... 194 C7
 LW/ROSE BN22 .... 11 D3
 PEAHV BN10 .... 222 A2
 ROTT BN2 .... 7 F4
 SEAF BN25 .... 225 F6
First Av *BEX* TN40 .... 196 A6
 HOVE BN3 .... 203 H6
 NEWHV BN9 .... 8 C4
 RYE TN31 .... 145 H1
First St *RRTW* TN3 .... 18 D8
Firtoft Cl *BURH* RH15 .... 89 H8
Fir Toll Cl *MAYF* TN20 .... 71 G1
Fir Toll Rd *MAYF* TN20 .... 71 G1
Fir Tree Cl *BEXW* TN39 .... 194 B8
 HAIL BN27 .... 189 H1
Firtree Rd *HAS* TN34 .... 5 E2
Fir Tree Rd *SBGH/RUST* TN4 .... 29 K1
Fir Tree Wy *HPPT/KEY* BN6 .... 119 G7
Firwood Cl *HTHF* TN21 .... 100 A3
 LW/ROSE BN22 .... 229 K2
Firwood Ri *HTHF* TN21 .... 100 A3
Fisher Cl *LGNY* BN23 .... 231 G4
Fishergate Cl *PTSD* BN41 .... 201 K4 🄸
Fishermans Wk *SHOR* BN43 .... 200 A6 🄸
Fishersgate Ter *PTSD* BN41 .... 201 K4 🄸
Fisher St *LEW* BN7 .... 2 C4
Fishmarket Rd *RYE* TN31 .... 113 J5
Fishponds La *RHAS* TN35 .... 139 G8
Fitch Dr *ROTT* BN2 .... 205 F2
Fitzgerald Av *STLEO* TN38 .... 232 B1
Fitzgerald Cl *EDN/EASTW* BN20 .... 10 B6 🄸
Fitzgerald Pk *SEAF* BN25 .... 232 B1
Fitzgerald Rd *LEW* BN7 .... 3 D2 🄸
Fitzherbert Dr *ROTT* BN2 .... 7 F2
Fitzjohns Rd *LEW* BN7 .... 2 A3
Fitzmaurice Av *LW/ROSE* BN22 .... 11 J2
Fitzroy Rd *LEW* BN7 .... 2 A3
Five Chimneys La *UCK* TN22 .... 69 J6
Flag Sq *SHOR* BN43 .... 200 C5
Flamsteed Rd *HAIL* BN27 .... 191 H2
Flaxmore Pl *SBGH/RUST* TN4 .... 20 A1 🄸
Fleming Cl *LGNY* BN23 .... 231 H1
Fletcher Av *STLEO* TN38 .... 169 G4
Fletching Cl *ROTT* BN2 .... 205 G5
Fletching Rd *LW/ROSE* BN22 .... 230 B1
Fletching St *MAYF* TN20 .... 56 B8
Flimwell Cl *LGNY* BN23 .... 216 B7
 ROTT BN2 .... 205 F6 🄸
 STLEO TN38 .... 196 E1
 WADH TN5 .... 47 H7
Flint Cl *PTSD* BN41 .... 202 A1
 SEAF BN25 .... 225 F5
The Flints *LEW* BN7 .... 181 H6
Flitterbrook La *HTHF* TN21 .... 101 J6
 HTHF TN21 .... 131 K1
Florance La *RRTW* TN3 .... 27 K5
Florence Av *HOVE* BN3 .... 202 C5
Florence Pl *BRI* BN1 .... 7 D1
Florence Rd *BRI* BN1 .... 6 C2
Folders Cl *BURH* RH15 .... 119 K2
Folders La *BURH* RH15 .... 119 J2
Foley Cl *LGNY* BN23 .... 231 F4 🄸
Folkestone Cl *SEAF* BN25 .... 225 K6 🄸
Folkestone Rd *RYE* TN31 .... 86 E8
Folkington Gdns *SLVH* TN37 .... 169 K6 🄸
Folkington Rd *POLE* BN26 .... 214 C6
Fonthill Av *HOVE* BN3 .... 203 G5
Fontridge La *BUR/ETCH* TN19 .... 76 B8
Fontwell Av *BEXW* TN39 .... 194 B6
Foords La *PEV* BN24 .... 216 C4
Foot's La *BUR/ETCH* TN19 .... 74 D8
Fordbrook HI *CROW* TN6 .... 69 G1
Fordcombe La *RRTW* TN3 .... 18 B8
Ford Manor Rd *LING* RH7 .... 13 F1
Ford Rd *STLEO* TN38 .... 197 F1
Fordoun Rd *EDN/EASTW* BN20 .... 236 C1
 PTSD BN41 .... 202 A1 🄸
Foredown Dr *PTSD* BN41 .... 202 A2
Foredown Rd *PTSD* BN41 .... 176 A8
 PTSD BN41 .... 202 A1
Forest Dene *CROW* TN6 .... 54 B2
Forest La *HTHF* TN21 .... 101 K6
Forest Pk *CROW* TN6 .... 53 F1
Forest Pl *HTHF* TN21 .... 98 D5
Forest Ri *CROW* TN6 .... 54 B2
Forest Rd *BRI* BN1 .... 179 F6
 FROW RH18 .... 36 B2
 RTWE/PEM TN2 .... 30 C2

Forest Vw *HAIL* BN27 .... 189 F3
 UCK TN22 .... 50 C8
Forest View Rd *EGRIN* RH19 .... 22 C5
Forest Wy *EGRIN* RH19 .... 23 F6
 HAS TN34 .... 4 C3
 HRTF TN7 .... 26 E5
 RTWE/PEM TN2 .... 21 K3
 RTWE/PEM TN2 .... 30 C2
Forewood La *BAT* TN33 .... 168 B3
Forewood Ri *BAT* TN33 .... 167 K5
Forge Cl *PTSD* BN41 .... 202 A1
 UCK TN22 .... 95 J5
Forge Fld *WADH* TN5 .... 59 H5
Forge La *RBTBR* TN52 .... 108 A2
Forge Ri *UCK* TN22 .... 95 J5
Forge Rd *RRTW* TN3 .... 27 K8
 SBGH/RUST TN4 .... 19 K2
Forge Wy *BURH* RH15 .... 89 F7
 SLVH TN37 .... 169 K6
Forstall *RRTW* TN3 .... 18 E7 🄸
Fort Hvn *SHOR* BN43 .... 201 F5
Fort La *LW/ROSE* BN22 .... 11 F1
Fort Ri *NEWHV* BN9 .... 9 D5
Fort Rd *LW/ROSE* BN22 .... 11 F1
 NEWHV BN9 .... 9 D5
Forward Cl *NEWHV* BN9 .... 223 K1
Foster Cl *SEAF* BN25 .... 225 F7
Foundry La *LEW* BN7 .... 3 E4
Foundry St *BRI* BN1 .... 6 C4
Fountains Cl *BRI* BN1 .... 204 C1 🄸
 LW/ROSE BN22 .... 215 K8
Founthill Av *ROTT* BN2 .... 220 E2
Founthill Rd *ROTT* BN2 .... 220 E2
Fourteen Acre La *RHAS* TN35 .... 140 B6
Fourth Av *HOVE* BN3 .... 203 G6
Fowey Cl *SHOR* BN43 .... 200 E5
Fowlers Cl *BEXW* TN39 .... 194 D6
Fowly La *UCK* TN22 .... 68 E4
Fox Cl *BURH* RH15 .... 119 F2 🄸
Foxcote *SLVH* TN37 .... 170 A7
Foxdown Rd *ROTT* BN2 .... 206 C4
Foxglove Cl *BURH* RH15 .... 88 D7
 RING/NEW BN8 .... 156 B4
Foxglove Rd *LGNY* BN23 .... 216 C3
Foxhill *BEXW* TN39 .... 194 D6
Fox HI *HWH* RH16 .... 90 A2
Foxhill *PEAHV* BN10 .... 222 B2
Fox Hill Cl *HWH* RH16 .... 90 A2
Fox Hill Village *HWH* RH16 .... 90 B3
Foxhole La *HAWK* TN18 .... 63 K3
 WADH TN5 .... 59 H4
Foxhunters Rd *PTSD* BN41 .... 175 J8 🄸
Fox Wy *PTSD* BN41 .... 175 K8
Framelle Mt *UCK* TN22 .... 96 D5
Framfield Cl *BRI* BN1 .... 179 F5
Framfield Rd *UCK* TN22 .... 68 D3
 UCK TN22 .... 95 K5
Framfield Wy *EAST* BN21 .... 229 J5
Francis St *BRI* BN1 .... 6 C3
Frankfield Ri *RTWE/PEM* TN2 .... 29 K2
Franklands Cl *BURH* RH15 .... 119 F3 🄸
Franklands Gdns *BURH* RH15 .... 119 G3
Franklands Wy *BURH* RH15 .... 119 G3
Franklin Rd *PTSD* BN41 .... 202 B4
 ROTT BN2 .... 7 E3
 SHOR BN43 .... 201 F3
Franklin St *ROTT* BN2 .... 7 E3
Frank's Hollow Rd *RRTW* TN3 .... 19 G2
Frant Av *BEXW* TN39 .... 194 B6
Frant Cl *BEXW* TN39 .... 194 B6
Frant Rd *HOVE* BN3 .... 203 F1
 RTWE/PEM TN2 .... 30 A4
Frary Wk *HTHF* TN21 .... 100 A8
Fraser Av *LGNY* BN23 .... 231 F4
Freckley Hollow *BAT* TN33 .... 166 A1
Frederick Pl *BRI* BN1 .... 6 C4
Frederick Rd *RHAS* TN35 .... 171 F8
Frederick St *BRI* BN1 .... 6 B4
Free Heath Rd *RRTW* TN3 .... 32 E8
Freehold St *SHOR* BN43 .... 200 B4
Freehold Ter *ROTT* BN2 .... 7 D2
Freek's La *BURH* RH15 .... 89 G5
Freeland Cl *SEAF* BN25 .... 224 C5
Freeman Av *LW/ROSE* BN22 .... 229 K2
Freemans Rd *PTSD* BN41 .... 201 K3
Freezeland La *BEXW* TN39 .... 194 E2
Fremlin Cl *SBGH/RUST* TN4 .... 19 F7
Frenches Farm Dr *HTHF* TN21 .... 100 A6
Frenchgate Cl *LW/ROSE* BN22 .... 230 A1 🄸
Frenchgate Rd *LW/ROSE* BN22 .... 230 A1
Freshfield Bank *FROW* RH18 .... 35 J1
Freshfield Cl *HAIL* BN27 .... 189 G5 🄸
Freshfield La *RHWH* RH17 .... 64 A3
Freshfield Pl *ROTT* BN2 .... 7 E5
Freshfield Rd *ROTT* BN2 .... 7 E5
Freshfield St *ROTT* BN2 .... 7 E4
Freshfield Wy *ROTT* BN2 .... 7 E5
Freshford Cl *LGNY* BN23 .... 230 E1
Freshway *LW/ROSE* BN22 .... 215 H8
Frewen Cl *RYE* TN31 .... 81 K4
Frewyn Cl *STLEO* TN38 .... 169 G7
Friar Cl *BRI* BN1 .... 178 B7
Friar Crs *BRI* BN1 .... 178 A8
Friar Rd *BRI* BN1 .... 178 B7
Friars' Av *PEAHV* BN10 .... 222 D5

Friars Bank RHAS TN35 ... 172 A4
Friars Cl HPPT/KEY BN6 ... 118 E7
Friars HI RHAS TN35 ... 171 J4
Friars Oak Rd HPPT/KEY BN6 ... 118 E6
Friars Rd WSEA TN36 ... 143 F4
Friars' Wk LEW BN7 ... 3 D4
Friar's Wy HAS TN34 ... 170 C7
  RTWE/PEM TN2 ... 20 D5
Friar Wk BRI BN1 ... 178 A7
Friday St LGNY BN23 ... 216 D7
Friezland Rd SBGH/RUST TN4 ... 29 H2
Frimley Cl ROTT BN2 ... 206 B4
Friston Av LW/ROSE BN22 ... 229 H2
Friston Cl EDN/EASTW BN20 ... 234 E2
  ROTT BN2 ... 179 G7
  SEAF BN25 ... 224 D7
Friston Downs EDN/EASTW BN20 .. 235 F1
Frith Pk EGRIN RH19 ... 12 C8
Frith Rd HOVE BN3 ... 203 F3
Frobisher Cl LGNY BN23 ... 231 F4
Frog Hole La MAYF TN20 ... 71 F6
Frog La RTW TN1 ... 30 A1
Fryatts Wy BEXW TN39 ... 194 E5
Fry Crs BURH RH15 ... 88 E6
Fryman's La RYE TN31 ... 159 F1
Fulford Cl STLEO TN38 ... 197 H3
Fuller Cl WADH TN5 ... 44 B6
Fuller Rd LEW BN7 ... 2 A2
Fullers La RYE TN31 ... 81 K5
Fullwood Av NEWHV BN9 ... 8 B3
Fulmar Cl HOVE BN3 ... 203 J2
Fulmar Dr EGRIN RH19 ... 12 E8
The Furlongs POLE BN26 ... 212 C8
Furnace Av RRTW TN3 ... 33 H8
Furnace La HTHF TN21 ... 129 H3
  RRTW TN3 ... 33 F7
  RYE TN31 ... 109 K6
Furnace Wy UCK TN22 ... 96 A4
Furness Rd EDN/EASTW BN20 ... 10 B5
Furzefield Av RRTW TN3 ... 18 E3
Furzefield Cha EGRIN RH19 ... 12 C5
Furzefield Rd EGRIN RH19 ... 12 B7
Furze HI HOVE BN3 ... 203 J5
Fyning Pl BEXW TN39 ... 194 B6
Fyrsway RHAS TN35 ... 172 D8
Fysie La BUR/ETCH TN19 ... 61 H8

G

Gableson Av BRI BN1 ... 177 G7
Gage Rdg FROW RH18 ... 35 J2
The Gages HAS TN34 ... 189 J4
Gainsborough Crs LGNY BN23 ... 230 E2
Gainsborough La POLE BN26 ... 214 D5
Gainsborough Rd BEX TN40 ... 195 K5
Galley Hill Vw BEX TN40 ... 95 K7
Galliers Cl BRI BN1 ... 178 C5
Gallipot HI HRTF TN7 ... 25 J8
The Gallops LEW BN7 ... 2 A4
Gallows Cl PEV BN24 ... 217 F5
Gallows La PEV BN24 ... 217 F5
Galveston Cl LGNY BN23 ... 231 G4
Gammons Wy BAT TN33 ... 138 A2
Gander Cl BURH RH15 ... 89 G6
Garden Cl BEX TN40 ... 195 J7
  EGRIN RH19 ... 22 D4
  PTSD BN41 ... 202 B3
  SHOR BN43 ... 200 E2
Gardener St PTSD BN41 ... 201 K3
Garden House La EGRIN RH19 ... 22 A2
Garden Rd RTW TN1 ... 20 B7
The Gardens PTSD BN41 ... 202 B3
  STHW BN42 ... 201 J4
Garden St LEW BN7 ... 2 C5
  RTW TN1 ... 20 B7
Garden Wood Rd EGRIN RH19 ... 22 A2
Gardner Cl LGNY BN23 ... 231 F4
Gardner Rd PTSD BN41 ... 201 K4
Gardner's HI RYE TN31 ... 85 H5
Gardner St BRI BN1 ... 6 C5
  HAIL BN27 ... 163 G5
Garfield Rd HAIL BN27 ... 189 G4
Garland Cl EGRIN RH19 ... 22 B2
Garlinge Rd SBGH/RUST TN4 ... 20 A2
Garnet Dr EDN/EASTW BN20 ... 229 H4
Garston Pk BUR/ETCH TN19 ... 75 K5
Garth Cl BEXW TN39 ... 195 K6
Gatehouse La BURH RH15 ... 88 C7
  HPPT/KEY BN6 ... 88 B6
  UCK TN22 ... 96 E5
  UCK TN22 ... 97 F6
Gatelands Dr BEXW TN39 ... 195 F5
The Gattons BURH RH15 ... 88 E8
Gaudick Cl EDN/EASTW BN20 ... 10 A6
Gaudick Rd EDN/EASTW BN20 ... 10 A6
Geering Rd PEV BN24 ... 216 C6
Geers Wd HTHF TN21 ... 99 K5
Gemma Cl HAIL BN27 ... 189 K4
Geneva Rd NEWHV BN9 ... 9 D4
Gensing Rd STLEO TN38 ... 4 A5
George HI RBTBR TN32 ... 78 H3
George St HAIL BN27 ... 189 H4
  HAS TN34 ... 5 E5
  HOVE BN3 ... 203 C5
  PTSD BN41 ... 201 K4
  PTSD BN41 ... 202 B4
  ROTT BN2 ... 7 D5
  WADH TN5 ... 44 B6
Georgian Cl BEX TN40 ... 195 K5
Georgian Wk STLEO TN38 ... 197 C3
Gerald Cl BURH RH15 ... 89 K8
Gerald Rd SEAF BN25 ... 232 B2
Gerard St BRI BN1 ... 6 C2
German Cl RYE TN31 ... 93 H2
Ghyll Rd CROW TN6 ... 39 F7
  HTHF TN21 ... 99 K5
Ghyllside ROTT BN2 ... 205 F2
Ghyllside Av SLVH TN37 ... 169 K7
Ghyllside Dr HAS TN34 ... 170 A7
  HAS TN34 ... 81 K4
Ghyll Side Rd RYE TN31 ... 81 K4
Ghyllside Wy HAS TN34 ... 170 A7
Gibb Cl BEX TN40 ... 196 A6
Gibbets Rd RRTW TN3 ... 18 D8
Gibbon Rd NEWHV BN9 ... 8 B3
Gibraltar Ri HTHF TN21 ... 100 A4
Giffards Cl EGRIN RH19 ... 22 D2
Gilbert Rd LW/ROSE BN22 ... 11 D3
  STLEO TN38 ... 197 J3
Gilberts Dr EDN/EASTW BN20 ... 235 F4
Gilbert Wy HAIL BN27 ... 189 G6
Gilda Crs POLE BN26 ... 215 F5
Gildredge Rd EAST BN21 ... 10 B4
  SEAF BN25 ... 225 C8
Gilham La FROW RH18 ... 35 J1
Gillham Wood Rd BEXW TN39 ... 194 C8
The Gilligans BURH RH15 ... 89 F6
Gillridge Gn CROW TN6 ... 39 H7
Gillsman's Dr STLEO TN38 ... 197 C2
Gillsman's HI STLEO TN38 ... 197 H2
Gillsman's Pk STLEO TN38 ... 197 C2
Gimble Wy RTWE/PEM TN2 ... 21 K3
Gingerbread La HAWK TN18 ... 47 K8
Gipps Cross La RRTW TN3 ... 18 D8
Githa Rd RHAS TN35 ... 199 F1
The Glades BEX TN40 ... 195 K5
  EGRIN RH19 ... 23 F2
The Glade HAIL BN27 ... 188 E5
  MAYF TN20 ... 72 A1
  UCK TN22 ... 95 K4
Gladstone Cl LW/ROSE BN22 ... 230 A2
Gladstone Pl ROTT BN2 ... 7 E2
Gladstone Rd BURH RH15 ... 89 J6
  CROW TN6 ... 53 H3
  HAS TN34 ... 5 E3
  PTSD BN41 ... 202 A4
  SBGH/RUST TN4 ... 19 F7
Gladys Av PEAHV BN10 ... 222 C5
Gladys Rd HOVE BN3 ... 202 C3
Glassenbury Dr BEX TN40 ... 196 A6
Glastonbury Rd HOVE BN3 ... 202 C5
Gleave Cl EGRIN RH19 ... 22 E1
Glebe Cl BEXW TN39 ... 194 C7
  EDN/EASTW BN20 ... 229 J8
  LEW BN7 ... 2 A5
  STHW BN42 ... 201 J4
Glebe Dr SEAF BN25 ... 225 F8
Glebelands Cl SHOR BN43 ... 200 C5
The Glebelands CROW TN6 ... 53 H1
The Glebe HAS TN34 ... 5 F3
  RTWE/PEM TN2 ... 21 K3
Glebe Vls HOVE BN3 ... 202 C4
Glen Cl POLE BN26 ... 214 E7
Glendale Av EAST BN21 ... 229 H5
Glendale Rd BURH RH15 ... 119 H1
  HOVE BN3 ... 203 H8
Glendor Rd HOVE BN3 ... 202 D5
Glendyne Cl EGRIN RH19 ... 22 E3
Glendyne Wy EGRIN RH19 ... 22 E3
Gleneagles Cl BEX TN40 ... 195 K6
  SEAF BN25 ... 224 B5
Gleneagles Dr HAIL BN27 ... 188 C3
  STLEO TN38 ... 197 C4
Glenfalls Av BRI BN1 ... 178 B4
Glengorse BAT TN33 ... 137 F8
Glenleigh Av BEXW TN39 ... 194 E5
Glenleigh Park Rd BEXW TN39 ... 195 F5
Glenleigh Wk RBTBR TN32 ... 78 A7
Glenmore Pk RTWE/PEM TN2 ... 29 K5
Glenmore Rd CROW TN6 ... 39 F8
Glenmore Rd E CROW TN6 ... 39 F8
Glen Ri BRI BN1 ... 177 G6
Glen Rise Cl BRI BN1 ... 177 G6
The Glen UCK TN22 ... 95 K2
Glenthorn Rd BEXW TN39 ... 195 F1
Glenview Cl RHAS TN35 ... 199 G3
Glen Vue EGRIN RH19 ... 22 C2
Glessing Rd PEV BN24 ... 216 C6
Gleton Av HOVE BN3 ... 202 C1
Gloucester Av BEX TN40 ... 196 B6
Gloucester Cl LW/ROSE BN22 ... 229 H1
Gloucester Pl BRI BN1 ... 6 C4
  ROTT BN2 ... 6 C4
Gloucester Rd BRI BN1 ... 6 B4
  BURH RH15 ... 89 F8
  WADH TN5 ... 44 B6
Gloucester St BRI BN1 ... 6 C4
Glovers La BEX TN40 ... 195 J4
Clynde Av LW/ROSE BN22 ... 22
  ROTT BN2 ... 22
Clyndebourne Av ROTT BN2 ... 22
Clyndebourne Gdns SLVH TN37 ... 169
Clynde Cl NEWHV BN9 ... 223
Clynde Rd ROTT BN2 ...
Clyne Ascent BEX TN40 ... 19
Clyne Barn Cl BEX TN40 ... 19
Clyne Dr BEX TN40 ... 19
Clyneigh Dr POLE BN26 ... 21
Clynleigh Rd PEV BN24 ... 21
Clynn Ri PEAHV BN10 ... 22
Clynn Rd PEAHV BN10 ... 22
Goatham La RYE TN31 ... 10
Godden Cl RYE TN31 ... 8
Godden Rd RING/NEW BN8 ... 9
Godfrey Cl LEW BN7 ...
Godwin Rd HOVE BN3 ... 20
  RHAS TN35 ... 19
The Goffs EAST BN21 ...
Goldbridge Rd RING/NEW BN8 ... 9
Goldcrest Dr UCK TN22 ...
Golden HI BURH RH15 ... 8
Golden Miller La POLE BN26 ... 2
Goldhurst Gn WSEA TN36 ... 14
Golding Rd LGNY BN23 ... 22
Gold La PEAHV BN10 ... 22
Goldsmid Rd HOVE BN3 ...
Goldsmith Cl LGNY BN23 ... 217
Goldsmiths Av CROW TN6 ...
Goldstone Cl HOVE BN3 ... 17
Goldstone Crs HOVE BN3 ... 20
Goldstone La HOVE BN3 ... 20
Goldstone Rd HOVE BN3 ... 20
Goldstone St HOVE BN3 ... 20
Goldstone Vls HOVE BN3 ... 20
Goldstone Wy HOVE BN3 ... 20
Golf Dr BRI BN1 ... 17
Goods Station Rd RTW TN1 ...
Goodtrees La EDEN TN8 ...
Goodwin Cl HAIL BN27 ... 18
Goodwins Cl EGRIN RH19 ...
The Goodwins RTWE/PEM TN2 ... 29
Goodwood Cl EDN/EASTW BN20 ... 22
Goodwood Wy ROTT BN2 ... 17
Gooseberry La RYE TN31 ... 8
Gordon Av SHOR BN43 ...
Gordon Rd BRI BN1 ... 2
  BURH RH15 ...
  CROW TN6 ...
  HAIL BN27 ... 18
  HAS TN34 ... 5
  PTSD BN41 ... 20
  SBGH/RUST TN4 ...
  SHOR BN43 ... 2
  UCK TN22 ...
Gore Park Av EAST BN21 ... 229
Gore Park Rd EAST BN21 ... 22
Gorham Av ROTT BN2 ... 22
Gorham Cl ROTT BN2 ... 22
Gorham Wy PEAHV BN10 ... 22
Gorringe Cl EDN/EASTW BN20 ... 2
  SHOR BN43 ... 2
Gorringe Dr EDN/EASTW BN20 ... 2
Gorringe Rd LW/ROSE BN22 ...
Gorringe Valley Rd
  EDN/EASTW BN20 ...
Gorse Cl EDN/EASTW BN20 ... 2
  PTSD BN41 ... 1
Gorse Dr SEAF BN25 ... 2
Gorse HI HTHF TN21 ... 1
Gorselands BAT TN33 ... 1
Gorse Rd RTWE/PEM TN2 ... 1
Gorsethorn Wy RHAS TN35 ... 1
The Gorseway BEXW TN39 ... 1
Gosford Wy POLE BN26 ... 2
Gote La RING/NEW BN8 ...
Goudhurst Cl LGNY BN23 ... 230
Gradwell End RING/NEW BN8 ...
Graffham Cl ROTT BN2 ... 2
Grafton St ROTT BN2 ...
Graham Av BRI BN1 ... 1
  PTSD BN41 ... 1
Graham Crs PTSD BN41 ... 2
Grampian Cl LGNY BN23 ... 2
  RTWE/PEM TN2 ...
Grand Av BEX TN40 ... 1
  HOVE BN3 ... 2
  HPPT/KEY BN6 ... 1
  SEAF BN25 ... 2
Grand Crs ROTT BN2 ... 2
Grand Junction Rd BRI BN1 ...
Grand Pde EAST BN21 ... 21
  POLE BN26 ... 21
  ROTT BN2 ...
  STLEO TN38 ...
Grand Parade Ms ROTT BN2 ...
Grange Av SLVH TN37 ... 1
Grange Cl BRI BN1 ...
  BURH RH15 ...
  CROW TN6 ...
  HTHF TN7 ...
Grange Court Dr BEXW TN39 ... 1
Grange Gdns SBGH/RUST TN4 ...

ge Rd EAST BN21 ... 10 B5
s TN34 ... 170 B6
VE BN3 ... 202 D4
W BN7 ... 2 C5
GH/RUST TN4 ... 19 H7
BEXW BN8 ... 123 H7
K TN22 ... 95 J4
range RING/NEW BN8 ... 123 H7
geways BRI BN1 ... 177 K6
tham Bank RING/NEW BN8 ... 123 J7
tham Cl RING/NEW BN8 ... 122 C4
tham Rd BRI BN1 ... 6 C1
t St ROTT BN2 ... 7 D3
ville Rd EDN/EASTW BN20 ... 10 B5
VE BN3 ...
W TN1 ... 20 B6
mere Ln LGNY BN23 ... 216 C7
sington Rd EDN/EASTW BN20 ... 10 B6
smere Rd PEAHV BN10 ... 221 J3
ett Ct BURH BN15 ... 119 F1
coats Ct CROW TN6 ... 53 H1
stone La RHAS TN35 ... 171 F8
ebrook Cl BEXW TN39 ... 194 B8
t Cliffe Rd LGNY BN23 ... 231 F2
t College St ROTT BN2 ... 7 E6
t Courtlands RRTW TN3 ... 18 E8
ter Paddock RING/NEW BN8 ... 155 K5
t Footway RRTW TN3 ... 18 D7
t Oak BUR/ETCH TN19 ... 62 A8
t Rough RING/NEW BN8 ... 92 E5
t Wd BAT TN33 ... 137 G7
lan Rd RTW TN1 ... 30 B1
nacres PEAHV BN10 ... 222 C1
AS TN35 ... 39 C8
OR BN43 ... 200 B3
nacres Dr HAIL BN27 ... 189 H3
NG/NEW BN8 ... 155 H7
nacres Wy HAIL BN27 ... 189 H3
nbank Av ROTT BN2 ... 221 F2
n Cl RING/NEW BN8 ... 155 K5
HW BN42 ... 201 H4
nfield Cl BRI BN1 ... 178 B6
GH/RUST TN4 ... 19 G6
n Field Cl STHW BN42 ... 201 H3
nfield Crs BRI BN1 ... 178 A6
nfield Dr UCK TN22 ... 95 K7
nfield Rd BUR/ETCH TN19 ... 76 A4
ST BN21 ... 229 J8
nfields HAIL BN27 ... 189 F2
nfields Cl SLVH TN37 ... 169 F3
n Ga PEAHV BN10 ... 222 B2
n Gv HAIL BN27 ... 189 G5
n Hedges Av EGRIN RH19 ... 22 B1
n Hedges Cl EGRIN RH19 ... 22 B1
nhill Pk HWH RH16 ... 90 C1
nhill Wy HWH RH16 ... 90 C1
AHV BN10 ... 222 B1
nlands Cl BURH BN15 ... 119 H3
nlands Dr BURH BN15 ... 119 H3
n La BEXW TN39 ... 194 C6
OW TN6 ... 39 K8
HF TN21 ... 100 B5
W BN7 ... 2 C5
LE BN26 ... 228 B2
NG/NEW BN8 ... 122 C4
NG/NEW BN8 ... 122 C2
NG/NEW BN8 ... 156 B2
BN25 ... 206 B5
F BN25 ... 232 A1
nleaf Gdns POLE BN26 ... 215 F4
nleas HOVE BN3 ... 202 C1
VE/PEM TN2 ... 21 J5
n Park Cnr RHWH RH17 ... 90 C7
n Rdg BRI BN1 ... 177 C6
n Rd RHWH RH17 ... 90 C6
n Sq WADH TN5 ... 44 B6
nstede Av EGRIN RH19 ... 12 D8
aways Crs SHOR BN43 ... 200 D2
nwell Cl SEAF BN25 ... 225 J1
nwich Rd HAIL BN27 ... 189 J4
nwich Wy PEAHV BN10 ... 222 A4
gs Wood Rd RTWE/PEM TN2 ... 20 E4
ory La PEV BN24 ... 217 G6
ory Wk BAT TN33 ... 138 A3
da Cl BEXW TN39 ... 194 C4
ville Rd PEV BN24 ... 217 K7
ille St BRI BN1 ... 6 B5

Gresham Cl EAST BN21 ... 229 H5
Gresham Wy STLEO TN38 ... 197 H3
Greville Rd RHAS TN35 ... 171 F8
Greyfriars HOVE BN3 ... 203 J3
Greyfriars Pl WSEA TN36 ... 143 H5
Greys Rd EDN/EASTW BN20 ... 229 J8
Grinstead La EGRIN RH19 ... 34 A3
Gromenfield RRTW TN3 ... 28 A4
Groombridge Hl RRTW TN3 ... 28 A3
Groombridge Rd RRTW TN3 ... 27 J3
Grosvenor Br SBGH/RUST TN4 ... 20 B6
Grosvenor Cl POLE BN26 ... 214 E6
Grosvenor Crs STLEO TN38 ... 197 G5
Grosvenor Gdns STLEO TN38 ... 197 G5
Grosvenor Pk RTW TN1 ... 20 A6
Grosvenor Rd EGRIN RH19 ... 22 B2
  SEAF BN25 ... 225 F7
Grosvenor St ROTT BN2 ... 7 D5
Grosvenor Wk RTW TN1 ... 20 A7
Grove Av RTW TN1 ... 30 A1
Grove Hl HAIL BN27 ... 161 H6
  ROTT BN2 ... 7 D4
Grove Hill Gdns RTW TN1 ... 30 B1
Grove Hill Rd RTW TN1 ... 20 A8
Grovelands Cl BURH BN15 ... 119 F2
Grovelands Rd HAIL BN27 ... 189 F2
Grove La RYE TN31 ... 85 J7
Grovely La HTHF TN21 ... 132 D2
Grove Rd BURH BN15 ... 119 F1
  EAST BN21 ... 10 B5
  EDEN TN8 ... 17 F2
  RHAS TN35 ... 171 G7
  SEAF BN25 ... 225 G8
Grove St ROTT BN2 ... 7 D4
The Grove BAT TN33 ... 137 F8
  BEXW TN39 ... 194 D6
  CROW TN6 ... 53 G2
  EDN/EASTW BN20 ... 214 E6
  EDN/EASTW BN20 ... 229 G4
  HAIL BN27 ... 189 G5
  MAYF TN20 ... 72 A1
  NEWHV BN9 ... 223 K1
  RTWE/PEM TN2 ... 21 K3
  RYE TN31 ... 113 J3
Growers End RING/NEW BN8 ... 93 H4
Guardsway Pl SEAF BN25 ... 225 F8
Guestling Rd LW/ROSE BN22 ... 11 F2
Guildford Rd RTW TN1 ... 20 B8
Guildford St BRI BN1 ... 6 B4
Guilford Rd BRI BN1 ... 6 B4
Guildeford La RYE TN31 ... 87 H8
Guldeford Rd RYE TN31 ... 114 A5
Gundreda Rd LEW BN7 ... 2 B3
Gun Rd UCK TN22 ... 97 J5
Gurth Rd HAS TN34 ... 5 F4
Gurth Rd RHAS TN35 ... 199 F2
Gwynne Gv BEX TN40 ... 196 A4
Gwynne Gdns EGRIN RH19 ... 22 A1

H

Hackenden Cl EGRIN RH19 ... 12 C3
Hackenden La EGRIN RH19 ... 12 C2
Hackhurst La HAIL BN27 ... 160 A6
Hackwood RBTBR TN32 ... 77 J7
Haddington Cl HOVE BN3 ... 203 G5
Haddington St HOVE BN3 ... 203 C4
Hadlow Av LGNY BN23 ... 216 B7
Hadlow Cl ROTT BN2 ... 7 J4
Hadlow Down Rd CROW TN6 ... 69 H1
Hadrian Av STHW BN42 ... 201 J3
Hailsham Gdns STLEO TN38 ... 169 H5
Hailsham Rd ROTT BN2 ... 207 G8
Hailsham Rd HAIL BN27 ... 165 F6
  HTHF TN21 ... 100 A3
  POLE BN26 ... 214 E4
  POLE BN26 ... 216 A3
Hairpin Cft PEAHV BN10 ... 222 B5
Half Mile Dro RING/NEW BN8 ... 156 C5
Halland Cl LW/ROSE BN22 ... 229 J2
Halland Rd ROTT BN2 ... 179 G7
Hallett Rd ROTT BN2 ... 7 K2
Halley Rd HAIL BN27 ... 191 J2
  HTHF TN21 ... 100 E3
Hall La UCK TN22 ... 70 A6
Hall's Hole Rd RTWE/PEM TN2 ... 20 E8
Hallyburton Rd HOVE BN3 ... 202 C5
Halsford Park Rd EGRIN RH19 ... 22 A1
Halton Crs HAS TN34 ... 5 F5
Halton Pl HAS TN34 ... 5 F5
Halton Rd LW/ROSE BN22 ... 11 E3
Halton Ter HAS TN34 ... 5 F2
Hamble Rd POLE BN26 ... 216 A6
Hambleton Cl LGNY BN23 ... 216 E8
Hambrook BURH BN15 ... 119 J3
Hamelsham Ct HAIL BN27 ... 189 F3
Hamilton Cl PTSD BN41 ... 175 K8
Hamilton Gdns RHAS TN35 ... 171 G8
Hamilton Pl BRI BN1 ... 6 B2
Hamilton Ter BEXW TN39 ... 195 F7
Hamlands Dr LW/ROSE BN22 ... 215 G8

Ham La BUR/ETCH TN19 ... 75 J4
  LEW BN7 ... 3 D5
  RING/NEW BN8 ... 155 G5
Hammer La HTHF TN21 ... 131 F3
Hammerwood Rd EGRIN RH19 ... 23 J5
Hammonds HAWK TN18 ... 63 G1
Hammonds Gdns BURH BN15 ... 119 F2
Hammonds Rdg BURH BN15 ... 118 E2
Hammy Cl SHOR BN43 ... 200 E3
Hammy La SHOR BN43 ... 200 E3
Hammy Rd SHOR BN43 ... 200 E3
Hampden Av LW/ROSE BN22 ... 230 A2
Hampden Cl BAT TN33 ... 136 B7
Hampden Park Dr LW/ROSE BN22 ... 229 K3
Hampden Rd ROTT BN2 ... 7 E3
Hampstead Rd BRI BN1 ... 203 J2
Hampton Pl BRI BN1 ... 6 A5
Hampton St BRI BN1 ... 6 A5
Hampton Wy EGRIN RH19 ... 22 D4
Ham Rd SHOR BN43 ... 200 C4
Hamsey Cl EDN/EASTW BN20 ... 229 G5
  ROTT BN2 ... 205 G6
Hamsey Crs LEW BN7 ... 2 A3
Hamsey La RING/NEW BN8 ... 153 K4
  SEAF BN25 ... 232 E1
Hamsey Rd ROTT BN2 ... 221 G3
Hamsland RHWH RH17 ... 48 A3
Hanging Birch La HTHF TN21 ... 99 H8
  HTHF TN21 ... 129 H1
Hangleton Cl HOVE BN3 ... 202 C1
Hangleton Gdns HOVE BN3 ... 202 C2
Hangleton La HOVE BN3 ... 202 B1
  PTSD BN41 ... 202 A1
Hangleton Manor Cl HOVE BN3 ... 202 B1
Hangleton Rd HOVE BN3 ... 202 D1
Hangleton Valley Dr HOVE BN3 ... 176 B8
Hangleton Wy HOVE BN3 ... 202 C1
Hankham Hall Rd PEV BN24 ... 216 D3
Hankham Rd PEV BN24 ... 216 C5
Hankham St PEV BN24 ... 216 C2
Hannington Pl HPPT/KEY BN6 ... 118 A4
Hanover Cl BEX TN40 ... 195 H6
  SEAF BN25 ... 224 C5
Hanover Crs ROTT BN2 ... 7 D3
Hanover Ms ROTT BN2 ... 7 D3
Hanover Rd LW/ROSE BN22 ... 11 E3
  RTW TN1 ... 20 A7
Hanover St ROTT BN2 ... 7 D3
Hanover Ter ROTT BN2 ... 7 D3
Hanson Rd NEWHV BN9 ... 8 B4
Harbour Farm WSEA TN36 ... 143 H5
Harbour Rd RYE TN31 ... 113 J7
Harbour View Cl SEAF BN25 ... 224 C5
Harbour View Rd NEWHV BN9 ... 8 B5
Harbour Wy SHOR BN43 ... 200 E5
  STLEO TN38 ... 196 A4
Harcourt Cl UCK TN22 ... 95 J5
Harcourt Rd UCK TN22 ... 95 K5
Harding Av LW/ROSE BN22 ... 11 D1
Hardwicke Rd HAS TN34 ... 5 F3
Hardwick Rd EAST BN21 ... 10 C5
  HOVE BN3 ... 176 D8
Hardwick Wy HOVE BN3 ... 176 D7
Hardy Cl SHOR BN43 ... 200 C5
Hardy Dr LGNY BN23 ... 231 G5
Harebeating La HAIL BN27 ... 189 H1
Harebeating Crs HAIL BN27 ... 189 H1
Harebeating Dr HAIL BN27 ... 161 G8
Harebeating Gdns HAIL BN27 ... 189 H1
Harebeating La HAIL BN27 ... 189 H1
Harebell Cl LGNY BN23 ... 216 D8
Harebell Dr PTSD BN41 ... 175 K8
Harecombe Ri CROW TN6 ... 53 G3
Harecombe Rd CROW TN6 ... 53 G3
Haremere Hl BUR/ETCH TN19 ... 77 H2
Harescroft RTWE/PEM TN2 ... 29 K4
Hare Wy SLVH TN37 ... 169 K6
Harewood Cl BEXW TN39 ... 194 B8
Harfield Cl NEWHV BN9 ... 224 A1
Hargate Cl RTWE/PEM TN2 ... 29 K4
Harison Rd SEAF BN25 ... 225 H7
Harkness Dr HAS TN34 ... 170 E6
Harlequin Gdns SLVH TN37 ... 169 H5
Harlequin La CROW TN6 ... 53 G3
Harlequin Pl CROW TN6 ... 53 G3
Harley La HTHF TN21 ... 100 A5
Harley Shute Rd STLEO TN38 ... 197 F4
Harley Wy STLEO TN38 ... 197 F5
Harmans Md EGRIN RH19 ... 22 E2
Harmers Hay Rd HAIL BN27 ... 189 G2
Harmers Hl RING/NEW BN8 ... 93 G4
Harmony St SBGH/RUST TN4 ... 19 H7
Harmsworth Crs HOVE BN3 ... 176 D8
Harold Cl PEV BN24 ... 218 C4
Harold Dr LGNY BN23 ... 231 F3
Harold Ms STLEO TN38 ... 4 A6
Harold Pl HAS TN34 ... 5 D5
Harold Rd RHAS TN35 ... 199 G1
Harpers Rd NEWHV BN9 ... 8 C3
Harrier La BAT TN33 ... 137 F7
Harries Rd RTWE/PEM TN2 ... 20 D4
Harrington Pl BRI BN1 ... 204 C1
Harrington Rd BRI BN1 ... 203 K1
Harrington Vls BRI BN1 ... 204 A1
Harris Ct EAST BN21 ... 10 C4

Harrisons La RING/NEW BN8 .... 155 K5 🖪
Harrow Cl SEAF BN25 .... 225 H7
Harrow La SLVH TN37 .... 169 J5
Hart Cl UCK TN22.......................... 95 G4
Hartfield Av BRI BN1 .... 178 B7
Hartfield La EAST BN21 .... 10 B3
Hartfield Meadow STLEO TN38 .. 168 E8 🖪
Hartfield Rd EAST BN21 .... 10 B4
    EDEN TN8 .... 15 K8
    FROW RH18................................ 36 A1
    ROTT BN2 .... 221 G2
    SEAF BN25 .... 225 H8
Hartington Pl EAST BN21................ 10 C5
    ROTT BN2 .... 7 E2
Hartington Rd ROTT BN2................. 7 E2
Hartington Ter ROTT BN2................ 7 E2
Hartington Vls HOVE BN3 .... 203 G3
Hartnokes HAWK TN18.................. 63 G1
Harvard Cl LEW BN7 .... 2 C2
Harvard Rd RING/NEW BN8.......... 155 J6
Harvest Cl PEAHV BN10 .... 222 A1 🖪
Harvesters HWH RH16 .... 89 K1
Harvest Hl EGRIN RH19 .... 22 C3
Harvest Wy SLVH TN37 .... 169 K6 🖪
Harvey Cl STLEO TN38 .... 169 G7
Harvey's La RING/NEW BN8 .... 125 H8
    UCK TN22 .... 126 B3 🖪
Harveys Wy LEW BN7....................... 3 E4
Harwood Cl LGNY BN23 .... 231 F4
Harwood Cl EGRIN RH19 .... 22 D4 🖪
Harwood's La EGRIN RH19 .... 22 D3
    EGRIN RH19............................... 22 D5
Haslam Crs BEX TN40 .... 196 A5
Hasletts Cl SBGH/RUST TN4........... 20 B5
Hassocks Cl LW/ROSE BN22......... 216 A7
Hassocks Rd HPPT/KEY BN6 .... 118 B6
Hastings Av SEAF BN25 .... 225 K6
Hastings La BAT TN33 .... 137 G8
    BEX TN40 .... 195 J6
    HAWK TN18................................ 63 F4
    ROTT BN2 .... 7 E2
    RTWE/PEM TN2 .... 21 K5
Hatch End RH18............................. 35 K1
Hatherley Rd SLVH TN37 .... 4 A5 🖪
Havelock Rd BEXW TN39 .... 195 H5
    BRI BN1 .... 6 B1
    HAS TN34 .... 5 D4
    LW/ROSE BN22 .... 11 D3 🖪
Haven Brow SEAF BN25 .... 225 H7
Haven Cl LW/ROSE BN22 .... 215 G8
    PEV BN24 .... 218 B5
Haven Rd STLEO TN38 .... 196 E5
Havenside SHOR BN43 .... 200 A6
Havering Cl RTWE/PEM TN2 .... 21 F5
Hawkenbury Cl RTWE/PEM TN2 .. 30 D1 🖪
Hawkenbury Md
    RTWE/PEM TN2 .... 30 D2 🖪
Hawkenbury Rd RTWE/PEM TN2 ... 30 E2
Hawkenbury Wy LEW BN7............... 2 A4
Hawkhurst Cl LGNY BN23 .... 230 D1
Hawkhurst Rd BRI BN1 .... 178 E5
    BUR/ETCH TN19 .... 178 A1
Hawkins Cl SHOR BN43 .... 201 G2
Hawkins Crs SHOR BN43 .... 201 G1
Hawkins Rd SHOR BN43 .... 201 G2
Hawkins Wy HAIL BN27 .... 189 G3
Hawksbridge Cl LW/ROSE BN22 .. 215 G8
Hawks Farm Cl HAIL BN27 .... 189 G1 🖪
Hawks Rd HAIL BN27 .... 189 G1
Hawkstown Cl HAIL BN27 .... 161 G8 🖪
Hawkstown Gdns HAIL BN27 .... 161 G8 🖪
Hawkstown Vw HAIL BN27 .... 161 G8
Hawkswood Dr HAIL BN27 .... 161 H8
Hawkswood Rd HAIL BN27 .... 161 G8
Hawth Cl SEAF BN25.................... 224 D7
Hawth Crs SEAF BN25 .... 224 D7
Hawth Gv SEAF BN25 .... 224 D8 🖪
Hawth Hl SEAF BN25 .... 224 C6
Hawthorn Av BEXW TN39 .... 194 C8
Hawthorn Cl BURH RH15 .... 89 G3
    ROTT BN2 .... 221 F1
Hawthorne Cl HTHF TN21 .... 100 B5 🖪
The Hawthornes RYE TN31 .... 109 J7
Hawthorn Ri NEWHV BN9 .... 8 B3 🖪
Hawthorn Rd RHAS TN35 .... 199 C3 🖪
The Hawthorns BURH RH15 .... 89 G6 🖪
    HAIL BN27 .... 189 F4
Hawthorn Wk RTWE/PEM TN2 ...... 20 E3 🖪
Hawthorn Wy PTSD BN41 .... 175 K8
Hawth Park Rd SEAF BN25 .... 224 D6 🖪
Hawth Ri SEAF BN25 .... 224 D6
Hawth Wy SEAF BN25 .... 224 C7
Hawthylands Crs HAIL BN27 .... 189 G1
Hawthylands Dr HAIL BN27........... 189 G1
Hawthylands Rd HAIL BN27 .... 189 G1
Haybourne Cl ROTT BN2 .... 205 F4 🖪
Haybourne Rd ROTT BN2............. 205 F4
Hayes Cl PTSD BN41 .... 202 B3
    RING/NEW BN8 .... 155 J6 🖪
Hayes La RYE TN31 .... 111 F6
Hayes Plat RYE TN31 .... 82 A6
Haystoun Cl LW/ROSE BN22 .... 229 H1

Haystoun Pk LW/ROSE BN22 .... 229 H1
Hayward Rd LEW BN7.................... 2 A2
Haywards Rd BRI BN1 .... 178 B5
Hazelbank RRTW TN3 .... 18 D8 🖪
Hazel Cl NEWHV BN9 .... 8 B3 🖪
    PTSD BN41 .... 176 A8
Hazeldene SEAF BN25 .... 225 H8
Hazeldene Meads BRI BN1 .... 177 J8
    BRI BN1 .... 203 J1
Hazeledene La RING/NEW BN8..... 92 D4
Hazel Gv BURH RH15................... 119 H2
    EDN/EASTW BN20 .... 215 F8
Hazelwood Av LW/ROSE BN22 .... 215 J8
Hazelwood Cl BEXW TN39 .... 194 A8 🖪
    RTWE/PEM TN2 .... 20 D3
Hazelwood Gdns HAS TN34......... 170 A6
Headland Av SEAF BN25.............. 225 H8
Headlands Cl PEAHV BN10 .... 222 D4 🖪
Heansill La HAWK TN18 .... 62 E3
Heathdown Cl PEAHV BN10 .... 222 C1
Heather Cl LGNY BN23 .... 216 C8
Heatherdune Rd BEXW TN39 .... 195 F6
Heather Wy RHAS TN35 .... 172 E7
Heathfield Av ROTT BN2 .... 221 G1
Heathfield Cl HAS TN34 .... 170 C6
Heathfield Crs PTSD BN41 .... 175 J7
Heathfield Dr PTSD BN41 .... 175 J8
Heathfield Gdns RBTBR TN32 ...... 78 B8
Heathfield Rd SEAF BN25 .... 225 G8
Heath Hill Av ROTT BN2 .... 205 G2
Heathlands RHAS TN35 .... 139 G8
Heathy Brow PEAHV BN10 .... 222 A2
Heavegate Rd CROW TN6 .... 52 E3
Hebe Rd SHOR BN43 .... 200 B4
Heighton Cl BEXW TN39 .... 194 C8
Heighton Crs NEWHV BN9 .... 223 J1
Heighton Rd NEWHV BN9 .... 223 K1
The Heights BRI BN1 .... 177 G6
    RHAS TN35 .... 171 H7
Helena Cl PTSD BN41 .... 202 B2
Helena Rd ROTT BN2 .... 206 A2 🖪
Hellingly Cl ROTT BN2 .... 205 F6
Hempstead Gdns UCK TN22 .... 95 K4 🖪
Hempstead La ROTT BN2 .... 88 D8
    UCK TN22.................................. 96 A3
Hempstead Ri UCK TN22 .... 95 J4 🖪
Hempstead Rd ROTT BN2 .... 221 G1
    UCK TN22.................................. 95 J4
Henderson Cl HAS TN34 .... 5 D1
Hendon St ROTT BN2 .... 7 E5
Henfield Cl ROTT BN2 .... 205 G7
Henfield Rd LW/ROSE BN22 .... 229 K1
Henfield Wy HOVE BN3 .... 176 E8
Henge Wy PTSD BN41 .... 202 J1
Hengist Cl LGNY BN23 .... 231 G3 🖪
Henley Cl RTWE/PEM TN2 .... 20 C7
    RYE TN31 .... 113 G5
Henley Rd ROTT BN2 .... 205 G7
Henley's Hl BAT TN33 .... 164 D2
Henry Burt Wy BURH RH15 .... 118 E2
Henwood Green Rd
    RTWE/PEM TN2 .... 21 K4
Henwoods Crs RTWE/PEM TN2 ... 21 K5
Herbert Rd BRI BN1 .... 204 A1
Herbrand Wk PEV BN24 .... 219 J2
Hereford St ROTT BN2 .... 7 D5
Hereward Rd LGNY BN23 .... 231 G2
Hereward Wy LEW BN7 .... 3 D3
Hermitage La EGRIN RH19 .... 22 D3
Hermitage Rd EGRIN RH19 .... 12 B8
Herne Down CROW TN6................ 53 H4
Herne Rd CROW TN6 .... 53 H3
Heron Cl LGNY BN23 .... 230 D1
    STLEO TN38 .... 197 F3
    UCK TN22.................................. 95 K6
Heron Pl EGRIN RH19 .... 22 D3
Heron Rdg POLE BN26 .... 215 G5
Heronsdale Rd ROTT BN2 .... 206 C3
Herontye Dr EGRIN RH19 .... 22 D3
Herring's Rd HTHF TN21 .... 133 G2
Hertford Cl STLEO TN38 .... 169 H7
Hertford Rd BRI BN1 .... 204 C1
Heston Av BRI BN1 .... 178 A4
Hever Cl LGNY BN23 .... 230 E1
Hever Crs BEXW TN39 .... 194 E6
Heyworth Cl ROTT BN2 .... 206 C3
Hickling Cl LGNY BN23 .... 216 C7 🖪
Hickman Wy SLVH TN37 .... 170 A7
Hide Hollow LGNY BN23 .... 216 E8
Higham Gdns RHAS TN35 .... 171 K3
Higham La RYE TN31 .... 81 J5
Highbank BRI BN1 .... 177 H6
High Bank RHAS TN35 .... 199 F1
High Bank RHAS TN35 .... 199 F1 🖪
High Beech Cl STLEO TN38 .... 169 G5
High Beeches RTWE/PEM TN2 ...... 20 D5
High Branches BEXW TN39 .... 194 D7
Highbridge La LEW BN7................ 121 K7
Highbrook Cl ROTT BN2 .... 204 E1
High Broom La CROW TN6 .... 53 J5
High Broom Rd CROW TN6 .... 53 G4
High Brooms Rd SBGH/RUST TN4 .. 20 C3
High Cl EDN/EASTW BN20 .... 235 G1
    PTSD BN41 .... 201 K2 🖪
Highcroft Crs HTHF TN21............. 100 A4

Highcroft Vls BRI BN1 ....
High Cross Flds CROW TN6 ....
Highdown STHW BN42................. 2●
Highdown Cl STHW BN42 .... 2●
Highdown Rd HOVE BN3 ....
    LEW BN7 ....
Highfield Cl HAWK TN18.............. ●
    RTWE/PEM TN2 .... ●
Highfield Crs BRI BN1 1
Highfield Dr HPPT/KEY BN6 1
    STLEO TN38 1
Highfield Rd EGRIN RH19 1
    HTHF TN21 .... 1●
    HTHF TN21 .... 1●
    SBGH/RUST TN4 .... ●
Highfields BRI BN1 .... 1●
    BUR/ETCH TN19 .... ●
    FROW RH18 .... ●
High Fords WSEA TN36 .... ●
High Fords Cl WSEA TN36 .... 14●
Highgate Hl HAWK TN18 .... ●
Highgate Rd FROW RH18.............. ●
Highgrove BAT TN33 .... 136●
    RTWE/PEM TN2 .... ●
High Hurst Cl RING/NEW BN8 .... ●
Highlands Av UCK TN22 .... ●
Highlands Cl BEXW TN39............. 1
    CROW TN6 .... ●
    HPPT/KEY BN6 .... ●
Highlands Dr BURH RH15 .... ●
Highlands Gdns STLEO TN38....... 1●
Highlands Rd PTSD BN41 .... 2●
    SEAF BN25 2
The Highlands BEXW TN39 1
Highlea Cl SLVH TN37 .... 165●
High Meadow RYE TN31 .... ●
High Pk RYE TN31 .... ●
High Park Av HOVE BN3 .... 1●
High Rocks La RRTW TN3 .... ●
Highsted Pk PEAHV BN10 .... 2●
High St BAT TN33......................... ●
    BAT TN33................................ ●
    BUR/ETCH TN19 .... ●
    BUR/ETCH TN19 .... ●
    CROW TN6 .... ●
    CROW TN6 .... ●
    EAST BN21 .... ●
    EDEN TN8 .... ●
    EGRIN RH19 .... ●
    HAIL BN27 .... 1●
    HAS TN34................................ ●
    HAWK TN18 .... ●
    HPPT/KEY BN6 .... ●
    HPPT/KEY BN6 .... ●
    HRTF TN7................................ ●
    HTHF TN21 .... 1●
    LEW BN7 .... ●
    MAYF TN20 .... ●
    NEWHV BN9 .... ●
    PEV BN24 .... 2●
    POLE BN26 .... 215●
    POLE BN26 .... 2●
    PTSD BN41 .... 2●
    RBTBR TN32 .... ●
    RING/NEW BN8........................ ●
    RING/NEW BN8........................ 1●
    RING/NEW BN8........................ 1●
    ROTT BN2 .... ●
    ROTT BN2 .... 2●
    RRTW TN3 .... ●
    RRTW TN3 .... ●
    RTW TN1 .... ●
    RTWE/PEM TN2 .... ●
    RYE TN31 .... ●
    SEAF BN25.............................. 2
    SHOR BN43 .... 2●
    UCK TN22................................ ●
    UCK TN22................................ ●
    UCK TN22................................ ●
    UCK TN22................................ ●
    WADH TN5 .... ●
    WADH TN5 .... ●
    WADH TN5 .... ●
    WSEA TN36 .... ●
Highview La UCK TN22................. ●
Highview Av North BRI BN1 1
Highview Av South BRI BN1 1
Highview Cl HAIL BN27................. 1
    HAS TN34................................ ●
Highview La UCK TN22................. ●
Highview Rd BRI BN1 .... 177●
    PEAHV BN10 .... ●
Highview Wy BRI BN1 .... 1●
Highwater Vw BAT TN33 .... ●
Highway Cl ROTT BN2 .... 2●
Highways PTSD BN41 .... 202●
The Highway PEAHV BN10 .... ●
    ROTT BN2 .... 2●
    ROTT BN2 .... 2●
High Weald Landscape Trail
    CROW TN6 .... ●
    EGRIN RH19 .... ●
    EGRIN RH19 .... ●
    HRTF TN7................................ ●
High Weald Wk RRTW TN3 .... ●
    RRTW TN3 .... ●

WE/PEM TN2	30 E3
GH/RUST TN4	19 J2
GH/RUST TN4	20 A1
GH/RUST TN4	29 K1
s, Wickham RHAS TN35	5 F3
woods Av BEXW TN39	194 B5
n Woods La RTWE/PEM TN2	31 F1
m Gn WSEA TN36	142 E4
y Cl POLE BN26	214 E6
ert Cl RTW TN1	20 C6
ers Farm La CROW TN6	53 K2
ove Rd ROTT BN2	207 G8
ry Cl EGRIN RH19	22 E1
ank Cl PTSD BN41	175 J8
orough Cl BEXW TN39	194 C7
row Rd BRI BN1	177 H7
ury Gdns WADH TN5	60 B2
t CROW TN6	53 G2
rest EGRIN RH19	12 C5
GH/RUST TN4	20 B3
rest BRI BN1	177 H6
E TN31	113 H4
rest Av BEXW TN39	195 F5
rest Cl RHWH RH17	91 H1
rest Dr RTWE/PEM TN2	20 D4
rest CROW TN6	53 C2
Crest Rd NEWHV BN9	8 C4
roft PTSD BN41	201 J1
Dr HOVE BN3	177 G8
Farm Wy STHW BN42	201 G1
arth SBGH/RUST TN4	20 A3
d UCK TN22	50 C7
se CROW TN6	53 K1
ti NEWHV BN9	9 F1
AF BN25	224 D6
olton EDN/EASTW BN20	229 F6
W BN7	2 A3
WHV BN9	9 F1
AS TN35	172 B7
TT BN2	220 E2
ide NEWHV BN9	9 D3
ide EDN/EASTW BN20	235 F2
SD BN41	202 B2
TT BN2	179 F8
TT BN2	204 E1
HW BN42	201 J2
ide Av SEAF BN25	225 J6
de Cl EGRIN RH19	12 C8
de Dr HTHF TN21	129 K4
de Rd BEX TN40	195 G6
S TN34	4 C1
S TN34	170 B5
de Wy BRI BN1	177 H7
t HAS TN34	5 E4
W TN11	20 B6
op BRI BN1	177 G6
op Cl PTSD BN41	201 J1
op Dr RYE TN31	113 H4
op BR2 ROTT BN2	205 H3
iew Rd SBGH/RUST TN4	19 C7
field LEW BN7	2 B5
glen Cl HAS TN34	4 C4
over Crs SEAF BN25	225 H7
over Rd SEAF BN25	225 H7
on Cl BRI BN1	204 D1
er Chantlers RRTW TN3	18 E3
dleys La CROW TN6	39 F6
d Rd LW/ROSE BN22	11 D3
ney Ri PEV BN24	217 G6
ington La EDN/EASTW BN20	229 G2
combe Cl LGNY BN23	216 C7
fern Av PEAHV BN10	222 A4
shrove Rd ROTT BN2	179 F8
Hoe SLVH TN37	169 J5
rth Rd HOVE BN3	202 E4
VY BN23	
ia La RRTW TN3	45 C1
rough La WSEA TN36	142 E4
rook Cl EDN/EASTW BN20	236 E3
en Cnr SBGH/RUST TN4	19 J2
en Park Rd SBGH/RUST TN4	19 K3
rth Rd HAS TN34	19 K2
Holdings LEW BN7	181 J6
Farm Cl HAS TN34	4 C2
nd Av BEXW TN39	194 B7
nd Ms HOVE BN3	203 J6
nd Rd HOVE BN3	203 J5
nd St ROTT BN2	7 D4
nds Wy EGRIN RH19	12 E7
er's HI BEX TN40	195 H6
Cl SBGH/RUST TN4	19 K7
ngbury Copse BRI BN1	178 B7
ngbury Crs BRI BN1	7 D1
ngbury Park Av BRI BN1	204 B1
ngbury Pl BRI BN1	204 C1
ngbury Ri BRI BN1	178 C8
ngbury Rl West BRI BN1	204 B1
ngbury Rd BRI BN1	7 D1
ngbury Ter BRI BN1	204 B1
agdean La BRI BN1	7 D2
agdean Rd ROTT BN2	7 D2
agdean St BRI BN1	7 D1

Hollingdean Ter BRI BN1	7 D1
Hollinghurst Cl SLVH TN37	169 J6
Hollinghurst Rd SLVH TN37	169 J7
Hollington Ct STLEO TN38	197 H3
Hollington Old La STLEO TN38	169 H7
Hollington Park Cl STLEO TN38	197 H2
Hollington Park Rd STLEO TN38	197 H2
Hollow La LING RH7	13 F3
	97 J7
Hollybank Gdns STLEO TN38	197 G3
Holly Cl BEXW TN39	194 B5
BRI BN1	177 K8
HAIL BN27	189 C5
HTHF TN21	100 A5
Holly Ct CROW TN6	53 G1
Hollydene Rd WADH TN5	44 B5
Holly Dr HTHF TN21	100 A5
Holly Rd LW/ROSE BN22	215 K8
Hollyshaw Cl RTWE/PEM TN2	30 C1
Holmbush Cl HWH RH16	90 A1
SHOR BN43	201 G1
Holmbush Wy STHW BN42	201 G2
Holmdale Rd NEWHV BN9	9 F1
Holmes Av HOVE BN3	202 E1
Holmes Cl SEAF BN25	224 D5
Holmesdale Cl WADH TN5	44 A6
Holmesdale Gdns HAS TN34	4 C4
Holmesdale Rd BEXW TN39	195 F7
BURH RH15	119 F2
Holmewood Rdg RRTW TN3	18 D8
Holmewood Rd SBGH/RUST TN4	20 C4
Holmhurst Cl SBGH/RUST TN4	19 K7
Holmhurst La SLVH TN37	169 J5
Holm Oak Cl BEXW TN39	194 D8
Holters Wy SEAF BN25	225 G6
Holton Hl ROTT BN2	206 B4
The Holt BURH RH15	119 J1
HAIL BN27	189 F5
SEAF BN25	225 G6
Holtview Rd ROTT BN2	205 J3
Holtye Av EGRIN RH19	12 D8
Holtye Rd EGRIN RH19	13 J8
EGRIN RH19	22 D1
Holyhead Cl HAIL BN27	189 F2
Holywell Cl EDN/EASTW BN20	236 E4
Holywell Rd EDN/EASTW BN20	236 D5
Homebush Av ROTT BN2	207 J8
ROTT BN2	221 G2
Home Farm La RTWE/PEM TN2	20 E3
Home Farm Rd BRI BN1	178 E8
Homefield Cl SEAF BN25	225 C7
Homefield Rd SEAF BN25	225 G7
Homelands Cl BEXW TN39	195 F5
Home Rd BRI BN1	203 K1
Homestall Rd EGRIN RH19	23 J3
Homestead La BURH RH15	89 J5
The Homestead RRTW TN3	28 A4
Homewood Cl LW/ROSE BN22	11 D1
Homewood Rd RRTW TN3	18 D8
Honeycrag Cl POLE BN26	214 E4
Honey Cft HOVE BN3	176 C7
Honey La RING/NEW BN8	186 A4
Honeypot La RING/NEW BN8	121 K4
Honeysuckle Cl HAIL BN27	189 G6
LGNY BN23	216 C3
SLVH TN37	170 A6
Honeyway Cl POLE BN26	214 E5
Hood Cl LGNY BN23	231 F4
Hoo Gdns EDN/EASTW BN20	229 G2
Hook Hl WADH TN5	45 J5
Hook La LYDD TN29	87 K5
Hookswood Cl CROW TN6	39 J8
Hoopers Cl LEW BN7	2 C2
Hoopers Ct STLEO TN38	197 F4
Hopfield Gdns UCK TN22	96 A3
Hop Gdn UCK TN22	67 J1
Hopgarden Cl HAS TN34	4 C4
Hoppers Croft La BUR/ETCH TN19	75 K5
Hopwood Gdns SBGH/RUST TN4	20 A5
Horam Park Cl HTHF TN21	129 K4
Horebeech La HTHF TN21	129 K4
Horizon Cl SBGH/RUST TN4	20 B1
Horleigh Green Rd MAYF TN20	71 G2
Horley Pl ROTT BN2	205 H3
Hornbeam BUR/ETCH TN19	75 K4
Hornbeam Av RTWE/PEM TN2	20 D2
Hornbuckles Cl RING/NEW BN8	122 C4
Hornby Rd ROTT BN2	205 G2
Horning Cl LGNY BN23	216 C7
Hornshurst Rd CROW TN6	55 F3
Horns Rd HAWK TN18	62 D3
Horntye Rd SLVH TN37	4 A3
Horse Br BAT TN33	192 C4
Horsegrove Av WADH TN5	60 D2
Horsegrove La CROW TN6	55 F3
Horseshoe Cl STLEO TN38	197 J1
Horseshoe La RYE TN31	82 C4
Horsewalk HAIL BN27	189 C6
Horsfield Rd LEW BN7	2 B2
Horsham Av PEAHV BN10	222 A5
Horsham Av North PEAHV BN10	222 B5
Horsham Cl ROTT BN2	205 G5
Horsted La RHWH RH17	48 D3
UCK TN22	124 E4
Horsted Pond La UCK TN22	95 G7

Horsye Rd LW/ROSE BN22	230 C4
Horton Rd BRI BN1	7 D1
Hoskins Pl EGRIN RH19	12 D7
Hosmers Fld CROW TN6	55 H2
Hospital Vls HWH RH16	90 B1
Houghton Green La RYE TN31	113 K1
Houghton La RYE TN31	85 J8
Houndean Cl LEW BN7	2 A5
Houndean Ri LEW BN7	2 A5
LEW BN7	181 J3
Hova Vls HOVE BN3	203 G5
Hove Park Gdns HOVE BN3	203 G3
Hove Park Rd HOVE BN3	203 H2
Hove Park Vls HOVE BN3	203 G3
Hove Park Wy HOVE BN3	203 H2
Hove Pl HOVE BN3	203 G6
Hove St HOVE BN3	203 F5
Howard Av BURH RH15	88 E7
Howard Cl HAIL BN27	189 J5
Howard Pl BRI BN1	6 B3
Howard Rd ROTT BN2	7 E3
Howards Crs BEXW TN39	194 B7
Howard Sq EAST BN21	10 C6
Howard Ter BRI BN1	6 B3
Howbourne La UCK TN22	69 G6
Howey Cl NEWHV BN9	9 F1
Howlett Cl STLEO TN38	169 G7
Howlett Dr HAIL BN27	189 G1
Howletts Cl LW/ROSE BN22	230 A2
How's Cl RYE TN31	109 K6
Hoyle Rd PEAHV BN10	222 B4
Hudson Cl LGNY BN23	231 H4
Huggett's La LW/ROSE BN22	215 G8
Hughenden Pl HAS TN34	5 D2
Hughenden Rd HAS TN34	5 D2
Hughes Rd ROTT BN2	7 D2
Hughes Wy UCK TN22	95 J3
Hugletts La HTHF TN21	101 G5
Humboldt Ct RTWE/PEM TN2	20 D6
Humphrey's Gap SHOR BN43	200 D5
Hundred Acre La HPPT/KEY BN6	120 D2
Hundredhouse La RYE TN31	110 D8
Hungershall Pk SBGH/RUST TN4	29 J1
Hunioke Av LW/ROSE BN22	11 D1
Hunston Cl ROTT BN2	206 C4
Hunters Wy RTWE/PEM TN2	29 K2
UCK TN22	95 H3
Hunting Cl BEX TN40	195 H6
Huntingdon Wy BURH RH15	89 K6
Huntley Mill Rd WADH TN5	46 B8
Huntleys Pk SBGH/RUST TN4	19 K5
Hurdis Rd SEAF BN25	224 B5
Hurrell Rd HAS TN34	5 F2
Hurst Crs PTSD BN41	202 A3
Hurst Farm Rd EGRIN RH19	23 J5
Hurstfield Cl HWH RH16	90 C1
Hurst La BRI BN1	178 D6
Hurst La BAT TN33	108 A8
EAST BN21	229 J7
HAIL BN27	163 J6
Hurst Rd EAST BN21	229 J6
HPPT/KEY BN6	118 D7
The Hurst RTWE/PEM TN2	20 E4
Hurstwood Cl BEX TN40	196 A4
Hurstwood La HWH RH16	90 B3
RHWH RH17	48 B2
SBGH/RUST TN4	19 J8
Hurstwood Pk SBGH/RUST TN4	19 K8
Hurstwood Rd UCK TN22	68 C5
Hurtis Hl CROW TN6	53 G4
Hutton Rd BRI BN1	178 C8
Hyde Cl LEW BN7	181 H6
Hyde Gdns EAST BN21	10 C5
Hydehurst Cl CROW TN6	53 H2
Hyde Rd EAST BN21	10 B5
The Hyde ROTT BN2	205 G2
Hyde Tynings Cl EDN/EASTW BN20	236 C3
The Hydneye LW/ROSE BN22	230 A2
Hylden Cl ROTT BN2	205 J3
Hyperion Av POLE BN26	214 D5
Hythe Av STLEO TN38	196 C6
Hythe Cl POLE BN26	215 H4
SBGH/RUST TN4	20 A2
SEAF BN25	225 K6
Hythe Crs SEAF BN25	225 K7
Hythe Rd BRI BN1	204 B1
Hythe Vw SEAF BN25	225 K7

I

Ian Cl BEX TN40	196 A4
Icklesham Dr STLEO TN38	168 E8
Iden Cl ROTT BN2	205 F6
Iden Hurst HPPT/KEY BN6	118 A4
Iden Rd RYE TN31	85 H8
Iden's La HTHF TN21	100 D3
Iden St LW/ROSE BN22	230 D1
Ifield Cl ROTT BN2	221 H1
Ifield Mill La PEV BN24	216 C6
Ifield Cl NEWHV BN9	223 J1
Iford Cl NEWHV BN9	
Impala Gdns SBGH/RUST TN4	20 B5

Ingham Dr *BRI* BN1 .... 178 E5
Ingleside *STLEO* TN38 .... 169 F7
Ingleside Dr *CROW* TN6 .... 53 G1
Inglewood Gdns *STLEO* TN38 .... 169 F7
Ingram Crs *HOVE* BN3 .... 202 D4 ▣
Ingram Crs East *HOVE* BN3 .... 202 D4
Ingram Crs West *HOVE* BN3 .... 202 D4
Ingrams Av *BEXW* TN39 .... 185 H4
Ingrams Wy *HAIL* BN27 .... 189 F6
Inholmes CI *BURH* RH15 .... 119 H1
Inholmes Park Rd *BURH* RH15 .... 89 H8
Inkpen La *FROW* RH18 .... 35 K2
Innham's Wd *CROW* TN6 .... 39 F7
Innings Dr *PEV* BN24 .... 217 K2
Innovation Dr *HPPT/KEY* BN6 .... 118 D1
Inverness Rd *ROTT* BN2 .... 7 E2 ▣
Inwood Crs *BRI* BN1 .... 203 J2
Irelands La *LEW* BN7 .... 2 B4 ▣
Ironlatch Av *STLEO* TN38 .... 197 G2
Ironlatch CI *STLEO* TN38 .... 197 G1
Ironstones *RRTW* TN3 .... 19 F8 ▣
Ironstone Wy *UCK* TN22 .... 96 A4 ▣
Isaac's La *BURH* RH15 .... 89 F5
Isabel CI *SEAF* BN25 .... 225 F6
Isabel Crs *HOVE* BN3 .... 202 D3
Isfield Rd *BRI* BN1 .... 204 D1
UCK TN22 .... 124 E7
Islingford PI *ROTT* BN2 .... 7 E4
Islingford Rd *ROTT* BN2 .... 7 D3
Islingword St *ROTT* BN2 .... 7 D4
Iveagh Crs *NEWHV* BN9 .... 9 D1
Ivor Rd *ROTT* BN2 .... 205 K2
Ivors La *RING/NEW* BN8 .... 154 A6
Ivory PI *ROTT* BN2 .... 7 D4
Ivy Dene La *EGRIN* RH19 .... 23 H5
Ivyhouse La *HAS* TN34 .... 170 E6
RHAS TN35 .... 170 E3
Ivy PI *HOVE* BN3 .... 203 J6 ▣
Ivy Ter *EAST* BN21 .... 10 B4 ▣

J

The Jackdaws *UCK* TN22 .... 96 A7 ▣
Jackies La *RING/NEW* BN8 .... 93 F4
Jack O'dandy CI *EAST* BN21 .... 229 H4 ▣
Jacks HI *HRTF* TN7 .... 37 K1
Jackson Ms *NEWHV* BN9 .... 8 C3 ▣
Jackson St *ROTT* BN2 .... 7 D3
Jacobs Acre *BEX* TN40 .... 195 H6 ▣
Jamaica St *LGNY* BN23 .... 231 G3
James Av *HAIL* BN27 .... 163 F5
Jameson Crs *STLEO* TN38 .... 169 H8
Jameson Rd *BEX* TN40 .... 195 J8
Jane Murray Wy *BURH* RH15 .... 118 E2
HPPT/KEY BN6 .... 118 E2
Janes CI *BURH* RH15 .... 89 J6
Janes La *BURH* RH15 .... 89 J6
Japonica CI *SHOR* BN43 .... 200 E2
Jardine Ct *CROW* TN6 .... 53 J3
Jarvisbrook CI *BEXW* TN39 .... 194 B6
Jason CI *LGNY* BN23 .... 230 D1
Jay CI *LGNY* BN23 .... 230 D1
Jay Rd *PEAHV* BN10 .... 222 D5
The Jays *BURH* RH15 .... 88 E7
UCK TN22 .... 95 K7 ▣
Jefferies La *BURH* RH15 .... 89 J6
Jefferies Wy *CROW* TN6 .... 39 H7
Jellicoe CI *LGNY* BN23 .... 231 G5
Jenner's La *RHAS* TN35 .... 171 H5
Jephson CI *EDN/EASTW* BN20 .... 237 F3 ▣
Jerome CI *LGNY* BN23 .... 231 F1
Jersey St *ROTT* BN2 .... 7 D4
Jervis Av *LGNY* BN23 .... 231 F5
Jesmond Rd *HOVE* BN3 .... 202 D4
Jesters *BURH* RH15 .... 89 J4
Jevington Dr *ROTT* BN2 .... 7 F1
SEAF BN25 .... 224 D7
Jevington Gdns *EDN/EASTW* BN20 .... 10 B6
Jevington Rd *POLE* BN26 .... 228 B3
Jew St *BRI* BN1 .... 6 C5 ▣
Job's La *HPPT/KEY* BN6 .... 88 A5
Joe's La *HAIL* BN27 .... 163 J6
John Dann CI *UCK* TN22 .... 97 J5
John Macadam Wy *SLVH* TN37 .... 169 H5
Johns CI *PEAHV* BN10 .... 222 B1
John's Cross Rd *RBTBR* TN32 .... 78 B8
RBTBR TN32 .... 106 B2
Johnson CI *STLEO* TN38 .... 169 G5
Johnson Dr *BURH* RH15 .... 89 K8
John St *ROTT* BN2 .... 7 D5
SBGH/RUST TN4 .... 20 A4
SHOR BN43 .... 200 B4
Jonas Dr *WADH* TN5 .... 44 A6
Jonas La *WADH* TN5 .... 44 A6
Jordans La East *LW/ROSE* BN22 .... 215 J3
Jordans La West *LW/ROSE* BN22 .... 215 H8
The Jordans *EGRIN* RH19 .... 22 C3
Jubilee Gdns *SEAF* BN25 .... 225 H6 ▣
Jubilee Rd *BEXW* TN39 .... 195 F4
BURH RH15 .... 118 E1
PTSD BN41 .... 201 K3
Judge's Ter *EGRIN* RH19 .... 22 C3 ▣

Juggs CI *LEW* BN7 .... 2 B5 ▣
Juggs Rd *LEW* BN7 .... 2 A6
LEW BN7 .... 2 B5 ▣
Julian Rd *HOVE* BN3 .... 6 A3
Junction CI *BURH* RH15 .... 89 J7
Junction Rd *BURH* RH15 .... 119 H1
EAST BN21 .... 10 C4 ▣
RBTBR TN32 .... 79 C1
RBTBR TN32 .... 97 K6
SLVH TN37 .... 169 J4
Junction St *POLE* BN26 .... 215 G5
Juniper CI *PTSD* BN41 .... 176 A8 ▣
RTWE/PEM TN2 .... 20 D2
SEAF BN25 .... 225 K8
STLEO TN38 .... 169 F8
Jury's Gap Rd *LYDD* TN29 .... 117 J7

K

Kammond Av *SEAF* BN25 .... 225 J6
Katherine Wy *SEAF* BN25 .... 224 E6
Keats CI *STLEO* TN38 .... 197 G5
Keats PI *EGRIN* RH19 .... 22 B2 ▣
Kedale Rd *SEAF* BN25 .... 225 F7
Keere St *LEW* BN7 .... 2 C5
Keld Av *UCK* TN22 .... 95 K5
Keld CI *UCK* TN22 .... 95 K5
Keld Dr *UCK* TN22 .... 95 K5
Kelly Rd *HOVE* BN3 .... 203 J2
Kemble Rd *RTWE/PEM* TN2 .... 20 C4
Kemps Farm Rd *CROW* TN6 .... 53 K2 ▣
Kemp St *BRI* BN1 .... 6 C4
Kemp Town PI *ROTT* BN2 .... 7 F6 ▣
Kendal Pk *SBGH/RUST* TN4 .... 19 J6
Kendal Rd *HOVE* BN3 .... 202 E3
Kenilworth CI *ROTT* BN2 .... 205 H1
Kenilworth Rd *STLEO* TN38 .... 197 J4
Kenmure Av *BRI* BN1 .... 178 B4
Kennedy Av *EGRIN* RH19 .... 12 B8
Kennedy CI *HTHF* TN21 .... 100 B5
Kennedy Rd *BEX* TN40 .... 195 K2
Kennedy Wy *NEWHV* BN9 .... 8 B3
Kennel La *BEXW* TN39 .... 194 B7
Kennett CI *POLE* BN26 .... 216 D4
Kensington Gdns *BRI* BN1 .... 6 C4 ▣
Kensington PI *BRI* BN1 .... 6 C4
Kensington St *BRI* BN1 .... 6 C4 ▣
Kent CI *BEX* TN40 .... 196 B6
SHOR BN43 .... 201 F4
WSEA TN36 .... 142 E4
Kent Fids *LEW* BN7 .... 181 H6
Kentish Gdns *RTWE/PEM* TN2 .... 29 J3
Kent La *RBTBR* TN32 .... 104 E4
Kenton Rd *HOVE* BN3 .... 202 C4
Kent Rd *SBGH/RUST* TN4 .... 20 A5 ▣
STLEO TN38 .... 169 G7
Kent's La *HPPT/KEY* BN6 .... 117 G4
Kent St *BAT* TN33 .... 138 B7
Kenwards *BRI* BN1 .... 178 E4
Kenwood CI *HAS* TN34 .... 170 E7 ▣
Keppel Rd *HAS* TN34 .... 5 D2
Kerrara Ter *LW/ROSE* BN22 .... 11 D2
Kestrel CI *BEX* TN40 .... 195 K7
HOVE BN3 .... 203 J3
The Kestrels *STLEO* TN38 .... 169 G6 ▣
Ketche's La *RHWH* RH17 .... 64 C4
UCK TN22 .... 64 E5
Kevin Gdns *ROTT* BN2 .... 206 B3
Kewhurst Av *BEXW* TN39 .... 194 B8
Kew St *BRI* BN1 .... 6 B4 ▣
Keymer Av *PEAHV* BN10 .... 222 C5
Keymer Ct *BURH* RH15 .... 119 H1 ▣
Keymer Gdns *BURH* RH15 .... 119 H2
Keymer Pde *BURH* RH15 .... 119 H1 ▣
Keymer Pde *HPPT/KEY* BN6 .... 119 H8
Keymer Rd *BRI* BN1 .... 178 C5
BURH RH15 .... 119 H3
HPPT/KEY BN6 .... 119 F8 ▣
Key West *LGNY* BN23 .... 231 G4
Kibbles La *SBGH/RUST* TN4 .... 19 J3
Kidd's HI *HRTF* TN7 .... 37 F6
Kildare CI *HAS* TN34 .... 170 E7
Kilda St *LW/ROSE* BN22 .... 11 D3
Kilnbarn Wy *HWH* RH16 .... 89 K1
Kiln CI *UCK* TN22 .... 95 K7 ▣
Kiln Dr *RYE* TN31 .... 113 H3
Kiln La *BAT* TN33 .... 192 E4
UCK TN22 .... 124 E6
Kiln Rd *RING/NEW* BN8 .... 156 B3
The Kiln *BURH* RH15 .... 89 J8
Kilnwood La *RING/NEW* BN8 .... 122 C4
Kilpatrick CI *LGNY* BN23 .... 216 E8
Kimberley Rd *ROTT* BN2 .... 7 E2
SEAF BN25 .... 224 D7
Kindersley CI *EGRIN* RH19 .... 13 F8 ▣
Kinfauns Av *LW/ROSE* BN22 .... 11 D1
King Edward Av *SLVH* TN37 .... 169 K7
King Edward La *SLVH* TN37 .... 4 A1 ▣

King Edward's Pde
EDN/EASTW BN20 .... 2? ▣
Kingfisher CI *UCK* TN22 .... 9?
Kingfisher Dr *LGNY* BN23 .... 2?
Kingfisher Ri *EGRIN* RH19 .... ?
King George Av *EGRIN* RH19 .... ?
King George Rd *SHOR* BN43 .... 2?
King George V HI *RTW* TN1 .... ?
King George Vi Av *HOVE* BN3 .... 1?
King George Vi Dr *HOVE* BN3 .... 1?
King Henry's Rd *LEW* BN7 .... ?
King PI *BRI* BN1 .... 6?
King's Av *EAST* BN21 .... ?
NEWHV BN9 .... ?
RYE TN31 .... 1?
Kingsbank La *RYE* TN31 .... 1?
Kingsbury Rd *BRI* BN1 .... 6?
Kingsbury St *BRI* BN1 .... 6?
Kings Cha *CROW* TN6 .... ?
Kings CI *BRI* BN1 .... 1?
EAST BN21 .... ?
PEAHV BN10 .... 222?
Kings Copse *EGRIN* RH19 .... 22?
Kingscott CI *BEXW* TN39 .... 1?
Kings Crs *SHOR* BN43 .... 2?
Kingsdale CI *BAT* TN33 .... 1?
SLVH TN37 .... 1?
King's Dr *EAST* BN21 .... ?
EAST BN21 .... ?
HPPT/KEY BN6 .... 1?
SHOR BN43 .... 2?
King's Esp *HOVE* BN3 .... 2?
Kings Gap *SHOR* BN43 .... 2?
King's Gdns *HOVE* BN3 .... 2?
King's Hill Rd *BUR/ETCH* TN19 .... ?
Kingsland CI *SHOR* BN43 .... 2?
Kingsley CI *SLVH* TN37 .... 1?
Kingsley Rd *BRI* BN1 .... ?
LEW BN7 .... ?
Kingsmead *SEAF* BN25 .... 224?
Kingsmead CI *SEAF* BN25 .... 225?
King's Mead La *SEAF* BN25 .... 2?
Kingsmead Wk *SEAF* BN25 .... 2?
Kingsmead Wy *SEAF* BN25 .... 2?
Kingsmere Wy *LGNY* BN23 .... 2?
Kings Ms *HOVE* BN3 .... 203?
Kings Ride *BURH* RH15 .... 1?
POLE BN26 .... 2?
SEAF BN25 .... 2?
King's Rd *BRI* BN1 .... ?
BRI BN1 .... ?
HWH RH16 .... ?
SLVH TN37 .... ?
STHW BN42 .... 2?
Kings Standing Wy
RTWE/PEM TN2 .... ?
Kingsthorpe Rd *HOVE* BN3 .... 2?
Kingston Av *SEAF* BN25 .... 2?
Kingston Bay Rd *SHOR* BN43 .... 2?
Kingston Broadway *SHOR* BN43 .... 2?
Kingston CI *BRI* BN1 .... 1?
HOVE BN3 .... 2?
SEAF BN25 .... 2?
SHOR BN43 .... 2?
Kingston Gn *SEAF* BN25 .... 2?
Kingston La *SHOR* BN43 .... 2?
Kingston Rdg *LEW* BN7 .... 1?
Kingston Rd *LEW* BN7 .... ?
LW/ROSE BN22 .... 2?
Kingston Wy *SEAF* BN25 .... 2?
SEAF BN25 .... 2?
SHOR BN43 .... 2?
King St *BRI* BN1 .... 6?
Kings Wk *SHOR* BN43 .... 2?
Kings Wy *BURH* RH15 .... 1?
Kingsway *HOVE* BN3 .... 2?
SEAF BN25 .... 2?
Kingswood Av *BEXW* TN39 .... 1?
Kingswood Rd *RTWE/PEM* TN2 .... ?
Kingswood St *ROTT* BN2 .... 6?
King Wood HI *RYE* TN31 .... 1?
Kinnibrugh Dr *LING* RH7 .... ?
Kinver La *BEX* TN40 .... 2?
Kipling Av *ROTT* BN2 .... 2?
Kipling Wy *EGRIN* RH19 .... ?
Kirby Dr *PEAHV* BN10 .... 2?
Kirdford CI *BURH* RH15 .... 119?
Kirkdale Rd *RTW* TN1 .... ?
Kirkstall CI *LW/ROSE* BN22 .... 2?
Kirkwood Wy *EDN/EASTW* BN20 .... 2?
Kitchenour La *RYE* TN31 .... ?
Kite CI *STLEO* TN38 .... 1?
Knebworth Rd *BEXW* TN39 .... 1?
Knelle Rd *RBTBR* TN32 .... ?
Knepp CI *ROTT* BN2 .... ?
Knightsbridge CI *SBGH/RUST* TN4 .... ?
Knights CI *RTWE/PEM* TN2 .... ?
Knights Gdn *HAIL* BN27 .... ?
Knights Meadow *UCK* TN22 .... 96?
Knights Pk *RTWE/PEM* TN2 .... ?
Knight's Rdg *RTWE/PEM* TN2 .... 2?
Knights Wy *RTWE/PEM* TN2 .... ?
Knock HI *TENT* TN30 .... ?
Knole Gv *EGRIN* RH19 .... ?

e Rd *BEX* TN40 .... 195 J8
TT BN2 .... 220 D2
CI *HOVE* BN3 .... 202 C2
Ri *STLEO* TN38 .... 197 H4
vle Av *RHAS* TN35 .... 172 D6
vle CI *CROW* TN6 .... 54 A3
TW TN3 .... 18 C8
vle HI *MAYF* TN20 .... 72 A2
vle Pk *CROW* TN6 .... 53 F1
vle Park Rd *MAYF* TN20 .... 72 A1
vle Rd *RHAS* TN35 .... 172 D6
le Rd *BRI* BN1 .... 203 K1
er Gdns *HPPT/KEY* BN6 .... 119 G8

L

rnum Av *HOVE* BN3 .... 202 D2
rnum Gdns *BEX* TN40 .... 196 A5
s HI *RING/NEW* BN8 .... 183 K3
roke Hurst *LING* RH7 .... 12 E2
es Mile Rd *RRTW* TN3 .... 27 F7
es Mile CI *BRI* BN1 .... 178 A5
es' Mile Rd *BRI* BN1 .... 177 K5
cross CI *SEAF* BN25 .... 225 K8
mead *BURH* RH15 .... 89 J6
Oak La *CRBK* TN17 .... 47 G3
s Gift Rd *SBGH/RUST* TN4 .... 19 H4
smith Rd *ROTT* BN2 .... 7 F2
wood La *HPPT/KEY* BN6 .... 118 E8
CI *BRI* BN1 .... 177 K8
Dr *PEAHV* BN10 .... 222 A3
House CI *BEXW* TN39 .... 194 C7
hurst La *BAT* TN33 .... 133 H3
ands CI *LW/ROSE* BN22 .... 230 B1
ands Dr *BEXW* TN39 .... 194 C7
Rd *SBGH/RUST* TN4 .... 19 J7
side *RTWE/PEM* TN2 .... 20 E5
YF TN30 .... 56 A2
View Rd *EGRIN* RH19 .... 12 D6
am CI *EAST* BN21 .... 10 A3
H TN37 .... 169 K6
ersart CI *RTWE/PEM* TN2 .... 20 D2
ert PI *LEW* BN7 .... 3 D2
ert La *LGNY* BN23 .... 217 F8
erts Rd *RTWE/PEM* TN2 .... 20 D3
bourn CI *EGRIN* RH19 .... 12 C6
bourne Rd *BRI* BN1 .... 204 D1
bourne CI *BRI* BN1 .... 204 D1
bourn Wy *RTWE/PEM* TN2 .... 30 D2
ington Rw *RRTW* TN3 .... 18 C8
aster Dr *EGRIN* RH19 .... 12 E8
aster Rd *BRI* BN1 .... 6 B3
EO TN38 .... 169 G6
aster St *LEW* BN7 .... 2 C4
ing CI *HAS* TN34 .... 4 B1
ing Wy *POLE* BN26 .... 214 E1
gate *RYE* TN31 .... 113 J5
port Rd *LEW* BN7 .... 2 C3
sdowne Wy *BEX* TN40 .... 195 K6
sdown Rd *SEAF* BN25 .... 225 J6
seer Rd *HOVE* BN3 .... 203 F3
dale CI *LGNY* BN23 .... 216 D2
dale Gdns *HOVE* BN3 .... 202 E5
dale Rd *HOVE* BN3 .... 202 E5
nam CI *HAS* TN34 .... 170 C7
/G/NEW BN8 .... 155 J6
ham Rd *HAS* TN34 .... 170 C7
BR TN38 .... 77 K7
nolm Rd *RRTW* TN3 .... 18 D8
ley CI *BEXW* TN39 .... 195 G3
ley Crs *ROTT* BN2 .... 206 A2
ney Gn *LGNY* BN23 .... 231 F3
ney Ri *LGNY* BN23 .... 230 E1
ney Rd *EAST* BN21 .... 11 D4
ridge Dr *EGRIN* RH19 .... 22 C3
SD BN41 .... 202 A1
ridge Wy *BURH* RH15 .... 88 C6
rcon La *BAT* TN33 .... 136 E7
ton Rd *RRTW* TN3 .... 18 D8
TW TN3 .... 18 E4
tye La *RING/NEW* BN8 .... 186 B5
downe Crs *HAIL* BN27 .... 189 F1
downe Dr *HAIL* BN27 .... 189 F1
downe Gdns *HAIL* BN27 .... 189 C1
downe Ms *HOVE* BN3 .... 203 J5
downe PI *HOVE* BN3 .... 203 J6
downe Rd *HAIL* BN27 .... 189 F1
VE BN3 .... 203 J5
T BN1 .... 20 C7
downe Sq *HOVE* BN3 .... 203 J6
W TN1 .... 20 B7
downe St *HOVE* BN3 .... 203 J5
downe Wy *HAIL* BN27 .... 161 F8
down PI *LEW* BN7 .... 3 D5
rre Rd *NEWHV* BN9 .... 8 B3
ing CI *LGNY* BN23 .... 230 D1
T BN2 .... 206 C4
EO TN38 .... 197 H2

Larch Gdns *LW/ROSE* BN22 .... 215 J8
Larke CI *SHOR* BN43 .... 201 F4
Larkfield *LW/ROSE* BN22 .... 215 J8
Larkfield Wy *BRI* BN1 .... 178 B7
Larkhill *BEX* TN40 .... 195 H7
Lark HI *HOVE* BN3 .... 176 D8
Larkspur Dr *LGNY* BN23 .... 216 C8
Larnach Rd *UCK* TN22 .... 95 K3
Lascelles Ter *EAST* BN21 .... 10 C6
Lashbrooks Rd *UCK* TN22 .... 95 H4
Latimer Rd *LW/ROSE* BN22 .... 11 E2
Laton Rd *HAS* TN34 .... 4 C2
Laughton CI *LW/ROSE* BN22 .... 216 B7
Laughton Rd *RING/NEW* BN8 ...... 156 B5
RING/NEW BN8 .... 157 K4
ROTT BN2 .... 206 C3
Laundry La *RHWH* RH17 .... 49 H3
Laurel Bank *SBGH/RUST* TN4 .... 20 B3
Laurel CI *BURH* RH15 .... 89 K6
Laurel Dene *EGRIN* RH19 .... 22 D2
Laurel La *WSEA* TN36 .... 141 K6
Laurel Rd *RTWE/PEM* TN2 .... 20 D4
The Laurels *UCK* TN22 .... 96 A3
Lauriston Rd *BRI* BN1 .... 203 K1
Lavant CI *BEXW* TN39 .... 194 B5
Lavender CI *LGNY* BN23 .... 216 C8
Lavender Gdns *WADH* TN5 .... 60 C2
Lavender HI *SHOR* BN43 .... 200 E2
Lavender St *ROTT* BN2 .... 7 D6
Lawes Av *NEWHV* BN9 .... 8 C3
Lawns Av *EAST* BN21 .... 229 J7
The Lawn *STLEO* TN38 .... 4 A5
Lawrence CI *LGNY* BN23 .... 230 E2
Lawrence Rd *HOVE* BN3 .... 202 E4
Laylands Rd *PTSD* BN41 .... 201 K4
Lea Av *RYE* TN31 .... 113 J6
Leaf Hall Rd *LW/ROSE* BN22 .... 11 D4
Leaf Rd *EAST* BN21 .... 10 C4
Leahurst Court Rd *BRI* BN1 .... 177 K8
Lealands Av *SLVH* TN37 .... 169 J6
Lealands CI *RRTW* TN3 .... 28 A1
Lealands Dr *UCK* TN22 .... 95 J3
Lea Rd *PEAHV* BN10 .... 222 A3
Leasam La *RYE* TN31 .... 113 H3
Leasingham Gdns *BEXW* TN39 .... 195 F6
The Leas *PEAHV* BN10 .... 222 E6
WADH TN5 .... 44 C5
Le Brun Rd *EAST* BN21 .... 10 B2
Ledsham Av *SLVH* TN37 .... 169 J6
Ledsham CI *SLVH* TN37 .... 169 J6
Ledsham Pk *SLVH* TN37 .... 169 J6
Ledsham Wy *SLVH* TN37 .... 169 J6
Leeds Av *LGNY* BN23 .... 230 E3
Leeds CI *RHAS* TN35 .... 171 G8
Leeds La *MAYF* TN20 .... 71 G5
Lee Rd *LEW* BN7 .... 2 B3
Leeves CI *HTHF* TN21 .... 100 A5
Leeves Wy *HTHF* TN21 .... 99 K5
Leeward Quay *LGNY* BN23 .... 231 G3
Lee Wy *NEWHV* BN9 .... 8 B2
Leggs' La *RRTW* TN3 .... 18 C6
Leicester Dr *RTWE/PEM* TN2 .... 29 K3
Leicester Rd *LEW* BN7 .... 2 B4
Leicester St *ROTT* BN2 .... 7 D5
Leicester Vls *HOVE* BN3 .... 202 C4
Leighton CI *SBGH/RUST* TN4 .... 20 A4
Leighton Rd *HOVE* BN3 .... 203 F3
RHWH RH17 .... 48 A6
Leneda Dr *RTWE/PEM* TN2 .... 29 J3
Lenham Av *ROTT* BN2 .... 220 E2
Lenham Rd East *ROTT* BN2 .... 220 E2
Lenham Rd West *ROTT* BN2 .... 220 D2
Lennox CI *EDN/EASTW* BN20 ...... 229 G6
Lennox Rd *HOVE* BN3 .... 202 E3
SHOR BN43 .... 200 E3
Lennox St *ROTT* BN2 .... 7 D5
Leopold Rd *BEXW* TN39 .... 195 G7
BRI BN1 .... 6 A6
Lepeland *HAIL* BN27 .... 189 F2
Lesley CI *BEX* TN40 .... 196 A4
Leslie St *LW/ROSE* BN22 .... 11 D3
Lesser Foxholes *SHOR* BN43 ...... 200 A2
Leveller Rd *RING/NEW* BN8 .... 93 H4
Levett Av *POLE* BN26 .... 215 H4
Levett CI *POLE* BN26 .... 215 H5
Levett Rd *POLE* BN26 .... 215 H5
Levetts La *RBTBR* TN32 .... 79 K2
Levett Wy *POLE* BN26 .... 215 H5
Lewes Av *BEXW* TN39 .... 195 F5
Lewes CI *LGNY* BN23 .... 221 H2
Lewes Crs *ROTT* BN2 .... 205 F7
Lewes Rd *BRI* BN1 .... 179 H5
EAST BN21 .... 10 B2
EGRIN RH19 .... 22 D3
FROW RH18 .... 23 J8
HPPT/KEY BN6 .... 151 F1
NEWHV BN9 .... 8 B2
POLE BN26 .... 214 A5
RHWH RH17 .... 48 A7
RHWH RH17 .... 49 H3
RING/NEW BN8 .... 155 J6
ROTT BN2 .... 7 D3
UCK TN22 .... 124 E5
Lewes St *ROTT* BN2 .... 7 D4
Lewis CI *NEWHV* BN9 .... 224 A1

Lewis Rd *STLEO* TN38 .... 169 H8
Lewry CI *NEWHV* BN9 .... 8 B3
Lexden Ct *SEAF* BN25 .... 225 H7
Lexden Dr *SEAF* BN25 .... 225 G6
Lexden Rd *SEAF* BN25 .... 225 G5
Leybourne Gdns *SLVH* TN37 .... 169 K7
Leybourne CI *ROTT* BN2 .... 205 H2
Leybourne Rd *ROTT* BN2 .... 205 H1
Leyland Rd *PEV* BN24 .... 218 A7
Leylands Pk *BURH* RH15 .... 89 H6
Leylands Rd *BURH* RH15 .... 89 G7
Library Wy *UCK* TN22 .... 95 J4
Lilac CI *LW/ROSE* BN22 .... 229 J1
Lillywhite CI *BURH* RH15 .... 89 F6
Limden CI *WADH* TN5 .... 59 H5
Lime CI *RRTW* TN3 .... 30 B8
STLEO TN38 .... 197 H2
UCK TN22 .... 95 K3
Lime Hill Rd *RTW* TN1 .... 20 A7
Limekiln Ct *CROW* TN6 .... 39 K8
Limes La *UCK* TN22 .... 69 F8
Limetree Av *LW/ROSE* BN22 .... 215 J8
Lime Tree Av *UCK* TN22 .... 95 K4
Lime Wy *HTHF* TN21 .... 100 B6
Limney Rd *ROTT* BN2 .... 205 F4
Linchmere Av *ROTT* BN2 .... 221 F2
Lincoln Av *PEAHV* BN10 .... 221 K4
Lincoln Av South *PEAHV* BN10 .... 221 K4
Lincoln CI *EDN/EASTW* BN20 ...... 236 C3
STLEO TN38 .... 169 G7
Lincoln Cottages *ROTT* BN2 .... 7 D4
Lincoln Rd *PTSD* BN41 .... 202 A4
Lincoln St *ROTT* BN2 .... 7 D4
Lincoln Wy *CROW* TN6 .... 53 J3
Linden Av *EGRIN* RH19 .... 22 A1
Linden Cha *UCK* TN22 .... 95 J4
Linden CI *LW/ROSE* BN22 .... 215 K8
RTWE/PEM TN2 .... 29 K1
Linden Ct *UCK* TN22 .... 95 J4
Linden Gdns *RTWE/PEM* TN2 .... 29 K2
Linden Gv *HAIL* BN27 .... 161 H8
Linden Park Rd *RTWE/PEM* TN2 ... 29 K2
Linden Rd *BEX* TN40 .... 195 H8
Lindfield Av *SEAF* BN25 .... 232 E1
Lindfield CI *ROTT* BN2 .... 220 E1
Lindfield Dr *HAIL* BN27 .... 189 G4
Lindfield Rd *LW/ROSE* BN22 .... 229 J2
Lindon CI *EDN/EASTW* BN20 ...... 235 F2
Lindsay CI *EDN/EASTW* BN20 ..... 236 C1
Lingfield Rd *EGRIN* RH19 .... 12 B8
Link Rd *EDN/EASTW* BN20 .... 236 D2
Links Av *NEWHV* BN9 .... 8 A3
Links CI *CROW* TN6 .... 53 F2
PTSD BN41 .... 202 B3
SEAF BN25 .... 225 H8
Links Dr *BEX* TN40 .... 195 K7
Links Rd *PTSD* BN41 .... 202 B3
SEAF BN25 .... 232 C1
The Links *STLEO* TN38 .... 197 G3
RYE TN31 .... 145 G1
The Link *EDN/EASTW* BN20 .... 235 G1
RYE TN31 .... 113 G6
Linkway *EDN/EASTW* BN20 .... 229 F4
Link Wy *RTWE/PEM* TN2 .... 20 E3
The Linkway *BRI* BN1 .... 7 D1
Linley CI *BEX* TN40 .... 195 J7
HAS TN34 .... 5 E2
Linley Dr *HAS* TN34 .... 5 E1
Linnet CI *LGNY* BN23 .... 230 E1
Linnet Gn *UCK* TN22 .... 95 K6
Linthouse CI *PEAHV* BN10 .... 222 C1
Linton Crs *HAS* TN34 .... 4 C4
Linton Rd *HAS* TN34 .... 4 C4
HOVE BN3 .... 202 E3
Lionel Rd *BEX* TN40 .... 195 K8
Lion HI *PEV* BN24 .... 216 C6
Lion La *LW/ROSE* BN22 .... 11 D4
Lion PI *SEAF* BN25 .... 232 B1
Lion St *RYE* TN31 .... 113 J6
Liphook CI *BRI* BN1 .... 7 E1
Lipscombe Rd *RTWE/PEM* TN2 .... 20 D5
Liptraps La *RTWE/PEM* TN2 .... 20 D4
Lismore Rd *EAST* BN21 .... 10 C5
Lister Av *EGRIN* RH19 .... 22 C5
Little Common Rd *BEXW* TN39 .... 194 C7
Little Copse Rd *HPPT/KEY* BN6 ... 118 E6
Little Crs *ROTT* BN2 .... 220 E2
Little East St *LEW* BN7 .... 3 D4
Little Footway *RRTW* TN3 .... 18 D8
Little High St *SHOR* BN43 .... 200 B4
Little King St *EGRIN* RH19 .... 22 C2
Little London St *HTHF* TN21 .... 129 J3
Little Mallett *RRTW* TN3 .... 18 D8
Little Md *RING/NEW* BN8 .... 153 K4
Little Mount Sion *RTW* TN1 .... 30 A1
Little Paddock *CROW* TN6 .... 53 G2
RING/NEW BN8 .... 155 K5
Little Pk *WADH* TN5 .... 44 A6
Little Preston St *BRI* BN1 .... 6 A5
Little Ridge Av *SLVH* TN37 .... 169 J5
Little Sunnyside *CROW* TN6 .... 53 H2
Little Trogers La *MAYF* TN20 .... 56 B7
Little Twitten *BEXW* TN39 .... 194 B8
Little Western St *BRI* BN1 .... 6 A5
Littlewood La *UCK* TN22 .... 68 E7

Littleworth Cl *ROTT* BN2 .... 206 C4
Livingstone Rd *BURH* RH15 .... 89 F8
  HOVE BN3 .... 203 G4
Livingstone St *ROTT* BN2 .... 7 F5
Lloyd Cl *HOVE* BN3 .... 203 H3
Lloyd Rd *HOVE* BN3 .... 203 H3
Lockitt Wy *LEW* BN7 .... 181 H6
Locks Crs *PTSD* BN41 .... 202 A3
Locks HI *PTSD* BN41 .... 202 A2
Locks Meadow *LING* RH7 .... 12 E2
Lockwood Cl *ROTT* BN2 .... 206 B4
Lockwood Crs *ROTT* BN2 .... 206 B4
Loder Cl *BRI* BN1 .... 204 A1
Loder Rd *BRI* BN1 .... 204 A1
Lodge Av *LW/ROSE* BN22 .... 229 H1
Lodge Cl *EGRIN* RH19 .... 22 A2
  LEW BN7 .... 2 A5
  PTSD BN41 .... 201 J1
Lodge Ct *SHOR* BN43 .... 200 B2
Lodge Hill La *HPPT/KEY* BN6 .... 119 J7
Lodge La *HPPT/KEY* BN6 .... 119 G8
Lodge Rd *RHAS* TN35 .... 199 F2
Lodsworth Cl *ROTT* BN2 .... 205 G4
Lomond Av *BRI* BN1 .... 178 B4
London Rd *BAT* TN33 .... 136 C1
  BEXW TN39 .... 195 G6
  BRI BN1 .... 6 C3
  BRI BN1 .... 177 J3
  BUR/ETCH TN19 .... 62 A8
  BURH RH15 .... 89 F8
  CROW TN6 .... 39 G7
  EGRIN RH19 .... 22 C2
  FROW RH18 .... 23 J7
  HAIL BN27 .... 189 G3
  HPPT/KEY BN6 .... 118 E6
  HPPT/KEY BN6 .... 148 C1
  RBTBR TN32 .... 78 B5
  RBTBR TN32 .... 106 D6
  RHWH RH17 .... 48 E7
  RING/NEW BN8 .... 127 H6
  SBGH/RUST TN4 .... 4 A4
  STLEO TN38 .... 67 H7
  UCK TN22 .... 47 H8
  WADH TN5 .... 47 H8
London Ter *BRI* BN1 .... 6 C3
Long Acre Cl *EAST* BN21 .... 229 J6
Longacre Cl *SLVH* TN37 .... 169 K5
Long Av *BEX* TN40 .... 196 B5
Longbury *UCK* TN22 .... 95 J6
Longfield Rd *RTWE/PEM* TN2 .... 20 E3
Longhill Cl *ROTT* BN2 .... 206 B7
Longhill Rd *ROTT* BN2 .... 206 A7
Longhurst *BURH* RH15 .... 119 K1
Longland Rd *EDN/EASTW* BN20 .... 229 H7
Long La *BAT* TN33 .... 138 A2
Long Meads *RRTW* TN3 .... 19 F8
Long Park Cnr *HPPT/KEY* BN6 .... 150 E1
Longridge Av *ROTT* BN2 .... 221 F3
Long Slip *RRTW* TN3 .... 18 E8
Longstone Rd *EAST* BN21 .... 10 C7
Longview *HTHF* TN21 .... 100 A6
Longview Wy *RTWE/PEM* TN2 .... 20 A8
Lonsdale Gdns *RTW* TN1 .... 20 A8
The Lookout *PEAHV* BN10 .... 208 B8
Lordine La *RBTBR* TN32 .... 80 D7
Lordslaine Cl *EDN/EASTW* BN20 .... 236 C3
Lords La *RHAS* TN35 .... 171 G8
The Lords *SEAF* BN25 .... 225 F5
Lordswell La *CROW* TN6 .... 53 G3
Lorna Rd *HOVE* BN3 .... 203 J4
Lorne Rd *BRI* BN1 .... 6 C2
Lorraine Rd *NEWHV* BN9 .... 9 D3
Lottbridge Dro *LW/ROSE* BN22 .... 11 F1
  LW/ROSE BN22 .... 230 A2
Love La *MAYF* TN20 .... 71 K1
  RYE TN31 .... 113 H5
Lover's Wk *BRI* BN1 .... 6 B2
Lowdells Cl *EGRIN* RH19 .... 12 A7
Lowdells Dr *EGRIN* RH19 .... 12 B7
Lowdells La *EGRIN* RH19 .... 12 A8
Lower Beach Rd *SHOR* BN43 .... 200 C5
Lower Bevendean Av *ROTT* BN2 .... 205 F2
Lower Chalvington Pl
  ROTT BN2 .... 205 F6
Lower Church Rd *BURH* RH15 .... 89 F8
Lower Dene *EGRIN* RH19 .... 22 D2
Lower Dr *SEAF* BN25 .... 225 G6
  STHW BN42 .... 201 H2
Lower Glen Rd *SLVH* TN37 .... 169 J7
Lower Green Rd *RRTW* TN3 .... 19 G6
  RTWE/PEM TN2 .... 21 K5
  SBGH/RUST TN4 .... 19 G7
Lower Hazelhurst *WADH* TN5 .... 45 K8
Lower High St *WADH* TN5 .... 44 C8
Lower Lake *BAT* TN33 .... 136 E7
Lower Market St *HOVE* BN3 .... 203 J6
Lower Mere *EGRIN* RH19 .... 22 D3
Lower Park Rd *HAS* TN34 .... 4 C3
Lower Pl *NEWHV* BN9 .... 8 C3
Lower Platts *WADH* TN5 .... 60 C2
Lower Rd *EAST* BN21 .... 229 J7
  HAIL BN27 .... 162 E8
Lower Rock Gdns *ROTT* BN2 .... 7 D6
Lower Saxonbury *CROW* TN6 .... 53 H1
Lower South Rd *SLVH* TN37 .... 4 A3

Lower Station Rd *RING/NEW* BN8 .... 92 E5
Lower Stoneham *RING/NEW* BN8 .... 3 E1
Lower St *BAT* TN33 .... 166 A7
  EDN/EASTW BN20 .... 235 F3
Lower Waites La *RHAS* TN35 .... 172 E7
Lowlands Rd *BURH* RH15 .... 89 H6
The Lowlands *HAIL* BN27 .... 189 F2
Lowther Cl *LGNY* BN23 .... 216 E8
Lowther Rd *BRI* BN1 .... 204 B1
Loxfield Cl *MAYF* TN20 .... 72 A1
Loxwood Cl *BEXW* TN39 .... 194 B6
  LW/ROSE BN22 .... 229 H2
Lucas *RHWH* RH17 .... 48 B6
Lucas Cl *EGRIN* RH19 .... 22 D2
Lucas Shadwell Wy *RYE* TN31 .... 144 B1
Lucerne Cl *PTSD* BN41 .... 202 A2
Lucerne Rd *BRI* BN1 .... 6 B1
Lucinda Wy *SEAF* BN25 .... 225 G6
Lucraft Rd *ROTT* BN2 .... 179 G6
Ludley HI *RYE* TN31 .... 110 E5
Ludlow Rd *ROTT* BN2 .... 205 H2
Ludpit La *BUR/ETCH* TN19 .... 77 G5
Lulham Cl *PEAHV* BN10 .... 222 A2
Lullington Av *HOVE* BN3 .... 202 E3
Lullington Cl *BEX* TN40 .... 196 B5
  EAST BN21 .... 229 H4
  SEAF BN25 .... 232 D1
Lullington Gdns *SLVH* TN37 .... 169 K6
Lunce's HI *RHWH* RH17 .... 90 B3
Lundy Wk *HAIL* BN27 .... 188 E1
Lurgashall *BURH* RH15 .... 119 J2
Lushington La *EAST* BN21 .... 10 C5
Lushington Rd *EAST* BN21 .... 10 C5
Lustrells Cl *ROTT* BN2 .... 220 E1
Lustrells Crs *ROTT* BN2 .... 220 D1
Lustrells V *ROTT* BN2 .... 220 E1
Luther St *ROTT* BN2 .... 7 E3
Luton Cl *EAST* BN21 .... 229 H5
Luxford Dr *CROW* TN6 .... 53 J5
Luxford La *CROW* TN6 .... 53 J5
Luxford Rd *CROW* TN6 .... 53 J4
Luxfords La *EGRIN* RH19 .... 23 F6
  EGRIN RH19 .... 23 F5
Lychgates Cl *BEX* TN40 .... 195 J6
Lydd Cl *LGNY* BN23 .... 230 E1
Lydd Rd *RYE* TN31 .... 145 G1
Lymden La *WADH* TN5 .... 59 J4
Lyminster Av *BRI* BN1 .... 178 B6
Lynchet Cl *BRI* BN1 .... 204 D1
Lynchet Down *BRI* BN1 .... 204 D1
Lynchets Crs *HOVE* BN3 .... 176 C8
The Lynchets *LEW* BN7 .... 3 E2
The Lynchette *SHOR* BN43 .... 200 C2
Lynchet Wk *BRI* BN1 .... 204 D1
Lyndhurst Av *HAS* TN34 .... 170 D7
Lyndhurst Rd *HOVE* BN3 .... 203 J4
Lynholm Rd *POLE* BN26 .... 215 G5
Lynton Cl *HPPT/KEY* BN6 .... 118 B6
Lynton Pk *EGRIN* RH19 .... 22 E1
Lynton St *ROTT* BN2 .... 7 D1
Lynwood *RRTW* TN3 .... 28 A5
Lynwood Cl *HAS* TN34 .... 170 A6
Lynwood Rd *ROTT* BN2 .... 221 F3
Lyon Cl *HOVE* BN3 .... 203 J4
Lytham Cl *STLEO* TN38 .... 197 G3

M

Maberley Rd *BEX* TN40 .... 195 H5
Mackerel HI *RYE* TN31 .... 83 K6
Mackerel's Rocks *RING/NEW* BN8 .... 93 K8
Mackie Av *BRI* BN1 .... 178 A5
  HPPT/KEY BN6 .... 119 G6
Macmichaels Wy
  BUR/ETCH TN19 .... 62 A8
Macmillan Dr *EAST* BN21 .... 229 H6
Madehurst Cl *ROTT* BN2 .... 7 F5
Madeira Dr *ROTT* BN2 .... 7 D6
Madeira Pk *RTW* TN1 .... 30 B1
Madeira Pl *ROTT* BN2 .... 7 D6
Maderia *SLVH* TN37 .... 4 A1
Mafeking Rd *ROTT* BN2 .... 7 E2
Magdalen Cl *LGNY* BN23 .... 216 D8
Magdalen Rd *BEX* TN40 .... 195 J7
  SLVH TN37 .... 4 B5
Magellan Wy *LGNY* BN23 .... 231 H5
Magnolia Cl *HTHF* TN21 .... 100 B6
Magnolia Dr *LW/ROSE* BN22 .... 229 J1
Magpie Cl *BEXW* TN39 .... 194 B5
  STLEO TN38 .... 197 F3
Magpie Rd *LGNY* BN23 .... 216 D8
Magreed La *HTHF* TN21 .... 100 E1
Maidstone Rd *RTWE/PEM* TN2 .... 21 J3
Main Rd *RHAS* TN35 .... 139 G7
  RHAS TN35 .... 141 F7
Mainstone Rd *HOVE* BN3 .... 202 E4
Main St *RYE* TN31 .... 81 K5
  RYE TN31 .... 85 H8
  RYE TN31 .... 112 B1
Maitland Cl *HAS* TN34 .... 170 B5
Major Cl *BRI* BN1 .... 7 D1
Major York's Rd *SBGH/RUST* TN4 .... 19 K8

Malcolm Gdns *POLE* BN26 2
Maldon Rd *BRI* BN1 2
Malines Av *PEAHV* BN10 2
Malines Av South *PEAHV* BN10 2
Mallard Cl *LW/ROSE* BN22 2
Mallard Dr *UCK* TN22 2
Mallard Pl *EGRIN* RH19 2
Mallett Cl *SEAF* BN25 232
Malling Cl *LEW* BN7 2
Malling Down *LEW* BN7 2
Malling HI *LEW* BN7 2
Malling St *LEW* BN7 2
Mallory Rd *HOVE* BN3 2
Malthouse La *HPPT/KEY* BN6 2
  ROTT BN2 2
  RYE TN31 1
Malthouse Wy *RING/NEW* BN8 1
The Maltings *BURH* RH15 1
Malton Wy *RTWE/PEM* TN2 2
Malvern St *HAS* TN34 20
Malvern Wy *HAS* TN34 1
Manchester Rd *BAT* TN33 1
Manchester St *ROTT* BN2 2
Manifold Rd *LW/ROSE* BN22 1
Manning Cl *EGRIN* RH19 2
Mann St *HAS* TN34 2
Manor Av *HPPT/KEY* BN6 1
Manor Cl *BURH* RH15 2
  EDN/EASTW BN20 2
  HTHF TN21 1
  RING/NEW BN8 150
  ROTT BN2 2
  SBGH/RUST TN4 2
  SEAF BN25 2
  STHW BN42 2
  UCK TN22 2
  WSEA TN36 1
Manor Dr *PEAHV* BN10 2
Manor End *UCK* TN22 2
Manor Gdns *ROTT* BN2 2
Manor Gn *ROTT* BN2 2
Manor Hall Rd *STHW* BN42 2
Manor HI *ROTT* BN2 2
Manor Paddock *ROTT* BN2 2
Manor Pk *SBGH/RUST* TN4 2
Manor Park Rd *HAIL* BN27 1
Manor Pl *ROTT* BN2 2
Manor Rd *BEX* TN40 1
  BURH RH15 2
  EGRIN RH19 2
  HAS TN34 2
  HTHF TN21 1
  LW/ROSE BN22 2
  PTSD BN41 2
  ROTT BN2 2
  SBGH/RUST TN4 2
  SBGH/RUST TN4 2
  SEAF BN25 2
Manor Rd North *SEAF* BN25 2
Manor Wy *CROW* TN6 2
  EDN/EASTW BN20 2
  POLE BN26 2
  ROTT BN2 2
  UCK TN22 2
Mansell Cl *BEXW* TN39 1
Mansell Rd *SHOR* BN43 2
Mansers La *HAIL* BN27 1
Mansfield Rd *LW/ROSE* BN22 2
Mansion Cl *BURH* RH15 2
Manston Wy *HAS* TN34 2
Mantell Cl *LEW* BN7 2
Manton Rd *ROTT* BN2 2
Manvers Rd *EDN/EASTW* BN20 2
Maple Av *BEXW* TN39 1
Maple Cl *BEXW* TN39 1
  BURH RH15 2
  ROTT BN2 2
  UCK TN22 6
Maple Ct *HAIL* BN27 1
Maple Dr *BURH* RH15 1
  EGRIN RH19 2
Maple Gdns *HOVE* BN3 2
Maple Hts *SLVH* TN37 1
Maplehurst Cl *SLVH* TN37 1
Maplehurst Dr *SLVH* TN37 1
Maplehurst Ri *SLVH* TN37 16
Maplehurst Rd *LW/ROSE* BN22 2
  PTSD BN41 2
Maple Leaf Cl *NEWHV* BN9 ....
Mapleleaf Gdns *POLE* BN26 215
Maple Wk *BEXW* TN39 1
Marbles Rd *RING/NEW* BN8 ....
Marchants Cl *HPPT/KEY* BN6 1
Marchants Dr *RYE* TN31 1
Marchants Rd *HPPT/KEY* BN6 1
Marchants Wy *BURH* RH15 1
Marcia Cl *EDN/EASTW* BN20 2
Marcus Gdns *STLEO* TN38 1
Marden's HI *CROW* TN6 ....
Mardyke *SHOR* BN43 2
Mare Bay Cl *STLEO* TN38 1
Maresfield Dr *PEV* BN24 2
Maresfield Rd *ROTT* BN2 2
Margaret St *ROTT* BN2 2
Margery Rd *HOVE* BN3 2

...na *BEX* TN40 .... 195 H8
...LEO TN58 .... 197 H5
...na Court Av *BEX* TN40 .... 195 H8
...na Wk *LGNY* BN23 .... 231 F3
...ne Rd *ROTT* BN2 .... 205 F8
...ne Av *HOVE* BN3 .... 202 C5
...ne CI *PEV* BN24 .... 218 C5
...TT BN2 .... 220 E2
...ne Crs *SEAF* BN25 .... 232 A1
...ne Dr *ROTT* BN2 .... 205 G8
...TT BN2 .... 205 G2
...AF BN25 .... 224 B5
...ne Gdns *ROTT* BN2 .... 7 D6 ▯
...ne Pde *LW/ROSE* BN22 .... 11 D5
...TT BN2 .... 7 E6
...BN24 .... 224 C7
...ne Rd *LW/ROSE* BN22 .... 11 D4 ▯
...W BN24 .... 218 A6
...ners CI *HAIL* BN27 .... 189 H4
...ne Sq *ROTT* BN2 .... 7 E6
...ne Terrace Ms *ROTT* BN2 .... 7 E6 ▯
...ne Vw *ROTT* BN2 .... 7 D5
...oram PI *SHOR* BN43 .... 200 C3 ▯
...t CI *SEAF* BN25 .... 232 E1 ▯
...t La *LEW* BN7 .... 3 D4 ▯
...et CI *HAIL* BN27 .... 189 H4
...et Rd *BAT* TN33 .... 136 C6
...E TN31 .... 113 J6 ▯
...et St *BRI* BN1 .... 6 C5 ▯▮
...W BN7 .... 3 D4
...WE/PEM TN2 .... 30 A1 ▯
...E TN31 .... 113 J6 ▯
...LEO TN58 .... 4 A6 ▯
...kland Wy *UCK* TN22 .... 95 G4
...t La *EAST* BN21 .... 10 C5
...lye La *HTHF* TN21 .... 100 B2
...HF TN21 .... 101 J8
...stakes Cnr *RING/NEW* BN8 .... 122 C2
...stakes La *RING/NEW* BN8 .... 122 C2
...wick Ter *STLEO* TN38 .... 197 J3
...borough CI *LGNY* BN23 .... 216 E8 ▯
...GH/RUST TN4 .... 19 J7
...LEO TN58 .... 197 H2
...borough Dr *BURH* RH15 .... 89 J3
...borough Ms *BRI* BN1 .... 6 C5 ▯
...borough PI *BRI* BN1 .... 6 C5 ▮▮
...borough St *BRI* BN1 .... 6 B5 ▯
...e Av *BURH* RH15 .... 89 G7 ▯
...ey CI *BAT* TN33 .... 137 F7
...ey Gdns *BAT* TN33 .... 137 F7
...ey La *BAT* TN33 .... 137 F7
...ey Ri *BAT* TN33 .... 137 F7
...ey Rd *RYE* TN31 .... 113 G5
...ne Rd *STLEO* TN58 .... 169 H8
...ne Rd *STLEO* TN58 .... 169 H7
...Marlinspike *SHOR* BN43 .... 200 D5
...ow Av *LW/ROSE* BN22 .... 11 D1
...ow Dr *SLVH* TN37 .... 169 J6
...ow Rd *ROTT* BN2 .... 205 G2
...oit CI *EGRIN* RH19 .... 12 C8
...pits La *BAT* TN33 .... 165 K4
...Marlpit *WADH* TN5 .... 44 A6
...nion Rd *HOVE* BN3 .... 202 E4
...den Rd *LGNY* BN23 .... 231 F2
...halls Rw *BRI* BN1 .... 6 C3 ▯
...hall Wy *HOVE* BN3 .... 202 E2
...hlands La *HTHF* TN21 .... 100 A3
...hfoot La *HAIL* BN27 .... 189 H3
...hlands Rd *RTWE/PEM* TN2 .... 30 D2
...elyne Rd *HAIL* BN27 .... 191 H3
...n Stamford Gn *RYE* TN31 .... 114 C3 ▯
...n Rd *RYE* TN31 .... 113 C6
...ck Rd *SEAF* BN25 .... 225 G7
...AF BN25 .... 225 G7
...ock Rd *BRI* BN1 .... 203 J2
...V/EASTW BN20 .... 236 D3
...ice Rd *SEAF* BN25 .... 232 B2
...field CI *EDN/EASTW* BN20 .... 229 C6 ▯
...ield La *RHAS* TN35 .... 171 C1
...Av *SEAF* BN25 .... 225 J8
...air CI *POLE* BN26 .... 214 E7
...ield *LING* RH7 .... 12 E2
...ield Av *PEAHV* BN10 .... 222 C5
...ield CI *BRI* BN1 .... 178 A6
...ield Crs *BRI* BN1 .... 178 A6
...ield Flat *HTHF* TN21 .... 98 E3 ▯
...ield La *STLEO* TN38 .... 196 E1 ▯

WADH TN5 .... 43 J7
Mayfield Pk *WADH* TN5 .... 43 K6
Mayfield PI *LW/ROSE* BN22 .... 10 C3
Mayfield Rd *CROW* TN6 .... 56 A1
SBGH/RUST TN4 .... 19 K7
Mayfield Wy *BEX* TN40 .... 195 K6
Mayhew Wy *LEW* BN7 .... 3 D2
Mayhouse Rd *BURH* RH15 .... 119 F2 ▯
Mayne Waye *HAS* TN34 .... 170 D7
Mayne La *BEXW* TN59 .... 195 F3
Mayo Ri *BEXW* TN59 .... 195 F3
Mayo Rd *ROTT* BN2 .... 7 D2
Maypole Cottages *UCK* TN22 .... 68 D3
Maypole Rd *EGRIN* RH19 .... 22 B1
EGRIN RH19 .... 23 J5
May Rd *ROTT* BN2 .... 7 F3
May Tree Gdns *BEX* TN40 .... 196 A5
Maytree Wk *HOVE* BN3 .... 202 D2
Maywood Av *LW/ROSE* BN22 .... 229 J1
Mcindoe Rd *EGRIN* RH19 .... 12 B8
Mcwilliam Rd *ROTT* BN2 .... 205 K2
Meades CI *LING* RH7 .... 12 E2 ▯
The Meades *LING* 13 F2
Meadow CI *HAIL* BN27 .... 189 G2
HOVE BN3 .... 177 G8
PTSD BN41 .... 202 A1 ▯
ROTT BN2 .... 206 B8
STLEO TN38 .... 197 H3
Meadow Crs *BEXW* TN59 .... 195 H4
Meadowcroft CI *EGRIN* RH19 ...... 22 A1
Meadow Hill Rd *RTW* TN1 .... 20 B8 ▯
Meadowlands Av *LW/ROSE* BN22 .. 229 J1
BURH RH15 .... 119 F2
Meadow Pde *ROTT* BN2 .... 206 C8
Meadow Rd *HAIL* BN27 .... 189 F5
RRTW TN3 .... 27 K4
SBGH/RUST TN4 .... 19 G7
SBGH/RUST TN4 .... 19 K2
Meadows *HPPT/KEY* BN6 .... 118 E6
Meadows Rd *LW/ROSE* BN22 .... 229 G1
The Meadows *HOVE* BN3 .... 176 B8
LEW BN7 .... 3 E2
SLVH TN37 .... 169 K5
The Meadow *RTWE/PEM* TN2 .... 21 K3
CROW TN6 .... 54 E4
Meadowview *ROTT* BN2 .... 205 F2
Meadow Vw *HTHF* TN21 .... 100 A6
RHAS TN35 .... 172 D7
SEAF BN25 .... 225 J7
Meads Av *BEXW* TN59 .... 194 B7
HOVE BN3 .... 176 B8
Meads Brow *EDN/EASTW* BN20 .... 236 D3 ▯
Meads CI *HOVE* BN3 .... 176 B8 ▯
Meads Rd *BEXW* TN59 .... 194 B7
EDN/EASTW BN20 .... 10 A6
SEAF BN25 .... 225 G8
Meads St *EDN/EASTW* BN20 .... 236 E3
The Meads *BRI* BN1 .... 178 E6
EGRIN RH19 .... 22 C4
RTWE/PEM TN2 .... 30 C1
The Mead *BEXW* TN59 .... 194 C7
Meadway CI *STHW* BN42 .... 201 G3
Meadway Crs *HOVE* BN3 .... 202 E1
The Meadway *ROTT* BN2 .... 205 G6
SHOR BN43 .... 200 C5
Mealla CI *LEW* BN7 .... 2 C2 ▯
Medina CI *PEV* BN24 .... 216 C6
Medina PI *HOVE* BN3 .... 203 G6
Medina Ter *HOVE* BN3 .... 203 G6 ▯
Medina Vis *HOVE* BN3 .... 203 G6
Medmerry Hi *ROTT* BN2 .... 205 F1
HAIL BN27 .... 189 F1
Medway Dr *EGRIN* RH19 .... 22 B5
FROW RH18 .... 36 A1
Medway Rd *PEV* BN24 .... 216 B6
Meeching Ri *HOVE* BN9 .... 8 C3
Meeching Rd *NEWHV* BN9 .... 9 D3
Meeds Rd *BURH* RH15 .... 119 G1
Meeting House La *BRI* BN1 .... 6 C5 ▯▮
Melbourne Rd *LW/ROSE* BN22 ..... 11 D4
Melbourne St *ROTT* BN2 .... 7 E2
Melfort Rd *CROW* TN6 .... 53 F2
Melrose Av *PTSD* BN41 .... 201 K2
Melrose CI *BRI* BN1 .... 204 D1
HAIL BN27 .... 189 F5
Melville Rd *HOVE* BN3 .... 6 A3
Melvill La *EDN/EASTW* BN20 ...... 229 G3
Mendip Av *LGNY* BN23 .... 216 D8
Mendip Gdns *HAS* TN34 .... 5 F1
Menzies Rd *SLVH* TN37 .... 169 J8 ▯
Meon CI *PEV* BN24 .... 216 B6
Mercatoria *STLEO* TN38 .... 4 A6 ▯
Mercers *HAWK* TN18 .... 63 G2
RRTW TN3 .... 18 E8
Mercer St *RTW* TN1 .... 20 B6 ▯
Mercread Rd *SEAF* BN25 .... 225 G6
Meres La *MAYF* TN20 .... 71 F8
MAYF TN20 .... 71 H3
Merevale *BRI* BN1 .... 204 C1
Mereworth Rd *SBGH/RUST* TN4 ... 20 A5
Meridian Rd *LEW* BN7 .... 2 B3
Meridian Wy *EGRIN* RH19 .... 12 D8

Merlin CI *HOVE* BN3 .... 203 J3
Merlin Wy *EGRIN* RH19 .... 12 E8
Mermaid St *RYE* TN31 .... 113 H6
Merrimede CI *STLEO* TN58 .... 197 H4
Merriments La *BUR/ETCH* TN19 .. 62 A7
Merrion CI *SBGH/RUST* TN4 .... 20 B4
Merrion Wy *SBGH/RUST* TN4 ...... 20 B4
Merston CI *ROTT* BN2 .... 206 B5
Metcalfe Av *NEWHV* BN9 .... 8 B2
Mews Ct *EGRIN* RH19 .... 22 D5
Mews Rd *STLEO* TN38 .... 4 A6 ▯
The Mews *RING/NEW* BN8 .... 127 J6
RTWE/PEM TN2 .... 21 J5
Meyners CI *HOVE* BN3 .... 176 B8 ▯
Michael Flds *FROW* RH18 .... 35 J1
Michelbourne CI *BURH* RH15 ...... 118 E2 ▯
Michel CI *EDN/EASTW* BN20 ...... 235 F2
Michel Dene CI
  EDN/EASTW BN20 .... 235 G2 ▯
Michel Dene Rd
  EDN/EASTW BN20 .... 235 F2
Michele CI *STLEO* TN58 .... 197 J2 ▯
Michele Gv *EAST* BN21 .... 10 A3
Michelham CI *LGNY* BN23 .... 216 B7 ▯
Micheltam Rd *UCK* TN22 .... 96 A2
Michelson CI *STLEO* TN58 .... 169 G7
Mickle Dr *UCK* TN22 .... 67 G5
Middle Furlong *SEAF* BN25 .... 225 G8
Middleham CI *RING/NEW* BN8 ..... 155 H7
Middleham Wy *LGNY* BN23 .... 216 D7 ▯
Middle Rd *BRI* BN1 .... 6 A1
  RHAS TN35 .... 171 G8
  RRTW TN3 .... 31 G6
  SHOR BN43 .... 200 E4
Middlesex Rd *BEX* TN40 .... 195 J8
Middle St *BRI* BN1 .... 6 B5 ▯
  BRI BN1 .... 179 K5
  HAS TN34 .... 5 D4 ▯
  PTSD BN41 .... 202 A5
  SHOR BN43 .... 200 C4
Middleton Av *HOVE* BN3 .... 202 C5
Middleton Dr *LGNY* BN23 .... 231 H4 ▯
Middleton Ri *BRI* BN1 .... 179 F6
Middle Wk *BURH* RH15 .... 89 H8
Middleway *HAIL* BN27 .... 163 J6
Middle Wy *LEW* BN7 .... 2 A4
Midfields CI *BURH* RH15 .... 89 H7 ▯
Midfields Dr *BURH* RH15 .... 89 H8
Midfields Wk *BURH* RH15 .... 89 H7 ▯
Midhurst Ri *BRI* BN1 .... 178 C5
Midhurst Rd *LW/ROSE* BN22 .... 230 A1
Midhurst Wk *HOVE* BN3 .... 176 E8 ▯
Midway Rd *ROTT* BN2 .... 205 K3
The Midway *SBGH/RUST* TN4 ...... 29 H1
Mighell St *ROTT* BN2 .... 7 D5 ▯
Milcote Av *HOVE* BN3 .... 202 E3
Mildenhall Dr *SLVH* TN37 .... 169 J7
Mildmay CI *RING/NEW* BN8 .... 155 J3
Mildmay Rd *LEW* BN7 .... 2 A4
Mile Oak Crs *STHW* BN42 .... 201 J2
Mile Oak Gdns *PTSD* BN41 .... 201 K2
Mile Oak Rd *PTSD* BN41 .... 175 J8
Milfoil Dr *LGNY* BN23 .... 216 D8 ▯
Military Rd *RYE* TN31 .... 113 K2
Milland CI *BEX* TN40 .... 195 K5
Milland Rd *HAIL* BN27 .... 189 G2
Mill Av *SHOR* BN43 .... 200 C2 ▯
Millbank *BURH* RH15 .... 89 H8
Millberg Rd *SEAF* BN25 .... 225 J7
Millbrook CI *HTHF* TN21 .... 130 A4
Millbrook Gdns *EDN/EASTW* BN20 .. 229 G5
Millbrook Rd *CROW* TN6 .... 39 J8
Mill Brooks *RING/NEW* BN8 .... 122 B4
Mill CI *EDN/EASTW* BN20 .... 234 E2
  EGRIN RH19 .... 22 C4
  HTHF TN21 .... 99 K4
  POLE BN26 .... 214 C2
  POY/PYE BN45 .... 148 B6
  PTSD BN41 .... 202 B2
  RBTBR TN32 .... 108 A1
  RHAS TN35 .... 139 G6
  RHAS TN35 .... 139 F5
Mill Crs *CROW* TN6 .... 39 H8 ▯
Millcroft *BRI* BN1 .... 177 H6
Millcroft Av *STHW* BN42 .... 201 J2
Millcroft Gdns *STHW* BN42 .... 201 H2
Millcross Rd *PTSD* BN41 .... 202 A2
Milldown Rd *SEAF* BN25 .... 225 G7
Mill Dr *CROW* TN6 .... 54 B3
  HOVE BN3 .... 177 F8
  SEAF BN25 .... 225 H8
Mill Dro *SEAF* BN25 .... 9 F5
  UCK TN22 .... 95 J5
Miller Rd *BRI* BN1 .... 6 A1
Miller's Hill Cottage La *RHAS* TN35 .. 139 F4
Millers Ri *HAIL* BN27 .... 189 F5
Miller's Rd *BRI* BN1 .... 6 A1 ▯
Millers Wy *BURH* RH15 .... 89 G7
Millfield *BAT* TN33 .... 165 K5
Millfield CI *RING/NEW* BN8 .... 93 G4
  SEAF BN25 .... 225 H7
Millfield Cottages *ROTT* BN2 ...... 7 F6 ▯
Millfield Ri *BEX* TN40 .... 195 H7
Mill Gap Rd *EAST* BN21 .... 10 B2

Mill Gdns *HTHF* TN21 .... 100 A6
  RING/NEW BN8 .... 155 J6
Millham Cl *BEXW* TN39 .... 194 E6
Mill Hi *SHOR* BN45 .... 174 E6
Mill Hill Cl *SHOR* BN43 .... 200 B2
Mill Hill Dr *SHOR* BN43 .... 200 B2
Mill Hill Gdns *SHOR* BN43 .... 200 B2
Mill La *BAT* TN33 .... 193 J1
  CROW TN6 .... 53 G1
  HAIL BN27 .... 161 F6
  HPPT/KEY BN6 .... 88 A8
  HPPT/KEY BN6 .... 149 K4
  LEW BN7 .... 208 B4
  LING RH7 .... 12 D1
  POY/PYE BN45 .... 148 B6
  PTSD BN41 .... 202 A1
  RHAS TN35 .... 139 G6
  RHAS TN35 .... 171 H6
  RING/NEW BN8 .... 122 B4
  RING/NEW BN8 .... 127 J6
  RING/NEW BN8 .... 154 C1
  RYE TN31 .... 83 K8
  SHOR BN43 .... 200 B3
  UCK TN22 .... 95 J5
Mill Md *RING/NEW* BN8 .... 155 J6
Mill Race *HPPT/KEY* BN6 .... 118 E3
The Millrace *POLE* BN26 .... 214 E7
Mill Ri *BRI* BN1 .... 177 H6
  RBTBR TN32 .... 78 A3
Mill Rd *BRI* BN1 .... 177 H5
  BURH RH15 .... 89 H7
  EAST BN21 .... 10 A2
  EAST BN21 .... 229 J6
  HAIL BN27 .... 189 H4
  HTHF TN21 .... 99 K4
  LEW BN7 .... 3 E2
  PTSD BN41 .... 202 A4
  RING/NEW BN8 .... 155 J6
  RYE TN31 .... 113 J4
  WSEA TN36 .... 142 E5
Millstream Cl *RRTW* TN3 .... 27 F1
Millstream Gdns *POLE* BN26 .... 214 E7
Mill St *BRI* BN1 .... 179 K4
Mill Vw *RING/NEW* BN8 .... 155 H7
Mill View Cl *PEV* BN24 .... 216 E5
Mill View Rd *BEXW* TN39 .... 195 G4
Millward Rd *PEV* BN24 .... 217 K8
Mill Wy *EGRIN* RH19 .... 22 C2
  POLE BN26 .... 214 D8
Milner Rd *ROTT* BN2 .... 7 E1
Milnthorpe Rd *EDN/EASTW* BN20 .... 236 E3
  HOVE BN3 .... 202 D3
Milton Crs *EAST* BN21 .... 229 H7
  EGRIN RH19 .... 22 A2
Milton Dr *RTWE/PEM* TN2 .... 20 B4
  STHW BN42 .... 201 J3
Milton Rd *EAST* BN21 .... 229 H7
  ROTT BN2 .... 7 D3
Milton St *EAST* BN21 .... 216 B5
Milward Crs *HAS* TN34 .... 5 E4
Milward Rd *HAS* TN34 .... 5 E4
Mimosa Cl *POLE* BN26 .... 215 F4
Mimram Rd *PEV* BN24 .... 216 B6
Mindleheim Av *EGRIN* RH19 .... 23 F1
The Minnels *HPPT/KEY* BN6 .... 119 F8
Minster Cl *POLE* BN26 .... 215 F4
The Mint *RYE* TN31 .... 113 H6
Mistley Cl *BEX* TN40 .... 196 B5
Mitchelldean *PEAHV* BN10 .... 222 A2
Mitten Rd *BEX* TN40 .... 195 H7
Moat Croft Rd *EAST* BN21 .... 10 A4
Moat Farm *RTWE/PEM* TN2 .... 30 A4
Moat La *BAT* TN33 .... 169 J1
  EDEN TN8 .... 15 K4
  HTHF TN21 .... 128 B2
Moat Rd *EGRIN* RH19 .... 22 C2
Mocatta Wy *BURH* RH15 .... 88 D6
Modena Rd *HOVE* BN3 .... 202 E4
Molesworth St *HOVE* BN3 .... 202 E3
Molyneux Park Rd *SBGH/RUST* TN4 .... 19 K7
Monarch Gdns *LGNY* BN23 .... 231 F2
  SEAF BN25 .... 225 H6
Monarchs Wy *BRI* BN1 .... 6 A5
  HOVE BN3 .... 203 H4
  PTSD BN41 .... 176 C5
  SHOR BN43 .... 174 D4
  STHW BN42 .... 175 H8
Mona Rd *LW/ROSE* BN22 .... 11 D3
Monceux Rd *EDN/EASTW* BN20 .... 229 H7
  HAIL BN27 .... 163 F5
Monckton Wy *LEW* BN7 .... 181 H6
Monger's Md *RING/NEW* BN8 .... 123 J7
Monk Cl *BRI* BN1 .... 179 F5
Monks La *WADH* TN5 .... 44 D4
Monks' Wk *WSEA* TN36 .... 142 E5
Monks Wy *RYE* TN31 .... 91 K5
Monmouth St *HOVE* BN3 .... 203 G4
Monson Rd *RTW* TN1 .... 20 B7
Monson Wy *RTW* TN1 .... 20 B7

Montacute Gdns *RTWE/PEM* TN2 .... 29 K1
Montacute Rd *LEW* BN7 .... 2 A5
  LEW BN7 .... 181 J5
  RTWE/PEM TN2 .... 30 A2
Montacute Wy *UCK* TN22 .... 95 K3
Montague Cl *SHOR* BN43 .... 201 G4
Montague Pl *ROTT* BN2 .... 7 E6
Montague St *ROTT* BN2 .... 7 E6
Montague Wy *PEV* BN24 .... 217 G6
Montargis Wy *CROW* TN6 .... 53 H2
Montefiore Rd *HOVE* BN3 .... 6 A3
Monteith Cl *RRTW* TN3 .... 18 E8
Montford Cl *SHOR* BN43 .... 201 G3
Montfort Cl *PEV* BN24 .... 217 G5
Montfort Rd *PEV* BN24 .... 217 G5
Montgomery Rd *RHAS* TN35 .... 171 G6
  SBGH/RUST TN4 .... 20 B4
Montgomery St *HOVE* BN3 .... 202 E4
Montpelier Crs *BRI* BN1 .... 6 A4
Montpelier Pl *BRI* BN1 .... 6 A5
Montpelier Rd *BRI* BN1 .... 6 A5
Montpelier St *BRI* BN1 .... 6 A4
Montpelier Ter *BRI* BN1 .... 6 A4
Montpelier Vls *BRI* BN1 .... 6 A4
Montreal Rd *ROTT* BN2 .... 7 D4
Monument Vw *ROTT* BN2 .... 7 F4
Moons Hl *BAT* TN33 .... 166 A5
Moon's La *EGRIN* RH19 .... 13 H4
Moore's La *RYE* TN31 .... 110 C4
Moor Hall Dr *BAT* TN33 .... 165 J5
Moor Hl *HAWK* TN18 .... 63 F3
The Moorings *SHOR* BN43 .... 201 F5
Moor La *RHAS* TN35 .... 139 G8
  RING/NEW BN8 .... 156 B8
Moor Pl *EGRIN* RH19 .... 22 B1
Moor Rd *RHAS* TN35 .... 139 G7
The Moor *HAWK* TN18 .... 63 F3
Morecambe Rd *BRI* BN1 .... 178 B5
Morestead *PEAHV* BN10 .... 222 C2
Morgan Cl *BEXW* TN39 .... 195 G3
Morgay Wood La *RHAS* TN35 .... 171 H1
Morlais Pl *WSEA* TN36 .... 143 H7
Morlais Rdg *WSEA* TN36 .... 143 H5
Morland Dr *RRTW* TN3 .... 33 K6
Morlands Cl *BAT* TN33 .... 166 A6
Morley Cl *LEW* BN7 .... 2 B6
Morley St *ROTT* BN2 .... 6 C4
Morningside Cl *SEAF* BN25 .... 225 G7
Mornington Crs *HOVE* BN3 .... 202 C4
Morris Rd *LEW* BN7 .... 3 E4
Mortain Rd *PEV* BN24 .... 217 G5
Mortimer Gdns *POLE* BN26 .... 214 E7
Mortimer Rd *HOVE* BN3 .... 202 E3
  LW/ROSE BN22 .... 10 C1
Morton Rd *EGRIN* RH19 .... 22 C4
Moscow Rd *RHAS* TN35 .... 171 F8
Motcombe La *EAST* BN21 .... 229 J7
Motcombe Rd *EAST* BN21 .... 229 J7
Motte Fld *HRTF* TN7 .... 26 A7
Mottins Hl *CROW* TN6 .... 54 B3
Moulsecoomb Wy *ROTT* BN2 .... 179 F8
Mountain Ash Cl *HAIL* BN27 .... 189 F3
Mountbatten Cl *RHAS* TN35 .... 171 G6
Mountbatten Dr *LGNY* BN23 .... 231 F4
Mount Caburn Crs *PEAHV* BN10 .... 222 B1
Mount Cl *NEWHV* BN9 .... 9 F2
Mount Dr *ROTT* BN2 .... 221 G1
Mount Edgcumbe Rd *SBGH/RUST* TN4 .... 20 A8
Mount Ephraim *RTW* TN1 .... 20 A7
Mount Ephraim Rd *RTW* TN1 .... 20 A7
Mountfield Gdns *RTWE/PEM* TN2 .... 20 B8
Mountfield La *RBTBR* TN32 .... 105 F4
Mountfield Rd *LEW* BN7 .... 3 D5
  RTWE/PEM TN2 .... 20 B8
Mountfields *BRI* BN1 .... 204 D1
Mount Harry Rd *LEW* BN7 .... 2 A3
Mount Idone Wy *BEXW* TN39 .... 194 E3
Mount Joy *BAT* TN33 .... 136 D6
Mountney Dr *PEV* BN24 .... 218 C5
Mountney Rd *EAST* BN21 .... 229 H7
Mount Pl *LEW* BN7 .... 2 C4
Mount Pleasant *CROW* TN6 .... 54 A7
  ROTT BN2 .... 7 D5
  UCK TN22 .... 97 J5
  WADH TN5 .... 44 A6
Mount Pleasant Av *ROTT* BN2 .... 20 B8
Mount Pleasant La *RRTW* TN3 .... 33 H5
Mount Pleasant Rd *HAS* TN34 .... 5 D2
  RTW TN1 .... 20 A8
Mountreed *MAYF* TN20 .... 71 F4
Mount Rd *EDN/EASTW* BN20 .... 237 F3
  NEWHV BN9 .... 9 F3
  RHAS TN35 .... 199 F1
Mount Sion *RTW* TN1 .... 30 A1
Mount St *BAT* TN33 .... 136 D6
  LEW BN7 .... 2 C5
The Mount *HAIL* BN27 .... 189 H5
  UCK TN22 .... 95 J3
Mount View Ter *HAIL* BN27 .... 189 H5
Mount Zion Pl *BRI* BN1 .... 6 B4
Moy Av *LW/ROSE* BN22 .... 10 C3

Moyne Cl *HOVE* BN3 .... 2...
Muirfield Ri *STLEO* TN38 .... 19...
Mulberry Cl *BEXW* TN39 .... 19...
  BRI BN1 .... 178...
  LW/ROSE BN22 .... 2...
  RTWE/PEM TN2 .... 2...
  SHOR BN43 .... 2...
Mulberry La *HPPT/KEY* BN6 .... 1...
Mulberry Wk *SLVH* TN37 .... 1...
Mulberry Wy *HTHF* TN21 .... 1...
Munns Dr *BURH* RH15 .... 8...
Munster Gn *RING/NEW* BN8 .... 123...
Murray Av *NEWHV* BN9 .... 8...
Murton-neale Cl *HAWK* TN18 .... 63...
Musgrave Av *EGRIN* RH19 .... 2...
Mushroom Fld *LEW* BN7 .... 18...
Mutton Hall Hi *HTHF* TN21 .... 1...
Mutton Hall La *HTHF* TN21 .... 1...
Mutton Hl *LING* RH7 .... 1...
Myrtle Rd *CROW* TN6 .... 5...

N

Namrik Ms *HOVE* BN3 .... 2...
Nanson Rd *BRI* BN1 .... 1...
Nan Tucks La *UCK* TN22 .... 9...
Naomi Cl *EDN/EASTW* BN20 .... 10...
Napier Rd *RTWE/PEM* TN2 .... 3...
  STLEO TN38 .... 1...
Natal Rd *ROTT* BN2 .... 2...
  ROTT BN2 .... 2...
Neath Rd *LYDD* TN29 .... 1...
Neaves La *RING/NEW* BN8 .... 9...
Neill's Cl *NEWHV* BN9 .... 8...
Neills Rd *RRTW* TN3 ....
Nellington Rd *RRTW* TN3 ....
Nelson Dr *LGNY* BN23 .... 231...
Nelson Rd *HAS* TN34 ....
  RTWE/PEM TN2 ....
Nelson Rw *ROTT* BN2 .... 7...
Nesbitt Rd *ROTT* BN2 ....
Netherfield Av *LGNY* BN23 .... 23...
Netherfield Gn *ROTT* BN2 .... 20...
Netherfield Hl *BAT* TN33 .... 13...
Netherfield Rd *BAT* TN33 .... 13...
Netherfield Wy *BAT* TN33 .... 13...
Nether La *UCK* TN22 .... 7...
Netherwood Cl *HAS* TN34 .... 17...
Nevill Av *HOVE* BN3 .... 2...
  LW/ROSE BN22 .... 2...
Nevill Cl *HOVE* BN3 .... 2...
Nevill Crs *LEW* BN7 ....
Nevill Ga *RTWE/PEM* TN2 ....
Nevill Gdns *HOVE* BN3 .... 2...
Nevill Pk *SBGH/RUST* TN4 ....
Nevill Pl *HOVE* BN3 .... 2...
Nevill Rdg *SBGH/RUST* TN4 ....
Nevill Rd *CROW* TN6 ....
  HOVE BN3 ....
  LEW BN7 ....
  ROTT BN2 .... 2...
  UCK TN22 ....
Nevill St *RTWE/PEM* TN2 .... 2...
Nevill Ter *RTWE/PEM* TN2 .... 29...
Nevill Wy *HOVE* BN3 ....
Newark Pl *ROTT* BN2 ....
New Barn Cl *HAIL* BN27 .... 18...
  PTSD BN41 ....
  SHOR BN43 .... 200...
New Barn La *UCK* TN22 ....
New Barn Rd *ROTT* BN2 .... 2...
  SHOR BN43 .... 2...
Newbury La *WADH* TN5 ....
New Church Rd *HOVE* BN3 .... 2...
Newcomen Rd *SBGH/RUST* TN4 .... 2...
New Cut *RBTBR* TN32 .... 10...
  RHAS TN35 .... 13...
New Dorset St *BRI* BN1 ....
Newells Cl *ROTT* BN2 ....
New England La *BAT* TN33 .... 13...
New England Ri *PTSD* BN41 .... 1...
New England Rd *BRI* BN1 ....
  SBGH/RUST TN4 ....
New England St *BRI* BN1 .... 6...
New Farthingdale *LING* RH7 ....
Newfield La *NEWHV* BN9 .... 8...
Newfield Rd *NEWHV* BN9 .... 8...
Newgate Rd *SLVH* TN37 ....
Newhache *LING* RH7 ....
Newhaven Rd *SEAF* BN25 .... 22...
Newhaven St *ROTT* BN2 ....
Newick Cl *SEAF* BN25 .... 232...
Newick Dr *RING/NEW* BN8 ....
Newick Hi *RING/NEW* BN8 ....
Newick La *MAYF* TN20 ....
Newick Rd *BRI* BN1 .... 1...
  EDN/EASTW BN20 .... 229...
Newlands *RRTW* TN3 ....
Newlands Av *BEXW* TN39 .... 19...

wlands Cl *HAS* TN34 .... 170 B6
PPT/KEY BN6 .... 119 C8
wlands Crs *EGRIN* RH19 .... 22 B1
wlands Ri *SBGH/RUST* TN4 ... 20 A5 🄰
wlands Rd *ROTT* BN2 .... 220 D2
BGH/RUST TN4 .... 20 B5
wlands Wy *SBGH/RUST* TN4 ... 20 B4 🄰
w Lydd Rd *RYE* TN31 .... 115 F8 🄱
wmans Wy *RHAS* TN35 .... 171 C7
wmarket Rd *ROTT* BN2 .... 7 E2 🄰
w Moorsite *RHAS* TN35 .... 139 H8
wnham Rd *HTHF* TN21 .... 100 A5
wnham Wy *HTHF* TN21 .... 100 A4
w Park Av *BEX* TN40 .... 195 H7
w Pl *EAST* BN21 .... 229 J8 🄱
CK TN22 .... 95 K8
w Pond Hl *HTHF* TN21 .... 99 H5
wport Rd *BURH* RH15 .... 89 F8
wport St *ROTT* BN2 .... 7 D3 🄰
w Rd *BRI* BN1 .... 6 C5 🄵🄱
ROW TN6 .... 39 H6
ROW TN26 .... 55 F3
AIL BN27 .... 161 H7
PPT/KEY BN6 .... 150 A2
EW BN7 .... 2 C4
N/ROSE BN22 .... 11 D4
OLE BN26 .... 215 G5
HAS TN35 .... 172 C1
HAS TN35 .... 199 C1
TON TN11 .... 17 J2
YE TN31 .... 81 J8
YE TN31 .... 113 K5
HOR BN43 .... 200 C4
CK TN22 .... 95 K8
v Steine *ROTT* BN2 .... 7 D6 🄰
OTT BN2 .... 7 D6 🄰
wtimber Dr *PTSD* BN41 .... 201 K2
wtimber Gdns *SHOR* BN43 ... 200 C2 🄰
vton Rd *EGRIN* RH19 .... 22 D5
vton Rd *LEW* BN7 .... 2 B3
EAHV BN10 .... 222 B4 🄱
vton St *BRI* BN1 .... 20 B7
wton Willows *RRTW* TN3 .... 28 A4
vtown Rd *HOVE* BN3 .... 203 D3
v Upperton Rd *EAST* BN21 ... 10 A3 🄱
v Way La *HPPT/KEY* BN6 .... 149 C1
v Winchelsea Rd *RYE* TN31 ... 143 H1
olson Dr *SHOR* BN43 .... 200 C3
htingale Cl *EGRIN* RH19 .... 22 B4 🄱
GNY BN23 .... 230 D1
ntingale La *BURH* RH15 .... 119 F3
ntingale La *UCK* TN22 .... 95 K7 🄰
St *BRI* BN1 .... 6 C5 🄱🄱
field Pl *ROTT* BN2 .... 205 F2
field Rd *BEXW* TN39 .... 194 D3
ells Av *HOVE* BN3 .... 203 J4
les La *HAIL* BN27 .... 162 H3
l Gn *BURH* RH15 .... 89 H7
l Ri *BURH* RH15 .... 89 H7
an Rd *ROTT* BN2 .... 206 B4
k Cl *RHAS* TN35 .... 171 G8 🄱
Nook *UCK* TN22 .... 95 K7 🄰
bury Cl *CROW* TN6 .... 39 C7
e Rd *NEWHV* BN9 .... 8 B4
folk Buildings *BRI* BN1 .... 6 A5 🄱
folk Cl *BEXW* TN39 .... 195 C4
folk Dr *STLEO* TN38 .... 169 C2 🄰
folk Ms *BRI* BN1 .... 6 A5 🄱
folk Rd *BRI* BN1 .... 6 A5
W TN1 .... 30 B1 🄰
folk Sq *BRI* BN1 .... 6 A5
folk St *BRI* BN1 .... 203 J6
folk Ter *BRI* BN1 .... 6 A4
ington Cl *RING/NEW* BN8 ..... 155 J5
ington Flds *RING/NEW* BN8 155 H4
ington La *RING/NEW* BN8 .... 155 J3
man Cl *BAT* TN33 .... 137 F7
EAF BN25 .... 224 C5 🄱
man Crs *SHOR* BN43 .... 200 C2
mandale *BEXW* TN39 .... 194 E8
mandy Cl *EGRIN* RH19 .... 22 D3 🄱
mandy Cl *SLVH* TN37 .... 4 A1
man Rd *BURH* RH15 .... 89 F8
OVE BN3 .... 202 D5
EWHV BN9 .... 8 C3
EV BN24 .... 218 A7
W TN1 .... 20 B6 🄱
LEO TN38 .... 4 A6
mansal Cl *SEAF* BN25 .... 225 H5 🄱
mansal Park Av *SEAF* BN25 225 C6
mansland *UCK* TN22 .... 67 H1
manton St *ROTT* BN2 .... 7 E3 🄰
stead Gdns *SBGH/RUST* TN4 ... 20 B4
champton Wy *STLEO* TN38 ... 169 H7 🄱
th Av *EDN/EASTW* BN20 .... 229 H5
th Bank *HPPT/KEY* BN6 ...... 118 E7
th Barnes La *LEW* BN7 .... 121 H4
th Beeches Rd *CROW* TN6 .... 53 J1
thbourne Cl *SHOR* BN43 ...... 200 C3 🄰
thbourne La *LW/ROSE* BN22 230 C4
thbridge St *RBTBR* TN32 ...... 78 B6
th Camp La *SEAF* BN25 .... 225 C6
thcliffe St *SEAF* BN25 .... 225 C7 🄰

North Cl *POLE* BN26 .... 215 G4
PTSD BN41 .... 201 K1
North Common Rd *RHWH* RH17 ... 91 F6
Northcote La *PEAHV* BN10 .... 221 K2 🄱
North Ct *HPPT/KEY* BN6 .... 118 E7
LEW BN7 .... 3 E4
Northdown Cl *NEWHV* BN9 .... 8 C4 🄱
Northdown Rd *NEWHV* BN9 .... 8 B4
North Dr *ROTT* BN2 .... 7 E4
Northease Cl *HOVE* BN3 .... 202 C1 🄱
Northease Dr *HOVE* BN3 .... 202 C1
Northease Gdns *HOVE* BN3 ... 176 D8 🄱
North End *HPPT/KEY* BN6 ...... 119 K7
Northern Av *POLE* BN26 .... 215 G4
North Farm La *RTWE/PEM* TN2 ... 20 D3
North Farm Rd *SBGH/RUST* TN4 ... 20 C4
Northfield *POLE* BN26 .... 214 E6
Northfield Cl *SEAF* BN25 .... 225 G6
Northfield Ri *HOVE* BN3 .... 176 C7
ROTT BN2 .... 220 D1
Northfields *RRTW* TN3 .... 18 E3
Northfield Wy *BRI* BN1 .... 178 B7
North Gdns *BRI* BN1 .... 6 B4
Northgate Cl *ROTT* BN2 .... 220 C1
Northgrove Rd *HAWK* TN18 ... 63 F1 🄱
North Heath Cl *HAIL* BN27 .... 189 H1 🄱
North Hill Rd *HAWK* TN18 ...... 62 C2
Northiam Ri *STLEO* TN38 .... 196 E1
Northiam Rd *EDN/EASTW* BN20 ... 229 H7
RYE TN31 .... 109 J4
North La *PTSD* BN41 .... 201 K1
RHAS TN35 .... 140 C6
North Pl *BRI* BN1 .... 6 C5 🄱
North Quay Rd *NEWHV* BN9 ... 9 D1
Northridge *RYE* TN31 .... 81 J5
North St *BEXW* TN39 .... 195 H4
BRI BN1 .... 6 B4 🄰
BRI BN1 .... 6 A1
HAIL BN27 .... 163 K1
PEV BN24 .... 218 A7
POLE BN26 .... 212 B8
PTSD BN41 .... 201 K1
RING/NEW BN8 .... 155 J5
STLEO TN38 .... 4 A3 🄱
North Ter *HAS* TN34 .... 5 F2
North Trade Rd *BAT* TN33 .... 135 K7
Northway *BURH* RH15 .... 89 J7
North Wy *LEW* BN7 .... 2 A3
NEWHV BN9 .... 8 C3
SEAF BN25 .... 225 G6
Northwood Av *ROTT* BN2 ...... 221 H2
Norton Cl *HOVE* BN3 .... 203 C5 🄱
Norton Dr *ROTT* BN2 .... 206 A2
Norton Rd *HOVE* BN3 .... 203 C5
NEWHV BN9 .... 9 E3
Norton Ter *NEWHV* BN9 .... 20 A2 🄱
Norway Rd *LW/ROSE* BN22 .... 11 F1
Norway St *PTSD* BN41 .... 202 B1
Norwich Cl *ROTT* BN2 .... 205 H1
Norwich Dr *ROTT* BN2 .... 205 H1
Nottidge Rd *SBGH/RUST* TN4 ... 29 H2 🄱
Novington La *LEW* BN7 .... 152 D2
Nunnery La *RTON* TN11 .... 17 J5
Nunnery Stable *LEW* BN7 .... 3 H2
Nursery Cl *HAIL* BN27 .... 189 H3 🄱
POLE BN26 .... 216 C5
PTSD BN41 .... 175 H7 🄱
SHOR BN43 .... 200 E3
WADH TN5 .... 47 F8
Nursery Fld *UCK* TN22 .... 68 C7
Nursery La *HAIL* BN27 .... 163 J6
UCK TN22 .... 50 C7
UCK TN22 .... 67 H6
UCK TN22 .... 95 K7
UCK TN22 .... 95 H4
Nursery Rd *SBGH/RUST* TN4 ... 20 B3
The Nursery *BURH* RH15 .... 89 J7
Nursery Wy *HTHF* TN21 .... 99 H5
Nuthatch Rd *LGNY* BN23 .... 216 D8
Nuthurst Cl *ROTT* BN2 .... 205 G3
Nuthurst Pl *ROTT* BN2 .... 205 G6
Nutley Av *ROTT* BN2 .... 221 C3
Nutley Cl *HOVE* BN3 .... 176 E8 🄱
RYE TN31 .... 113 K5
Nutley Mill Rd *PEV* BN24 .... 218 D6
Nye Cl *CROW* TN6 .... 53 H2

Nye La *HPPT/KEY* BN6 .... 150 E3
Nye Rd *BURH* RH15 .... 89 H8
Nyetimber Hl *ROTT* BN2 .... 205 F1

O

Oakapple Rd *STHW* BN42 .... 201 G1
Oak Cl *BRI* BN1 .... 177 K8
Oak Cft *EGRIN* RH19 .... 22 E3
Oakdale Rd *SBGH/RUST* TN4 ... 19 K7
Oakdene Av *PTSD* BN41 .... 175 H8
Oakdene Cl *PTSD* BN41 .... 175 H8
Oakdene Crs *PTSD* BN41 .... 175 H8
Oakdene Gdns *PTSD* BN41 .... 175 H8
Oakdene Ri *PTSD* BN41 .... 175 H7
Oakdene Wy *PTSD* BN41 .... 175 H8
Oak End Cl *SBGH/RUST* TN4 ... 20 A1
Oakenden La *EDEN* TN8 .... 16 D2
Oakenfield *BURH* RH15 .... 89 F6
Oakfield *HAWK* TN18 .... 63 F1
Oakfield Court Rd
  RTWE/PEM TN2 .... 20 C8 🄰
Oakfield Rd *RHAS* TN35 .... 171 F8 🄱
The Oak Fld *RHAS* TN35 .... 172 E2
The Oakfield *RYE* TN31 .... 113 H3
Oakfield Wy *BEXW* TN39 .... 194 B5
  EGRIN RH19 .... 12 B3
Oak Hall Pk *BURH* RH15 .... 119 H2
Oakhill Dr *RYE* TN31 .... 109 K6
Oakhurst Cl *HAS* TN34 .... 170 B6
Oakhurst Dr *CROW* TN6 .... 39 J6
Oakhurst Gdns *EGRIN* RH19 ... 22 A1
Oakhurst Rd *BAT* TN33 .... 136 D5
Oakland Dr *RBTBR* TN32 .... 77 H7
Oaklands *PEV* BN24 .... 216 E5
Oaklands Av *ROTT* BN2 .... 221 F2
Oaklands Cl *POLE* BN26 .... 215 G5 🄱
Oaklands Rd *HAWK* TN18 .... 63 F2
  RRTW TN3 .... 27 K5
Oaklands Wy *HAIL* BN27 .... 189 F5 🄱
Oaklea Cl *SLVH* TN37 .... 169 K7
Oakleaf Dr *POLE* BN26 .... 215 F4
Oaklea Wy *UCK* TN22 .... 95 H4
Oakleigh Dr *HTHF* TN21 .... 100 B5 🄱
Oakleigh Rd *BEXW* TN39 .... 194 B7
Oakley Cl *EGRIN* RH19 .... 23 F4
Oakmead Rd *BURH* RH15 .... 119 F2
Oakmede Wy *RING/NEW* BN8 155 H6
Oak Rd *RTWE/PEM* TN2 .... 20 D4
Oakroyd Cl *BURH* RH15 .... 89 J6
Oaks Cl *BUR/ETCH* TN19 .... 77 F2
The Oaks *BURH* RH15 .... 88 C7
  EGRIN RH19 .... 22 E3
  HTHF TN21 .... 100 B5
  SLVH TN37 .... 170 A6
Oaktree *RING/NEW* BN8 .... 123 J7 🄱
Oak Tree Cl *RTW* TN1 .... 30 A2
Oak Tree Ct *UCK* TN22 .... 95 K3
Oak Tree La *LGNY* BN23 .... 216 D7
Oak Tree Wy *HAIL* BN27 .... 189 H1
Oakwood Av *BEXW* TN39 .... 195 C4 🄱
Oakwood Cl *BURH* RH15 .... 119 H1
  HAS TN34 .... 5 D1
Oakwood Dr *UCK* TN22 .... 96 A3
Oakwood Pk *UCK* TN22 .... 50 C6
Oakwood Ri *RTWE/PEM* TN2 ... 20 E4
Oakwood Rd *BURH* RH15 .... 119 H1
Oast Cl *RTWE/PEM* TN2 .... 20 D4
Oasthouse Cl *HAS* TN34 .... 170 A6 🄱
Oast House Dr *RYE* TN31 .... 113 F7
Oast House Fld *WSEA* TN36 ... 141 K5
Oast House Rd *WSEA* TN36 ... 141 K6 🄱
Oban Rd *SLVH* TN37 .... 169 J8
Observatory Vw *HAIL* BN27 ... 189 J5
Ochiltree Cl *HAS* TN34 .... 170 D7
Ochiltree Rd *HAS* TN34 .... 170 D7
Ockenden Wy *HPPT/KEY* BN6 ... 118 E8
Ockley Hl *HPPT/KEY* BN6 ...... 119 H5
Ockley La *BURH* RH15 .... 119 H4
  HPPT/KEY BN6 .... 119 G2
Ockley Rd *HAWK* TN18 .... 63 G1
Ockley Wy *HPPT/KEY* BN6 ..... 119 G2
Ocklynge Cl *BEXW* TN39 .... 194 C6
Ocklynge Rd *EAST* BN21 .... 229 J7
Ockman La *RYE* TN31 .... 113 J6 🄱
Offa Rd *RHAS* TN35 .... 171 C8
Offham Cl *LW/ROSE* BN22 ..... 216 A7
  SEAF BN25 .... 225 C6 🄱
Offham Rd *LEW* BN7 .... 2 A3
Okehurst Rd *EAST* BN21 .... 229 H8
Oldaker Rd *RING/NEW* BN8 .... 93 H4
Old Barn Cl *EDN/EASTW* BN20 229 C2
Old Barn Wy *STHW* BN42 .... 201 K4
Old Boat Wk *BRI* BN1 .... 178 C4
Old Camp Rd *EDN/EASTW* BN20 236 C1
Old Church Rd *RTWE/PEM* TN2 ... 21 K2
  STLEO TN38 .... 169 H7
Old Court Cl *BRI* BN1 .... 178 A7
Old Dr *POLE* BN26 .... 214 E5
Old Dro *LGNY* BN23 .... 216 D8
Olde Place Ms *ROTT* BN2 .... 220 C2
Old Farm Rd *BEXW* TN39 .... 195 C5

BRI BN1 .... **178** A6
Oldfield Av *EDN/EASTW* BN20 .... **215** F8
Oldfield Crs *HAIL* BN27 .... **189** G2
STHW BN42 .... **201** C4
Oldfield Rd *HAIL/NEW* BN8 .... **215** F7
Old Forest La *CROW* TN6 .... **54** C3
Old Forewood La *BAT* TN33 ...... **168** A4
Old Forge La *UCK* TN22 .... **67** F3
Old Fort Rd *BRI* BN43 .... **200** D5
Old Gardens Cl *RTWE/PEM* TN2 ... **30** B3
Old Ghyll Rd *HTHF* TN21 .... **100** A6
Old Harrow Rd *SLVH* TN37 .... **169** J7
Old Heath Cl *RING/NEW* BN8 ... **126** E5
The Old Hop Gdn *RYE* TN31 ...... **112** C1
Old House Gdns *HAS* TN34 .... **170** C7
Old House La *RRTW* TN3 .... **18** B6
Oldlands *HPPT/KEY* BN6 .... **119** G7
Oldlands Hl *UCK* TN22 .... **67** J1
Old La *CROW* TN6 .... **39** F8
CROW TN6 .... **53** K2
MAYF TN20 .... **71** K1
Old London Rd *BRI* BN1 .... **177** K6
RHAS TN35 .... **171** G7 🔒
Old Lydd Rd *RYE* TN31 .... **145** G3
Old Malling Wy *LEW* BN7 .... **2** C2
Old Manor Cl *BEX* TN40 .... **195** J7
Old Mansion Cl *EDN/EASTW* BN20 .. **229** F3
Old Mill Cl *BRI* BN1 .... **177** K6
HAIL BN27 .... **161** F8 🔒
Old Mill La *POLE* BN26 .... **214** D8
Old Mill Pk *BEXW* TN39 .... **195** F5
Old Motcombe Ms *EAST* BN21 .. **229** J7 🔒
Old Orchard Pl *HAIL* BN27 .... **189** G4
Old Orchard Rd *EAST* BN21 .... **10** B5
Old Patcham Ms *BRI* BN1 .... **177** K5
Old Rectory Gdns *STHW* BN42 ... **201** C4
Old River Wy *WSEA* TN36 .... **143** H4
Old Rd *EGRIN* RH19 .... **22** D3
HAIL BN27 .... **162** A7
Old Roar Rd *SLVH* TN37 .... **169** K7
Old School La *RING/NEW* BN8 .. **155** K5 🔒
Old School La *POLE* BN26 .... **215** F4 🔒
Old School Pl *BURH* RH15 .... **119** F1
Old Shoreham Rd *BRI* BN1 .... **3** H3
HOVE BN3 .... **203** H3
STHW BN42 .... **201** J3
Old Steine *BRI* BN1 .... **6** C5 🔒
Old Swan La *HAIL* BN27 .... **189** J6
Old Timbers La *UCK* TN22 .... **95** J5
Old Top Rd *RHAS* TN35 .... **171** G7
Old Wardsdown *WADH* TN5 .... **47** F8
Old Willingdon Rd
EDN/EASTW BN20 .... **234** E2
Old Wish Rd *EAST* BN21 .... **10** B6 🔒
Oliver Cl *CROW* TN6 .... **53** J2
ROTT BN2 .... **7** E5
Olive Rd *HOVE* BN3 .... **202** D3
Olives Meadow *UCK* TN22 .... **95** K4
Onslow Rd *HOVE* BN3 .... **203** H2
Orange Rw *BRI* BN1 .... **6** C5 🔒
Orchard Av *HOVE* BN3 .... **203** F2
Orchard Cl *HAS* TN34 .... **5** D1
RTWE/PEM TN2 .... **20** D4
SHOR BN43 .... **200** B3
STHW BN42 .... **201** J3
Orchard Gdns *HOVE* BN3 .... **203** G2
Orchard La *HPPT/KEY* BN6 .... **119** J7
HPPT/KEY BN6 .... **119** F7
Orchard Ms *NEWHV* BN9 .... **224** A1 🔒
Orchard Ri *RRTW* TN3 .... **27** K4
Orchard Rd *BEX* TN40 .... **195** H5
BURH RH15 .... **89** F8
HOVE BN3 .... **203** F2
LEW BN7 .... **3** E3
The Orchard *BUR/ETCH* TN19 ... **77** G2
RYE TN31 .... **109** K7
UCK TN22 .... **50** C7
Orchard Wy *BURH* RH15 .... **89** F8 🔒
EGRIN RH19 .... **22** C2
RYE TN31 .... **112** C2
Orchid Cl *LGNY* BN23 .... **216** C8
Orchidhurst *RTWE/PEM* TN2 ...... **20** D4 🔒
Orchid Vw *BRI* BN1 .... **178** D5
Oriental Pl *BRI* BN1 .... **6** A5
Orion Cl *HAIL* BN27 .... **189** J3
Ormerod Av *STLEO* TN38 .... **169** H7
Ormonde Wy *SHOR* BN43 .... **200** A5
Orpen Rd *HOVE* BN3 .... **203** J2
Osbern Cl *BEXW* TN39 .... **194** B8
Osborne Cl *HAS* TN34 .... **4** C2
Osborne Hl *CROW* TN6 .... **54** A3
Osborne Rd *BRI* BN1 .... **204** A1
CROW TN6 .... **54** A2 🔒
EDN/EASTW BN20 .... **229** G7
Osborne Vls *HOVE* BN3 .... **203** G6
Osmers Hl *WADH* TN5 .... **44** B4
Osmunda Bank *EGRIN* RH19 ...... **12** C5
Osprey Dr *UCK* TN22 .... **96** A6
Osprey Pl *RTWE/PEM* TN2 .... **21** F5
Otham Court La *POLE* BN26 ..... **215** F3
Otham Rd *LW/ROSE* BN22 .... **230** B1
Otteham Cl *POLE* BN26 .... **215** G5

Oulton Cl *LGNY* BN23 .... **216** C8
Ousedale Cl *LEW* BN7 .... **2** B4
Outlook Av *PEAHV* BN10 .... **222** K5
The Outlook *EDN/EASTW* BN20 ... **234** E2
Oval Cl *PEAHV* BN10 .... **222** B1
Overdown Ri *PTSD* BN41 .... **175** J7
Overhill *STHW* BN42 .... **201** H2
Overhill Dr *BRI* BN1 .... **177** K6
Overhill Gdns *BRI* BN1 .... **177** K6
Overhill Wy *BRI* BN1 .... **177** K5
Overmead *SHOR* BN43 .... **200** B3
Over St *BRI* BN1 .... **6** C4
Overton Shaw *EGRIN* RH19 .... **12** C8
Ovingdean Cl *ROTT* BN2 .... **206** A6
Ovingdean Rd *ROTT* BN2 .... **206** A7
Owen Cl *BURH* RH15 .... **119** F2
Oxbottom Cl *RING/NEW* BN8 ..... **93** F5
Oxen Av *SHOR* BN43 .... **200** C3
Oxenbridge La *BUR/ETCH* TN19 ... **77** K5
Oxendean Gdns *LW/ROSE* BN22 ... **215** G7
Oxford Ct *BRI* BN1 .... **6** C3 🔒
Oxford Ms *HOVE* BN3 .... **203** H4
Oxford Pl *BRI* BN1 .... **6** C3 🔒
Oxford Rd *LW/ROSE* BN22 .... **11** D3 🔒
STLEO TN38 .... **169** H8
Oxford St *BRI* BN1 .... **6** C3
Ox Lea *RRTW* TN3 .... **18** E8
Oyster Creek *RYE* TN31 .... **114** B8

P

Packham Wy *BURH* RH15 .... **89** F7 🔒
Paddock Cl *RRTW* TN3 .... **17** K6
Paddock Gdns *EGRIN* RH19 .... **22** C4
POLE BN26 .... **214** E7
Paddock La *LEW* BN7 .... **2** C4 🔒
Paddock Rd *LEW* BN7 .... **2** C4 🔒
The Paddocks *EDEN* TN8 .... **15** H4
HAIL BN27 .... **189** F1
LEW BN7 .... **121** C5 🔒
LEW BN7 .... **208** C3
The Paddock *HOVE* BN3 .... **203** H2
LW/ROSE BN22 .... **230** A1
RTWE/PEM TN2 .... **21** J5
RYE TN31 .... **81** K4
SHOR BN43 .... **200** A2
UCK TN22 .... **67** G7
Padgham La *HTHF* TN21 .... **133** F5
Pages Av *BEXW* TN39 .... **194** E8
Pages Hl *HTHF* TN21 .... **99** J1
Pages Hl *HTHF* TN21 .... **99** H2
Pages La *BEXW* TN39 .... **194** D8
The Pagets *RING/NEW* BN8 .... **93** H4
Pagham Cl *PEV* BN24 .... **216** C7
Pain's Flat *RHWH* RH17 .... **88** D3
Palace Pl *BRI* BN1 .... **6** C5 🔒
Palesgate La *CROW* TN6 .... **54** C3
Palliser Rd *LGNY* BN23 .... **231** F5 🔒
Palma Cl *POLE* BN26 .... **215** F4
Palmeira Av *HOVE* BN3 .... **203** H5
Palmeira Sq *HOVE* BN3 .... **203** H6
Palmerston Rd *NEWHV* BN9 .... **9** F1
Pangdean La *HPPT/KEY* BN6 ..... **88** C2
Pangdene Cl *BURH* RH15 .... **118** E2
Pankhurst Av *ROTT* BN2 .... **7** E4
Pankhurst Cl *BEXW* TN39 .... **195** F3 🔒
Pankhurst Rd *BEXW* TN39 .... **195** F3
Pannel La *RHAS* TN35 .... **172** E1
Pannell Cl *EGRIN* RH19 .... **22** B2
Pannett *BURH* RH15 .... **88** C7 🔒
The Pantiles *RTWE/PEM* TN2 ..... **30** A1 🔒
The Parade *PEV* BN24 .... **218** B6
Paradise Cl *EDN/EASTW* BN20 ... **236** D1
Paradise Dr *EAST* BN21 .... **10** A5
EDN/EASTW BN20 .... **236** D2
The Paragon *EDN/EASTW* BN20 .. **214** E8
Parham Cl *ROTT* BN2 .... **7** F5
Park Av *BEXW* TN39 .... **195** G8
EAST BN21 .... **229** H4
HAS TN34 .... **4** B1
HOVE BN3 .... **202** D4
HPPT/KEY BN6 .... **150** B1
PEAHV BN10 .... **221** K3
SHOR BN43 .... **200** D3
Park Cl *BRI* BN1 .... **179** F6
BURH RH15 .... **89** F8
EDN/EASTW BN20 .... **229** J8 🔒
HAIL BN27 .... **189** G5
HAS TN34 .... **4** B1
HOVE BN3 .... **176** D8
PTSD BN41 .... **202** A2
SBGH/RUST TN4 .... **29** J1
Park Crs *CROW* TN6 .... **39** H8 🔒
FROW RH18 .... **36** A1
HAS TN34 .... **4** B1
PTSD BN41 .... **201** K3
ROTT BN2 .... **220** C2
Park Crescent Pl *ROTT* BN2 .... **7** D3
Park Crescent Rd *ROTT* BN2 .... **7** D3
Park Crescent Ter *ROTT* BN2 .... **7** D3
Park Cft *POLE* BN26 .... **215** F7
Park Dr *HAS* TN34 .... **4** B2

Park Drive Cl *NEWHV* BN9 .... **224** ●
Parker Cl *EAST* BN21 .... **10** ●
Parker Rd *HAS* TN34 .... **5** ●
Park Farm Cl *BUR/ETCH* TN19 ... **77** ●
Parkfield Av *LW/ROSE* BN22 .... **230** ●
Park Ga *HAIL* BN27 .... **161** ●
Park Hl *ROTT* BN2 .... ● ●
Park House Gdns *SBGH/RUST* TN4 .. **29** ●
Parkhurst Rd *BEXW* TN39 .... **195** ●
Parklands *SHOR* BN43 .... **200** ●
UCK TN22 .... **67** ●
Parklands Rd *HPPT/KEY* BN6 .... **119** ●
Park La *BAT* TN33 .... **138** ●
BEXW TN39 .... **195** ●
EAST BN21 .... **229** ●
RBTBR TN32 .... **107** ●
RING/NEW BN8 .... **155** ●
STHW BN42 .... **201** ●
Parkmore Ter *BRI* BN1 .... ● ●
Park Ri *HOVE* BN3 .... **176** ●
Park Rd *BEXW* TN39 .... **195** ●
BRI BN1 .... **178** ●
BURH RH15 .... **89** ●
CROW TN6 .... **54** ●
EGRIN RH19 .... **12** ●
EGRIN RH19 .... **13** ●
FROW RH18 .... **36** ●
HAIL BN27 .... **161** ●
HTHF TN21 .... **100** ●
LEW BN7 .... ● ●
PEAHV BN10 .... **222** ●
ROTT BN2 .... **206** ●
SBGH/RUST TN4 .... **29** ●
SBGH/RUST TN4 .... **29** ●
SEAF BN25 .... **224** ●
SHOR BN43 .... **200** ●
Park Road Ter *ROTT* BN2 .... ● ●
Park Shaw *BAT* TN33 .... **138** ●
Parkside *EGRIN* RH19 .... **13** ●
HPPT/KEY BN6 .... **119** ●
HTHF TN21 .... **100** ●
SHOR BN43 .... **200** ●
Parkside Rd *SEAF* BN25 .... **225** ●
The Parks *PTSD* BN41 .... **176** A●
Parkstone Rd *HAS* TN34 .... **170** ●
Park St *BRI* BN1 .... **178** ●
ROTT BN2 .... ● ●
RTWE/PEM TN2 .... **20** ●
The Park *CROW* TN6 .... **53** ●
ROTT BN2 .... **220** ●
Park Vw *HAS* TN34 .... **8** ●
RYE TN31 .... **81** ●
RYE TN31 .... **112** ●
UCK TN22 .... **67** ●
Park View Cl *PEAHV* BN10 .... **221** ●
Park View Ri *PEAHV* BN10 .... **221** ●
Parkview Rd *HOVE* BN3 .... **202** ●
Parkview Rd *UCK* TN22 .... **9** ●
Parkway *EDN/EASTW* BN20 ..... **229** ●
Park Wy *HAS* TN34 .... **4** ●
STHW BN42 .... **201** ●
Park Way Cl *STHW* BN42 .... **201** ●
Parkwood *RYE* TN31 .... **81** ●
Parkwood Cl *RTWE/PEM* TN2 ...... **20** ●
Park Wood Rd *HAS* TN34 .... **170** ●
Parrock La *HRTF* TN7 .... **37** ●
Parry Cl *LGNY* BN23 .... **217** ●
Parsonage Cl *SBGH/RUST* TN4 ... **19** ●
Parsonage La *RHAS* TN35 .... **138** ●
RRTW TN3 .... **33** ●
WSEA TN36 .... **143** ●
Parsonage Rd *EAST* BN21 .... **229** ●
SBGH/RUST TN4 .... **1** ●
Parsons Cl *STLEO* TN38 .... **169** ●
Pashley Rd *EDN/EASTW* BN20 ... **234** ●
Paston Pl *ROTT* BN2 .... ● ●
Patcham By-pass *BRI* BN1 .... **177** ●
Patcham Gra *BRI* BN1 .... **177** ●
Patcham Mill Rd *PEV* BN24 ...... **217** ●
Patchdean *BRI* BN1 .... **177** ●
Paton Rd *BEXW* TN39 .... **194** ●
Paul Cl *HAIL* BN27 .... **161** ●
Pavilion Buildings *BRI* BN1 .... **6** C●
Pavilion Cl *HPPT/KEY* BN6 ...... **118** ●
Pavilion Pde *ROTT* BN2 .... **6** C●
Pavilion St *ROTT* BN2 .... **6** C●
Pavilion Wy *EGRIN* RH19 .... **2** ●
Paxhill Cl *STLEO* TN38 .... **169** ●
Paygate Rd *BAT* TN33 .... **138** ●
Payne Av *HOVE* BN3 .... **203** ●
Paynsbridge Wy *HTHF* TN21 .... **129** ●
Paynters Wy *RING/NEW* BN8 ...... ● ●
Paynton Rd *SLVH* TN37 .... **169** ●
Paythorne Cl *STHW* BN42 .... **201** ●
Payton Dr *BURH* RH15 .... **119** ●
Peace Cl *BRI* BN1 .... ● ●
Peacock La *BRI* BN1 .... **177** ●
Peakdean Cl *EDN/EASTW* BN20 ... **236** ●
Peakdean La *EDN/EASTW* BN20 ... **236** ●
Pearse Rd *RRTW* TN3 .... ● ●
Peartree Cl *BURH* RH15 .... **89** ●
Peartree Fld *WSEA* TN36 .... **141** ●
Peartree Hl *WADH* TN5 .... **5** ●
Peartree La *BEXW* TN39 .... **19** ●
Pebble Rd *PEV* BN24 .... **21** ●

osham Dr BEX TN40 ...... 196 B5
osham La BEX TN40 ...... 196 A5
ckham Cl LEW BN7 ...... 2 C2
elings La PEV BN24 ...... 216 C5
el Rd ROTT BN2 ...... 205 G7
asus Wy EGRIN RH19 ...... 12 E8
ler Av NEWHV BN9 ...... 8 B4
well Cl HAS TN34 ...... 4 C2
ham Cl PEAHV BN10 ...... 222 C2
 EV BN24 ...... 217 G6
ham Crs HAIL BN27 ...... 189 H5
 AS TN34 ...... 5 E5
ham Pl HAS TN34 ...... 5 D5
ham Ri PEAHV BN10 ...... 222 B2
ham Rd SEAF BN25 ...... 232 A1
ham Sq BRI BN1 ...... 6 C4
ham Ter LEW BN7 ...... 2 C3
ham Yd SEAF BN25 ...... 232 A1
lbrook Rd LEW BN7 ...... 2 A2
 Cl WADH TN5 ...... 44 C5
lings Farm Cl CROW TN6 ...... 53 K1
lings Ri CROW TN6 ...... 39 K8
wood Rd RYE TN31 ...... 145 J1
nbroke Av HOVE BN3 ...... 203 F5
nbroke La HAIL BN27 ...... 161 H8
nbroke Crs HOVE BN3 ...... 203 F4
nbroke Gdns HOVE BN3 ...... 203 F5
nbury Cl RTWE/PEM TN2 ...... 21 K4
nbury Gra RTWE/PEM TN2 ...... 21 G5
nbury Gv BEXW TN39 ...... 195 F4
nbury Rd LGNY BN23 ...... 230 E2
 TWE/PEM TN2 ...... 20 C8
nnybridge La MAYF TN20 ...... 56 D6
nny La BEX TN40 ...... 196 B6
rith Wy LGNY BN23 ...... 216 F2
nsford Dr LGNY BN23 ...... 230 E1
nshurst Rd RTON TN11 ...... 18 B1
atland Cl LGNY BN23 ...... 216 E8
 LVH TN37 ...... 169 K6
opercombe Rd
 DN/EASTW BN20 ...... 229 G7
oper Dr BURH RH15 ...... 118 E1
 URH RH15 ...... 119 F2
ch La RRTW TN3 ...... 33 F2
cival Crs LW/ROSE BN22 ...... 216 A8
cival Rd LW/ROSE BN22 ...... 216 A8
cival Ter ROTT BN2 ...... 7 F6
cy Rd RHAS TN35 ...... 171 F8
ryfields BURH RH15 ...... 88 E7
ry Av EGRIN RH19 ...... 12 C8
ry Hl ROTT BN2 ...... 221 F1
ryman's La RHWH RH17 ...... 49 H8
th Cl SEAF BN25 ...... 225 K8
th Rd SLVH TN37 ...... 169 J8
er James La RYE TN31 ...... 145 G1
er James La RHAS TN35 ...... 172 B4
t Cl ROTT BN2 ...... 205 G5
t La WSEA TN36 ...... 142 B7
t Level Rd RHAS TN35 ...... 172 E5
 WSEA TN36 ...... 143 G8
t Rd RHAS TN35 ...... 171 K4
 HAS TN35 ...... 173 J1
worth Dr BURH RH15 ...... 89 G7
worth Pl LW/ROSE BN22 ...... 229 K1
worth Rd BRI BN1 ...... 178 C5
ensey Bay Rd LGNY BN23 ...... 231 F3
ensey Cl SEAF BN25 ...... 225 J7
ensey Park Rd PEV BN24 ...... 217 G4
ensey Rd EAST BN21 ...... 11 D4
 EWHV BN9 ...... 8 A5
 OLE BN26 ...... 215 G5
 OTT BN2 ...... 7 E2
 TLEO TN38 ...... 4 A5
 Peverells SEAF BN25 ...... 225 H6
ton Cl LGNY BN23 ...... 231 G4
enix Cswy LEW BN7 ...... 3 D4
enix Crs STHW BN42 ...... 201 G3
enix La EGRIN RH19 ...... 23 J5
enix Pl LEW BN7 ...... 3 D4
 OTT BN2 ...... 7 D4
enix Ri ROTT BN2 ...... 7 D4
enix Wy STHW BN42 ...... 201 G3
llis Av PEAHV BN10 ...... 222 A4
ardy La BAT TN33 ...... 136 E7
cadilly La MAYF TN20 ...... 72 D2
ketts La UCK TN22 ...... 66 D4
xforde La WADH TN5 ...... 60 C2
on St ROTT BN2 ...... 7 E3
dinghoe Av PEAHV BN10 ...... 222 C5
dinghoe Cl PEAHV BN10 ...... 222 C4

Piddinghoe Md NEWHV BN9 ...... 8 B2
Pilmer Rd CROW TN6 ...... 39 H8
Pilot Rd HAS TN34 ...... 170 D7
Piltdown Cl BEXW TN39 ...... 195 G7
 HAS TN34 ...... 4 C5
Piltdown Ri UCK TN22 ...... 95 K3
Piltdown Rd ROTT BN2 ...... 205 G5
Piltdown Wy LW/ROSE BN22 ...... 216 B7
Pinders Rd RHAS TN35 ...... 199 G1
Pine Av HAS TN34 ...... 5 F1
Pine Gv CROW TN6 ...... 53 G1
Pinehurst BURH RH15 ...... 119 G2
Pine Tree Cl HPPT/KEY BN6 ...... 118 B6
Pine Tree Rd HTHF TN21 ...... 100 A4
Pine Wk UCK TN22 ...... 95 K3
Pine Wy HAIL BN27 ...... 189 F4
Pine Way Cl EGRIN RH19 ...... 22 C3
Pinewood Cha CROW TN6 ...... 39 F8
Pinewood Cl LW/ROSE BN22 ...... 229 J1
 SEAF BN25 ...... 225 G7
Pinewood Gdns SBGH/RUST TN4 ...... 20 A1
Pinewood Rd RTWE/PEM TN2 ...... 20 D6
Pinewoods BEXW TN39 ...... 194 D7
Pinewood Wy HWH RH16 ...... 89 K1
 STLEO TN38 ...... 169 F8
Pinfold Cl ROTT BN2 ...... 206 B5
Pinton Hl WADH TN5 ...... 45 K8
Pinwell Rd LEW BN7 ...... 3 D5
Pipers Cl SEAF BN25 ...... 225 H6
 HOVE BN3 ...... 176 B8
 WADH TN5 ...... 44 C7
Pipers Fld UCK TN22 ...... 95 K7
Piper's Ga UCK TN22 ...... 95 K7
Pipit Meadow UCK TN22 ...... 95 K6
Pitreavie Dr HAIL BN27 ...... 189 F3
Pit Rd HPPT/KEY BN6 ...... 118 A6
Pitt Dr SEAF BN25 ...... 225 H6
Pitt Gdns ROTT BN2 ...... 206 A3
Place La SEAF BN25 ...... 225 F8
Plainfields Av BRI BN1 ...... 178 B4
Plaistow Cl ROTT BN2 ...... 205 G5
The Plat RYE TN31 ...... 81 K5
The Platt LING RH7 ...... 12 E3
Plaw Hatch La EGRIN RH19 ...... 34 C6
Playden Cl ROTT BN2 ...... 205 F7
Playden Gdns HAS TN34 ...... 170 E7
Playden La RYE TN31 ...... 85 H8
Pleasant View Rd CROW TN6 ...... 39 G7
Plemont Gdns BEXW TN39 ...... 195 F5
Pleyden Ri BEXW TN39 ...... 193 J7
Plough La SLVH TN37 ...... 12 E1
Plough Rd LING RH7 ...... 12 E1
Plover Cl LGNY BN23 ...... 230 D1
Plover Ct STLEO TN38 ...... 169 F8
Plumpton Bostall LEW BN7 ...... 152 A5
Plumpton Cl BEX TN40 ...... 195 H5
 LW/ROSE BN22 ...... 216 B2
Plumpton La LEW BN7 ...... 152 B3
Plumpton Rd ROTT BN2 ...... 7 F4
Plymouth Av ROTT BN2 ...... 205 G2
Plymouth Cl LGNY BN23 ...... 231 G3
Plynlimmon Rd HAS TN34 ...... 5 J6
Pocock's Rd EAST BN21 ...... 229 J6
Polegate By-pass POLE BN26 ...... 214 E4
Polesden Rd RTWE/PEM TN2 ...... 30 D1
Polley Cl RTWE/PEM TN2 ...... 21 K4
Pollington Pl CROW TN6 ...... 53 H1
Pomper La HPPT/KEY BN6 ...... 118 A1
Pond Cl RYE TN31 ...... 109 K6
Pond Rd SHOR BN43 ...... 200 C4
Pond Wy EGRIN RH19 ...... 23 F2
Ponswood Rd STLEO TN38 ...... 197 J1
Pont Cl HTHF TN21 ...... 99 J5
Pook Reed La HTHF TN21 ...... 100 A5
Pool Va BRI BN1 ...... 6 C6
Poona Rd RTWE/PEM TN2 ...... 30 D1
Poplar Av HOVE BN3 ...... 176 B8
Poplar Cl BRI BN1 ...... 204 A1
 HOVE BN3 ...... 176 D8
The Poplars HPPT/KEY BN6 ...... 119 G8
Poppinghole La RBTBR TN32 ...... 106 D2
Popps La BEXW TN39 ...... 194 B8
Porters Wy POLE BN26 ...... 215 F5
Portfield Av BRI BN1 ...... 178 B5
Portfield Cl BEX TN40 ...... 195 J6
Port Hall Av BRI BN1 ...... 6 A2
Port Hall Ms BRI BN1 ...... 6 A2
Port Hall Pl BRI BN1 ...... 6 A2
Port Hall Rd HOVE BN3 ...... 6 A2
Port Hall St BRI BN1 ...... 6 A2
Portland Av HOVE BN3 ...... 202 D4
Portland Cl HAIL BN27 ...... 189 F2
Portland Pl HAS TN34 ...... 5 D4
 ROTT BN2 ...... 7 E6
Portland Rd BURH RH15 ...... 89 F8
 EGRIN RH19 ...... 22 C3
 HOVE BN3 ...... 202 C3
The Portlands LGNY BN23 ...... 231 G4
Portland St BRI BN1 ...... 6 B5
Portland Vls HOVE BN3 ...... 202 C4
Port Rd LW/ROSE BN22 ...... 230 B2
Portsdown Wy EDN/EASTW BN20 ...... 229 K1
Port Vw NEWHV BN9 ...... 223 K1
Possingworth Cl HTHF TN21 ...... 98 D3
Post Horn La FROW RH18 ...... 36 A2

Post Office Rd HAWK TN18 ...... 63 F1
Potato La RING/NEW BN8 ...... 155 K6
Potman's La BEXW TN39 ...... 194 D1
Pottens Mill La MAYF TN20 ...... 73 F7
The Potteries UCK TN22 ...... 95 K7
Potters Fld RING/NEW BN8 ...... 155 J5
Potters La BURH RH15 ...... 119 F2
 LEW BN7 ...... 2 C5
Pottery Cl RYE TN31 ...... 139 H1
Pottery La RYE TN31 ...... 139 H1
Pottingfield Rd RYE TN31 ...... 113 G5
Pound Cl LGNY BN23 ...... 231 G5
Poundfield Rd CROW TN6 ...... 53 K1
Pound La RING/NEW BN8 ...... 157 K4
 UCK TN22 ...... 97 F5
Poundsbridge Hl RRTW TN3 ...... 18 B5
The Pound BURH RH15 ...... 89 F7
Poveys Cl BURH RH15 ...... 88 D8
Powdermill Cl RTWE/PEM TN2 ...... 20 C5
Powdermill La BAT TN33 ...... 166 D3
 RYE TN31 ...... 109 F8
Powder Mill La SBGH/RUST TN4 ...... 20 B4
Powell Gdns NEWHV BN9 ...... 9 E1
Powell Rd RING/NEW BN8 ...... 93 H4
Powis Gv BRI BN1 ...... 6 A3
Powis Rd BRI BN1 ...... 6 A4
Powis Sq BRI BN1 ...... 6 A4
Powis Vls BRI BN1 ...... 6 B4
Poynings Cl SEAF BN25 ...... 232 E1
Poynings Dr HOVE BN3 ...... 176 E8
Poynter Rd HOVE BN3 ...... 203 F3
Pratt's Folly La CROW TN6 ...... 53 G2
Precincts Castle LEW BN7 ...... 2 C4
Preemans La UCK TN22 ...... 68 A1
Preston Dro BRI BN1 ...... 204 A1
Preston Gv UCK TN22 ...... 96 D5
Preston Park Av BRI BN1 ...... 6 B1
Preston Rd BEXW TN39 ...... 195 G4
 BRI BN1 ...... 6 A1
 BRI BN1 ...... 203 K1
Preston St BRI BN1 ...... 6 A5
Prestonville Rd BRI BN1 ...... 6 B3
Prideaux Rd EAST BN21 ...... 10 A2
Primrose Cl BURH RH15 ...... 88 D7
 LGNY BN23 ...... 216 C8
Primrose Hl BEXW TN39 ...... 194 E5
 RHAS TN35 ...... 172 E6
Primrose La FROW RH18 ...... 36 A2
Prince Albert St BRI BN1 ...... 6 C5
Prince Charles Cl STHW BN42 ...... 201 J2
Prince Charles Rd LEW BN7 ...... 3 E2
Prince Edward's Rd LEW BN7 ...... 2 B4
Prince Regent's Cl ROTT BN2 ...... 205 F7
Princes Av HOVE BN3 ...... 203 F5
Princes Cl SEAF BN25 ...... 225 F7
 UCK TN22 ...... 95 G4
Princes Crs HOVE BN3 ...... 203 F5
 ROTT BN2 ...... 7 D2
Prince's Pl BRI BN1 ...... 6 C5
Princes Rd LGNY BN23 ...... 231 F4
 ROTT BN2 ...... 7 D2
 SLVH TN37 ...... 4 B5
Princess Dr SEAF BN25 ...... 224 E6
Princes Sq HOVE BN3 ...... 203 F5
Prince's St ROTT BN2 ...... 6 C5
 RTWE/PEM TN2 ...... 20 C8
Prince's Ter ROTT BN2 ...... 205 F7
Prince William Pde LGNY BN23 ...... 231 F5
Prinkle La HAIL BN27 ...... 163 K2
Prinsep Rd HOVE BN3 ...... 203 F3
Prior's Wy EDEN TN8 ...... 15 G5
Priory Av HAS TN34 ...... 4 C3
Priory Cl HAS TN34 ...... 4 C3
 PEV BN24 ...... 218 A6
Priory Crs LEW BN7 ...... 2 C5
Priory Hts EDN/EASTW BN20 ...... 229 F6
Priory La LGNY BN23 ...... 217 F8
Priory Orch LGNY BN23 ...... 231 F3
Priory Rd BURH RH15 ...... 119 G2
 FROW RH18 ...... 34 H1
 HAS TN34 ...... 5 E4
 HPPT/KEY BN6 ...... 118 E2
 LGNY BN23 ...... 217 F8
Priory St HAS TN34 ...... 4 C4
 LEW BN7 ...... 2 C5
Promenade PEAHV BN10 ...... 221 K5
The Promenade PEV BN24 ...... 218 A7
Prospect Gdns EAST BN21 ...... 229 J7
Prospect Pk SBGH/RUST TN4 ...... 19 K2
Prospect Pl HAS TN34 ...... 4 C5
Prospect Rd HTHF TN21 ...... 100 B5
 RTWE/PEM TN2 ...... 20 B8
 SBGH/RUST TN4 ...... 19 G2
Providence Pl BRI BN1 ...... 6 C3
Prowting Md BEXW TN39 ...... 194 B7
Pudding Cake La UCK TN22 ...... 95 J4
Pulborough Av LW/ROSE BN22 ...... 229 K2
Pulborough Cl ROTT BN2 ...... 205 G4
Pump La UCK TN22 ...... 127 F1
Purbeck Cl LGNY BN23 ...... 216 D8
Pyecombe St POY/PYE BN45 ...... 149 F5

Q

Quadrant *BRI* BN1 .... 6 B5
The Quadrant *EAST* BN21 .... 10 A3 ⊡
   HPPT/KEY BN6 .... 119 G7
Quantock Cl *LGNY* BN23 .... 216 E8 ⊡
   RTWE/PEM TN2 .... 20 D6
Quantock Gdns *HAS* TN34 .... 5 F1
Quarry Bank Rd *BRI* BN1 .... 204 C1 ⊡
Quarry Cl *BURH* RH15 .... 89 K8
Quarry Crs *HAS* TN34 .... 5 E5
Quarry HI *STLEO* TN38 .... 197 J4
Quarry La *SEAF* BN25 .... 225 H6
Quarry Ri *EGRIN* RH19 .... 12 E8
Quarry Rd *HAS* TN34 .... 5 D3
   NEWHV BN9 .... 8 C5
   RTW TN1 .... 20 B6
Quebec Cl *BEXW* TN39 .... 195 F6 ⊡
   LGNY BN23 .... 231 G4 ⊡
Quebec Rd *STLEO* TN38 .... 169 H7
Quebec St *ROTT* BN2 .... 7 D4
Queen Alexandra Av *HOVE* BN3 .. 177 F8 ⊡
Queen Anne's Cl *LEW* BN7 .... 2 C4 ⊡
Queen Caroline Cl *HOVE* BN3 .... 177 F8 ⊡
Queen Elizabeth Av *BURH* RH15 .. 119 F1
Queen Mary Av *HOVE* BN3 .... 177 F8
Queens Ap *UCK* TN22 .... 95 K2 ⊡
Queensbury Ms *BRI* BN1 .... 6 A5 ⊡
Queen's Colonnade Gdns
   EAST BN21 .... 11 D4 ⊡
Queens Cottages *WADH* TN5 ...... 44 A6
Queens Ct *HAWK* TN18 .... 63 G1
Queens Crs *BURH* RH15 .... 119 G1
   LGNY BN23 .... 230 E4
Queensdown School Rd *BRI* BN1 .. 178 D8
Queens Dr *HPPT/KEY* BN6 .... 67 F7
   UCK TN22 .... 67 F7
Queen's Gdns *BRI* BN1 .... 6 C4 ⊡
   HOVE BN3 .... 203 H6
   SBGH/RUST TN4 .... 20 B5
Queensmount *MAYF* TN20 .... 71 F4
Queens Park Gdns *SEAF* BN25 .... 224 D7 ⊡
Queen's Park Ri *ROTT* BN2 .... 7 E4
Queen's Park Rd *ROTT* BN2 .... 7 D5
Queen's Park Ter *ROTT* BN2 .... 7 D5
Queen's Pl *BRI* BN1 .... 6 B5
   HOVE BN3 .... 203 H6
   SHOR BN43 .... 200 C5
Queen Sq *BRI* BN1 .... 6 B5
Queen's Rd *BRI* BN1 .... 6 B4
   CROW TN6 .... 53 H5
   EGRIN RH19 .... 22 C3
   HAIL BN27 .... 163 F6
   HAS TN34 .... 5 D5 ⊡
   HAWK TN18 .... 63 G1
   LEW BN7 .... 3 D2
   LGNY BN23 .... 230 E4
   SBGH/RUST TN4 .... 20 B5
   STHW BN42 .... 201 H2
Queensway *EGRIN* RH19 .... 22 C3 ⊡
   ROTT BN2 .... 7 F4
   SEAF BN25 .... 225 H6
   STLEO TN38 .... 169 F6
Queen Victoria Av *HOVE* BN3 ..... 177 F8
Querneby Cl *SHOR* BN43 .... 201 G4 ⊡
Quickbourne La *RYE* TN31 .... 82 A4
Quinnell Dr *HAIL* BN27 .... 189 C1
Quintin Cl *HAIL* BN27 .... 189 F6 ⊡

R

Radcliffe Cl *SLVH* TN37 .... 4 A1
Radinden Dr *HOVE* BN3 .... 203 J2
Radinden Manor Rd *HOVE* BN3 .... 203 J3
Radnor Ms *STLEO* TN38 .... 197 F2 ⊡
Ragged Dog La *HTHF* TN21 .... 99 F3
Railway Ap *EGRIN* RH19 .... 22 B2
   NEWHV BN9 .... 9 D3
Railway La *LEW* BN7 .... 3 D4
Railway Rd *NEWHV* BN9 .... 9 D3
Railway St *BRI* BN1 .... 6 B4 ⊡
Raleigh Cl *LGNY* BN23 .... 231 F4
   SHOR BN43 .... 200 B5
Ramsay Wy *LGNY* BN23 .... 231 F4
Ramslye Rd *SBGH/RUST* TN4 ...... 29 H2
Randolph La *RYE* TN31 .... 85 G8
Ranelagh Vls *HOVE* BN3 .... 203 G3
Rangemore Dr *EAST* BN21 .... 229 J4
Rangemore Rd *RTWE/PEM* TN2 ... 20 D4
Ranmore Cl *HAS* TN34 .... 170 B5
Rannoch Rd *CROW* TN6 .... 53 F1
Rannoch Rd West *CROW* TN6 ...... 53 F1 ⊡
Ranscombe Hi *RING/NEW* BN8 ... 183 F5
Ransombe La *RING/NEW* BN8 .... 183 G5
Ranworth Cl *LGNY* BN23 .... 216 C7 ⊡
Raphael Rd *HOVE* BN3 .... 202 E4
Rapson's Rd *EDN/EASTW* BN20 ... 214 E8
Rastrick Cl *BURH* RH15 .... 119 F2
Rattle Rd *PEV* BN24 .... 216 E6
Ratton Dr *EDN/EASTW* BN20 ..... 229 G4

Ratton Rd *EAST* BN21 .... 10 A3
Raven Ct *BAT* TN33 .... 137 F7 ⊡
   STLEO TN38 .... 169 F8
Ravensbourne Av *SHOR* BN43 ... 200 C2
Ravensbourne Cl *SHOR* BN43 .... 200 C2 ⊡
Ravens Cl *BEXW* TN39 .... 194 B8
Ravens Cft *EDN/EASTW* BN20 ... 237 F3 ⊡
Raven's Rd *SHOR* BN43 .... 200 C4
Ravenswood Av *RTW* TN1 .... 20 C5
Ravenswood Dr *ROTT* BN2 .... 206 C5
Ravenswood Rd *BURH* RH15 .... 89 H8
Ravine Cl *HAS* TN34 .... 5 E1
Rayford Cl *PEAHV* BN10 .... 222 B4 ⊡
Raymond Cl *SEAF* BN25 .... 225 H6
Readers La *RYE* TN31 .... 85 F6
Reading Rd *ROTT* BN2 .... 205 G7
Rectory Cl *BUR/ETCH* TN19 .... 75 K5
   EDN/EASTW BN20 .... 229 J8
   NEWHV BN9 .... 8 B6
   RING/NEW BN8 .... 127 J6
   SHOR BN43 .... 201 G4
   STLEO TN38 .... 197 J2 ⊡
Rectory Fld *HRTF* TN7 .... 26 A7
Rectory La *RYE* TN31 .... 82 D6
   RYE TN31 .... 113 H3
   WSEA TN36 .... 142 E5
Rectory Rd *NEWHV* BN9 .... 223 K1
   SHOR BN43 .... 200 D3
Rectory Wy *BEX* TN40 .... 195 J6
Redbridge La *CROW* TN6 .... 53 F6
Redbrook La *UCK* TN22 .... 69 F7
Redcross St *BRI* BN1 .... 6 C4
Redford Cl *LGNY* BN23 .... 231 F2 ⊡
Redgeland Ri *STLEO* TN38 .... 197 G1
Redgill La *RING/NEW* BN8 .... 93 F2
Redhill Cl *BRI* BN1 .... 177 H6
Redhill Dr *BRI* BN1 .... 177 H7
Red Lake Ter *RHAS* TN35 .... 171 G7 ⊡
Redleaf Cl *RTWE/PEM* TN2 .... 20 D5
Red Oak *HAWK* TN18 .... 62 E3
Redoubt Rd *LW/ROSE* BN22 .... 11 E3
Redvers Rd *ROTT* BN2 .... 7 F1
Redwell Av *BEXW* TN39 .... 195 G3 ⊡
Redwings La *RTWE/PEM* TN2 ...... 21 K1
Redwood Dr *HWH* RH16 .... 89 K1
Reedham Rd *LGNY* BN23 .... 216 C7 ⊡
Reedswood Rd *RYE* TN31 .... 109 K7
   STLEO TN38 .... 197 F3
Reeves HI *BRI* BN1 .... 178 E6
Reeves Ter *WADH* TN5 .... 60 C2 ⊡
Regal Ct *RYE* TN31 .... 22 D3
Regency Cl *UCK* TN22 .... 95 J4
Regency Gdns *STLEO* TN38 .... 197 H3
Regency Ms *BRI* BN1 .... 6 A5
   EDN/EASTW BN20 .... 10 C6 ⊡
Regency Rd *BRI* BN1 .... 6 A5
Regency Sq *BRI* BN1 .... 6 A5
Regent Hi *BRI* BN1 .... 6 B5
Regent Pl *STLEO* TN38 .... 169 G4
Regent Rw *BRI* BN1 .... 6 B5 ⊡
Regents Cl *SEAF* BN25 .... 225 F6
Regent St *BRI* BN1 .... 6 C5 ⊡
Reginald Rd *BEXW* TN39 .... 195 G7
Regnum Cl *LW/ROSE* BN22 .... 215 K7
Reigate Rd *BRI* BN1 .... 203 J2
Resting Oak Hi *RING/NEW* BN8 . 122 D7
Reynolds Dr *BEX* TN40 .... 195 K6
Reynolds La *SBGH/RUST* TN4 ...... 19 K5
   LGNY BN23 .... 230 E2
Reynolds Rd *HOVE* BN3 .... 202 E4
   LGNY BN23 .... 230 E2
Reynoldstown La *POLE* BN26 .... 214 E5 ⊡
Riccards La *BAT* TN33 .... 137 L3
Rices Hi *EGRIN* RH19 .... 22 C2
Richardson Rd *HOVE* BN3 .... 202 C4
   SBGH/RUST TN4 .... 20 A5
Richborough Cl *HAS* TN34 .... 170 A7 ⊡
Richington Wy *SEAF* BN25 .... 225 J6
Richland Cl *RHAS* TN35 .... 171 G7
Richmead Gdns *MAYF* TN20 .... 72 B3
Richmond Av *BEXW* TN39 .... 194 E8
Richmond Cl *BEXW* TN39 .... 195 F8
Richmond Pde *ROTT* BN2 .... 7 D4 ⊡
Richmond Pl *ROTT* BN2 .... 6 C4
Richmond Rd *BEXW* TN39 .... 194 E8
   ROTT BN2 .... 7 D2
   SEAF BN25 .... 224 E8
Richmond St *HAS* TN34 .... 199 F1 ⊡
   ROTT BN2 .... 7 D4
Richmond Ter *SEAF* BN25 .... 225 F8 ⊡
Richmond Wy *EGRIN* RH19 .... 22 D3
Riddens Cl *LEW* BN7 .... 121 C6
Riddens La *LEW* BN7 .... 121 G5
Riddlesdale Av *SBGH/RUST* TN4 .. 20 A5
Riders Bolt *BEXW* TN39 .... 194 D6
The Ride *BRI* BN1 .... 179 J4
Ridge Cl *PTSD* BN41 .... 175 K7 ⊡
   UCK TN22 .... 50 C6
Ridge Lands Cl
   EDN/EASTW BN20 .... 229 H8 ⊡
Ridge Rd *BRI* BN1 .... 179 K3
Ridgeside Av *BRI* BN1 .... 177 K6
The Ridge *HAS* TN34 .... 170 E7
   SLVH TN37 .... 169 K5
   WSEA TN36 .... 143 H6
Ridge Vw *BRI* BN1 .... 179 F6

Ridge Wy *HWH* RH16 .... 90 ⊡
Ridgeway *BUR/ETCH* TN19 .... 6 ⊡
   EGRIN RH19 .... 2 ⊡
   PTSD BN41 .... 201 ⊡
   RTWE/PEM TN2 .... 21 ⊡
Ridgeway Cl *HTHF* TN21 .... 10 ⊡
   STHW BN42 .... 20 ⊡
The Ridgewaye *SBGH/RUST* TN4 .. 2 ⊡
Ridgeway Gdns *ROTT* BN2 .... 206 ⊡
The Ridgeway *BURH* RH15 .... 89 ⊡
   EDN/EASTW BN20 .... 22 ⊡
   HAIL BN27 .... 163 ⊡
   SEAF BN25 .... 225 ⊡
The Ridge West *SLVH* TN37 ...... 16 ⊡
Ridgewood Av *ROTT* BN2 .... 20 ⊡
Ridgewood Cl *UCK* TN22 .... 95 ⊡
Ridgewood Gdns *BEX* TN40 .... 19 ⊡
   HAS TN34 .... 17 ⊡
Ridgway Cl *ROTT* BN2 .... 20 ⊡
Ridgway Paddock *LEW* BN7 ...... 18 ⊡
The Ridgway *ROTT* BN2 .... 20 ⊡
The Ridings *BEXW* TN39 .... 19 ⊡
   BURH RH15 .... 11 ⊡
   PEAHV BN10 .... 22 ⊡
   RING/NEW BN8 .... 9 ⊡
   RTWE/PEM TN2 .... 2 ⊡
   SEAF BN25 .... 225 ⊡
   SLVH TN37 .... 169 K ⊡
Rigden Rd *HOVE* BN3 .... 20 ⊡
Riley Rd *ROTT* BN2 .... 2 ⊡
Rill Wk *EGRIN* RH19 .... 2 ⊡
Ringmer Cl *BRI* BN1 .... 17 ⊡
Ringmer Rd *BRI* BN1 .... 17 ⊡
   NEWHV BN9 .... 8 ⊡
   SEAF BN25 .... 23 ⊡
Ringmer Wy *LGNY* BN23 .... 216 ⊡
Ringwood Cl *LW/ROSE* BN22 .... 1 ⊡
Ringwood Rd *BEXW* TN39 .... 19 ⊡
   LW/ROSE BN22 .... 1 ⊡
Ripe La *RING/NEW* BN8 .... 158 ⊡
Risden La *HAWK* TN18 .... 6 ⊡
Riseden Rd *WADH* TN5 .... 5 ⊡
Rise Park Gdns *LGNY* BN23 ...... 23 ⊡
The Rise *EGRIN* RH19 .... 2 ⊡
   PTSD BN41 .... 20 ⊡
The Rising *LGNY* BN23 .... 23 ⊡
River Cl *SHOR* BN43 .... 20 ⊡
Riverdale *LEW* BN7 .... 2 ⊡
River La *POLE* BN26 .... 21 ⊡
Riverside *FROW* RH18 .... 2 ⊡
   NEWHV BN9 .... 9 ⊡
   PTSD BN41 .... 20 ⊡
   SHOR BN43 .... 20 ⊡
   UCK TN22 .... 9 ⊡
Riverside Gdns *CROW* TN6 .... 5 ⊡
Riverside Rd *SHOR* BN43 .... 20 ⊡
River Wy *UCK* TN22 .... 9 ⊡
Rixons Cl *RHWH* RH17 .... 4 ⊡
Rixons Orch *RHWH* RH17 .... 4 ⊡
Roadean Cl *SEAF* BN25 .... 225 ⊡
Robert's Hi *WSEA* TN36 .... 14 ⊡
Robertson Pas *HAS* TN34 .... 5 ⊡
Robertson Rd *BRI* BN1 .... 20 ⊡
Robertsons Hi *HAS* TN34 .... 5 ⊡
Robertson St *HAS* TN34 .... 4 ⊡
Robertson Ter *HAS* TN34 .... 5 ⊡
Robert St *BRI* BN1 .... 6 ⊡
Robert Tressell Cl *HAS* TN34 .... ⊡
Robian Cl *UCK* TN22 .... 6 ⊡
Robin Cl *EGRIN* RH19 .... 2 ⊡
   LGNY BN23 .... 230 ⊡
Robin Davis Cl *ROTT* BN2 .... 20 ⊡
Robin Dene *ROTT* BN2 .... 20 ⊡
Robin Hl *BEXW* TN39 .... 19 ⊡
Robin Post La *POLE* BN26 .... 21 ⊡
Robin Rd *HPPT/KEY* BN6 .... 11 ⊡
Robinson Rd *NEWHV* BN9 .... ⊡
Roborough Cl *LW/ROSE* BN22 ..... 1 ⊡
Robsack Av *STLEO* TN38 .... 19 ⊡
Rochdale Rd *RTW* TN1 .... 2 ⊡
Rochester Cl *EDN/EASTW* BN20 .. 236 ⊡
Rochester Gdns *HOVE* BN3 ...... 203 ⊡
Rochester Rd *SLVH* TN37 .... 197 ⊡
Rochester St *ROTT* BN2 .... ⊡
Rochester Wy *CROW* TN6 .... 54 ⊡
Rochford Wy *SEAF* BN25 .... 224 ⊡
Rochmans Wy *CROW* TN6 .... 53 ⊡
Rockall Av *LGNY* BN23 .... 231 ⊡
Rockall Dr *HAIL* BN27 .... 189 ⊡
Rock-a-nore Pde *RHAS* TN35 .... 199 ⊡
Rock-a-nore Rd *HAS* TN34 .... ⊡
Rock Channel *RYE* TN31 .... 11 ⊡
Rock Cl *RHAS* TN35 .... 17 ⊡
Rock Gv *ROTT* BN2 .... ⊡
Rockhurst Dr *EDN/EASTW* BN20 .. 225 ⊡
Rockington Wy *CROW* TN6 .... 53 ⊡
Rocklands La *RHAS* TN35 .... 199 ⊡
Rock La *RHAS* TN35 .... 17 ⊡
Rockmead Rd *RHAS* TN35 .... 172 ⊡
Rock Pl *ROTT* BN2 .... ⊡
Rocks Hi *RBTBR* TN32 .... 7 ⊡
Rocks La *UCK* TN22 .... 6 ⊡
Rocks Park Rd *UCK* TN22 .... 9 ⊡
The Rocks *EGRIN* RH19 .... 2 ⊡
Rock St *ROTT* BN2 .... 20 ⊡

ck Villa Rd *RTW* TN1 .... 20 A7 ◫
cky La *HWH* RH16 .... 89 J2
derick Av *PEAHV* BN10 .... 222 B2
derick Av North *PEAHV* BN10.. 222 B1
dmell Av *ROTT* BN2 .... 221 C2
dmell Rd *RTWE/PEM* TN2 ...... 30 A2
EAF BN25 .... 232 D1
dmill Dr *EAST* BN21 .... 229 J6
dmill Rd *EAST* BN21 .... 229 J6
dney Cl *LGNY* BN23 .... 231 G4 ◫
dwell *CROW* TN6 .... 54 A2 ◫
ebuck St *HAS* TN34 .... 5 F4 ◫
edale Rd *BRI* BN1 .... 7 D1
edean Cl *BEXW* TN39 .... 195 F6
edean Crs *ROTT* BN2 .... 205 H7
edean Hts *ROTT* BN2 .... 205 H7
edean Pth *ROTT* BN2 .... 205 J8
edean Rd *ROTT* BN2 .... 205 H8
TWE/PEM TN2 .... 30 A2
edean V *ROTT* BN2 .... 205 J8
efe Dr *BURH* RH15 .... 89 K8
maine Cl *BURH* RH15 .... 89 K6
man Cl *SEAF* BN25 .... 224 C5 ◫
man Crs *STHW* BN42 .... 201 H3
man Rd *HOVE* BN3 .... 202 C5
THW BN42 .... 201 H3
mans Av *PEV* BN24 .... 217 F5
mans Wy *STHW* BN42 .... 201 H3
.... 96 A4
many Cl *PTSD* BN41 .... 202 A3
nney Cl *SEAF* BN25 .... 225 K8 ◫
nney Gdns *POLE* BN26 .... 213 G5
OTT BN2 .... 220 D2
nney St *LW/ROSE* BN22 .... 11 E2 ◫
okery Cl *BRI* BN1 .... 204 C1
okery Cl *BRI* BN1 .... 6 A1
EWHV BN9 .... 223 K1 ◫
okery La *WSEA* TN36 .... 143 F4
okery Wy *HWH* RH16 .... 90 A2
EWHV BN9 .... 224 A1
EAF BN25 .... 224 C6
okhurst Rd *BEX* TN40 .... 196 A6
okley Cl *RTWE/PEM* TN2 .... 30 D1 ◫
okwood Cl *UCK* TN22 .... 96 A3 ◫
oppers *RRTW* TN3 .... 18 E4
petackle *SHOR* BN43 .... 200 B4
YE TN31 .... 113 J5
HOR BN43 .... 200 B4
sebarn Cl *BURH* RH15 .... 119 J2
sebery Av *LW/ROSE* BN22.... 229 K2
OTT BN2 .... 205 K3
sedale Pl *LW/ROSE* BN22 .... 215 J8 ◫
sedene Cl *ROTT* BN2 .... 206 D5
se Hi *ROTT* BN2 .... 7 D3
se Hill Cl *BRI* BN1 .... 6 C3
se Hill Ter *BRI* BN1 .... 6 C3
sehill Wk *RTW* TN1 .... 20 A8 ◫
selands *BEXW* TN39 .... 194 E5 ◫
MAYF TN20 .... 71 K2
selands Cl *LW/ROSE* BN22 .... 11 E2 ◫
semary *LW/ROSE* BN22 .... 11 E1 ◫
semary Dr *SHOR* BN43 .... 200 C4
semary La *RHAS* TN35 .... 172 D5
VADH TN5 .... 46 E6
semount Cl *SEAF* BN25 .... 224 B5
setti Rd *PEV* BN24 .... 217 J4
severe Rd *LW/ROSE* BN22.... 11 E1 ◫
se Wk *SEAF* BN25 .... 225 G7
se Walk Cl *NEWHV* BN9 ...... 8 B3
* Rose Wk *NEWHV* BN9 ...... 8 C3
ssdale *RTWE/PEM* TN2 ...... 20 C6
sslyn Av *SHOR* BN43 .... 200 D4
sslyn Ct *SHOR* BN43 .... 200 C3
sslyn Rd *SHOR* BN43 .... 200 C4
sthbury Rd *HOVE* BN3 .... 202 C4
ther Av *POLE* BN26 .... 216 A6
ther Cl *BUR/ETCH* TN19 ...... 75 K5
ROW TN6 .... 53 J4
therfield Av *BEX* TN40 .... 195 J7
W/ROSE BN22 .... 216 B7
therfield Cl *BRI* BN1 .... 178 C6
therfield Crs *BRI* BN1 .... 178 C6
therfield La *MAYF* TN20 ...... 55 K7
therfield Rd *CROW* TN6 ...... 54 C3
therhill *CROW* TN6 .... 53 J3
therhurst La *CROW* TN6 ...... 54 E5
thermead *MAYF* TN20 .... 71 K2
ther Rd *SEAF* BN25 .... 232 C1
ther Vw *BUR/ETCH* TN19 .... 75 K4
therview *RBTBR* TN32 .... 78 C6
hsay Rd *STLEO* TN38 .... 4 A5 ◫
hwell Ct *NEWHV* BN9 ...... 8 A3
* n Rw *LEW* BN7 .... 2 B5
unda Rd *LGNY* BN23 .... 230 E3
Rotyngs *ROTT* BN2 .... 220 C1
ugh Brow *SEAF* BN25 .... 225 H7
ugh Fld *EGRIN* RH19 .... 12 B7 ◫
Rough *RING/NEW* BN8 .... 93 K1
andacres Wy *BEX* TN40 .... 195 K5
Roundel *SLVH* TN37 .... 170 A6
andhay Av *PEAHV* BN10 ...... 222 D5 ◫
andhill Crs *ROTT* BN2 .... 7 D2

Round Hill Rd *ROTT* BN2 .... 7 D2 ◫
Roundhill Rd *RTWE/PEM* TN2...... 30 D2
Round Hill St *ROTT* BN2 .... 7 D2 ◫
Roundway *BRI* BN1 .... 179 F6
Roundwood Rd *SLVH* TN37 ...... 169 J6
Rowan Av *HOVE* BN3 .... 202 D2
LW/ROSE BN22 .... 215 J8
Rowan Cl *HAS* TN34 .... 170 A5
HTHF TN21 .... 100 A6
PTSD BN41 .... 201 J2
SEAF BN25 .... 225 K8 ◫
Rowan Gdns *BEX* TN40 .... 196 A5
Rowan Tree Rd *RTWE/PEM* TN2 ... 29 J2 ◫
Rowan Wy *ROTT* BN2 .... 206 B8
Rowbarns *BAT* TN33 .... 136 C5
Rowe Av *PEAHV* BN10 .... 222 A3
Rowley Hl *RTWE/PEM* TN2 .... 21 K2
Rowsley Rd *EDN/EASTW* BN20 .... 236 D4
Royal Cha *SBGH/RUST* TN4 .... 19 K7
Royal Crs *ROTT* BN2 .... 7 E6
Royal Crescent Ms *ROTT* BN2 .... 7 E6
Royal Dr *SEAF* BN25 .... 225 F5
Royal George Pde *SHOR* BN43 .... 200 E2
Royal George Rd *BURH* RH15 .... 88 E8
Royal Military Canal Pth
TENT TN30 .... 86 C5
Royal Military Rd *WSEA* TN36 .... 143 G3
Royal Oak La *UCK* TN22 ...... 68 D2
Royal Pde *LW/ROSE* BN22 .... 11 F2
Royal Sovereign Vw
LGNY BN23 .... 231 G5 ◫
Royal Sussex Crs
EDN/EASTW BN20 .... 229 G6
Royles Cl *ROTT* BN2 .... 220 D1
Royston Cl *EDN/EASTW* BN20 .... 234 E2
Royston Gdns *BEX* TN40 .... 196 A6
Rudyard Cl *ROTT* BN2 .... 206 B3
Rudyard Rd *ROTT* BN2 .... 206 B3
Rue De Bayeux *BAT* TN33 .... 136 D6 ◫
Rufus Cl *LEW* BN7 .... 2 C4
Rugby Cl *SEAF* BN25 .... 225 J7
Rugby Pl *ROTT* BN2 .... 205 J7
Rugby Rd *BRI* BN1 .... 6 B3 ◫
Rumbolds La *HWH* RH16 ...... 89 K1
Rusbridge La *LEW* BN7 ...... 3 E4 ◫
Ruscombe Cl *SBGH/RUST* TN4 .... 19 K1 ◫
Rushetts *RRTW* TN3 .... 18 D7
Rushey Cl *RING/NEW* BN8 .... 155 K6
Rushlake Cl *BRI* BN1 .... 179 F6
Rushlake Crs *EAST* BN21 ...... 229 J5
Rushlake Rd *BRI* BN1 .... 179 F5
Rushlye Cl *RRTW* TN3 .... 31 F6
Rushmere Ri *STLEO* TN38 .... 197 F2
Ruskin Rd *EDN/EASTW* BN20 .... 229 G2
HOVE BN3 .... 202 A4
Rusper Rd *BRI* BN1 .... 178 E5
EDN/EASTW BN20 .... 229 G5
Ruspers *BURH* RH15 .... 119 K1
Russell Av *BRI* BN1 .... 6 B3 ◫
Russell Pl *BRI* BN1 .... 6 B5 ◫
Russell Rd *BRI* BN1 .... 6 B5 ◫
Russell Sq *BRI* BN1 .... 6 B5 ◫
Russell St *HAS* TN34 .... 5 D5
Russet Cl *POLE* BN26 .... 215 H5
Rusthall Gra *SBGH/RUST* TN4 .... 19 H7 ◫
Rusthall High St *SBGH/RUST* TN4.... 19 F7
Rusthall Pk *SBGH/RUST* TN4 .... 19 H7
Rusthall Rd *SBGH/RUST* TN4 .... 19 H8
Rustic Cl *PEAHV* BN10 .... 222 A1
Rustic Rd *PEAHV* BN10 .... 222 A1
Rustington Rd *BRI* BN1 .... 178 B6
Rustwick *SBGH/RUST* TN4 .... 19 F7
Rutland Cl *EAST* BN21 .... 229 J5
Rutland Gdns *HOVE* BN3 ...... 202 A4
Rutland Rd *HOVE* BN3 .... 203 F4
Rydal Cl *SBGH/RUST* TN4 .... 19 J6
Rydal Rd *SBGH/RUST* TN4 .... 19 J6
Rydal Wy *LGNY* BN23 .... 216 C7
Ryde Rd *ROTT* BN2 .... 7 F3
Ryders *RRTW* TN3 .... 18 E3
Rye Cl *POLE* BN26 .... 215 H4
ROTT BN2 .... 221 H1
SEAF BN25 .... 225 K7
Ryefield Cl *EAST* BN21 .... 229 H4
Ryelands Dr *ROTT* BN2 .... 178 E8
Rye Rd *HAWK* TN18 .... 63 K3
RHAS TN35 .... 171 G7
RYE TN31 .... 113 F1
TENT TN30 .... 85 G1
Rye St *LW/ROSE* BN22 .... 11 E1
Rylstone Rd *LW/ROSE* BN22 .... 11 E3
Rymers Cl *RTWE/PEM* TN2 .... 20 D4
Rymill Rd *STLEO* TN38 .... 169 H8
Ryst Wood Rd *FROW* RH18 .... 36 B1

S

Sackville Cl *EGRIN* RH19 .... 12 A8
LEW BN7 .... 2 C4 ◫
Sackville Gdns *HOVE* BN3 ...... 202 E5
Sackville Rd *BEXW* TN39 .... 195 G8
HAIL BN27 .... 189 H5

HOVE BN3 .... 203 F5
LW/ROSE BN22 .... 230 A1
Saddlers Cl *BURH* RH15 .... 119 K2
Saddler's Wall La *LYDD* TN29.... 87 K2
Sadlers Wy *RING/NEW* BN8 .... 155 J7
Sadler Wy *ROTT* BN2 .... 205 G5
Saffron Cl *SHOR* BN43 .... 201 F2
Saffron Gdns *POLE* BN26 ...... 212 C8
Saffrons Pk *EDN/EASTW* BN20 .... 10 A6
Saffrons Rd *EAST* BN21 .... 10 A4
The Saffrons *BURH* RH15 ...... 88 E6
St Agnes Rd *EGRIN* RH19 ...... 22 C1
St Andrews Cl *HAIL* BN27 ...... 189 F7
St Andrews Ct *SBGH/RUST* TN4 .... 20 A2 ◫
St Andrew's Dr *SEAF* BN25 ...... 224 B5
St Andrew's La *LEW* BN7 .... 3 D5 ◫
LEW BN7 .... 3 D4 ◫
St Andrews Park Rd
SBGH/RUST TN4 .... 20 A2
St Andrew's Rd *BEX* TN40 ...... 195 H6
BRI BN1 .... 6 C1 ◫
BURH RH15 .... 89 K8 ◫
PTSD BN41 .... 202 A4
St Anne's Crs *LEW* BN7 .... 2 B4 ◫
St Anne's Rd *EAST* BN21 ...... 10 A3
LW/ROSE BN22 .... 215 G8
St Anthony's Av *LGNY* BN23 .... 230 E4
St Aubyns *HOVE* BN3 .... 203 F5
St Aubyn's Crs *PTSD* BN41 ...... 202 A4
St Aubyn's Md *ROTT* BN2 ...... 220 D2
St Aubyn's Rd *LW/ROSE* BN22 .... 11 D4 ◫
PTSD BN41 .... 201 K4
St Aubyns South *HOVE* BN3 .... 203 F6 ◫
St Augustine's Cl *BEXW* TN39 .... 194 E8 ◫
St Barnabas' Cl *RTW* TN1 ...... 20 B6 ◫
St Boswells Cl *HAIL* BN27 ...... 188 E3
St Catherine's Cl *SLVH* TN37 .... 4 B4 ◫
St Crispians *SEAF* BN25 .... 224 E8
St Cuthmans Cl *ROTT* BN2 .... 205 F5
St David's Av *BEX* TN40 .... 195 H6
St Davids Cl *LW/ROSE* BN22 .... 215 J7
St David's Rd *SBGH/RUST* TN4 .... 20 B5
St Edward's Cl *EGRIN* RH19 .... 22 A2
St Francis Cha *BEXW* TN39 .... 195 F6
St Francis Cl *HWH* RH16 ...... 90 A1
St George's La *HPPT/KEY* BN6 .... 118 B6
St George's Ms *BRI* BN1 .... 6 C4 ◫
St George's Pk *RTWE/PEM* TN2 .... 29 K3
St George's Pl *BRI* BN1 .... 6 C4 ◫
HPPT/KEY BN6 .... 118 B6
St George's Rd *BEXW* TN39 .... 195 H6
HAS TN34 .... 5 E3
LW/ROSE BN22 .... 11 D3 ◫
ROTT BN2 .... 7 E6
St George's Ter *ROTT* BN2 ...... 7 E6
St Giles Cl *EDN/EASTW* BN20 .... 204 E3
WSEA TN36 .... 142 E4
St Gregory Cl *EDN/EASTW* BN20.... 236 C1
St Helen's Av *HAS* TN34 .... 4 C1
St Helen's Crs *HAS* TN34 ...... 4 C2
HOVE BN3 .... 176 C8
St Helen's Down *HAS* TN34 .... 5 E1
St Helen's Dr *HOVE* BN3 .... 176 C8
St Helen's Park Rd *HAS* TN34 .... 5 D1
St Helen's Rd *ROTT* BN2 ...... 7 F3
SLVH TN37 .... 4 B1
St Helens Wood Rd *HAS* TN34 .... 170 B6
St Heliers Av *HOVE* BN3 .... 202 D4
St James' Av *BEX* TN40.......... 195 J5
St James' Crs *BEX* TN40 .... 195 J4
St James' Pk *RTW* TN1 .... 20 C6
RTWE/PEM TN2 .... 20 C6
St James' Rd *BEX* TN40 .... 195 H5
LW/ROSE BN22 .... 11 E3 ◫
RTW TN1 .... 20 C7
Stjames' Rd *RTW* TN1 .... 20 C6
St James's Av *ROTT* BN2 .... 7 D6
St James's Rd *EGRIN* RH19 .... 22 B2
HAS TN34 .... 5 D3
St James's St *ROTT* BN2 ...... 6 C5 ◫ ◫
St James's Street Ms *ROTT* BN2 .... 7 D5 ◫◫
St James St *LEW* BN7 .... 2 C5
St John Bank *RING/NEW* BN8 .... 122 B3
St John's Av *BURH* RH15 ...... 89 F8
St John's Cl *CROW* TN6 .... 39 G8
EGRIN RH19 .... 22 C1
St John's Dr *PEV* BN24 .... 217 F5
St John's Hl *LEW* BN7 .... 2 C4
St John's Pk *SBGH/RUST* TN4 .... 20 A3
St John's Pl *HOVE* BN3 .... 203 H5 ◫
ROTT BN2 .... 7 D5 ◫
St John's Rd *BEX* TN40 .... 195 H5
BURH RH15 .... 89 G8
CROW TN6 .... 38 E6
EDN/EASTW BN20 .... 236 D3
EGRIN RH19 .... 22 C1
HOVE BN3 .... 203 H6
POLE BN26 .... 215 F5
SBGH/RUST TN4 .... 20 A4
SEAF BN25 .... 232 A1
SLVH TN37 .... 4 A5
St John's Ter *LEW* BN7 .... 2 C4
St John St *LEW* BN7 .... 3 D4
St Joseph's Cl *HOVE* BN3 ...... 203 F3
St Julians Cl *SHOR* BN43 ...... 201 F4

St Julian's La SHOR BN43 ... 201 F4
St Keyna Av HOVE BN3 ... 202 C5
St Lawrence Cl PEAHV BN10 ... 221 K2
St Lawrence Rd BEXW TN39 ... 195 G4
St Lawrence Wy HPPT/KEY BN6 ... 118 A4
St Leonard's Av HOVE BN3 ... 202 B5
St Leonards Cl NEWHV BN9 ... 224 A1
St Leonard's Gdns HOVE BN3 ... 202 C5
St Leonard's Pl EDN/EASTW BN20 ... 229 H8
St Leonard's Rd EAST BN21 ... 10 C4
  HOVE BN3 ... 202 B5
  NEWHV BN9 ... 224 A1
  ROTT BN2 ... 7 E2
St Leonards Ter POLE BN26 ... 214 E4
St Louie Cl STHW BN42 ... 201 K3
St Luke's Rd ROTT BN2 ... 7 E4
  SBGH/RUST TN4 ... 20 B5
St Luke's Ter ROTT BN2 ... 7 E4
St Margaret's Av EGRIN RH19 ... 12 C5
St Margaret's Pl BRI BN1 ... 6 B5
St Margaret's Ri SEAF BN25 ... 224 B5
St Margaret's Rd EGRIN RH19 ... 12 D8
  SLVH TN37 ... 4 B5
St Marks Cl SLVH TN37 ... 194 C7
St Mark's Fld UCK TN22 ... 69 K6
St Mark's Rd RTWE/PEM TN2 ... 29 K4
St Mark's St ROTT BN2 ... 205 F7
St Martins Cl NEWHV BN9 ... 9 D1
St Martins Pl ROTT BN2 ... 7 D3
St Martins St LW/ROSE BN22 ... 215 J8
St Mary-in-the-Fields MAYF TN20 ... 72 B1
St Mary Magdalene St ROTT BN2 ... 7 D2
St Marys Av HAIL BN27 ... 189 H4
St Mary's Cl LW/ROSE BN22 ... 229 G1
  RYE TN31 ... 139 J1
  SHOR BN43 ... 200 C4
  WADH TN5 ... 60 B2
St Mary's Cottages
  EDN/EASTW BN20 ... 229 J8
Saint Marys Garth UCK TN22 ... 68 E7
St Mary's La BEXW TN39 ... 194 E2
  RRTW TN3 ... 18 E3
  WADH TN5 ... 60 B2
St Mary's Pl ROTT BN2 ... 7 D5
St Mary's Rd EAST BN21 ... 229 J7
  HAS TN34 ... 5 E3
  SHOR BN43 ... 200 C4
St Mary's Rd West BURH RH15 ... 88 E7
St Mary's Sq ROTT BN2 ... 7 F6
St Mary's Ter HAS TN34 ... 5 E3
St Matthew's Gdns STLEO TN38 ... 197 J2
St Matthew's Rd STLEO TN38 ... 197 J2
St Mellion Cl HAIL BN27 ... 188 E3
St Michaels Cl CROW TN6 ... 53 K3
  PEV BN24 ... 216 B5
St Michael's Pl BRI BN1 ... 6 A4
St Michaels Rd EGRIN RH19 ... 22 C1
  PTSD BN41 ... 202 A4
  SBGH/RUST TN4 ... 20 B4
St Michael's Ter LEW BN7 ... 3 D5
St Nicholas La LEW BN7 ... 3 D4
St Nicholas Rd BRI BN1 ... 6 B4
  PTSD BN41 ... 202 A4
St Nicolas Cl PEV BN24 ... 217 J5
St Nicolas Cl SHOR BN43 ... 200 A3
St Olive's Cl HTHF TN21 ... 99 G4
St Pancras Gdns LEW BN7 ... 2 B5
St Pancras Rd LEW BN7 ... 181 G6
St Pancras Rd LEW BN7 ... 2 B5
St Patrick's Crs BEX TN40 ... 195 H6
St Patrick's Rd HOVE BN3 ... 203 F4
St Pauls Cl LW/ROSE BN22 ... 215 J8
St Paul's Pl SLVH TN37 ... 4 B5
St Paul's St ROTT BN2 ... 7 D2
  SBGH/RUST TN4 ... 19 G7
St Peter's Av PEAHV BN10 ... 221 K3
St Peter's Cl HOVE BN3 ... 202 E1
  SEAF BN25 ... 225 F6
St Peters Crs BEX TN40 ... 195 J6
St Peters Pl LEW BN7 ... 2 C5
  LEW BN7 ... 2 C4
St Peters Rd BURH RH15 ... 89 G7
  PTSD BN41 ... 202 A4
  SEAF BN25 ... 225 F6
  SLVH TN37 ... 4 A4
St Peters Rw RRTW TN3 ... 17 K6
St Peter's St BRI BN1 ... 6 C3
  RTWE/PEM TN2 ... 20 C8
St Philip's Av LW/ROSE BN22 ... 11 D2
St Philips Ms HOVE BN3 ... 202 E4
St Richards Rd CROW TN6 ... 53 J4
  PTSD BN41 ... 202 A4
St Saviour's Rd STLEO TN38 ... 197 F5
Saints Hl RTON TN11 ... 17 J2
St Stephons Ct RTW TN1 ... 20 B6
St Swithun's Cl EGRIN RH19 ... 22 D2
St Swithun's Ter LEW BN7 ... 2 C5
St Thomas's St WSEA TN36 ... 143 F4
St Vincents Pl EDN/EASTW BN20 ... 10 A6
St Vincents Rd STLEO TN38 ... 197 G4
St Wilfred's Pl SEAF BN25 ... 232 D1
St Wilfreds Rd BURH RH15 ... 89 H7
St Wilfrid's Gn HAIL BN27 ... 189 G3

Salcey Cl STLEO TN38 ... 197 F1
Salehurst Gdns STLEO TN58 ... 196 E1
Salehurst Rd EAST BN21 ... 229 H8
Salisbury Cl LW/ROSE BN22 ... 229 H1
Salisbury Rd BEXW TN39 ... 195 G6
  EDN/EASTW BN20 ... 236 C3
  HOVE BN3 ... 203 H5
  RRTW TN3 ... 18 D8
  SBGH/RUST TN4 ... 20 C3
  SEAF BN25 ... 225 F8
  SLVH TN37 ... 4 A3
Saltcote St RYE TN31 ... 113 J3
Saltdean Cl BEXW TN39 ... 194 D8
Saltdean Dr ROTT BN2 ... 220 E2
Saltdean Park Rd ROTT BN2 ... 221 F2
Saltdean V ROTT BN2 ... 207 G8
  ROTT BN2 ... 221 F1
Saltdean Wy BEXW TN39 ... 194 C8
The Saltings SHOR BN43 ... 200 A5
Saltwood Rd SEAF BN25 ... 225 K7
Salvador Cl LGNY BN23 ... 231 G4
Salvington Crs BEXW TN39 ... 194 E7
Sancroft Rd EDN/EASTW BN20 ... 229 G8
The Sanctuary
  EDN/EASTW BN20 ... 229 G7
Sandbanks Cl HAIL BN27 ... 189 F6
Sandbanks Gdns HAIL BN27 ... 189 G6
Sandbanks Gv HAIL BN27 ... 189 G5
Sandbanks Rd HAIL BN27 ... 189 F6
Sandbanks Wy HAIL BN27 ... 189 G5
Sandfield Rd RTON TN11 ... 17 H4
Sandgate Cl SEAF BN25 ... 225 K6
Sandgate Rd BRI BN1 ... 204 B1
Sandhawes Hl EGRIN RH19 ... 12 E7
Sandhill La CROW TN6 ... 40 C4
  HAIL BN27 ... 132 C6
Sand Hill La RING/NEW BN8 ... 126 C5
  UCK TN22 ... 126 E2
Sandhurst Av ROTT BN2 ... 206 A2
Sandhurst Cl RTWE/PEM TN2 ... 20 C4
Sandhurst Gdns HAS TN34 ... 170 C5
Sandhurst La BEXW TN39 ... 193 K7
Sandhurst Pk RTWE/PEM TN2 ... 20 D5
Sandhurst Rd RTWE/PEM TN2 ... 20 D4
Sandore Cl SEAF BN25 ... 225 H7
Sandore Rd SEAF BN25 ... 225 H7
Sandown Cl LGNY BN23 ... 216 C7
  RTWE/PEM TN2 ... 21 F5
Sandown Gv RTWE/PEM TN2 ... 21 F5
Sandown Pk RTWE/PEM TN2 ... 21 F6
Sandown Rd RHAS TN35 ... 171 F8
  ROTT BN2 ... 7 F3
  STHW BN42 ... 201 G3
Sandown Wy BEX TN40 ... 195 K5
Sandridge CROW TN6 ... 53 H2
Sandringham Cl HOVE BN3 ... 177 F8
  SEAF BN25 ... 225 H5
Sandringham Dr HOVE BN3 ... 177 F8
Sandringham Hts STLEO TN38 ... 168 B3
Sand Rd RRTW TN3 ... 33 J7
Sandrock Hl BAT TN33 ... 168 B7
Sandrock Pk HAS TN34 ... 170 C6
Sandrock Rd RTWE/PEM TN2 ... 20 C7
Sandrocks Wy HWH RH16 ... 90 A1
Sandwich Dr STLEO TN38 ... 197 G4
Sandwich St LW/ROSE BN22 ... 11 E1
Sandy Cl SLVH TN37 ... 169 J2
Sandy Cross La HTHF TN21 ... 100 B6
Sandy La EGRIN RH19 ... 22 C2
  HRTF TN7 ... 26 D5
  HTHF TN21 ... 129 J2
  RHWH RH17 ... 49 G3
  UCK TN22 ... 96 C3
Sandy V HWH RH16 ... 89 K1
San Feliu Ct EGRIN RH19 ... 23 F1
Santa Cruz Dr LGNY BN23 ... 231 G4
Sanyhils Av BRI BN1 ... 178 A4
Saunders Cl HAS TN34 ... 5 E3
  UCK TN22 ... 95 G3
Saunders Hl BRI BN1 ... 178 E4
Saunders Park Vw ROTT BN2 ... 7 E1
Saunders Rd SBGH/RUST TN4 ... 29 J2
Saunders Wy RYE TN31 ... 145 J1
Sawyers Cl BURH RH15 ... 119 K2
Saxby Cl LGNY BN23 ... 231 F2
Saxby Rd BEXW TN39 ... 195 F7
  BURH RH15 ... 88 D7
Saxonbury Cl CROW TN6 ... 53 H2
Saxon Cl EAST BN21 ... 229 H5
  ROTT BN2 ... 221 F1
Saxon La SEAF BN25 ... 232 A1
Saxon Ri BEX TN40 ... 195 K7
Saxon Rd HOVE BN3 ... 202 C5
  NEWHV BN9 ... 8 C3
  RHAS TN35 ... 171 G8
Saxons SHOR BN43 ... 200 C3
Saxon Shore Wy HAS TN34 ... 5 F4
  RHAS TN35 ... 173 H3
  RHAS TN35 ... 199 G2
  RYE TN31 ... 114 A3
  WSEA TN36 ... 143 F5
Saxon St SLVH TN37 ... 4 A6
Saxonwood Rd BAT TN33 ... 136 C6
Sayerland La POLE BN26 ... 215 F3
Sayerland Rd POLE BN26 ... 214 E4

The Sayers EGRIN RH19 ... 22
Scanlon Cl EDN/EASTW BN20 ... 215
Scarborough Rd BRI BN1 ... 203
Scarletts Cl UCK TN22 ... 95
Schofield Wy LGNY BN23 ... 231
School Cl BURH RH15 ... 119
  STHW BN42 ... 201
School Fld RING/NEW BN8 ... 123
School Gdns RING/NEW BN8 ... 123
School Hl RING/NEW BN8 ... 123
  RRTW TN3 ... 33
  WSEA TN36 ... 142
School La CROW TN6 ... 38
  EGRIN RH19 ... 21
  FROW RH18 ... 35
  POLE BN26 ... 215
  POY/PYE BN45 ... 149
  RHWH RH17 ... 48
  RYE TN31 ... 112
  RYE TN31 ... 113
  UCK TN22 ... 50
  UCK TN22 ... 62
  UCK TN22 ... 97
School Pl BEX TN40 ... 196
School Ri ROTT BN2 ... 205
  RTWE/PEM TN2 ... 29
School Rd HOVE BN3 ... 202
  RHAS TN35 ... 171
School Ter HAWK TN18 ... 167
Schwerte Wy SLVH TN37 ... 4
Scotland St ROTT BN2 ... 7
Scotsford Hl MAYF TN20 ... 72
Scotsford Rd HTHF TN21 ... 101
Scott Rd HOVE BN3 ... 202
Scotts Acre RYE TN31 ... 115
Scotts Wy RTWE/PEM TN2 ... 29
Scraper's Hl RING/NEW BN8 ... 159
Scutes Cl HAS TN34 ... 5
Seabeach La LW/ROSE BN22 ... 11
Seabourne Rd BEX TN40 ... 196
Seafield Cl SEAF BN25 ... 225
Seafield Rd HOVE BN3 ... 203
Seaford Rd HOVE BN3 ... 202
  LW/ROSE BN22 ... 11
  NEWHV BN9 ... 9
Seagrave Cl SEAF BN25 ... 224
Seagrove Wy SEAF BN25 ... 225
Seahaven Gdns SHOR BN43 ... 200
Searle Av PEAHV BN10 ... 222
Sea Rd BEX TN40 ... 195
  PEV BN24 ... 218
  RHAS TN35 ... 173
  RYE TN31 ... 145
  STLEO TN38 ... 197
  WSEA TN36 ... 143
Seasaw Wy ROTT BN2 ... 205
Seaside LW/ROSE BN22 ... 11
Seaside Rd EAST BN21 ... 11
  STLEO TN38 ... 197
Seaside Wy STLEO TN38 ... 197
Seaview Av PEAHV BN10 ... 222
Seaview Rd NEWHV BN9 ... 9
  PEAHV BN10 ... 222
  ROTT BN2 ... 205
Seaville Dr LGNY BN23 ... 230
  PEV BN24 ... 218
Second Av BEX TN40 ... 196
  HOVE BN3 ... 8
  NEWHV BN9 ... 8
  RYE TN31 ... 145
Second Rd PEAHV BN10 ... 221
Sedgebrook Gdns HAS TN34 ... 4
Sedgewick Rd BEXW TN39 ... 195
  BRI BN1 ... 178
Sedlescombe Gdns STLEO TN38 ... 197
Sedlescombe Rd North BAT TN33 ... 137
  SLVH TN37 ... 4
Sedlescombe Rd South
  STLEO TN38 ... 197
Sefton Cha CROW TN6 ... 39
Sefton Cl PTSD BN41 ... 175
Sefton Wy CROW TN6 ... 39
Segrave Cl LEW BN7 ... 2
Selba Dr ROTT BN2 ... 205
Selborne Pl HOVE BN3 ... 203
Selborne Rd HOVE BN3 ... 203
Selby Gdns UCK TN22 ... 95
Selby Ri UCK TN22 ... 95
Selby Rd EAST BN21 ... 229
  UCK TN22 ... 95
Selham Cl BRI BN1 ... 179
Selham Dr BRI BN1 ... 178
Selhurst Rd ROTT BN2 ... 206
Sellbourne Pk RRTW TN3 ... 30
Selmeston Cl HAS TN34 ... 4
Selmestone Rd ROTT BN2 ... 205
Selmeston Pl ROTT BN2 ... 205
Selmeston Rd EAST BN21 ... 229
Selsey Cl BRI BN1 ... 179
Selsfield Cl EAST BN21 ... 229
Selsfield Dr ROTT BN2 ... 178
Selwyn Dr EAST BN21 ... 10
Selwyn Rd EAST BN21 ... 10
Semley Rd BRI BN1 ... 6
  HPPT/KEY BN6 ... 118

npstead La RBTBR TN32 .... 80 E8
lac Rd NEWHV BN9 .... 9 D3 🄳
lac Wy SLVH TN37 .... 169 K6
fords Fld RING/NEW BN8 .... 122 C1 🄳
elands CI ROTT BN2 .... 205 G4 🄳
enoaks Rd LGNY BN23 .... 230 E2
en Acre CI SLVH TN37 .... 169 H6
en Sisters Rd LW/ROSE BN22 ... 215 G8
lle St ROTT BN2 .... 7 E3
rell Av BEX TN40 .... 195 H6
mour Sq ROTT BN2 .... 7 F6 🄳
mour St ROTT BN2 .... 7 F6 🄳🄳
ftesbury PI BRI BN1 .... 6 C2
ftesbury Rd BRI BN1 .... 6 C2
BGH/RUST TN4 .... 20 A5
kespeare St HOVE BN3 .... 203 F3
lesbrook La FROW RH18 .... 35 K2
lfleet CI LGNY BN23 .... 216 C8
ndon CI RTWE/PEM TN2 .... 20 C7
nklin CI LGNY BN23 .... 216 C7
nkley Rd ROTT BN2 .... 7 E2
nnon CI PEAHV BN10 .... 221 K2
nnow Wy LGNY BN23 .... 231 G5
rpthorne Crs PTSD BN41 .... 202 B1
wfield CROW TN6 .... 53 K2 🄳
Shaw RTWE/PEM TN2 .... 30 C1
ddingdean CI BURH RH15 .... 89 G7 🄳
en Rd LW/ROSE BN22 .... 11 D3
epbell CI PTSD BN41 .... 176 A8
epfair LEW BN7 .... 2 A3
ep Pen La SEAF BN25 .... 225 H8
ep Pln CROW TN6 .... 53 F4
epsetting La HTHF TN21 .... 99 J4
epstreet La BUR/ETCH TN19.... 60 C7
ep Wk ROTT BN2 .... 220 C2
epwash La UCK TN22 .... 98 A3
erwater Crs UCK TN34 .... 170 A7
ffield Dr UCK TN22 .... 65 F7
ffield Mill La UCK TN22 .... 65 G3
ffield Park Wy LW/ROSE BN22... 216 B7 🄳
ffield Rd SBGH/RUST TN4 .... 19 K1
lling Rd CROW TN6 .... 39 G8
idale Av PTSD BN41 .... 202 A4
idale Crs PTSD BN41 .... 202 A4
idale Rd PTSD BN41 .... 201 K3
ley CI LEW BN7 .... 2 B4
ley Rd EGRIN RH19 .... 22 B2
OVE BN3 .... 202 E4
NG/NEW BN8 .... 155 J6
I La HAS TN34 .... 5 E5
nfield Wy BRI BN1 .... 204 C1
oham Av ROTT BN2 .... 221 F2
oham La POLE BN26 .... 215 H4
pherd's CI BEXW TN39 .... 194 B7
EWHV BN9 .... 223 G2 🄳
pherds Cot PEAHV BN10 .... 222 C1 🄳
pherds Ctt BRI BN1 .... 177 H8
phersgrove La EGRIN RH19 ...... 13 K6
pherds Md BURH RH15 .... 89 F7 🄳
pherd St STLEO TN38 .... 4 A6 🄳
pherds Wk CROW TN6 .... 54 A2 🄳
PPT/KEY BN6 .... 118 E6
TWE/PEM TN2 .... 20 D7 🄳
pherds Wy RHAS TN35 .... 172 D7
NG/NEW BN8 .... 122 A4
NG/NEW BN8 .... 155 K6
CK TN22 .... 95 J6
oppard Wy PTSD BN41 .... 175 K8
opeys HWH RH16 .... 89 K1
opey Wk HAIL BN27 .... 161 F8
Shepway SEAF BN25 .... 225 J7
raton CI EAST BN21 .... 10 B5 🄳
rbourne CI HOVE BN3 .... 176 C8
rbourne Rd LW/ROSE BN22 .... 176 C8
rbourne Wy HOVE BN3 .... 176 C8
idan CI EGRIN RH19 .... 22 A2
idan Ter HOVE BN3 .... 203 F5
ingham CI RBTBR TN32 .... 108 A1
man Br POLE BN26 .... 213 F4
rington Rd ROTT BN2 .... 206 C3
wood CI HAS TN34 .... 5 D4
wood Gn HAIL BN27 .... 189 G5 🄳
wood PI RRTW TN3 .... 18 C8 🄳
wood Ri SEAF BN25 .... 225 G7
wood Rd RTWE/PEM TN2 .... 20 D7 🄳
WE/PEM TN2 .... 20 E6
AF BN25 .... 225 G7
wood Wy RTWE/PEM TN2 .... 20 D5
ewater La LGNY BN23 .... 216 C8
gle Ct STLEO TN38 .... 169 F4
gle Rd SHOR BN43 .... 200 D5
ley La BEXW TN39 .... 194 C8
ley Mill CI PEV BN24 .... 216 C6
ley Rd ROTT BN2 .... 206 B4
St BRI BN1 .... 6 B5 🄳
RIN RH19 .... 22 C3
WHV BN9 .... 8 C2 🄳
OR BN43 .... 200 B4
ea Vw BAT TN33 .... 136 E7
ey Av HOVE BN3 .... 203 G1
ey CI SHOR BN43 .... 201 F5

Shirley Dr HOVE BN3 .... 203 H2
SLVH TN37 .... 169 J7
Shirley Gdns SBGH/RUST TN4 .. 19 G7 🄳
Shirley Gv SBGH/RUST TN4 .... 19 H6
Shirley Rd HOVE BN3 .... 203 H3
Shirleys HPPT/KEY BN6 .... 151 F1
Shirley St HOVE BN3 .... 203 G4
Short Brow SEAF BN25 .... 225 H7
Short Brow La LW/ROSE BN22 .. 215 G8 🄳
Shortdean PI EAST BN21 .... 229 J7 🄳
Shortgate La RING/NEW BN8 ... 157 H1
Shortgate Rd ROTT BN2 .... 179 G7
Shortlands CI LW/ROSE BN22 .. 229 H2 🄳
Shovelstrode La EGRIN RH19 .... 23 J1
Showfields Rd RTWE/PEM TN2 .. 29 K2
The Shrublands BEXW TN39 .... 194 D8
Shrub La WADH TN5 .... 59 K6
Sicklehatch La HTHF TN21 .... 130 A1
Sidcup CI LGNY BN23 .... 230 E1 🄳
Sidehill Dr PTSD BN41 .... 201 J1
Sidley Gn BEXW TN39 .... 195 H4
Sidley Rd LW/ROSE BN22 .... 11 E2
Sidley St BEXW TN39 .... 195 G4
Sidney CI RTWE/PEM TN2 .... 29 J3
Silchester Rd STLEO TN38 .... 4 C5
Sillwood PI BRI BN1 .... 6 A5 🄳
Sillwood Rd BRI BN1 .... 6 A5 🄳
Sillwood St BRI BN1 .... 6 A5 🄳
Silva CI BEX TN40 .... 196 B5
Silvan Rd STLEO TN38 .... 169 F8 🄳
Silverdale HPPT/KEY BN6 .... 119 H8
Silverdale Av HOVE BN3 .... 203 J4
Silverdale La SBGH/RUST TN4 .. 20 B5
Silverdale Rd BURH RH15 .... 119 H1
EDN/EASTW BN20 .... 10 B6
HOVE BN3 .... 203 J4
SBGH/RUST TN4 .... 20 B5
Silverhill Av SLVH TN37 .... 169 K7
Silverlands Rd SLVH TN37 .... 197 J1
Silvester Rd BEX TN40 .... 195 H6
Silwood CI RTWE/PEM TN2 .... 20 E4
Simons CI CROW TN6 .... 53 J2 🄳
Singleton Mill Rd PEV BN24 ..... 216 D6
Singleton Rd BRI BN1 .... 178 B5
Singleton Wy BURH RH15 .... 119 J2
Sir David's Pk SBGH/RUST TN4 .. 19 J2
Six Bells Ms RYE TN31 .... 82 A6
Skinner's La BAT TN33 .... 166 B4
Skyline Vw PEAHV BN10 .... 222 C2
The Slade RRTW TN3 .... 33 J8
Sleepers Stile Rd WADH TN5 .... 44 E2
Slider's La UCK TN22 .... 64 E4
The Slides STLEO TN38 .... 169 G8
Slimbridge Rd BURH RH15 .... 89 F8
Slindon Av PEAHV BN10 .... 222 C5
Slindon Crs LGNY BN23 .... 231 F2 🄳
Slinford CI ROTT BN2 .... 7 F5
Slip Mill Rd HAWK TN18 .... 62 E1
Sliverick's La HTHF TN21 .... 133 H4
Sloe La POLE BN26 .... 212 D8
Slonk Hill Rd SHOR BN43 .... 200 D1
Slugwash La HWH RH17 .... 90 D6
Smarts La RTON TN11 .... 17 J2
Smeatons La WSEA TN36 .... 143 H6
Smith CI BAT TN33 .... 166 A6
Smithy's CI SLVH TN37 .... 169 K6 🄳
The Smithy UCK TN22 .... 95 H5
Smolletts EGRIN RH19 .... 22 A3 🄳
Smugglers CI POLE BN26 .... 212 C8
Smugglers La CROW TN6 .... 39 F6
Smugglers Ms HAWK TN18 .... 63 C3
Smugglers Wy RHAS TN35 ...... 172 E7
Snape La WADH TN5 .... 58 A2
Snape Vw WADH TN5 .... 44 B7
Snatt's Rd UCK TN22 .... 95 J2
Snednore LEW BN7 .... 181 J6
Snowdon CI LGNY BN23 .... 216 E8
Solomon's La RBTBR TN32 ..... 106 C7
Solway HAIL BN27 .... 189 F1
Solway Av BRI BN1 .... 178 A4
Somerhill Av HOVE BN3 .... 203 J6
Somerhill Rd HOVE BN3 .... 203 J5
Somerset Rd SBGH/RUST TN4 ... 20 A5
Somerset St ROTT BN2 .... 7 E5
Somerville CI LGNY BN23 .... 231 F4 🄳
Somerville Gdns SBGH/RUST TN4. 19 K7
Sompting CI ROTT BN2 .... 205 G4 🄳
Sorrel CI LGNY BN23 .... 216 D8 🄳
Sorrel Dr LGNY BN23 .... 216 D8
Southall Av ROTT BN2 .... 7 F1
Southampton CI LGNY BN23 .... 231 G3 🄳
Southampton St ROTT BN2 .... 7 D4
South Av EDN/EASTW BN20 .... 229 G6
HPPT/KEY BN6 .... 118 A6
ROTT BN2 .... 7 E5
South Bank HPPT/KEY BN6 ..... 118 G8
Southbourne Rd LW/ROSE BN22. 11 E1
South Brooks Rd LYDD TN29 ... 147 J3
South Cliff EDN/EASTW BN20 .. 237 F3
South Cliff Av EDN/EASTW BN20. 10 B6 🄳
South CI BURH RH15 .... 88 E8
HAIL BN27 .... 189 G5
PEV BN24 .... 218 C5
South Coast Rd PEAHV BN10 .. 221 H3
ROTT BN2 .... 221 G3

Southcourt Av BEXW TN39 ...... 194 E8
Southdown Av BRI BN1 .... 6 C1
EDN/EASTW BN20 .... 215 F8
HAS TN34 .... 5 F1
LEW BN7 .... 2 A5
PEAHV BN10 .... 222 D5
PTSD BN41 .... 202 B3 🄳
Southdown CI HWH RH16 .... 89 K1
NEWHV BN9 .... 8 B4
Southdown PI BRI BN1 .... 6 C1 🄳
Southdown Rd BRI BN1 .... 6 C1
EDN/EASTW BN20 .... 229 G4
NEWHV BN9 .... 8 B4
PTSD BN41 .... 201 K1
SEAF BN25 .... 232 C2
SHOR BN43 .... 200 C4
STHW BN42 .... 201 H4
South Downs LEW BN7 .... 121 H6 🄳
South Downs Rd LEW BN7 .... 3 D3
South Downs Wy
EDN/EASTW BN20 .... 236 B2
HFD BN5 .... 175 J1
HPPT/KEY BN6 .... 150 D4
LEW BN7 .... 180 D3
LEW BN7 .... 207 H1
POLE BN26 .... 213 H8
POY/PYE BN45 .... 149 K5
RING/NEW BN8 .... 209 J3
RING/NEW BN8 .... 211 K6
SEAF BN25 .... 226 D8
SHOR BN43 .... 174 E1
South Dr BURH RH15 .... 88 E8
Southerden CI HAIL BN27 .... 189 H4
Southern Av POLE BN26 .... 215 G5
Southern Rd LW/ROSE BN22 ... 230 A1 🄳
Southfield POLE BN26 .... 214 E6
Southfield Rd SBGH/RUST TN4 .. 20 A5
Southfields RRTW TN3 .... 18 E4
WADH TN5 .... 44 B5
Southfields Rd EAST BN21 .... 10 A4
Southfields Wy SBGH/RUST TN4. 20 B3
South Gv RTW TN1 .... 30 A1 🄳
Southlands EGRIN RH19 .... 22 C4
Southlands Av BEXW TN39 ...... 195 F4
Southlands Rd BEXW TN39 ...... 195 F4
South La HTHF TN21 .... 133 G1
NEWHV BN9 .... 9 D3 🄳
South Lodge CI BURH RH15 ..... 89 F7 🄳
South Lynn Dr EAST BN21 .... 10 B3
Southmead CI MAYF TN20 .... 56 D8
Southmount ROTT BN2 .... 7 D1
Southon CI PTSD BN41 .... 175 J8
Southover High St LEW BN7 .... 2 C5 🄳
Southover Pl ROTT BN2 .... 7 D3
Southover Rd LEW BN7 .... 2 C4
Southover St ROTT BN2 .... 7 D4
Southridge Ri CROW TN6 .... 53 G3
Southridge Rd CROW TN6 .... 53 G3
South Rd BRI BN1 .... 6 A1
HAIL BN27 .... 189 F5
NEWHV BN9 .... 9 D3 🄳
RHWH RH17 .... 90 E7
South Rough RING/NEW BN8 ... 93 G5
South St BRI BN1 .... 6 C5
BRI BN1 .... 179 K5
CROW TN6 .... 53 H2
CROW TN6 .... 55 F4
EAST BN21 .... 10 B5 🄳
HPPT/KEY BN6 .... 119 K8
LEW BN7 .... 3 E4
MAYF TN20 .... 72 B1
PTSD BN41 .... 201 K2
RING/NEW BN8 .... 127 H7
SEAF BN25 .... 232 A1
SLVH TN37 .... 4 A5
South Ter HAS TN34 .... 5 D4
South Undercliff RYE TN31 ...... 113 J6
South Vw HPPT/KEY BN6 .... 119 K6
South View CI BUR/ETCH TN19 .. 61 K8
Southview CI CROW TN6 .... 53 G2 🄳
SHOR BN43 .... 201 F4
STHW BN42 .... 201 H2 🄳
Southview Dr UCK TN22 .... 95 J5
South View Rd CROW TN6 .... 53 G2
Southview Rd PEAHV BN10 ..... 222 B3
South View Rd SBGH/RUST TN4 .. 20 B3
Southview Rd STHW BN42 .... 201 H3
South View Rd WADH TN5 .... 44 B5
Southwater CI ROTT BN2 .... 7 F4
Southwater Rd SLVH TN37 .... 4 A4
Southway BURH RH15 .... 88 D8
LEW BN7 .... 2 A4
NEWHV BN9 .... 9 D3 🄳
SEAF BN25 .... 232 E2
Southwick CI EGRIN RH19 .... 22 B1
Southwick Sq STHW BN42 .... 201 H4
Southwick St STHW BN42 .... 201 H4
Southwood Av SBGH/RUST TN4. 20 A5
Southwood CI STLEO TN38 ..... 197 J2 🄳
South Woodlands BRI BN1 ...... 177 K7
Southwood Rd SBGH/RUST TN4. 19 F6
Sovereign CI HAS TN34 .... 170 D7
SEAF BN25 .... 225 H6 🄳
The Spaldings STLEO TN38 ..... 197 F2
The Sparrows PEAHV BN10 ..... 222 C2 🄳

Sparrow Wy HPPT/KEY BN6 .... 88 D8
Spatham La HPPT/KEY BN6 .... 120 B8
Speldhurst Hl RRTW TN5 .... 19 F5
Speldhurst Rd RRTW TN5 .... 18 D6
  SBGH/RUST TN4 .... 19 K3
Spencer Av HOVE BN3 .... 176 C8
Spencer Rd EAST BN21 .... 10 C5
Spences Fld LEW BN7 .... 3 E3
Spences La LEW BN7 .... 3 E3
Spicers Cl BURH RH15 .... 89 F6 🔢
Spindlewood Cl BEXW TN39 .... 194 B7
Spinnals Gv STHW BN42 .... 201 G4
Spinney Cl HPPT/KEY BN6 .... 118 C6
The Spinneys HTHF TN21 .... 100 B5 🔢
  LEW BN7 .... 3 E3
The Spinney BAT TN33 .... 137 F8
  BEXW TN39 .... 194 C8
  HAS TN34 .... 4 C3
  HOVE BN3 .... 177 H8
  HPPT/KEY BN6 .... 119 F6
  RBTBR TN32 .... 77 K8
Spital Rd LEW BN7 .... 2 B4
Spithurst Rd RING/NEW BN8 ...... 123 J4
Spoote La POLE TN6 .... 15 G3
Spotted Cow La UCK TN22 .... 69 G6
Spout Hl CROW TN6 .... 55 H2
Spray Hl RRTW TN5 .... 33 K7
Spray's La BAT TN33 .... 138 D7
Springate Rd STHW BN42 .... 201 J3
Spring Cl EDN/EASTW BN20 .... 229 G2
Springett Av RING/NEW BN8 ...... 155 J6
Springfield EGRIN RH19 .... 12 B7
Springfield Av PEAHV BN10 .... 221 J3
Springfield Cl CROW TN6 .... 53 K1 🔢
  PEV BN24 .... 217 G5
Springfield Rd BEX TN40 .... 195 H5
  BRI BN1 .... 6 C2
  LW/ROSE BN22 .... 11 D3 🔢
  RRTW TN3 .... 28 A4
  SBGH/RUST TN4 .... 19 K2
  STLEO TN38 .... 197 J2
Springfields WADH TN5 .... 60 C2
Springfield Valley Rd STLEO TN38 .. 197 J2
Spring Gdns BRI BN1 .... 6 C5
  LEW BN7 .... 3 D4 🔢
Springhead RTWE/PEM TN2 .... 20 D6
Springhead Wy CROW TN6 .... 53 C5
Spring Hl RTON TN11 .... 17 J5
  RYE TN31 .... 81 K4
Spring La BEXW TN39 .... 194 B6
  BUR/ETCH TN19 .... 74 E3
  HPPT/KEY BN6 .... 149 K3
  UCK TN22 .... 70 D6
Spring Lodge Cl LGNY BN23 ...... 231 F1 🔢
Spring Meadow FROW RH18 .... 35 K2
Springside Wk STLEO TN38 ...... 197 G2
Spring St BRI BN1 .... 6 A5 🔢
  SLVH TN37 .... 4 A3 🔢
Spring Wy EGRIN RH19 .... 12 C7
Springwood Rd HTHF TN21 .... 99 K3
Spruce Cl LW/ROSE BN22 .... 229 J1
The Stennings EGRIN RH19 .... 12 A8
Stephens Cl RING/NEW BN8 ...... 155 J6 🔢
Stephenson Dr EGRIN RH19 .... 22 D5
Stephens Rd BRI BN1 .... 204 C1
  SBGH/RUST TN4 .... 20 A6
Stevens Cl BEXW TN39 .... 195 H4
Stevenson Cl LGNY BN23 .... 217 F8 🔢
Stevenson Rd ROTT BN2 .... 7 J7
  SLVH TN37 .... 169 J8 🔢
Stewards Inn La LEW BN7 .... 2 C5 🔢
Stewart Rd SBGH/RUST TN4 .... 20 C4
Steyne Cl SEAF BN25 .... 232 B1
Steyne Rd SEAF BN25 .... 232 A1
Steyning Av HOVE BN3 .... 176 E8
  PEAHV BN10 .... 222 B4
Steyning Cl SEAF BN25 .... 232 A1
Steyning Rd ROTT BN2 .... 220 C2
  SEAF BN25 .... 232 E1
The Stiles HAIL BN27 .... 189 H4
Still La SBGH/RUST TN4 .... 19 K1 🔢
Stirling Av SEAF BN25 .... 225 K7
Stirling Cl BURH RH15 .... 89 J7
  SEAF BN25 .... 225 K8 🔢
Stirling Court Rd BURH RH15 ...... 89 J7
Stirling Pl HOVE BN3 .... 203 F5
Stirling Wy EGRIN RH19 .... 13 F8
Stock Dl RHAS TN35 .... 172 E7
Stockland Green Rd RRTW TN3 .... 19 G5
Stockland La UCK TN22 .... 69 K5
Stockleigh Rd STLEO TN38 .... 4 A5
Stocks Meadow BAT TN33 .... 166 A6
Stockwell Rd EGRIN RH19 .... 22 C5
Stoddards La RYE TN31 .... 82 C6
Stoke Cl SEAF BN25 .... 225 J8
Stoke Manor Cl SEAF BN25 .... 225 J8
Stonebeach Ri STLEO TN38 .... 169 G4
Stone Br TENT TN30 .... 86 D1
Stonebridge La UCK TN22 .... 97 H6
Stonecott Cl CROW TN6 .... 53 H3
Stonecroft Cl HOVE BN3 .... 176 D7
Stone Cross Rd CROW TN6 .... 53 H5
Stonecross Rd ROTT BN2 .... 179 C7
Stone Cross Rd WADH TN5 .... 44 C8
Stonedene Cl FROW RH18 .... 36 B1
Stonefield Pl HAS TN34 .... 5 D4 🔢

Stonefield Rd HAS TN34 ....
Stonefield Wy BURH RH15 8
Stonegate Cl LW/ROSE BN22 21
Stonegate Rd WADH TN5 5
Stonegate Wy HTHF TN21 10
Stoneham Cl LEW BN7 ....
Stoneham Rd HOVE BN3 20
Stonehouse Dr BAT TN33 16
  STLEO TN38 19
Stonehurst Ct ROTT BN2 7
Stonehurst La MAYF TN20 7
  UCK TN22 7
Stoneleigh Av BRI BN1 17
Stoneleigh Cl BRI BN1 17
  EGRIN RH19 22
Stonelink Cl STLEO TN38 16
Stonepark Dr FROW RH18 3
Stonepound Rd HPPT/KEY BN6 .. 11
Stone Quarry Rd RHWH RH17 4
Stonery Cl PTSD BN41 20
Stonery Rd PTSD BN41 20
Stonestile La RHAS TN35 13
Stone St BRI BN1 ....
  HAS TN34 5
  RTW TN1 2
Stonewall Park Rd RRTW TN3 1
Stonewood Cl SEAF BN25 225
Stoney La SHOR BN43 20
Stonhouse Dr STLEO TN38 16
Storrington Cl HOVE BN3 202
Straight Half Mile UCK TN22 6
Strand RYE TN31 11
Strand Hl WSEA TN36 14
Strand Meadow BUR/ETCH TN19.. 7
The Strand ROTT BN2 20
Stratford St RTW TN1 ....
Strawberry Cl RRTW TN3 ....
Strawberry Flds RYE TN31 8
Stream La BAT TN33 13
  HAWK TN18 6
  RHAS TN35 17
Streamside Cl HAS TN34 ....
Streat Bostall HPPT/KEY BN6 15
Streatfield Gdns HTHF TN21 9
Streatfield Rd HTHF TN21 9
  UCK TN22 ....
Streat La HPPT/KEY BN6 12
  HPPT/KEY BN6 19
Streele La UCK TN22 9
Streele Vw UCK TN22 9
Street End La HTHF TN20 10
  MAYF TN20 ....
Streetlands BAT TN33 13
The Street BAT TN33 13
  HPPT/KEY BN6 15
  LEW BN7 18
  RING/NEW BN8 15
  SHOR BN43 20
  TENT TN30 8
  UCK TN22 ....
Stringer Wy BRI BN1 17
The Stringwalk HAIL BN27 18
Stroma Gdns HAIL BN27 18
Strood Ga RHWH RH17 ....
Strood Rd SLVH TN37 ....
Stuart Av EAST BN21 22
Stuart Cl RTWE/PEM TN2 ....
Stuart Wy EGRIN RH19 2
Stubb La RYE TN31 13
Studdens La HAIL BN27 16
Sturdee Cl LGNY BN23 ....
Sudeley Pl ROTT BN2 ....
Sudeley St ROTT BN2 ....
Sudeley Ter ROTT BN2 .... 7 F
Suffolk Rd BEXW TN39 19
Suffolk St HOVE BN3 20
Sullington Cl ROTT BN2 17
Sullington Wy SHOR BN43 20
Sumach Cl LW/ROSE BN22 22
Summer Cl PTSD BN41 20
Summercourt HAIL BN27 189
Summerdale Rd HOVE BN3 20
Summerdown Cl
  EDN/EASTW BN20 22
Summerdown La
  EDN/EASTW BN20 22
Summerdown Rd
  EDN/EASTW BN20 22
Summerfields SLVH TN37 4
Summerfields Av HAIL BN27 18
Summerheath Rd HAIL BN27 18
Summerhill Av SBGH/RUST TN4 .. 19
Summerhill Rd LW/ROSE BN22 2
Summerlands Rd LW/ROSE BN22.. 22
Summersdeane STHW BN42 20
Summervale Rd SBGH/RUST TN4.. 2
Sun La HAS TN34 5
Sunningdale Cl BEX TN40 19
  HAIL BN27 18
  SEAF BN25 232
Sunningdale Dr STLEO TN38 19
Sunninghill Av HOVE BN3 20
Sunninghill Cl HOVE BN3 202
Sunnybrooke Cl UCK TN22 95

nycroft Cl *RHWH* RH17 .... 91 G1
nydale Av *BRI* BN1 .... 178 B5
nydale Cl *BRI* BN1 .... 178 B5
nyside Rd *SBGH/RUST* TN4 .... 19 G7
set Cl *PEAHV* BN10 .... 222 A2
EV BN24 .... 218 B5
star La *POLE* BN26 .... 214 D5
St *LEW* BN7 .... 2 C4
view Av *PEAHV* BN10 .... 222 C5
renden Cl *BRI* BN1 .... 178 A7
renden Crs *BRI* BN1 .... 177 K8
renden Holt *BRI* BN1 .... 178 A8
renden Pk *BRI* BN1 .... 178 B7
renden Rd *BRI* BN1 .... 178 A8
rey Cl *RTWE/PEM* TN2 .... 29 K3
rey Rd *SEAF* BN25 .... 224 D7
rey St *BRI* BN1 .... 6 E4
ry St *SHOR* BN43 .... 200 C4
s Rd *RING/NEW* BN8 .... 127 J6
an's Rd *EAST* BN21 .... 10 C4
sex Av *HAIL* BN27 .... 189 C5
sex Border Pth *BRI* BN1 .... 176 E1
DEN TN8 .... 14 C3
RRIN RH19 .... 22 E6
AWK TN18 .... 63 G5
SD BN41 .... 175 H5
HW RH17 .... 48 B3
RTW TN3 .... 17 F7
ENT TN30 .... 84 D4
ADH TN5 .... 43 K3
ADH TN5 .... 46 E7
sex *BEXW* TN39 .... 194 E6
AIL BN27 .... 189 C5
TWE/PEM TN2 .... 30 C2
sex Gdns *EDN/EASTW* BN20 .... 235 C2
sex Ms *RTWE/PEM* TN2 .... 30 A1
sex Pl *ROTT* BN2 .... 7 D4
sex Rd *HOVE* BN3 .... 203 C6
LEO TN38 .... 197 H5
sex Sq *ROTT* BN2 .... 205 F7
sex St *ROTT* BN2 .... 7 D5
sex Wy *BURH* RH15 .... 88 E6
EAHV BN10 .... 221 J4
erland Av *PEAHV* BN10 .... 222 A4
erland Cl *BEXW* TN39 .... 194 E7
erland Rd *ROTT* BN2 .... 7 E5
TW TN1 .... 30 B1
on Av *PEAHV* BN10 .... 222 A4
AF BN25 .... 232 C1
on Av North *PEAHV* BN10 .... 222 A3
on Cl *ROTT* BN2 .... 206 B2
on Croft La *SEAF* BN25 .... 225 F8
on Dro *SEAF* BN25 .... 225 C7
on Park Rd *SEAF* BN25 .... 225 F8
on Pl *SEAF* TN40 .... 195 K7
on Rd *EAST* BN21 .... 10 C4
AF BN25 .... 225 C8
Suttons *RYE* TN31 .... 145 H2
LEO TN38 .... 197 C1
ines Wy *HTHF* TN21 .... 100 A5
nham La *BAT* TN33 .... 168 B3
llow Bank *STLEO* TN38 .... 197 C1
llow Cl *LGNY* BN23 .... 230 C1
llow Cl *UCK* TN22 .... 95 K6
llow Dr *BAT* TN33 .... 137 F7
TWE/PEM TN2 .... 21 F5
llowfield *LING* RH7 .... 12 E1
Swallows *PEAHV* BN10 .... 222 A2
nborough Dr *ROTT* BN2 .... 205 C2
nborough Dro *LEW* BN7 .... 181 J8
nborough Hollow *LEW* BN7 .... 181 K7
nborough Pl *ROTT* BN2 .... 205 C4
n Cl *RING/NEW* BN8 .... 122 C4
nley Cl *LGNY* BN23 .... 230 D1
nn Cl *BURH* RH15 .... 89 K8
nnee Cl *PEAHV* BN10 .... 222 C2
AF BN25 .... 232 C1
nsbrook La *HTHF* TN21 .... 160 C2
ns Chyll RH18 .... 23 J8
n Ter *HAS* TN34 .... 5 E4
ylands Av *CROW* TN6 .... 53 H4
eps Hill *RTWE/PEM* TN2 .... 21 F6
ethaws La *CROW* TN6 .... 52 E5
etings La *RRTW* TN3 .... 45 F2
etlands *HPPT/KEY* BN6 .... 119 H6
e La *HTHF* TN21 .... 73 J8
t Cl *CROW* TN6 .... 53 F2
PT/KEY BN6 .... 88 D8
K TN22 .... 95 K6
aburne Av *LW/ROSE* BN22 .... 215 C5
s Gdns *SHOR* BN43 .... 200 A4
sland Hl *EGRIN* RH19 .... 12 C5
nford Dr *STLEO* TN38 .... 169 C6
on Wy *CROW* TN6 .... 54 D3
more Cl *BEXW* TN39 .... 194 B6
HF TN21 .... 100 B5
ROSE BN22 .... 215 J8
SD BN41 .... 176 B8
TT BN2 .... 206 B3
AF BN25 .... 225 K8
LEO TN38 .... 197 H2
more Ct *UCK* TN22 .... 95 K3
more Dr *EGRIN* RH19 .... 22 E2
IL BN27 .... 189 C5
Sycamores *PEAHV* BN10 .... 222 C2

Sydney Cl *STLEO* TN38 .... 169 J8
Sydney Little Rd *STLEO* TN38 .... 168 E7
Sydney Rd *LW/ROSE* BN22 .... 11 D4
Sydney St *BRI* BN1 .... 6 C4
Sylvester Wy *HOVE* BN3 .... 176 B8
Symbister Rd *PTSD* BN41 .... 202 B4

T

Tackleway *HAS* TN34 .... 5 F4
Taddington Rd *LW/ROSE* BN22 .... 11 E3
Tainter's Brook *UCK* TN22 .... 96 A3
Talbot Pk *RTWE/PEM* TN2 .... 20 D6
Talbot Rd *BRI* BN1 .... 178 E5
Talbot Rd *TN18* 63 F3
Talbot Ter *LEW* BN7 .... 2 C4
Tall Ash Dr *SLVH* TN37 .... 169 K7
Tamarack Cl *LW/ROSE* BN22 .... 229 J1
Tamar Cl *PEV* BN24 .... 216 B6
Tamplin Ter *ROTT* BN2 .... 7 D4
Tamworth Rd *HOVE* BN3 .... 202 E4
Tanbridge Rd *LGNY* BN23 .... 231 C2
Tandridge Rd *HOVE* BN3 .... 202 D5
Tangier La *RRTW* TN3 .... 30 D5
Tanglewood Coppice
BEXW TN39 .... 194 D8
Tangmere Cl *BEXW* TN39 .... 194 D8
Tangmere Rd *BRI* BN1 .... 178 B5
Tanhouse La *RYE* TN31 .... 111 K1
Tanners Brook *LEW* BN7 .... 3 D5
Tanners Fld *RHWH* RH17 .... 90 C6
Tanners Wy *CROW* TN6 .... 53 J2
Tanyard Av *EGRIN* RH19 .... 22 E1
Tanyard La *RHWH* RH17 .... 49 C7
SBGH/RUST TN4 .... 19 K2
WSEA TN36 .... 142 E3
Tapsell's La *WADH* TN5 .... 43 J6
Tarmount La *SHOR* BN43 .... 200 C4
Tarner Rd *ROTT* BN2 .... 7 D4
Tarragon Wy *SHOR* BN43 .... 201 F2
Tarring Rd *NEWHV* BN9 .... 223 J1
Tas Combe Wy *EDN/EASTW* BN20 .... 229 C1
Tate Crs *BURH* RH15 .... 89 F6
Tates *HAWK* TN18 .... 63 G2
Taunton Rd *ROTT* BN2 .... 205 C2
Taunton Wy *ROTT* BN2 .... 205 H2
Tavistock Down *BRI* BN1 .... 204 D1
Taylor Cl *STLEO* TN38 .... 169 C7
Taylor St *SBGH/RUST* TN4 .... 19 K3
Tea Garden La *RRTW* TN3 .... 29 C2
Teal Ct *STLEO* TN38 .... 169 F8
Tedder Rd *SBGH/RUST* TN4 .... 20 B4
Teg Cl *PTSD* BN41 .... 202 B1
Telegraph St *ROTT* BN2 .... 7 E6
Telford Rd *STLEO* TN38 .... 169 H6
Telham Cl *HAS* TN34 .... 170 D6
Telham La *BAT* TN33 .... 167 K2
Telscombe Cliffs Wy *PEAHV* BN10 .... 221 J4
Telscombe Pk *PEAHV* BN10 .... 222 B1
Telscombe Wy *LGNY* BN23 .... 231 C1
PEAHV BN10 .... 222 B1
Temple Gdns *HOVE* BN3 .... 6 A4
Temple Gv *BURH* RH15 .... 88 D7
Temple St *BRI* BN1 .... 6 A5
Tenantry Down Rd *ROTT* BN2 .... 205 F4
Tenantry Rd *ROTT* BN2 .... 7 F2
Tennis Cl *HAIL* BN27 .... 189 C4
Tennis Rd *HOVE* BN3 .... 202 D5
Tennyson Rd *EGRIN* RH19 .... 22 A4
Tenterden Cl *LGNY* BN23 .... 230 E1
Tenterden Ri *HAS* TN34 .... 4 B1
Terminus Av *BEXW* TN39 .... 194 E8
Terminus Pl *BRI* BN1 .... 6 B3
Terminus Rd *BEXW* TN39 .... 195 F8
BRI BN1 .... 6 B3
EAST BN21 .... 10 B4
Terminus St *BRI* BN1 .... 6 B4
Terrace Rd *SLVH* TN37 .... 4 A5
Thackeray Cl *LGNY* BN23 .... 217 F8
Thakeham Cl *BEX* TN40 .... 196 B5
Thames Cl *ROTT* BN2 .... 7 D5
Thanet Wy *HAS* TN34 .... 4 C2
Thatchers Cl *BURH* RH15 .... 119 C5
The Thatchings *POLE* BN26 .... 215 F6
Theobalds *HAWK* TN18 .... 63 F1
Theobalds Gn *HTHF* TN21 .... 100 A6
Theobalds Rd *BURH* RH15 .... 89 J5
Theodore Cl *RTWE/PEM* TN2 .... 20 E4
Third Av *HOVE* BN3 .... 203 C6
NEWHV BN9 .... 8 C4
Third Rd *PEAHV* BN10 .... 221 K4
Third St *RRTW* TN3 .... 18 D8
Thirlmere Rd *SBGH/RUST* TN4 .... 19 H6
Thomas Brassey Cl *SLVH* TN37 .... 169 J6
Thomas St *LEW* BN7 .... 3 E4
SBGH/RUST TN4 .... 20 A6
Thomas Turner Dr
RING/NEW BN8 .... 127 J6
Thompson Rd *BRI* BN1 .... 7 E1
NEWHV BN9 .... 224 A1
Thornbank Crs *BEXW* TN39 .... 194 E8
Thornbush Crs *PTSD* BN41 .... 176 A8

Thorndean Rd *ROTT* BN2 .... 178 E8
Thorne Crs *BEXW* TN39 .... 194 D2
Thornfield Gdns *RTWE/PEM* TN2 .... 21 F6
Thornhill Av *BRI* BN1 .... 178 B4
Thornhill Cl *HOVE* BN3 .... 202 D1
Thornhill Ri *PTSD* BN41 .... 175 K7
Thornhill Wy *PTSD* BN41 .... 175 K8
The Thorns *RHAS* TN35 .... 171 K3
Thornwell Rd *POLE* BN26 .... 213 J4
Thornwood Cl *LW/ROSE* BN22 .... 229 K1
Thorny Cl *HTHF* TN21 .... 100 A4
Three Leg Cross Rd *WADH* TN5 .... 46 B8
Three Oaks La *WADH* TN5 .... 43 J4
Thurrock Cl *EDN/EASTW* BN20 .... 215 G2
Thyme Cl *SHOR* BN43 .... 201 F2
Thyssel La *RYE* TN43 .... 81 K5
Tibbs Mill La *UCK* TN22 .... 69 C2
Ticehurst Av *BEXW* TN39 .... 195 J6
Ticehurst Rd *ROTT* BN2 .... 205 C6
Tichborne St *BRI* BN1 .... 6 C5
Tickerage La *UCK* TN22 .... 97 H5
Tidebrook Gdns *LGNY* BN23 .... 231 C1
Tideswell Rd *EAST* BN21 .... 10 C4
Tidy St *BRI* BN1 .... 6 C2
Tilbury Pl *ROTT* BN2 .... 7 D5
Tilbury Wy *ROTT* BN2 .... 7 D4
Tile Barn Cl *UCK* TN22 .... 124 D3
Tile Barn Rd *STLEO* TN38 .... 169 G7
Tilehurst Dr *HAIL* BN27 .... 189 F3
Tilekiln La *RHAS* TN35 .... 171 H7
Tilers Cl *BURH* RH15 .... 89 K8
Tilgate Cl *EAST* BN21 .... 229 J4
ROTT BN2 .... 7 F4
Tilgate Dr *BEXW* TN39 .... 194 C8
Tilley La *HAIL* BN27 .... 164 A6
Tillingham Av *RYE* TN31 .... 113 H6
Tillingham La *RYE* TN31 .... 109 K3
Tillingham Vw *RYE* TN31 .... 109 J7
Tillingham Wy *PEV* BN24 .... 216 B6
Tillstone Cl *ROTT* BN2 .... 204 E1
Tillstone St *ROTT* BN2 .... 7 D5
Tilsmore Cnr *HTHF* TN21 .... 99 K4
Tilsmore Rd *HTHF* TN21 .... 99 K4
Timberlaine Rd *PEV* BN24 .... 217 K7
Timberley Rd *LW/ROSE* BN22 .... 229 J2
Timbers Ct *HAIL* BN27 .... 189 H4
Timber Yard Cottages *LEW* BN7 .... 3 E4
Tindal Cl *BURH* RH15 .... 89 K8
Tinker's La *UCK* TN22 .... 70 C7
WADH TN5 .... 46 B8
Tintern Cl *BRI* BN1 .... 7 D1
LW/ROSE BN22 .... 215 J8
Tisbury Rd *HOVE* BN3 .... 203 H5
Titchfield Cl *BURH* RH15 .... 119 K2
Tithe Barn Fld *WSEA* TN36 .... 141 K6
Titian Rd *HOVE* BN3 .... 202 E4
Tiverton Dr *BEX* TN40 .... 195 K6
Tivoli Crs *BRI* BN1 .... 203 J1
Tivoli Crs North *BRI* BN1 .... 203 J1
Tivoli Pl *BRI* BN1 .... 203 J1
Tivoli Rd *BRI* BN1 .... 203 J1
Tolhurst La *WADH* TN5 .... 59 J2
Tolkien Rd *LGNY* BN23 .... 231 F1
Tollgate *PEAHV* BN10 .... 222 A2
Tollgates *BAT* TN33 .... 136 B7
Toll La *UCK* TN22 .... 67 F2
Tollwood Pk *CROW* TN6 .... 53 K2
Tollwood Rd *CROW* TN6 .... 53 K3
Toll Wood Rd *HTHF* TN21 .... 129 K4
Tompset's Bank *FROW* RH18 .... 35 K3
Tomtits La *FROW* RH18 .... 35 J2
Tonbridge Rd *RTWE/PEM* TN2 .... 21 H4
Tonbridge Wy *RYE* TN31 .... 145 G1
Tongdean Av *HOVE* BN3 .... 177 H8
Tongdean La *BRI* BN1 .... 177 J7
Tongdean Ri *BRI* BN1 .... 177 H7
Tongdean Rd *HOVE* BN3 .... 177 G8
Tongswood Dr *HAWK* TN18 .... 63 J2
Top Cross Rd *BEX* TN40 .... 196 B4
Top Dr *UCK* TN22 .... 67 C5
Torcross Cl *ROTT* BN2 .... 205 F2
Torfield Rd *EAST* BN21 .... 10 A3
Toronto Ter *LEW* BN7 .... 2 C4
ROTT BN2 .... 7 D4
Torrance Cl *HOVE* BN3 .... 202 E2
Tor Rd *PEAHV* BN10 .... 222 B1
Tor Rd West *PEAHV* BN10 .... 222 A1
Totland Rd *ROTT* BN2 .... 7 F3
Tottington Wy *SHOR* BN43 .... 200 E2
Tott Yew Rd *EDN/EASTW* BN20 .... 215 F7
Tovey Cl *EAST* BN21 .... 229 J5
Tower Cl *EGRIN* RH19 .... 22 C1
PEV BN24 .... 218 C5
Towergate *BRI* BN1 .... 203 K1
Tower Ride *UCK* TN22 .... 95 K2
Tower Rd *ROTT* BN2 .... 7 E4
STLEO TN38 .... 4 A3
Tower Rd West *STLEO* TN38 .... 197 J3
Towerscroft Av *SLVH* TN37 .... 169 J6
Tower St *HTHF* TN21 .... 100 B5
RYE TN31 .... 113 J5
Tower Vw *UCK* TN22 .... 95 K3
Town Hl *RRTW* TN3 .... 33 J7
Trafalgar Cl *PEAHV* BN10 .... 222 B2
STLEO TN38 .... 169 G4

Trafalgar Ct *BRI* BN1 .... 6 C4 🔢
Trafalgar Ga *ROTT* BN2 .... 205 G8
Trafalgar La *BRI* BN1 .... 6 C4
Trafalgar Pl *BRI* BN1 .... 6 C4 🔢
Trafalgar St *BRI* BN1 .... 6 C4
Tram Rd *RYE* TN31 .... 144 C1
Transit Rd *NEWHV* BN9 .... 9 D3
Travellers La *RHAS* TN35 .... 171 F7
Trebilco Cl *RTWE/PEM* TN2 .... 20 D4 🔢
Treblers Rd *CROW* TN6 .... 54 B4
Tredcroft Rd *HOVE* BN3 .... 203 G1
Tree Tops Cl *ROTT* BN2 .... 206 B3
Tremola Av *ROTT* BN2 .... 220 E1
Trenches Rd *CROW* TN6 .... 53 H2
Treyford Cl *ROTT* BN2 .... 206 B2
The Triangle *EDN/EASTW* BN20 .. 215 F8 🔢
Trinity Cl *RTWE/PEM* TN2 .... 20 D7
Trinity Fld *RING/NEW* BN8 ..... 155 K5
Trinity Pl *EAST* BN21 .... 10 C5
Trinity Rd *HPPT/KEY* BN6 .... 118 A5
Trinity St *ROTT* BN2 .... 7 D5
Trinity Trees *EAST* BN21 .... 10 C5
Tristan Gdns *SBGH/RUST* TN4 .. 19 H7 🔢
Troon Cl *SEAF* BN25 .... 224 B5 🔢
Trossachs Cl *LGNY* BN23 .... 216 E3
Troy Cl *CROW* TN6 .... 53 J2 🔢
Truleigh Cl *ROTT* BN2 .... 206 C4
Truleigh Dr *PTSD* BN41 .... 175 K7
Truleigh Wy *SHOR* BN43 .... 200 D2
Truman Dr *STLEO* TN38 .... 169 G5
Trumpet La *HAIL* BN27 .... 163 J1
Tubwell La *CROW* TN6 .... 54 B4
HTHF TN21 .... 129 K1
Tudor Av *STLEO* TN38 .... 197 H4
Tudor Cl *EGRIN* RH19 .... 22 D4 🔢
HOVE BN3 .... 202 E1
SEAF BN25 .... 224 E7
Tudor Ct *RTWE/PEM* TN2 .... 29 J2 🔢
Tudor Gdns *BURH* RH15 .... 89 F7 🔢
Tudor Wk *UCK* TN22 .... 96 D6
Tugwell Rd *LW/ROSE* BN22 ..... 230 A1
Tumulus Rd *ROTT* BN2 .... 221 F1
Tunbridge Wells Rd *CROW* TN6 .. 55 J5
MAYF TN20 .... 55 K6
Tunnel Rd *RTW* TN1 .... 20 B6
Turkey La *BURH* RH15 .... 89 H8 🔢
Turkey Rd *BEXW* TN39 .... 194 C4
Turk's Br *HTHF* TN21 .... 74 A3
Turnberry Cl *STLEO* TN38 .... 197 G4
Turnberry Dr *HAIL* BN27 .... 189 F3
Turner Cl *BEX* TN40 .... 195 J6
LGNY BN23 .... 230 E2 🔢
Turner Ct *EGRIN* RH19 .... 12 E8
Turners Green La *WADH* TN5 .... 44 B5
Turners Green Rd *WADH* TN5 ..... 44 B4
Turners Wy *BURH* RH15 .... 89 F7 🔢
Turnpike Cl *PEAHV* BN10 .... 222 B3
RING/NEW BN8 .... 156 B3
Turton Cl *ROTT* BN2 .... 7 F5
Tutts Barn La *LW/ROSE* BN22 .. 10 B2
Tuxford Rd *SBGH/RUST* TN4 .... 19 F6
Twineham Ct *ROTT* BN2 .... 205 G4
Twineham Rd *EAST* BN21 .... 229 J4
Twitten Cl *STHW* BN42 .... 201 H4 🔢
Twitten *BURH* RH15 .... 89 H7 🔢
The Twitten *BURH* RH15 .... 89 H7 🔢
CROW TN6 .... 53 G2 🔢
STHW BN42 .... 201 H4
Twyford Crs *SLVH* TN37 .... 169 K7
Twyford Rd *BRI* BN1 .... 178 E5
Twyfords *CROW* TN6 .... 53 G2 🔢
Twyhurst Ct *EGRIN* RH19 .... 12 B8 🔢
Tye Cl *ROTT* BN2 .... 221 G3
Tyedean Rd *PEAHV* BN10 ...... 221 J3
Tye Hill Rd *POLE* BN26 .... 187 J7
Tye Vw *PEAHV* BN10 .... 221 K2 🔢
Tylers La *UCK* TN22 .... 66 E2
Tyndale Av *BEXW* TN39 .... 194 B8

U

Uckfield Cl *ROTT* BN2 .... 205 G5
Uckfield Rd *CROW* TN6 .... 52 D5
RING/NEW BN8 .... 155 G4
Uckham La *BAT* TN33 .... 136 E5
Udimore Rd *RYE* TN31 .... 109 K7
RYE TN31 .... 112 E7
Undercliff *STLEO* TN38 .... 197 J5
Underdown Rd *STHW* BN42 .... 201 H3
Underhill *UCK* TN22 .... 67 H6
Underhill La *HPPT/KEY* BN6 ... 149 K3
Under Rd *HAIL* BN27 .... 162 C8
Union Cl *HAIL* BN27 .... 189 C1
Union Rd *ROTT* BN2 .... 7 D5
Union St *BRI* BN1 .... 6 C5 🔢
STLEO TN38 .... 4 A5 🔢
Upland Rd *EDN/EASTW* BN20 .. 229 G8
Uplands Cl *BEXW* TN39 .... 194 E5
Uplands Pk *HTHF* TN21 .... 100 E2
Uplands Rd *BRI* BN1 .... 204 D1
UCK TN22 .... 95 J2
Upper Abbey Rd *ROTT* BN2 .... 7 F6
Upper Av *EAST* BN21 .... 10 C3

Upper Bannings Rd *ROTT* BN2 .... 207 H8
Upper Bedford St *ROTT* BN2... 7 E6
Upper Belgrave Rd *SEAF* BN25 .. 225 C6
Upper Bevendean Av *ROTT* BN2 .. 205 F2
Upper Broomgrove Rd *HAS* TN54 .. 5 F1
Upper Carlisle Rd
EDN/EASTW BN20 .... 236 C3
Upper Chalvington Pl *ROTT* BN2 .. 205 F6
Upper Church Rd *SLVH* TN37 .. 169 J7
Upper Chyngton Gdns
SEAF BN25 .... 225 J6 🔢
Upper Clarence Rd *SLVH* TN37 .. 4 A2
Upper Cl *FROW* RH18 .... 35 K1
Upper Cumberland Wk *RTW* TN1... 30 B2
The Upper Dr *HOVE* BN3 .... 203 H3
Upper Duke's Dr
EDN/EASTW BN20 .... 236 D4
Upper Dunstan Rd
SBGH/RUST TN4 .... 20 B5
Upper Gardner St *BRI* BN1 ..... 6 C4 🔢
Upper Glen Rd *SLVH* TN37 .... 169 H6
Upper Gloucester Rd *BRI* BN1 .. 6 B4 🔢
Upper Greenwoods La
HTHF TN21 .... 101 H5
Upper Grosvenor Rd
RTW TN1 .... 20 B6
Upper Hamilton Rd *BRI* BN1 .... 6 A2
Upper Hollingdean Rd *BRI* BN1 .. 7 D1
Upper Horsebridge Rd *HAIL* BN27 .. 161 F8
Upper King's Dr
EDN/EASTW BN20 .... 229 G2
Upper Kingston La *STHW* BN42 .. 201 G2
Upper Lake *BAT* TN33 .... 136 D7
Upper Lewes Rd *ROTT* BN2 .... 7 D3
Upper Market St *HOVE* BN3 .... 203 J6 🔢
Upper Maze Hl *STLEO* TN38 .. 197 J3
Upper Nellington *RRTW* TN3 ... 19 F7
Upper North St *BRI* BN1 .... 6 B5 🔢
Upper Park Pl *ROTT* BN2 .... 7 D5 🔢
Upper Park Rd *SLVH* TN37 .... 4 A3
Upper Profit *RRTW* TN3 .... 18 E8
Upper Ratton Dr
EDN/EASTW BN20 .... 229 G3
Upper Rock Gdns *ROTT* BN2 ..... 7 D6
Upper St James's St *ROTT* BN2 .. 7 D6
Upper St Johns Rd *BURH* RH15 .. 89 G8
Upper Sea Rd *BEX* TN40 .... 195 J7
Upper Sherwood Rd *SEAF* BN25 .. 225 J7
Upper Shoreham Rd *SHOR* BN43 .. 200 B3
STHW BN42 .... 201 G2
Upper South Rd *SLVH* TN37 ..... 4 A3
Upper Station Rd *HTHF* TN21 .. 100 A4
Upper Stephens *RRTW* TN3 .... 18 E8
Upper Stoneham *RING/NEW* BN8 .. 3 F1
Upper St *EDN/EASTW* BN20 .... 235 F3
Upper Sudeley St *ROTT* BN2 ..... 7 F6 🔢
Upperton Gdns *EAST* BN21 .... 10 B4
Upperton La *EAST* BN21 .... 10 B4
Upperton Rd *EAST* BN21 .... 10 A3
Upper Valley Rd *NEWHV* BN9 ... 8 B4
Upper Wellington Rd *ROTT* BN2 ... 7 E3
Upper Winfield Av *BRI* BN1 .... 178 A5
Upper Wish Hl *EDN/EASTW* BN20 .. 229 G2
Upton Av *STHW* BN42 .... 201 H2
Upton Quarry *RRTW* TN3 .... 18 D8 🔢
Upwick Rd *EDN/EASTW* BN20 .. 229 H8

V

Vale Av *BRI* BN1 .... 177 K4
RTW TN1 .... 20 A8 🔢
SBGH/RUST TN4 .... 19 K2
Valebridge Cl *BURH* RH15 ...... 89 J5 🔢
Valebridge Dr *BURH* RH15 ...... 89 J6 🔢
Valebridge Rd *BURH* RH15 ...... 89 J6
Vale Cl *SEAF* BN25 .... 225 H7
Vale Gdns *PTSD* BN41 .... 202 A4
Valence Rd *LEW* BN7 .... 2 B4
Valentine Dr *BURH* RH15 .... 88 E7
Valerie Cl *PTSD* BN41 .... 202 A1
Vale Rd *BAT* TN33 .... 136 B6
KWH RH16 .... 89 K1
MAYF TN20 .... 72 B1
PTSD BN41 .... 202 B4
ROTT BN2 .... 207 G8
RTW TN1 .... 20 A8
SBGH/RUST TN4 .... 19 K2
SEAF BN25 .... 225 G7
SLVH TN37 .... 4 A2
The Vale *ROTT* BN2 .... 206 B6
Vale View Rd *HTHF* TN21 ...... 100 B5 🔢
Valiance Cl *BURH* RH15 .... 88 E7
Valiance Gdns *HOVE* BN3 ...... 203 F5
Vallance Rd *HOVE* BN3 .... 203 F5
Valley Cl *BRI* BN1 .... 177 H7
NEWHV BN9 .... 8 B2
Valley Dene *NEWHV* BN9 .... 8 B3
Valley Dr *BRI* BN1 .... 177 H7
SEAF BN25 .... 225 H6
Valley Ri *SEAF* BN25 .... 225 G7
Valley Rd *CROW* TN6 .... 53 H2
LEW BN7 .... 2 A5

NEWHV BN9 .... 8 B2
Peahv BN10 22
PTSD BN41 20
SBGH/RUST TN4 11
Valley Side Rd *HAS* TN54 17
Valley Vw *SBGH/RUST* TN4 2
Valley View Cl *CROW* TN6 5
Val Prinseps Rd *PEV* BN24 21
Vanguard Wy *CROW* TN6 5
EGRIN RH19 1
LING RH7 5
POLE BN26 21
RING/NEW BN8 15
SEAF BN25 22
SEAF BN25 22
UCK TN22 6
UCK TN22 9
Varndean Cl *BRI* BN1 17
Varndean Dr *BRI* BN1 17
Varndean Gdns *BRI* BN1 17
Varndean Holt *BRI* BN1 17
Varndean Rd *BRI* BN1 17
Vega Cl *HAIL* BN27 18
Ventnor Cl *LGNY* BN23 21
Ventnor Vls *HOVE* BN3 20
Venture Cl *BEX* TN40 19
Verbania Wy *EGRIN* RH19 2
Verdant Cl *SLVH* TN37 2
Vere Rd *BRI* BN1 1
Vermont Rd *SBGH/RUST* TN4 ... 19
Vernon Av *PEAHV* BN10 22
ROTT BN2 20
Vernon Cl *LGNY* BN23 231
Vernon Rd *RTW* TN1 2
UCK TN22 9
Vernons Rd *RING/NEW* BN8 9
Vernon Ter *BRI* BN1 6
Veronica Wy *ROTT* BN2 7
Viaduct Rd *BRI* BN1 7
ROTT BN2 7
Vian Av *LGNY* BN23 230
Vicarage Cl *NEWHV* BN9 223
RING/NEW BN8 15
SEAF BN25 22
Vicarage Dr *EDN/EASTW* BN20 .. 22
Vicarage La *BUR/ETCH* TN19... 7
EDN/EASTW BN20 229
HAIL BN27 16
HAIL BN27 18
RHAS TN35 13
ROTT BN2 220
Vicarage Rd *BUR/ETCH* TN19... 7
EDN/EASTW BN20 22
HAIL BN27 18
HAS TN34 1
SBGH/RUST TN4 1
Vicarage Ter *ROTT* BN2 220
Vicarage Wy *BUR/ETCH* TN19... 6
RING/NEW BN8 15
Victor Cl *SEAF* BN25 22
Victoria Av *BURH* RH15 88
PEAHV BN10 22
RHAS TN35 17
Victoria Cl *BURH* RH15 88
BURH RH15 11
POLE BN26 21
Victoria Dr *EAST* BN21 1
EDN/EASTW BN20 22
Victoria Gdns *BURH* RH15 11
EDN/EASTW BN20 229
Victoria Gv *HOVE* BN3 203
Victoria Pl *BRI* BN1 6
Victoria Rd *BEXW* TN39 19
BRI BN1 1
BURH RH15 11
CROW TN6 5
EDN/EASTW BN20 229
HAIL BN27 18
HAIL BN27 16
MAYF TN20 7
POLE BN26 21
PTSD BN41 20
RTW TN1 20
SBGH/RUST TN4 1
SHOR BN43 20
SLVH TN37 4
STHW BN42 20
Victoria St *BRI* BN1 .... 2C
Victoria Wy *BURH* RH15 11
EGRIN RH19 1
WSEA TN36 14
Victory Ms *ROTT* BN2 20
View Bank *RHAS* TN35 15
View Rd *PEAHV* BN10 22
View Ter *LING* RH7 5
Viking Cl *SEAF* BN25 22
The Village Barn *BRI* BN1 19
The Village Ms *BEXW* TN39 19
The Village *EDN/EASTW* BN20 . 21
Village Wy *BRI* BN1 17
Villa Rd *SLVH* TN37 .... 2C
Villiers Cl *ROTT* BN2 .... 2C
Vincent Cl *LGNY* BN23 231
Vinehall Cl *HAS* TN34 17

Woodlands Cl *HAIL* BN27	189	H1
HPPT/KEY BN6	119	F7
HTHF TN21	100	B6
PEAHV BN10	222	A2
UCK TN22	95	K3
Woodlands Rd *EGRIN* RH19	12	E2
HPPT/KEY BN6	119	F7
The Woodlands *BRI* BN1	177	K6
HAS TN34	170	B6
Woodlands Wy *HAS* TN34	170	B5
Woodland Vale Rd *STLEO* TN38	4	A4
Woodland Wk *ROTT* BN2	206	A7
Woodland Wy *BAT* TN33	178	A7
BRI BN1	53	H3
CROW TN6	53	H3
HTHF TN21	100	B5
RHAS TN35	172	D6
Wood La *HAIL* BN27	164	B8
Woodleigh Rd *BURH* RH15	89	J7
Woodpecker Crs *HPPT/KEY* BN6	88	D8
Woodpecker Dr *HAIL* BN27	189	F3
Woodpecker Rd *LGNY* BN23	230	C1
Woodpecker Wy *UCK* TN22	95	K6
Woodruff Av *HOVE* BN3	203	H1
Woodsgate Av *BEX* TN40	195	H5
BEXW TN39	195	H5
Woodsgate Pk *BEXW* TN39	195	F5
Woodsgate Wy *RTWE/PEM* TN2	21	H5
Woods Hill Cl *EGRIN* RH19	23	H5
Woods Hill La *EGRIN* RH19	23	H5
Woodside *CROW* TN6	53	C1
Woodside Av *BRI* BN1	203	J1
Woodside Rd *SBGH/RUST* TN4	19	H7
Woodside Wy *HAIL* BN27	189	F7
Woodspring Cl *SLVH* TN37	169	J2
Woodstock *EGRIN* RH19	22	A1
Woodstock Rd *BEXW* TN39	194	B5
Wood St *EGRIN* RH19	22	B2
RTW TN1	20	B7
Woodview *SHOR* BN43	200	C3
Woodview Cl *BRI* BN1	178	E5
Woodville Rd *BEXW* TN39	195	G8
Woodward Cl *LGNY* BN23	231	F4
Woodwards Cl *BURH* RH15	119	H2
Woolley Cl *SBGH/RUST* TN4	19	K2
Woolley Rd *SBGH/RUST* TN4	19	K2
Woolven Cl *BURH* RH15	118	E2
Worcester Vls *HOVE* BN3	202	B4
Wordsworth Dr *LGNY* BN23	231	F1
Wordsworth Ri *EGRIN* RH19	22	A2
Wordsworth St *HOVE* BN3	203	F4
Workhouse La *WSEA* TN36	141	H1

hdean Rd *BRI* BN1	203	J1
herenden Rd *MAYF* TN20	72	E2
hy Bush *BURH* RH15	88	E7
URH RH15	88	E6
hyham Rd *ROTT* BN2	221	F3
hyham Cl *LW/ROSE* BN22	230	A2
hyham Rd *RRTW* TN3	27	J5
tersham La *RYE* TN31	85	H6
tersham Rd *RYE* TN31	85	G3
elsfield Rd *HWH* RH16	90	A1
OTT BN2	207	F8
burn Cl *HAIL* BN27	189	F2
burn Pl *BRI* BN1	179	G6
burn Wy *LW/ROSE* BN22	215	J8
de Rd *BAT* TN33	165	K8
fe Cl *CROW* TN6	53	J3
seley Rd *BRI* BN1	178	E5
TSD BN41	201	K3
BGH/RUST TN4	20	C4
stonbury Dr *HOVE* BN3	6	A3
stonbury Wy *BURH* RH15	119	G1
lverstone Dr *BRI* BN1	204	D1
odburn Rd *EGRIN* RH19	23	F3
odbury Av *BRI* BN1	178	A7
odbury Av *EGRIN* RH19	23	F3
odbury Cl *EGRIN* RH19	23	F3
odbury Park Gdns		
BGH/RUST TN4	20	B6
odbury Park Rd		
BGH/RUST TN4	20	A6
odcombe *HAS* TN34	170	C7
odcote Rd *FROW* RH18	55	J1
odcrest Rd *BURH* RH15	119	F2
odcroft *BURH* RH15	89	F6
odcroft Dr *EAST* BN21	229	H4
odgate Meadow *LEW* BN7	121	G4
odgate Rd *LW/ROSE* BN22	11	D2
odhams Cl *BAT* TN33	136	D7
odhill Pk *RTWE/PEM* TN2	21	J5
odhouse Rd *HOVE* BN3	202	D4
odland Av *BURH* RH15	89	J7
OVE BN3	177	C7
W/ROSE BN22	229	H3
odland Cl *BURH* RH15	89	J7
OVE BN3	203	G1
BGH/RUST TN4	20	B4
odland Dr *HOVE* BN3	177	C8
odland Ms *HTHF* TN21	100	B5
odland Ri *BEX* TN40	195	K7
odland Rd *SBGH/RUST* TN4	20	C4
odlands *HOVE* BN3	203	H1

Worsham La *BEX* TN40	196	A4
Worsted La *EGRIN* RH19	23	F4
Wray Cl *EGRIN* RH19	23	H5
Wren Cl *HTHF* TN21	100	A4
Wren Ct *BAT* TN33	137	F7
STLEO TN38	169	F8
Wrestwood Av *LW/ROSE* BN22	229	H2
Wrestwood Rd *BEX* TN40	195	J5
Wrotham Cl *HAS* TN34	170	B6
LGNY BN23	230	E2
Wroxham Rd *LGNY* BN23	216	C7
Wyatts La *RHWH* RH17	48	B6
Wyberlye Rd *BURH* RH15	89	G7
Wybourne Ri *RTWE/PEM* TN2	30	B2
Wychurst Gdns *BEX* TN40	195	J5
Wykeham Rd *HAS* TN34	4	C4
Wykeham Wy *BURH* RH15	119	J1
Wyndham St *ROTT* BN2	7	D6
Wynnes Ms *HOVE* BN3	203	F4
The Wyshe *POY/PYE* BN45	149	H5
Wythwood *HWH* RH16	90	A2

Y

Yardley St *BRI* BN1	6	C2
Yates Cl *RYE* TN31	145	J1
Yeomans *RING/NEW* BN8	156	B4
Yew Tree Cl *HAS* TN34	170	B5
HTHF TN21	100	A5
RING/NEW BN8	156	A4
Yewtree La *CROW* TN6	55	H3
Yew Tree Rd *SBGH/RUST* TN4	20	A3
Yielding's Cl *EAST* BN21	229	J6
York Av *EGRIN* RH19	22	E3
HOVE BN3	6	A4
York Gdns *HAS* TN34	5	D5
York Gv *BRI* BN1	6	B3
York Hl *BRI* BN1	6	C3
York Pl *BRI* BN1	6	C4
York Rd *BEX* TN40	196	B6
BRI BN1	6	A4
EAST BN21	10	B5
PEAHV BN10	222	D5
RTW TN1	20	A7
SLVH TN37	4	A2
York Vls *BRI* BN1	6	B3
Youngsmere Cl *BRI* BN1	178	C5

Index - featured places

ootsford School		
BURH RH15	89	F5
C Cinema		
HAS TN34	5	D5
C Cinema		
RTW TN1	20	A8
ur District Council		
STHW BN42	201	H4
ion Doctors Surgery		
ROTT BN2	7	D4
rington House Hospital		
HOVE BN3	202	E5
riston County		
Primary School		
POLE BN26	212	C8
Alfriston Gallery		
POLE BN26	212	D8
Saints Hospital		
EDN/EASTW BN20	236	E4
Saints Infant School		
BEXW TN39	195	G4
Saints Junior School		
RHAS TN35	199	F1
in Gallery		
SBGH/RUST TN4	30	A1
berstone Hospital		
HAIL BN27	161	J5
bulance Station		
LW/ROSE BN22	10	C3
dale Shopping Centre		
EAST BN21	10	C4
hur Blackman Clinic		
SLVH TN37	169	J7
down Forest Health Centre		
FROW RH18	23	J8
wyn Business Centre		
BURH RH15	89	G6
embly Hall Theatre		
RTWE/PEM TN2	20	B8
Atman Clinic		
SBGH/RUST TN4	20	A5

The Audrey Wickens		
School of Music		
EAST BN21	10	A4
The Avenue Surgery		
BURH RH15	119	F1
Bad Apple Theatre Co		
RTW TN1	20	C7
Baldwins Hill CP School		
EGRIN RH19	12	A8
Balfour Junior School		
BRI BN1	178	B8
Bandstand		
EAST BN21	11	D5
Barclays Business Centre		
HTHF TN21	100	A3
Barcombe Primary School		
RING/NEW BN8	123	H6
The Barry Clinic		
SBGH/RUST TN4	20	A5
Barton School		
STLEO TN38	197	J2
Battle Abbey		
Preparatory School		
BEX TN40	195	K6
Battle Abbey School		
BAT TN33	136	D7
Battle Hospital		
BAT TN33	136	A7
Battle & Langton School		
BAT TN33	136	C7
Battle Museum		
BAT TN33	136	D7
Beacon Community College		
CROW TN6	39	K8
Beacon Community College		
CROW TN6	53	J1
Beckley Gallery		
RYE TN31	83	G7
Beckley School		
RYE TN31	82	E7

Bedgebury Junior School		
CRBK TN17	47	J2
Beeching Park		
Industrial Estate		
BEXW TN39	195	G7
Bellerbys College		
HOVE BN3	203	H4
Bellerbys College Mayfield		
WADH TN5	43	J7
Bell Tower Industrial Estate		
ROTT BN2	205	C7
Belmont Surgery		
WADH TN5	44	C7
Benfield County Junior School		
PTSD BN41	202	B3
Benfield Valley Golf Course		
PTSD BN41	176	B8
Bennett Memorial		
Diocesan School		
SBGH/RUST TN4	19	J5
Bentley Wildfowl		
& Motor Museum		
RING/NEW BN8	126	B7
Bethany House Surgery		
HAIL BN27	189	H2
Bevendean County Primary Sch		
ROTT BN2	205	C2
Bexhill Amateur Athletic Club		
BEXW TN39	195	C6
Bexhill C of E Primary		
Junior School		
BEX TN40	195	H7
Bexhill College		
BEXW TN59	195	F4
Bexhill Costume Museum		
BEX TN40	195	J7
Bexhill High School		
BEXW TN59	195	C6
Bexhill Hospital		
BEX TN40	195	H5

Bexhill Leisure Centre
BEXW TN39 .... 195 G6

Bexhill Sailing Club
BEX TN40 .... 195 J8

Bexhill Squash Rackets Club
BEX TN40 .... 195 K7

The Bishop Bell C of E School
LGNY BN23 .... 231 F2

Bishops Down CP School
SBGH/RUST TN4 .... 19 J6

Blackboys C of E School
UCK TN22 .... 97 J5

Blackwell CP School
EGRIN RH19 .... 12 C8

Blatchington Mill School
HOVE BN3 .... 203 F2

Bodiam Castle (Nt)
RBTBR TN32 .... 80 B3

Bodiam Manor School
RBTBR TN32 .... 80 A3

Bodiam Primary School
RBTBR TN32 .... 80 A3

Boltons Clinic
MAYF TN20 .... 71 F5

Boltons Clinic
STLEO TN38 .... 197 J2

Booth Museum
of Natural History
BRI BN1 .... 6 A2

Bourne County Primary School
LW/ROSE BN22 .... 11 D4

Bowden House School
SEAF BN25 .... 225 F7

Brambletye School
EGRIN RH19 .... 23 G6

Braybon Business Park
BURH RH15 .... 118 E1

Brede County Primary School
RYE TN31 .... 109 K7

Brighton Business Centre
BRI BN1 .... 6 C2

The Brighton Centre
BRI BN1 .... 6 B5

Brighton College
ROTT BN2 .... 7 E5

Brighton College of Technology
BRI BN1 .... 6 C4

Brighton College of Technology
HOVE BN3 .... 202 D3

Brighton College of Technology
HOVE BN3 .... 203 G5

Brighton County Court
ROTT BN2 .... 6 C5

Brighton Fishing Museum
BRI BN1 .... 6 B6

Brighton General Hospital
ROTT BN2 .... 7 F3

Brighton & Hove Council
BRI BN1 .... 178 C5

Brighton & Hove Council
HOVE BN3 .... 202 E2

Brighton & Hove Council
HOVE BN3 .... 203 G4

Brighton & Hove Council
HOVE BN3 .... 203 H5

Brighton & Hove Council
PTSD BN41 .... 201 K2

Brighton & Hove Council
PTSD BN41 .... 202 B3

Brighton & Hove Council
ROTT BN2 .... 7 E3

Brighton & Hove Council
ROTT BN2 .... 179 F8

Brighton & Hove Girls Day School
BRI BN1 .... 6 A4

Brighton & Hove Golf Course
HOVE BN3 .... 176 D5

Brighton & Hove
Progressive Synagogue
HOVE BN3 .... 203 J5

Brighton Hove & Sussex
6th Form College
HOVE BN3 .... 6 A2

Brighton Islamic Centre
& Mosque
HOVE BN3 .... 6 A3

Brighton Library & Museum
BRI BN1 .... 6 C5

Brighton Municipal Market
ROTT BN2 .... 7 D5

Brighton Racecourse
ROTT BN2 .... 205 H3

Brighton Rugby Club
BRI BN1 .... 177 G5

Brighton Technical College
BRI BN1 .... 6 B2

Brighton Youth Centre
ROTT BN2 .... 7 D5

Broad Oak Primary School
HTHF TN21 .... 101 F1

Broadwater CP School
RTWE/PEM TN2 .... 29 K3

Broadway Surgery
ROTT BN2 .... 205 G7

The Brook Health Centre
CROW TN6 .... 54 A2

Broomham School
RHAS TN35 .... 140 E8

Broomhill Bank School
RRTW TN3 .... 19 G5

Bross Estate
NEWHV BN9 .... 9 E2

Buchanan Hospital
STLEO TN38 .... 197 J2

Buckingham Middle School
SHOR BN43 .... 200 D3

Burfield Park Industrial Estate
HAIL BN27 .... 189 F4

Burgess Hill Clinic
BURH RH15 .... 119 F1

Burgess Hill School
BURH RH15 .... 119 H1

Burgess Hill Town Football Club
BURH RH15 .... 89 H6

Burrswood Medical Centre
RRTW TN3 .... 27 J3

Burwash School
BUR/ETCH TN19 .... 75 K5

Buxted C of E Primary School
UCK TN22 .... 68 B8

Camber Castle
RYE TN31 .... 143 J1

Cambridge Gardens College
HAS TN34 .... 4 C5

The Cameron Practice
EAST BN21 .... 10 C5

Campion Gallery
RYE TN31 .... 113 H6

Cardinal Newman School
HOVE BN3 .... 203 J3

Carlton Hill CP School
ROTT BN2 .... 7 D5

Castledean School
BRI BN1 .... 204 C1

Catsfield C of E Primary School
BAT TN33 .... 166 D3

Causeway Secondary School
LW/ROSE BN22 .... 216 B8

The Cavendish School
EAST BN21 .... 229 J6

Centenary Industrial Estate
BRI BN1 .... 7 D1

The Central Hove Surgery
HOVE BN3 .... 203 G5

Central Library
EAST BN21 .... 10 B4

Chailey Comprehensive School
RING/NEW BN8 .... 122 B4

Chailey Heritage
Clinical Services
RING/NEW BN8 .... 92 A4

Chailey Heritage School
RING/NEW BN8 .... 92 A4

Chalklin Business Park
RTWE/PEM TN2 .... 20 E3

Chantry CP School
BEX TN40 .... 195 H6

Charlwoods Industrial Estate
EGRIN RH19 .... 12 C8

Charter Medical Centre
HOVE BN3 .... 203 J4

Charters Ancaster School
BEX TN40 .... 195 K6

Chartham Park Golf Club
EGRIN RH19 .... 12 A5

Chaucer Industrial Estate
POLE BN26 .... 215 J5

Chelsea College
SHOR BN43 .... 200 A4

Chiddingly CP School
RING/NEW BN8 .... 159 H3

Chiddingly Cricket Club
RING/NEW BN8 .... 159 H2

Child Clinic
BRI BN1 .... 6 C5

Churchfields Industrial Estate
STLEO TN38 .... 168 E7

Churchill Square Shopping Centre
BRI BN1 6

Church of England School
RHWH RH17 49

Church Surgery
ROTT BN2 7

Churchwood Primary School
STLEO TN38 169

Churchwood Surgery
STLEO TN38 169

Cinema
EAST BN21 10

Cinque Ports Surgery
RYE TN31 113

Circe Health & Beauty Clinic
UCK TN22 95

Civic Centre
SHOR BN43 200

Clanricarde Medical Centre
RTW TN1 20

Claremont CP School
RTWE/PEM TN2 30

Claverham Community College
BAT TN33 136

Clermont C P U School
BRI BN1 203

Cliffe Business Centre
LEW BN7 3

Cliffe Industrial Estate
LEW BN7 3

Club House
EDN/EASTW BN20 236

Cofe Primary School
MAYF TN20 56

Coghurst Hall County Primary
RHAS TN35 171

Coldean Junior & Infant School
BRI BN1 178

Colebrook Industrial Estate
RTWE/PEM TN2 21

The College of St Barnabas
LING RH7 12

Community Mental
Health Centre
BURH RH15 89

The Congress Theatre
EAST BN21 10

Conquest Hospital
HAS TN34 170

Conway Court Clinic
HOVE BN3 203

Coombe Road County
Primary Sch
ROTT BN2 7

Cornerstones
Independent School
HOVE BN3 203

Corn Exchange Theatre
BRI BN1 6

The Cottage Clinic
BEX TN40 195

Cottage Surgery
PEAHV BN10 222

Cottesmore St Marys
RC Primary Schl
HOVE BN3 203

Count Primary School
BURH RH15 119

County Hall
LEW BN7 3

County Middle School
STHW BN42 201

County Primary School
BRI BN1 204

County Primary School
RING/NEW BN8 157

Cradle Hill Cp School
SEAF BN25 225

The Craftsman Gallery
HPPT/KEY BN6 119

Cross In Hand C of E
Primary Sch
HTHF TN21 99

Crowborough Beacon Golf Club
CROW TN6 53

Crowborough War
Memorial Hospital
CROW TN6 53

Crowhurst School
BAT TN33 168

Crown Court
HOVE BN3 203

Crown Prosecution Service
EAST BN21 10

nnor House School
RHWH RH17 .... **49** F6
Cyril Richings Business
Centre 202-210
SHOR BN43 .... **200** D4
e Hill Hotel & Golf Club
WADH TN5 .... **60** D2
ington School
HTHF TN21 .... **103** F8
rigdor County Infants School
HOVE BN3 .... **203** J4
aton County Primary School
NEWHV BN9 .... **9** E1
ronshire Park Cricket Ground
EAST BN21 .... **10** B6
ronshire Park Theatre
EAST BN21 .... **10** C6
chling Gallery
HPPT/KEY BN6 .... **119** J8
chling Health Centre
HPPT/KEY BN6 .... **119** K8
chling Museum
HPPT/KEY BN6 .... **119** J8
chling Primary School
HPPT/KEY BN6 .... **119** K8
glas Moat Practice
SBGH/RUST TN4 .... **30** A1
vnland Medical Centre
POLE BN26 .... **215** F5
vnlands School
HPPT/KEY BN6 .... **119** F8
vns County First School
BRI BN1 .... **6** C2
vns Junior School
BRI BN1 .... **6** C1
vns Leisure Centre
SEAF BN25 .... **225** H7
vns Park School
PTSD BN41 .... **202** A1
vns Special School
EDN/EASTW BN20 .... **229** G7
vns View School
ROTT BN2 .... **205** K3
sillas Zoo Park
POLE BN26 .... **212** E5

EAST BN21 .... **10** B4

ROTT BN2 .... **7** D5
lley Infants School
RHAS TN35 .... **5** F3
nnings Squash Club
EGRIN RH19 .... **22** C5
gates Industrial Estate
WADH TN5 .... **44** A6
Eastbourne Clinic
EDN/EASTW BN20 .... **10** B5
tbourne College
EDN/EASTW BN20 .... **10** B6
tbourne College
EDN/EASTW BN20 .... **10** B5
tbourne College
EDN/EASTW BN20 .... **10** A6
tbourne College of Arts
& Tech
EAST BN21 .... **229** K4
tbourne County Court
EAST BN21 .... **10** B4
tbourne District
eneral Hospital
EAST BN21 .... **229** K4
tbourne Downs Golf Club
EDN/EASTW BN20 .... **236** A3
tbourne & Hailsham
Magistrates Court
EAST BN21 .... **10** A5
tbourne Health Authority
EAST BN21 .... **10** B3
tbourne Hospitals N H S Trust
EAST BN21 .... **10** C3
tbourne Pier
EAST BN21 .... **11** D5
tbourne Rugby
ootball Club
LW/ROSE BN22 .... **229** J3
tbourne Saffrons
ports Club
EAST BN21 .... **10** A5
tbourne Sovereign
ailing Club Ltd
LW/ROSE BN22 .... **11** F3
tbourne United
ootball Club
LW/ROSE BN22 .... **11** F2

East Court
EGRIN RH19 .... **22** D1
East Grinstead Health Clinic
EGRIN RH19 .... **22** C1
East Grinstead Sports Club
EGRIN RH19 .... **22** A6
East Hoathly C of E School
RING/NEW BN8 .... **127** H6
East Hoathly Surgery
RING/NEW BN8 .... **127** J6
East Sussex Brighton
& Hove Health Authority
LEW BN7 .... **3** D4
East Sussex County Council
HOVE BN3 .... **176** D8
East Sussex County Council
HTHF TN21 .... **100** C3
East Sussex County Council
LEW BN7 .... **2** B5
East Sussex County Council
LEW BN7 .... **3** E6
East Sussex County Council
LEW BN7 .... **3** D4
East Sussex County Council
NEWHV BN9 .... **8** C3
East Sussex County Council
NEWHV BN9 .... **9** E2
East Sussex County Council
PEAHV BN10 .... **222** B4
East Sussex County Council
PEAHV BN10 .... **222** D5
East Sussex County Council
POLE BN26 .... **215** F5
East Sussex County Council
ROTT BN2 .... **205** F5
East Sussex County Council
SEAF BN25 .... **225** F8
East Sussex County
Music School
LEW BN7 .... **2** C5
East Sussex Health Authority
NEWHV BN9 .... **9** D2
East Sussex National Golf Club
UCK TN22 .... **125** K3
E F International School
of English
SLVH TN37 .... **4** B5
Elm Grove CP School
ROTT BN2 .... **7** E6
Elphinstone Junior School
HAS TN34 .... **5** J4
Emerson College
FROW RH18 .... **24** B8
Enterprise Shopping Centre
EAST BN21 .... **10** B4
Escotts County Primary School
EGRIN RH19 .... **22** E2
Esperance Private Hospital
EAST BN21 .... **10** C5
Etchingham C of E
Primary School
BUR/ETCH TN19 .... **77** H1
Euro Business Park
NEWHV BN9 .... **9** D2
Eversfield Hospital
STLEO TN38 .... **197** H5
Evolution Health Centre
BRI BN1 .... **6** A4
Fairfax Gallery
RTW TN1 .... **30** A1
Fairfield Surgery
BUR/ETCH TN19 .... **75** J5
Fairlight County Primary School
ROTT BN2 .... **7** E2
Felix Gallery
LEW BN7 .... **3** D4
Fermor School
CROW TN6 .... **53** J1
Ferryfield Industrial Estate
NEWHV BN9 .... **9** E3
Filching Manor
POLE BN26 .... **228** C1
Filsham Valley
Secondary School
STLEO TN38 .... **197** G4
Firle C of E School
RING/NEW BN8 .... **184** B7
Firle Place
RING/NEW BN8 .... **184** D8
The Firs Surgery
HTHF TN21 .... **99** J3
The Fishermans Museum
HAS TN34 .... **5** F5

Fishersgate First School
PTSD BN41 .... **201** K4
Five Ashes Primary School
MAYF TN20 .... **71** F5
Fletching C of E School
UCK TN22 .... **65** K8
The Fold School
HOVE BN3 .... **202** C4
Fonthill Lodge School
EGRIN RH19 .... **22** A5
Fordcombe C of E
Primary School
RRTW TN3 .... **17** K6
Forest Row Business Park
FROW RH18 .... **23** K8
Forest Row C of E Infant School
FROW RH18 .... **35** K1
Fort
NEWHV BN9 .... **9** D5
Foxhill Surgery
PEAHV BN10 .... **222** A2
Framfield C of E School
UCK TN22 .... **96** D5
Frant C of E School
RRTW TN3 .... **30** B7
Freda Gardham Cp School
RYE TN31 .... **113** K5
Gallery
ROTT BN2 .... **7** E6
The Gallery
BEXW TN39 .... **195** G8
The Gallery
BRI BN1 .... **6** A5
The Gallery
HOVE BN3 .... **203** F4
The Gallery
SBGH/RUST TN4 .... **20** A1
Gattons CP School
BURH RH15 .... **88** E8
Gemini Business Centre
HOVE BN3 .... **203** F3
Gerald Dale Motor
Sports Centre
STLEO TN38 .... **169** C6
Glebe CP School
STHW BN42 .... **201** G4
Glennys Estate
LW/ROSE BN22 .... **11** E2
Glynde Palace
RING/NEW BN8 .... **184** A4
Goldsmith Leisure Centre
CROW TN6 .... **39** H7
Goldstone Junior School
HOVE BN3 .... **202** D2
The Good Start School
POY/PYE BN45 .... **148** B6
Graham Gallery
SBGH/RUST TN4 .... **20** A8
Graham Whitehouse Practice
BURH RH15 .... **88** E7
Granary Business Centre
HAIL BN27 .... **160** E5
Grays County Infants School
NEWHV BN9 .... **9** D4
Greenfield School
FROW RH18 .... **35** C2
Green Street Clinic
EAST BN21 .... **229** H7
Grosvenor Medical Centre
RTW TN1 .... **20** A7
Grovelands County
Primary School
HAIL BN27 .... **189** F2
Grove Park School
CROW TN6 .... **53** C2
The Grove School
STLEO TN38 .... **197** C2
Guestling School
RHAS TN35 .... **171** K3
Guestling Surgery
RHAS TN35 .... **171** K3
Hailsham School
HAIL BN27 .... **189** G3
Hailsham Town Council
HAIL BN27 .... **189** H4
Hailsham Whitehouse
CP School
HAIL BN27 .... **189** G3
Ham Business Centre
SHOR BN43 .... **200** D4
Hamilton Lodge School
ROTT BN2 .... **7** F5
Hammerwood Park
EGRIN RH19 .... **24** C1

Hampden Park Infants School
LW/ROSE BN22 .... 229 K1
Hampden Park
Secondary School
LW/ROSE BN22 .... 229 K1
Hampden Park Sports Centre
LW/ROSE BN22 .... 229 J1
Hamsey CP School
RING/NEW BN8 .... 153 K3
Hangleton County Junior
& Infant School
HOVE BN3 .... 202 D1
Hankham CP School
PEV BN24 .... 216 C3
Harlands Farm County
Primary School
UCK TN22 .... 95 K6
Harvington Business Park
LW/ROSE BN22 .... 230 A3
Hassocks County Infant School
HPPT/KEY BN6 .... 119 F7
Hassocks Golf Club
HPPT/KEY BN6 .... 118 E6
Hasting Medical Centre
HAS TN34 .... 5 D4
Hastings Castle
HAS TN34 .... 5 E4
Hastings College of Arts
& Technology
HAS TN34 .... 5 F3
Hastings College of Arts
& Technology
STLEO TN38 .... 197 J5
Hastings Education College
STLEO TN38 .... 197 G4
Hastings Golf Club
BAT TN33 .... 169 G3
Hastings Indoor Market
HAS TN34 .... 5 D5
Hastings Museum & Art Gallery
HAS TN34 .... 4 C5
Hastings & St Leonards
Sailing Club
STLEO TN38 .... 197 J5
Hastings Town Football Club
HAS TN34 .... 170 D7
Hawkes Farm Cp School
HAIL BN27 .... 189 G1
Hawkhurst C of E
Primary School
HAWK TN18 .... 63 F3
Hawkhurst Squash Club
HAWK TN18 .... 62 E1
Hazel Cottage Clinic
ROTT BN2 .... 205 K3
Hazel Court School
LGNY BN23 .... 216 C8
Heathfield C of E
Primary School
HTHF TN21 .... 100 D5
Heathfield School
HTHF TN21 .... 100 E4
Helenswood Lower School
SLVH TN37 .... 170 A4
Helenswood Upper School
HAS TN34 .... 170 D7
Hellingly CP School
HAIL BN27 .... 160 E6
Hellingly Hospital
HAIL BN27 .... 161 J6
Herbert Hone Clinic
ROTT BN2 .... 7 D3
Herne School
CROW TN6 .... 53 H3
Herons Dale School
SHOR BN43 .... 201 F2
Herstmonceux Castle
HAIL BN27 .... 191 J2
Herstmonceux C of E School
HAIL BN27 .... 163 F6
High Beech Hotel
& Country Club
STLEO TN38 .... 169 G5
Highfield Business Park
STLEO TN38 .... 168 E7
Highfield County Junior School
LW/ROSE BN22 .... 230 A2
High Hurstwood C of E School
UCK TN22 .... 68 C2
High Schools
BRI BN1 .... 6 A4
Highwoods Golf Club Ltd
BEXW TN39 .... 194 E4

Hillcrest School
RHAS TN35 .... 171 H6
Hillside School
PTSD BN41 .... 202 A1
Hippodrome Bingo
BRI BN1 .... 6 B5
Hoddern County Junior School
PEAHV BN10 .... 222 A3
Hollington Junior School
STLEO TN38 .... 169 H7
Hollington Lodge Country Club
SLVH TN37 .... 169 H4
Holmbush County Infants School
SHOR BN43 .... 201 F2
Holmewood House School
RRTW TN3 .... 28 E1
Homecare Business Centre
LEW BN7 .... 3 E4
Home Farm Business Centre
BRI BN1 .... 178 E8
Homeopathic Hospital
RTW TN1 .... 20 A8
Horsted Keynes C of E School
RHWH RH17 .... 48 A5
Hospital
HAWK TN18 .... 62 D1
Hove Business Centre
HOVE BN3 .... 203 G3
Hove General Hospital
HOVE BN3 .... 203 F4
Hove Medical Centre
HOVE BN3 .... 202 C1
Hove Metal Galleries
HOVE BN3 .... 6 A3
Hove Park Upper School
HOVE BN3 .... 203 F2
Hove Polyclinic
HOVE BN3 .... 202 E2
Hove Rugby Football Club
HOVE BN3 .... 203 C2
How We Lived Then
Museum of Shops
EAST BN21 .... 10 C5
Hubbard School
EGRIN RH19 .... 22 C2
Hurstpierpoint College
HPPT/KEY BN6 .... 118 B3
Hurstwood Park Hospital
HWH RH16 .... 90 C1
Icklesham Primary School
WSEA TN36 .... 141 J5
Iford & Kingston C of E School
LEW BN7 .... 181 J6
The Imber Sports Centre
EGRIN RH19 .... 12 B8
The Indooer Market
HAS TN34 .... 5 D5
Indoor Market
SLVH TN37 .... 4 A5
Inglesea School
STLEO TN38 .... 169 G7
Inside Out Theatre Co Ltd
STLEO TN38 .... 4 A4
International Lawn Tennis Centre
EAST BN21 .... 10 C5
Jarvis Brook Cp School
CROW TN6 .... 54 A4
Jempsons Trading Estate
RYE TN31 .... 113 H6
Kent & Sussex Hospital
SBGH/RUST TN4 .... 20 A7
King Offa CP School
BEXW TN39 .... 195 G6
Kings Manor School
SHOR BN43 .... 201 G3
Kingstanding Business Park
RTON TN11 .... 21 F1
Kingston Buci School
SHOR BN43 .... 200 D3
Kingswood Surgery
RTWE/PEM TN2 .... 20 C8
Knoll Business Centre
HOVE BN3 .... 202 C3
Lamberhurst C of E School
RRTW TN3 .... 33 K5
Lamberhurst Golf Club
RRTW TN3 .... 33 K5
Lamberhurst Surgery
RRTW TN3 .... 33 J6
Langney CP School
LGNY BN23 .... 231 F2
Langney Shopping Centre
LGNY BN23 .... 216 D8

Langney Sports Club
LGNY BN23 217
Langton Green Cp School
RRTW TN3 18
Lansdowne Road Clinic
RTW TN1 20
Law Courts
ROTT BN2 7
Lawn Tennis Club
EAST BN21 10
Leap Cross Small
Business Centre
HAIL BN27 189
Lewes Business Centre
LEW BN7 3
Lewes Castle & Museums
LEW BN7 2
Lewes District Council
NEWHV BN9 8
Lewes District Council
SEAF BN25 225
Lewes Gallery
LEW BN7 2
Lewes Grammar School
LEW BN7 2
Lewes Leisure Centre
LEW BN7 3
Lewes Little Theatre
LEW BN7 2
Lewes Magistrates Court
LEW BN7 3
Lewes Sports Club
LEW BN7 2
Lewes Tertiary College
LEW BN7 3
Lewes Victoria Hospital
LEW BN7 2
Lewes Wallands Cp School
LEW BN7 2
Lexden Lodge Industrial Estate
CROW TN6 54
Life Boat Museum
EAST BN21 10
Lindfield School
LW/ROSE BN22 229
Liongate Clinic
SBGH/RUST TN4 20
Little Common Primary School
BEXW TN39 194
Little Horsted School
UCK TN22 125
Little Ridge School
SLVH TN37 169
Little Ridge Surgery
SLVH TN37 169
Little Theatre
SEAF BN25 232
London Meed CP School
BURH RH15 119
Longhill School
ROTT BN2 206
Longley Industrial Estate
BRI BN1 6
Lower Glen Surgery
SLVH TN37 169
L T C International College
EAST BN21 10
Malthouse Business Park
RYE TN31 112
Manor Cp School
UCK TN22 95
Manor Farm Business Centre
POY/PYE BN45 148
Manor Field CP School
BURH RH15 89
Manor House Hospital
HOVE BN3 203
Manor Oak Surgery
HTHF TN21 129
Manor Park Medical Centre
POLE BN26 214
Marefield Leisure Centre
UCK TN22 67
Maresfield Bonners School
UCK TN22 67
Marine Clinic
ROTT BN2 220
Mark Cross C of E School
CROW TN6 42
Market Place
BURH RH15 119
Marlborough House School
HAWK TN18 62

lipins Museum
HOR BN43 .... 200 B5
shlands CP School
AIL BN27 .... 189 J3
tins Oak Surgery
AT TN33 .... 136 D7
field Gallery
MAYF TN20 .... 56 B8
nards Green Cp School
THF TN21 .... 130 A1
dows Memorial School
BGH/RUST TN4 .... 19 K1
Meadows Surgery
URH RH15 .... 88 D7
Mead School
TWE/PEM TN2 .... 30 A2
ds School
GRIN RH19 .... 22 C4
Meads Surgery
CK TN22 .... 95 J4
Medical Centre
EV BN24 .... 218 A6
ching Valley Cp School
EWHV BN9 .... 8 B3
abowl
EX TN40 .... 196 B7
norial Art Gallery
AS TN34 .... 5 D5
cateria Business Centre
TLEO TN38 .... 4 A6
idian CP School
PEAHV BN10 .... 222 B2
idian Leisure Centre
PEAHV BN10 .... 222 B4
idian Surgery
PEAHV BN10 .... 222 A3
Mews Clinic
AST BN21 .... 10 A3
ael Hall School
ROW RH18 .... 35 H2
elham Priory
AIL BN27 .... 188 A4
dle Street Primary School
RI BN1 .... 6 B5
Sussex Golf Club
PPT/KEY BN6 .... 120 C6
Oak Clinic
TSD BN41 .... 175 J8
Oak Junior School
TSD BN41 .... 175 J8
rook Business Park
ROW TN6 .... 54 B3
View Hospital
OVE BN3 .... 202 D2
tfield Surgery
GRIN RH19 .... 22 C1
a House School
DN/EASTW BN20 .... 236 D2
ey Street Health Centre
OTT BN2 .... 7 D4
Mosque
TLEO TN38 .... 4 A5
combe County
fant School
AST BN21 .... 229 H6
iscoomb Clinic
OTT BN2 .... 179 F8
isecoomb County
unior Sch
OTT BN2 .... 179 F8
ntfield & Whatlington C of E
rimary School
BTBR TN32 .... 106 D4
nt Pleasant Hospital
LVH TN37 .... 169 H7
nt School
ADH TN5 .... 43 H5
den School
OVE BN3 .... 203 J2
eum
HOR BN43 .... 200 A4
eum of Local History
AS TN34 .... 5 E4
erfield C of E
rimary School
AT TN33 .... 135 G1
ll Golf Club
TWE/PEM TN2 .... 30 D4
haven Flea Market
EWHV BN9 .... 8 C4
haven Health Centre
EWHV BN9 .... 9 D3
haven Town Council
EWHV BN9 .... 8 C3

Newick Health Centre
RING/NEW BN8 .... 93 H4
Newick House Special School
BURH RH15 .... 119 J2
Newick School
RING/NEW BN8 .... 93 G5
Newlands Preparatory School
SEAF BN25 .... 225 J7
Newlands Senior School
SEAF BN25 .... 225 H7
New Life School
EGRIN RH19 .... 22 B1
Newmans Loner School
HOVE BN3 .... 203 J3
New Venture Theatre
BRI BN1 .... 6 A5
Ninfield C of E School
BAT TN33 .... 166 A6
Northbourne Medical Centre
SHOR BN43 .... 200 D3
Northease Manor School
LEW BN7 .... 208 B2
North Farm Industrial Estate
RTWE/PEM TN2 .... 20 E2
Northfield Business Park
HAIL BN27 .... 159 K7
Northiam Primary School
RYE TN31 .... 81 K6
Nutley Primary School
UCK TN22 .... 50 C7
Oakmeads Community School
BURH RH15 .... 119 G1
Ocklynge County Junior School
EAST BN21 .... 229 H5
Odeon Cinema
BRI BN1 .... 6 B5
Old Grammar School
LEW BN7 .... 2 C4
The Old Museum
RYE TN31 .... 110 D1
Old Salehurst School
RBTBR TN32 .... 78 B6
Old School Surgery
SEAF BN25 .... 232 A1
Old Town Art Gallery
HAS TN34 .... 5 E4
The Open University
HAS TN34 .... 22 C2
Orchard Business Centre
RTWE/PEM TN2 .... 20 D3
Ore Business Park
HAS TN34 .... 5 F2
Our Lady of Lourdes School
ROTT BN2 .... 220 C1
Ovingdean Hall School
ROTT BN2 .... 206 A7
Park College Eastbourne
EAST BN21 .... 229 J4
Parklands Junior
& Infant School
LW/ROSE BN22 .... 229 J2
Park Mead School
HAIL BN27 .... 187 K3
Parkside County
Primary School
HTHF TN21 .... 100 C6
Park View Leisure Centre
HOVE BN3 .... 202 D4
Pashley Down County
Infant School
EDN/EASTW BN20 .... 229 G7
Patcham CP School
BRI BN1 .... 178 A5
Patcham First School
BRI BN1 .... 177 K5
Patcham High School
BRI BN1 .... 178 A5
Patcham House School
BRI BN1 .... 177 K5
The Pavilion Clinic
BRI BN1 .... 6 A5
Paxton Business Centre
HOVE BN3 .... 202 C3
Peacehaven Infant School
PEAHV BN10 .... 222 A4
Peacehaven Sports Centre
PEAHV BN10 .... 222 C4
Peacehaven Town Council
PEAHV BN10 .... 222 B3
Peacock Industrial Estate
HOVE BN3 .... 203 J4
Peasmarsh C of E
Primary School
RYE TN31 .... 112 B2

Pebsham Primary School
BEX TN40 .... 196 B6
Pells C of E Infant School
LEW BN7 .... 2 B3
Pells Primary School
LEW BN7 .... 2 C3
Pembury Hospital
RTWE/PEM TN2 .... 21 G4
Pembury Primary School
RTWE/PEM TN2 .... 21 K3
Penns Gallery
EAST BN21 .... 10 B5
Peter Gladwin School
PTSD BN41 .... 201 K1
Pevensey Bay Sailing Club
PEV BN24 .... 231 K1
Pevensey Castle
PEV BN24 .... 217 J5
Pevensey & Westham
C of E Primary School
PEV BN24 .... 217 H5
Phoenix Industrial Estate
LEW BN7 .... 3 D3
The Picture House
UCK TN22 .... 95 J4
The Piltdown Golf Club
UCK TN22 .... 94 E1
Playden School
RYE TN31 .... 113 J1
Plumpton New Primary School
LEW BN7 .... 121 H6
Polegate CP School
POLE BN26 .... 215 F4
Polegate Town Council Office
POLE BN26 .... 214 E6
Portland Business Park
HOVE BN3 .... 202 C4
Portland Industrial Estate
HOVE BN3 .... 202 D3
Portland Road Industrial Estate
HOVE BN3 .... 202 C3
Portland Surgery
HOVE BN3 .... 202 E4
Portslade Community College
PTSD BN41 .... 175 K8
Portslade Community College
PTSD BN41 .... 201 K2
Portslade Community College
STHW BN42 .... 201 J1
Portslade Health Centre
PTSD BN41 .... 202 A4
Practice
SBGH/RUST TN4 .... 30 A1
Premier Gallery
EAST BN21 .... 10 B5
Preston Furniture Gallery
BRI BN1 .... 204 A1
Preston Park Clinic
BRI BN1 .... 6 C1
Preston Park Surgery
BRI BN1 .... 6 C2
Prince Regent
Swimming Complex
BRI BN1 .... 6 C5
The Princes Royal Hospital
HWH RH16 .... 90 B1
Priory Hill Shopping Centre
HAS TN34 .... 5 D4
Priory School
LEW BN7 .... 3 D5
Punnetts Town School
HTHF TN21 .... 101 H5
Queensdown School
BRI BN1 .... 178 D8
Queens Park County
Primary School
ROTT BN2 .... 7 E5
Queen Victoria Hospital
N H S Trust
EGRIN RH19 .... 12 D8
Quintin Medical Centre
HAIL BN27 .... 161 H8
Ranalah Estate
NEWHV BN9 .... 9 E2
Ratton County
Secondary School
EAST BN21 .... 229 H4
Red Lake CP School
RHAS TN35 .... 171 G7
Regent Business Centre
BURH RH15 .... 118 E1
Rich Industrial Estate
NEWHV BN9 .... 9 E1

Ringmer Business Centre
RING/NEW BN8............................... **156** A5

Ringmer CP School
RING/NEW BN8............................... **155** K6

Ringmer Football Club
RING/NEW BN8............................... **155** J6

Ringmer Parish Council
RING/NEW BN8............................... **155** J6

Riverbank Business Centre
SHOR BN43................................... **200** A4

River Lodge Surgery
LEW BN7.. **3** D4

Riverside Business Centre
SHOR BN43................................... **200** C5

Riverside Industrial Estate
LEW BN7.. **3** D3

Robertsbridge Community
College
RBTBR TN32..................................... **77** K7

Roborough Day Hospital
EAST BN21....................................... **10** C3

Robsack Infant School
STLEO TN38................................... **197** F1

Rock & Bowl Bowling Alley
EGRIN RH19...................................... **22** C2

Rocks Park CP School
UCK TN22.. **95** H3

Rockys Leisure Centre
HAS TN34.. **4** C5

Rodmell Primary School
LEW BN7... **208** D2

Roebuck House Surgery
HAS TN34.. **5** F4

Roedean School
ROTT BN2....................................... **205** K8

Rose Hill School
SBGH/RUST TN4.............................. **19** J6

Roselands County Infants School
LW/ROSE BN22................................. **11** D2

Rother District Council
BAT TN33....................................... **136** C6

Rotherfield CP School
CROW TN6.. **55** F3

Rotherfield Surgery
CROW TN6.. **55** F3

Rottingdean Football Club
ROTT BN2....................................... **206** C8

Rottingdean Primary School
ROTT BN2....................................... **220** D1

Rottingdean Surgery
ROTT BN2....................................... **206** B8

Royal Alexandra Hospital
BRI BN1.. **6** B4

Royal Ashdown Forest Golf Club
FROW RH18...................................... **36** A2

Royal Eastbourne Golf Club
EDN/EASTW BN20......................... **236** D1

Royal George Clinic
BURH RH15...................................... **88** E8

Royal Hippodrome Theatre
LW/ROSE BN22................................. **11** D4

Royal Sussex County
Hospital Nhs Trust
ROTT BN2.. **7** F6

Royal Victoria Place
Shopping Centre
RTW TN1.. **20** B7

Rudyard Kipling
Primary School
ROTT BN2....................................... **206** B4

Rugby Club
EGRIN RH19...................................... **22** A6

Rusthall Medical Centre
SBGH/RUST TN4.............................. **19** F7

Rutherfords Business Park
BAT TN33....................................... **137** H4

Rye Art Gallery
RYE TN31.. **113** J6

Rye Bay Club House
WSEA TN36..................................... **143** G6

Rye Castle Museum
RYE TN31.. **113** J6

Rye Community Clinic
RYE TN31.. **113** H6

Rye Football & Cricket Club
RYE TN31.. **113** J5

Rye Golf Club
RYE TN31.. **114** D8

Rye Harbour Sailing Club
RYE TN31.. **114** C8

Rye Industrial Estate
RYE TN31.. **113** K7

Sackville School
EGRIN RH19...................................... **22** E2

Sacred Heart School
RTWE/PEM TN2................................. **20** E7

Sacred Heart School
WADH TN5.. **43** K6

St Andrews C of E Infant School
LW/ROSE BN22................................. **11** E1

St Andrews C of E School
HOVE BN3....................................... **203** G5

St Andrews Medical Centre
SBGH/RUST TN4.............................. **20** A2

St Andrews School
EDN/EASTW BN20......................... **236** D4

St Andrews Surgery
LEW BN7.. **3** D5

St Annes Special School
LEW BN7.. **2** B5

St Aubyns School
ROTT BN2....................................... **220** D2

St Augustine School
SBGH/RUST TN4.............................. **20** A4

St Barnabas C of E
Primary School
RTW TN1.. **20** B6

St Bartholomews C of E
Primary School
BRI BN1.. **6** C3

St Bedes School
EDN/EASTW BN20......................... **236** E4

St Bedes School
HAIL BN27....................................... **187** J3

St Bernadettes First
Middle Va School
BRI BN1.. **203** K1

St Christophers School
HOVE BN3....................................... **203** F4

St Dominics Gallery
HPPT/KEY BN6............................... **119** J8

St Faith Clinic
ROTT BN2....................................... **205** F7

St Georges School
RTWE/PEM TN2................................. **21** G6

St Giles College
EDN/EASTW BN20........................... **10** B6

St Gregorys RC School
SBGH/RUST TN4.............................. **20** A4

St James's Junior
& Infant School
RTWE/PEM TN2................................. **20** C7

St Johns Church School
CROW TN6.. **38** E7

St Johns Infant School
SBGH/RUST TN4.............................. **20** A6

St Johns Primary School
SBGH/RUST TN4.............................. **20** B4

St Johns Residential School
ROTT BN2.. **7** F5

St John the Baptist RC
Primary School
ROTT BN2.. **7** F5

St Josephs RC School
LW/ROSE BN22................................. **11** E2

St Leonards C of E
Primary School
STLEO TN38................................... **197** H4

St Leonards Football Club
HAS TN34.. **5** E1

St Lukes Junior & Infant School
ROTT BN2.. **7** E4

St Lukes School
SBGH/RUST TN4.............................. **20** C4

St Lukes Swimming Pool
ROTT BN2.. **7** E4

St Marks C of E Primary School
ROTT BN2....................................... **205** F6

St Marks C of E Primary School
SBGH/RUST TN4.............................. **29** H2

St Marks C of E Primary School
UCK TN22.. **70** A6

St Martins C of E Primary School
ROTT BN2.. **7** E2

St Mary Magdalene School
BEX TN40....................................... **195** K5

St Mary Magdalene School
BRI BN1.. **6** A5

St Marys C of E School
EGRIN RH19...................................... **22** B1

St Marys Hall School for Girls
ROTT BN2.. **7** F6

St Marys Primary Catholic School
CROW TN6.. **53** H1

St Marys RC School
PTSD BN41..................................... **202** A4

St Marys School
BEX TN40....................................... **195** K5

St Marys School
HTHF TN21..................................... **130**

St Mary the Virgin School
HRTF TN7.. **25**

St Michaels Cp School
HRTF TN7.. **26**

St Nicholas & St. Mary School
SHOR BN43..................................... **200**

St Pancras RC Primary School
LEW BN7.. **2**

St Pauls C of E Infant School
RRTW TN3.. **19**

St Pauls C of E Junior School
SBGH/RUST TN4.............................. **19**

St Pauls C of E School
BRI BN1.. **6**

St Pauls School
SLVH TN37.. **4**

St Peters County Infant School
PTSD BN41..................................... **202**

St Peters Primary School
RING/NEW BN8............................... **92**

St Peters Primary School
RTWE/PEM TN2................................. **20**

St Peters RC School
EGRIN RH19...................................... **22**

St Peters R C School
SHOR BN43..................................... **200**

St Phillips R C Primary School
UCK TN22.. **95**

St Richards School
BEX TN40....................................... **195**

St Thomas A Becket RC
Infants School
EAST BN21....................................... **10**

St Thomas A Becket RC
Junior School
EAST BN21....................................... **10**

St Thomas C of E
Primary School
RRTW TN3.. **28**

St Thomas C of E
Primary School
WSEA TN36..................................... **143**

St Vincent School
STLEO TN38................................... **197**

St Wilfrids RC School
BURH RH15..................................... **119**

Salehurst C of E
Primary School
RBTBR TN32..................................... **78**

Saltdean County
Primary School
ROTT BN2....................................... **221**

Salvation Army
LW/ROSE BN22................................. **11**

Sandown Court School
RTWE/PEM TN2................................. **20**

Sandown School
RHAS TN35..................................... **171**

Saxonborough Surgery
CROW TN6.. **53**

Saxon Mount School
STLEO TN38................................... **197**

The Seaford Business Centre
SEAF BN25..................................... **225**

Seaford CP School
SEAF BN25..................................... **225**

Seaford Day Hospital
SEAF BN25..................................... **225**

Seaford Golf Club
SEAF BN25..................................... **225**

Seaford Head Community
College
SEAF BN25..................................... **232**

Seaford Head Community
College
SEAF BN25..................................... **232**

Seaford Head Lower School
SEAF BN25..................................... **232**

Seaford Health Centre
SEAF BN25..................................... **225**

Seaford Sports & Leisure Centre
SEAF BN25..................................... **225**

Sea Life Centre
ROTT BN2.. **7**

Sea Road Surgery
BEX TN40....................................... **195**

Seaside Medical Centre
LW/ROSE BN22................................. **11**

Secondary School
ROTT BN2....................................... **205**

Sedlescombe C of E School
BAT TN33....................................... **138**

escombe Golf Club
  AT TN33 .... **138** A6
Seven Dials Medical Centre
  RI BN1 .... **6** A4
kill Surgery
  HAS TN35 .... **171** G7
dindean Business Centre
  URH RH15 .... **89** F6
dingdean First School
  URH RH15 .... **89** G6
a Cashin Gallery
  RI BN1 .... **6** B4
ffs Gallery
  AIL BN27 .... **189** H4
wood Park Infant School
  TWE/PEM TN2 .... **20** D5
wood Park Primary School
  TWE/PEM TN2 .... **20** D5
ship Street Surgery
  RIN RH19 .... **22** C3
eham Beach County
st School
  IOR BN43 .... **200** D5
eham College
  IOR BN43 .... **201** G4
eham County First School
  IOR BN43 .... **200** B3
eham Football Club
  SD BN41 .... **202** A4
eham Health Centre
  IOR BN43 .... **200** B4
y Primary School
  EXW TN39 .... **195** H5
y Sports Club
  EXW TN39 .... **195** H4
y Surgery
  EXW TN39 .... **195** G4
rhill Natural Health Centre
  LEO TN38 .... **197** J1
Springs Medical Practice
  VH TN37 .... **4** A4
sons Industrial Estate
  VE TN31 .... **114** A8
kinners School
  CH/RUST TN4 .... **20** A5
ers Hill Manor
eparatory School
  AYF TN20 .... **71** F3
rhill County Junior School
  VE BN3 .... **203** J5
ndown Business Park
  W BN7 .... **3** D3
ndown CP School
  WHV BN9 .... **8** C3
Downs Health Clinic
  I BN1 .... **6** B4
Malling Primary School
  W BN7 .... **3** D2
over C of E Primary School
  W BN7 .... **2** D1
Saxon Howe Surgery
  LEO TN38 .... **197** F4
way County Junior School
  PT/KEY BN6 .... **88** D8
wick Business Centre
  SD BN41 .... **201** H5
wick Manor Hall
unty First School
  HW BN42 .... **201** J4
dustrial Park
  WE/PEM TN2 .... **20** E3
hurst Primary School
  TW TN3 .... **18** E4
ey School
  HF TN21 .... **99** H8
gfield Industrial Estate
  WH RH17 .... **90** B6
h Club
  ST BN21 .... **10** A5
es Farm Industrial Estate
  K TN22 .... **127** G2
rd County Junior School
  /ROSE BN22 .... **10** C1
ord Junior School
  I BN1 .... **6** B2
ey Deason Leisure Centre
  TT BN2 .... **205** G6
cross School
  TBR TN32 .... **108** A1
nson Gallery
  E TN13 .... **113** H6
rt Gallery
  K TN40 .... **195** H8

Stone Cross CP School
  PEV BN24 .... **216** B6
Stonegate C of E Primary School
  WADH TN5 .... **59** H6
Stonelands School of Ballet
  & Theatre
  HOVE BN3 .... **203** G5
Summerfields Business Centre
  SLVH TN37 .... **4** B4
Summerfield Sports Centre
  HAS TN34 .... **4** B4
Sussex County Cricket Club
  HOVE BN3 .... **203** H4
Sussex Eye Hospital
  ROTT BN2 .... **7** F6
Sussex House Industrial Estate
  HOVE BN3 .... **202** E3
Sussex Nuffield Hospital
  HOVE BN3 .... **202** E5
Sussex Nuffield Hospital
  ROTT BN2 .... **205** K3
Sussex Private Clinic
  STLEO TN38 .... **197** J3
The Sussex Toy
  & Model Museum
  BRI BN1 .... **6** C4
Sussex University
  LEW BN7 .... **3** E3
Sutton Industrial Park
  WSEA TN36 .... **143** G4
Swan Barn Business Centre
  HAIL BN27 .... **189** J5
Sydney West Sports Centre
  BURH RH15 .... **89** G7
Synagogue
  EAST BN21 .... **10** C4
Synagogue
  BRI BN1 .... **6** B6
TA Centre
  LW/ROSE BN22 .... **11** D3
Teacher Training Sch
  HAS TN34 .... **5** E3
Telscombe Cliffs Primary School
  PEAHV BN10 .... **221** K3
Temple Grove with
  St Nicholas School
  UCK TN22 .... **52** A8
Tennis Club
  CROW TN6 .... **53** G1
Thomas Peacocke
  Community College
  RYE TN31 .... **113** H5
Ticehurst Clinic
  HOVE BN3 .... **203** F5
Ticehurst C of E Primary School
  WADH TN5 .... **60** B3
Tideway School
  NEWHV BN9 .... **8** B4
Tilling Green School
  RYE TN31 .... **113** G6
Tobias School of Art
  EGRIN RH19 .... **22** C5
Tollgate Junior School
  LGNY BN23 .... **230** E4
Torfield School
  HAS TN34 .... **5** F3
Towner Art Gallery & Local History
  Museum
  EDN/EASTW BN20 .... **229** J8
Tree Tops Tree Surgery
  STLEO TN38 .... **169** G8
Trinity Theatre
  & Arts Association
  RTW TN1 .... **20** A8
Tunbridge Wells Borderers
  Sports Club
  RTWE/PEM TN2 .... **30** A3
Tunbridge Wells Centre
  RTW TN1 .... **20** A7
Tunbridge Wells Golf Club
  SBCH/RUST TN4 .... **19** J8
Tunbridge Wells Grammar
  School for Boys
  SBCH/RUST TN4 .... **20** A3
Tunbridge Wells Grammar
  School for Girls
  SBCH/RUST TN4 .... **19** K5
Tunbridge Wells Hockey Club
  RTW TN1 .... **30** B2
Tunbridge Wells
  Independent Hospital
  RRTW TN3 .... **17** K8

Tunbridge Wells Museum
  & Art Gallery
  SBGH/RUST TN4 .... **20** A7
Tunbridge Wells Nuffield Hospital
  RTWE/PEM TN2 .... **20** D8
Tunbridge Wells Sports Centre
  SBGH/RUST TN4 .... **20** A4
Uckfield Civic Centre
  UCK TN22 .... **95** J4
Uckfield Community Hospital
  UCK TN22 .... **95** K5
Uckfield Community School
  UCK TN22 .... **95** K3
Uckfield Holy Cross School
  UCK TN22 .... **95** J4
Uckfield Rugby Football Club
  UCK TN22 .... **96** A3
Uckfield Sports Centre
  UCK TN22 .... **95** J4
University
  EDN/EASTW BN20 .... **10** A6
University of Brighton
  BRI BN1 .... **179** H6
University of Brighton
  EAST BN21 .... **10** B3
University of Brighton
  EDN/EASTW BN20 .... **236** D4
University of Brighton
  EDN/EASTW BN20 .... **236** D2
University of Brighton
  ROTT BN2 .... **204** D1
University of Sussex
  BRI BN1 .... **179** J4
Uplands Community College
  WADH TN5 .... **44** B7
Uplands School
  BRI BN1 .... **204** D1
Utopia Leisure Centre
  UCK TN22 .... **95** K3
Vals Swim School
  BEXW TN39 .... **195** G3
Varndean College
  BRI BN1 .... **178** A8
Varndean High School
  BRI BN1 .... **178** B8
Venture Industrial Park
  STLEO TN38 .... **197** H1
Vicarage Field Surgery
  HAIL BN27 .... **189** H3
Virgin Cinemas
  BRI BN1 .... **205** F8
Virgin Cinemas
  LGNY BN23 .... **231** G2
Wadhurst Business Park
  WADH TN5 .... **43** H4
Wadhurst C of E Primary School
  WADH TN5 .... **44** B6
Warrior Square Surgery
  SLVH TN37 .... **4** A5
Waterhall Golf Course
  BRI BN1 .... **177** G4
Waytefield Clinic
  BRI BN1 .... **203** K1
Wealden College
  CROW TN6 .... **53** H3
Wealden District Council
  HAIL BN27 .... **189** H3
Wealden Industrial Estate
  CROW TN6 .... **54** A3
Websters Gallery
  EAST BN21 .... **11** D4
Welfare Clinic
  HOVE BN3 .... **202** D1
Wellington Square
  Medical Centre
  HAS TN34 .... **5** D5
Wellshurst Golf & Country Club
  HAIL BN27 .... **161** F1
Westdene Primary School
  BRI BN1 .... **177** H6
Westerleigh School
  STLEO TN38 .... **197** H3
Westham Medical Centre
  PEV BN24 .... **217** H6
West Hove Middle School
  HOVE BN3 .... **202** D4
West Kent College
  of Further Edu
  SBGH/RUST TN4 .... **20** A4
West Pier (Under Repair)
  BRI BN1 .... **6** A6
West Rise Junior & Infant School
  LGNY BN23 .... **230** D1

Notes

Notes